CHILDREN'S
BRITANNICA

CHILDREN'S BRITANNICA

Volume 2
Ariosto to Bering Sea

Encyclopædia Britannica, Inc.

AUCKLAND / CHICAGO / GENEVA / LONDON / MANILA / PARIS
ROME / SEOUL / SYDNEY / TOKYO / TORONTO

First edition 1960
Second edition 1969
Third edition 1973
Fourth edition 1988

First revision 1989

International Standard Book Number: 0-85229-209-0
Library of Congress Catalogue Card Number: 88-82585

Printed in U.S.A.

ARIOSTO, LUDOVICO (1474–1533), was a celebrated Italian poet of the Renaissance. He was born at Reggio, in Lombardy, the son of a noble family. As a young man he studied law but later turned to writing. In 1503 he entered the service of Cardinal Ippolito d'Este. During the 14 years of his service with the cardinal, he wrote his immortal poem, *Orlando Furioso* ("Orlando in Passion"), which was first published in 1516. The poem tells of the heroic adventures of knights during the age of Charlemagne. It was declared a masterpiece through all of Italy.

After completing this epic, Ariosto entered the service of the cardinal's brother Alfonso, Duke of Ferrara, and turned his attention to writing comedies based on Latin models. These comedies helped to make drama a major literary form. More important than the comedies, however, are Ariosto's seven satires. Most of what is known of his personality has been learned from these works. In them it is revealed that he was not interested in politics and preferred a leisurely life.

In 1522, driven by poverty, Ariosto accepted a post as governor of a faraway province in the Apennines. He returned to Ferrara in 1525 and spent his remaining years in peaceful retirement. His epic influenced the Romantic poetry of Edmund Spenser, Sir Walter Scott, and Lord Byron.

ARISTOPHANES (*c.*448–*c.*380 BC) was the greatest writer of comedy plays in ancient Greece. He lived at the same time as the great Greek writers of tragedy, Sophocles and Euripides. Aristophanes' comedies are full of references to current affairs of his day, but people enjoy them and laugh at them now as much as the Greeks did when they were first acted.

Very little is known about the personal life of Aristophanes. He was born in the city of Athens but spent much of his youth on the nearby island of Aegina. He staged his first comedy play *The Banqueters* in 427 at one of the annual festival competitions for plays in Athens and won second prize. This and many of his other comedies are lost, but 11 plays have come down to us.

Aristophanes wrote his comedies not only to make people laugh but also to show up what he considered to be the faults and foolishness of the politicians and philosophers of his day. He was writing at a time when Athens and its allies were fighting a long and bitter war against a league of states headed by Sparta. Many people in Athens suffered because of the war, especially the women whose husbands were away in battle. Aristophanes' play *Lysistrata* (produced at Athens in 411) presents the women's sufferings in a comical way by making them "declare war" on their men to stop them from fighting. In *The Clouds* (first produced in 423), Aristophanes makes fun of the philosopher Socrates. In *The Birds* (414), Aristophanes' characters escape from troubled Athens to "Cloud cuckoo-land", a city in the sky ruled by birds. In *The Wasps* (422), Aristophanes makes fun of the Athenian law courts. In *The Frogs* (405), he comically criticizes the tragedies of Aeschylus and Euripides. In his plays, Aristophanes proved himself to be very inventive and more willing to experiment than many later writers.

ARISTOTLE (384–322 BC) was one of the great philosophers of ancient Greece. (A philosopher is a man who loves wisdom and who spends his life studying and trying to understand and explain the truth about the world around him.) Aristotle was born in 384 BC at Stagira in northern Greece. His father was a doctor at the court of the king of Macedon, Philip II. When he was 17 Aristotle went to Athens to become a pupil of another great philosopher, Plato. There he stayed for the next 20 years until Plato died. During this time he studied biology, mathematics, and all branches of philosophy, and taught and wrote about these subjects.

In 342 BC Aristotle went to be tutor to King Philip's son Alexander, who was then 14. Aristotle taught Alexander to love and respect the great qualities that the Greeks most admired, such as learning and freedom of ideas. In 336 BC, King Philip was murdered, and Alexander had to give up his studies to become king.

SCALA

Raphael's Vatican fresco, *The School of Athens*, shows the Greek philosopher Aristotle with his teacher Plato.

Aristotle therefore went back to Athens and started his own school of philosophy. He and his pupils were often seen walking under the trees during their discussions. From this habit they became known as the "Peripatetics", from the Greek word meaning "walks".

In 323 BC Aristotle retired from Athens to his mother's home at Chalchis on the island of Euboea and died the next year when he was 62.

Aristotle's Ideas

The ideas of Plato and Aristotle were very different. Plato was interested in what man's life ought to be. Aristotle thought more about what it was actually like, and about how to solve some of the problems that men find in their lives. In other words, Aristotle was rather like a modern scientist: he did not start by imagining what the world would be like if a certain idea were true; instead he looked at the facts of the real world and then tried to work out new ideas from these facts. Logic, which lays down the rules of reasoning, began with Aristotle and has lasted virtually unchanged for nearly 2,000 years.

Aristotle was interested in other things as well as science and philosophy. He wrote books on the art of public speaking and on poetry. He also studied the great plays of his time and people came to take his ideas about drama as rules for writing good plays.

Aristotle's three most famous works are called *Physics, Metaphysics*, and *Politics*. Writers of the Middle Ages based many of their ideas about nature and human life on his teaching.

ARITHMETIC is the branch of mathematics concerned with numbers. It is one of the most useful branches, since numbers are used by almost everybody. We use numbers when shopping, or at home when cooking or gardening. Tradesmen, storekeepers, accountants, scientists, engineers, architects and many others all use numbers in their work.

Writing Numbers

One of the first problems that early societies of human beings encountered was to find a way of recording numbers. The most obvious way was to make a mark somewhere for each object you were counting. So picture (a) could represent five sheep. Sometimes 5 could be recorded as five knots in a piece of string (b). When two men did business they would record an agreed amount as notches on a stick.

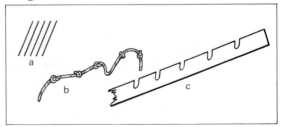

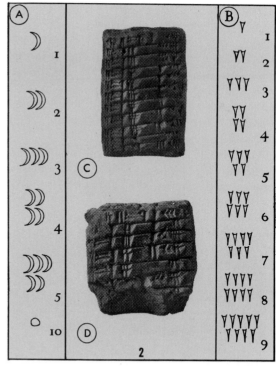

These illustrations show the numerals and calculations used by the ancient Egyptians and Babylonians. **Left:** (1A) Egyptian signs known as ideographs with the numbers they stand for; (1B) Egyptian numerals in Hieratic script; between (1A) and (1B) arithmetical problem written on papyrus, c. 1600 BC. **Right:** (2A) early Babylonian numerals; (2B) late cuneiform (wedge-shaped) numerals; (2C) and (2D) part of a Babylonian multiplication table found on broken clay tablets.

The stick was then split down the middle so that each man had a record of the agreement. (We still talk about "notching up" a score.)

As people began to invent ways of writing, they also invented more sophisticated ways of recording numbers, especially when the numbers they wanted to record became larger. The Egyptians probably began by making simple marks on papyrus, but they invented a much better system which used a different symbol to stand for ten. The number written out in words as "thirty-four" could be recorded as three tens and four ones. This way they recorded up to ninety-nine, then used another symbol for one hundred.

$$\cap = 10 \qquad \cap\cap\cap|||| = 34 \qquad \textcircled{e} = 100$$

The Babylonians had a similar system, based on wedge-shaped marks made on clay tablets. They used a larger wedge to stand for sixty, because they counted in sixties. (We count in tens.)

The Mayans of Central America based their system on fives. So did the Romans, whose well-known numerals were based on finger counting. The numbers from one to four (I II III IIII) represented the appropriate number

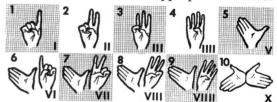

Roman numerals were based on counting with fingers.

of fingers, and the picture for five (V) represented one hand. The symbol for ten, although it became X, was based on two "Vs", that is, two hands. In the Middle Ages, Roman numerals were put on clocks, but the clockmakers found that numerals like IIII and VIIII were sometimes too large to fit on, so they invented the idea of writing a small numeral *before* a large numeral, and *subtracting* it instead of adding it. So IV meant 5−1, or 4, and IX meant 10−1, or 9. Some old clocks still have Roman numerals, and you can see the date written in Roman numerals on some old books and buildings.

Our own system of writing numerals came from the Hindus through the Arabs, and was also originally based on single marks for numbers. One, two, three were originally like this (a), and when written quickly they became something like this (b).

It is not hard to see how these turned into the numerals we know today.

Calculating

Apart from deciding how to record numbers, people also invented ways of calculating with them. The word "calculate" comes from the Latin word *calculus*, meaning "pebble", and the Romans calculated with pebbles placed in grooves made in the earth or sand. In spite of their somewhat clumsy system of numerals, they calculated in hundreds, tens, and ones, using a groove for each. This arrangement represented 137 like this (a).

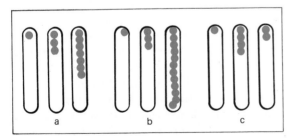

If they then wished to add 5, they would place five more pebbles in the right-hand (ones) groove (b). But ten pebbles in the "ones" groove could be exchanged for one pebble in the "tens" groove: and this gave 142 (c).

Later, the sand abacus, as it was called, was replaced by the bead abacus. (See ABACUS.)

Many methods have been invented for calculating, even on paper. Around the 14th century, multiplication was done in this way. To multiply 36 by 43, you wrote the numbers on a diagram called a "grating", whose Italian name was *gelosia*. Since 3×4=12, the 12 is written in the top left-hand square. The other squares are filled in, in the same way. Now all the digits are added up diagonally as indicated by the arrows, starting at bottom right, and carrying tens where necessary.

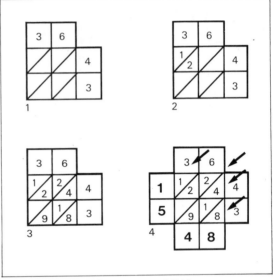

The answer can be seen as 1548.

Since about the beginning of the 19th century, different methods for calculating have been taught in schools. People with a lot of calculations to do have generally tried to find something to help them do them more quickly, particularly multiplication and division. At one time logarithms were taught in secondary schools or high schools (see LOGARITHM). Engineers used to use slide rules. Nowadays most people use electronic calculators for anything they cannot do easily in their heads (see CALCULATOR), and for anything very complicated people use computers (see COMPUTER).

The Laws of Arithmetic

The main operations of arithmetic, or the "four rules" as they are often called, are addition, subtraction, multiplication, and division. There are separate articles on these four subjects. There you will find the basic concepts and some ideas about methods of calculation. There is also some information under DECIMALS, FRACTIONS, and MATHEMATICS.

The calculator has made working out arithmetical problems a good deal easier than it used to be.

Here we shall discuss some connections between the four operations, some of which are useful when calculating.

There is an obvious link between addition and subtraction, since one is the "opposite" of the other. For instance, you can get from 12 to 17 by *adding* 5, and back from 17 to 12 by *subtracting* 5. This can be recorded as:

$$12+5=17$$
$$17-5=12$$

But you can also get to 17 by starting with 5 and adding 12, and back again by subtracting 12, so we can write two more number sentences for this relationship:

$$5+12=17$$
$$17-12=\ 5$$

There is a similar relationship between multiplication and division. So for example the following four sentences are all linked, in the same way as the above sentences are:

$$4\times3=12$$
$$12\div3=\ 4$$
$$3\times4=12$$
$$12\div4=\ 3$$

In fact, whenever we do division we tend to do it by multiplication. If we wish to know $24\div3$ we can ask, "How many threes make 24?", in other words,

$$?\times3=24,$$

and this is equivalent to saying

$$24\div3=?$$

This is one of the things that makes the *mul-*

tiplication tables so useful, because they can also be used for division. There are not as many to learn as there seem to be. For instance, if you know

$$7\times8=56$$

then you also know that

$$8\times7=56,$$

because multiplication is *commutative*, that is, two numbers when multiplied either way round give the same answer. (Addition of numbers is also commutative: $7+3=3+7$.)

Now suppose you did not know 7×8, but you knew $7\times4=28$. How would you get 7×8 from this? Well, you could double it. There are various ways of explaining why you can do this. One is to write

$$7\times8=7\times(4\times2)=(7\times4)\times2.$$

This uses the fact that if you have three numbers to multiply together, then you can start with the first two, or with the last two. This property of multiplication is called the *associative* property, because the 4 in the middle can be "associated" with either the 7 or the 2. Addition of numbers is also associative. (But note that subtraction and division are *not* commutative or associative.)

Another property connects multiplication and division, and it is known as the *distributive* property. It says, for instance, that if we want to calculate 3×14 then, because 14 is the same as $10+4$, we can calculate 3×10 and 3×4 and add the results together:

$$3\times14=3\times(10+4)$$
$$=(3\times10)+(3\times4)$$
$$=30+12=42.$$

This makes it easy to do a lot of calculation in our heads, and it was the basis of paper-and-pencil methods of multiplication, including the *gelosia* method described earlier.

There are other interesting properties of numbers which are useful for calculation. The following additions all give the same answer:

$36+49,\ 37+48,\ 38+47,\ 39+46,\ 40+45,\ \ldots$

This means that if we wish to add $99+67$ we can replace it by $100+66$.

Similarly, the following subtractions are all equal:

$$77-43,\ 76-42,\ 75-41,\ 74-40,\ \ldots$$

They all come to 34.

Thus we can replace $100-37$ by $99-36$ and still get 63.

"Tricks" like this, which rely on a knowledge of relationships between numbers, can make mental arithmetic much easier.

Powers and Roots

There is an old story about a mathematician in China who, when offered a reward for some service by the Emperor, asked for 1 grain of rice to be placed on the first square of a chessboard, 2 grains on the second, 4 on the third, 8 on the fourth, and so on, doubling the number of grains every time. You may like to calculate how many grains were to be placed on the 64th square. (The Emperor, not being a mathematician, readily agreed, but found out that it took more rice than there was in China!)

Numbers grow very quickly when they are doubled. The first few are:

1	$=1$	$1\times2\times2\times2\times2$	$=16$
1×2	$=2$	$1\times2\times2\times2\times2\times2$	$=32$
$1\times2\times2$	$=4$	$1\times2\times2\times2\times2\times2\times2$	$=64$
$1\times2\times2\times2$	$=8$		

Now, it takes time and space to keep writing out so many twos, so we have a shorthand for this. We write:

$$1\times2 \qquad =2^1$$
$$1\times2\times2 \qquad =2^2$$
$$1\times2\times2\times2 \qquad =2^3$$
$$1\times2\times2\times2\times2=2^4$$

and so on. And we read 2^4 as "two to the fourth power" or just "two to the fourth", followed by "two to the fifth (power)", etc. The exceptions to this are 2^2 which is called "two squared" and 2^3 which is "two cubed". (We do not often write 2^1, but it could be called "two to the first power". You can also see that if we extend the idea backwards then 1 on its own could be written 2^0.) You can see from this discussion that continuous doubling of rice grains will give 2^{63} rice grains on the last square of a chessboard.

These numbers are called *powers of 2*, and we can also have powers of other numbers. The column headings of our whole numbers, ones, tens, hundreds, thousands, etc, are powers of 10, and we can write

$1=10^0$	$100=10^2$
$10=10^1$	$1000=10^3$

Some calculators use *scientific notation* for decimals, which is based on powers of 10. A number like 8 000 000 000 would appear on the calculator as

$$8.\ 09$$

and means 8×10^9, that is $8\times1\ 000\ 000\ 000$. 8,324 in scientific notation would be 8.324×10^3; 423.6 would be 4.236×10^2.

It is easy to multiply and divide powers of a number (see LOGARITHM). The little number *indicating* the power is also called the *index* (plural indices), and writing numbers this way is sometimes called *index notation*.

To calculate the area of a square whose side is 5cm (see AREA AND VOLUME) we multiply 5×5 to get 25cm^2. We can write 5×5 as 5^2, and this is why it is called "5 squared". In the same way the volume of a cube with an edge of 5cm is $5\times5\times5$cm^3, and this is why we call 5^3 "5 cubed".

Sometimes we know the area of a square and want to know the side. To do this we find the *square root* (see MATHEMATICS). In the same way if we know the volume of a cube and want to know the edge we find the *cube root*. Or if we want to find out which number raised to the fourth power gives 81

$$\square^4=81$$

we must find the *fourth root* of 81. That one is easy to find (the answer is 3), but generally to find roots or powers of numbers it is best to use a scientific calculator, which has a special function for this.

Number Theory

Arithmetic to a mathematician is not only about calculating with numbers, but is also that branch of mathematics that deals with interesting things about numbers. This sort of arithmetic is described in the article NUMBER.

ARIZONA is situated in the southwestern part of the United States. It is a state of mountains, plateaus, and desert, yet it contains some of the most beautiful scenery in the nation. Most spectacular of all its sites is the Grand Canyon of the Colorado River, in the northwest part of the state. In addition to this

ZEFA

The spectacular Grand Canyon in north-central Arizona is the largest land gorge in the world.

natural wonder are the Painted Desert, the Petrified Forest, and the Oak Creek Canyon.

The population of Arizona is small, just over 3 million in the early 1980s. But it is one of the fastest growing states. Between 1970 and 1980 its population increased by 53 per cent. Most of the increase took place in the two major cities: Phoenix, the capital, and Tucson. Arizona has become a popular place for other Americans to settle in because it is one of the "Sun-belt" states, places where winter is far less severe than in the north and northeast. Another source of population increase has been immigration from Mexico, which borders the state on the south.

The Land

Arizona is bordered on the north by Utah, on the east by New Mexico, on the west by Nevada and California, and on the south by the Mexican state of Sonora. The northeast corner of the state meets Utah, Colorado, and New Mexico, the only place in the United States where so many states touch each other.

From north to south Arizona stretches 635 kilometers (395 miles). Its greatest width is 551 kilometers (343 miles). Of its total area of 295,259 square kilometers (114,000 square miles), only 1,274 square kilometers (492 square miles) is water surface.

The state has two distinct natural regions:

the Colorado Plateau, and the Basin and Range. The plateau covers about one-third of Arizona in the north. It is studded with lofty mountain ranges and great, flat-topped mesas (rocks). In this region are the Grand and Oak Creek canyons, the Painted Desert, and the Petrified Forest. Humphreys Peak, the highest in the state at 3,862 meters (12,670 feet), is near Flagstaff.

The Basin and Range region occupies the southern two-thirds of Arizona. Its northern part is an irregular belt of mountains running at a diagonal across the state, from northwest to southeast. This belt of mountains is from 110 to 240 kilometers (70 to 150 miles) wide. Its peaks rise to heights of 1,200 to 1,800 meters (4,000 to 6,000 feet). To the south of the mountains is a large area of desert plains, valleys, detached mountain ranges, and solitary peaks. It is in this arid region that most of the state's population lives.

The climate of Arizona varies markedly from region to region. The southern basin is very hot in the summer and warm in winter. The east-central portion of the state on the other hand can have very cold winters with high snowfall. Rainfall ranges from about 7.5 centimeters (3 inches) in the southwest around Yuma to 45 centimeters (18 inches) in the central part of the state around Flagstaff.

In spite of the lack of rainfall in the south, agriculture is still profitable owing to massive irrigation projects. Crops, including citrus fruits, are grown throughout the year.

The diversity of the state's regions has given rise to a varied plant and animal life. Coyotes, mountain lions, deer, antelope, and wildcats are found in the north. The southern desert is home to such interesting species as scorpions, tarantulas, and Gila monsters (a poisonous lizard). There are also rattlesnakes, other reptiles, and a large variety of birds.

The People

Arizona has been home to a variety of native populations for several thousand years. When Spanish explorers and gold-seekers arrived in the 16th century, they found a number of populous Indian tribes, including the Hopi,

Papago, and Pima. Later, the Apache, Navajo, and other tribes arrived. Today there are 21 reservations set aside for the Indians. Largest of these is for the Navajo, in the northeastern section of the state. The Hopi are believed to be the oldest existing tribe in the United States. One of their villages, Oraibi, is the oldest continuously inhabited town in the country.

The total Indian population in the early 1980s was about 153,000. Most live on reservations or in small towns and villages. Only 28,000 inhabit the larger cities.

Non-Indian immigration began in the early 1800s. Gold and silver discoveries in the 1850s brought in more settlers, but many of these left after the gold and silver mines were worked out. The coming of the transcontinental railroad in the 1880s brought more people, but growth was really quite slow until after World War II. In 1940 there were only 65,414 residents in Phoenix. Forty years later the metropolitan area had swollen to more than 1.5 million. Tucson has experienced similar, though less spectacular, growth in the past 40 years. The improvement in Arizona's economy in this period has helped to lure thousands of Mexicans to the state, mostly to the cities.

The Cities

Three-quarters of Arizona's population lives in two areas: Maricopa County, with Phoenix at its center; and Pima County, where the major city is Tucson. Maricopa County has by far the larger population of the two and is still growing rapidly. Besides Phoenix, the county includes the sizeable settlements of Scottsdale, Mesa, Glendale, Avendale, Tempe, and Sun City, a well-known retirement spot.

Tucson, to the southeast of Phoenix, is about half the size of the capital in population. Yuma, in the southwest corner of the state, is smaller still, with a population of about 43,000. And Flagstaff, in the north-central part of the state, has only about 35,000 residents. Because of Arizona's popularity as a winter refuge, the population increases annually between November and April.

The Economy

Until World War II, Arizona was primarily a mining state. Silver and gold proved insignificant after a few years of fierce exploitation. Copper, however, endured as the most profitable of minerals. Arizona was the greatest of the copper-mining states, accounting at one time for 12 per cent of world production. Other productive industries have been cotton growing, citrus fruit farming, and cattle raising. During World War II manufacturing made swift inroads, and today Arizona's factories produce processed foods, aircraft, aircraft parts, electrical machinery, animal and vegetable oils, and electronic equipment. Of these, electronics has proved to be the most profitable.

Agriculturally, the state is also quite productive. Well over 400,000 hectares (1 million acres) have been made productive by irrigation. The size of an average farm is 2,400 hectares (6,000 acres), but much of the land is given over to cattle grazing.

The Water Problem

The prosperity of Arizona's desert region depends in large part upon water. With annual precipitation less than 25 centimeters (10 inches), other sources of water had to be found. The first usable source was ground water. Persistent use of this water in the late 19th and early 20th centuries led to a lowering of the water table (the level water lies at in the ground) to dangerous levels—so dangerous that huge cracks, many running for miles, opened in the land. And the earth itself sank at many places. If irrigation were to continue, other means of getting water had to be found.

Even before Arizona became a state in 1912, it depended on the federal government to build water diversion projects to bring water to the desert. Several dams, the first of which was completed in 1911, store vast amounts of water to be sent to the desert as needed. Arizona now shares with California the rights to water from the Colorado River under the Central Arizona Project, approved by Congress in 1968. This project, when finished,

Arizona Highway Department

This open-pit copper mine at Morenci is one of the largest in the United States. It is over 400 m (1,320 ft) deep.

will consist of a 643-kilometer (400-mile) system of aqueducts and dams to divert water to the Phoenix and Tucson areas. Ninety per cent of the water is to be used for agriculture.

Natural Wonders

Apart from the Grand Canyon, which is covered in a separate article, the two most picturesque natural wonders of Arizona are the Painted Desert and the Petrified Forest.

The Painted Desert is a section of the high plateau in the north-central part of the state. It is about 240 kilometers (150 miles) long and from 24 to 80 kilometers (15 to 50 miles) wide. It covers an area of 19,400 square kilometers (7,500 square miles). It gets its name from the brilliantly colored shales, marls, and sandstones, which are banded with vivid red, yellow, blue, white, and lavender. The desert is a wild and barren region of rolling hills, cliffs, and flat-topped mesas. The Hopi and Navajo reservations occupy a large part of the Painted Desert, and members of these tribes use the brightly colored sands for their ceremonial paintings.

The Petrified Forest National Park is in eastern Arizona, 29 kilometers (18 miles) east of Holbrook. It occupies an area of 381 square kilometers (147 square miles). The park includes the Black Forest section of the Painted Desert; a region of colorful, wind-eroded hills; and the Mesa, Jasper, Crystal, and Rainbow forests which are filled with fossilized leaves, logs, and plants. There are also ancient Pueblo Indian ruins and a Rainbow Forest Museum. The fossilized wood in the forest has been produced by the mineral replacement of wood fibers, normally by silicon dioxide. This replacement is so accurate that the internal structure and external shapes of the plants and trees has been faithfully and colorfully preserved.

Education

The first schools in the state were founded by Catholic missionaries from Mexico. No public (state) school existed until 1871, after Arizona had become a territory of the United States. Organization of the public school system began in 1883.

There are today three state universities: the University of Arizona at Tucson, Arizona State University at Tempe, and Northern Arizona University at Flagstaff. There are more than a dozen two-year colleges around the state. Schools for Indian children are provided by the federal Bureau of Indian Affairs.

History of Arizona

When the first Spaniards came to Arizona in 1539 looking for cities of gold, they found Indian civilizations that were centuries old.

ZEFA

The San Xavier Mission, known as the "White Dove of the Desert", near Tucson, Arizona, founded by the Spanish.

The Indians lived in *pueblos* that looked something like modern apartment buildings. They were a settled people who irrigated the land for agriculture.

The first Spaniard, Marcos de Niza, was followed by others coming north from Mexico. For nearly 300 years the Spanish continued to explore the territory and to establish permanent residences there, with cattle, sheep, and horses. They were less successful than in neighboring New Mexico, but in 1692 the famed mission of San Xavier del Bac was founded near present-day Tucson. A fort was built there in 1776, and Tucson beame a Spanish town from that time.

The first English-speaking white men came to Arizona early in the 1800s looking for fur-bearing animals. Settlement remained slow;

Arizona was merely an extension of the more prosperous New Mexico colony.

After the Mexican War of 1846–48, the territory was given to the United States by the Treaty of Guadalupe Hidalgo. A territorial government was formally organized in 1863 when the territory was officially separated from New Mexico. Phoenix was made the capital in 1869.

Discoveries of gold, silver, and copper drew many settlers from the east. Silver mines near Tombstone proved profitable, but the most enduring wealth came from the copper mines at Ajo, Morenci, Globe, Superior, Bisbee, and Jerome.

Statehood was granted in 1912. Arizona was among the first states to pass laws giving women the right to vote, regulating the employment of women and children in dangerous occupations, and providing for workers' compensation.

World War II was the turning point in Arizona's history. Thousands of servicemen trained at the eight military bases in the state. After the war many of them returned to live there with their families. The war was also the impetus for new manufacturing, improvement of the road system, and the building of new airfields.

FACT AND FIGURES

AREA: 295,259 square kilometers (114,000 square miles).
POPULATION: 3,053,000 (1984).
MOUNTAINS: Humphreys Peak, 3,862 meters (12,670 feet).
RIVERS: Colorado, Gila, Santa Cruz, San Pedro.
CITIES: Phoenix (789,704); Tucson (330,537), Mesa (152,453), Tempe (106,743), Glendale (97,172), Scottsdale (88,412), and Yuma (42,433).

ARKANSAS is a state partly of the old South and partly of the new West. Its eastern sections consist of rolling plains that were once home to large cotton plantations similar to those of the Deep South just to the east, across the Mississippi River.

The northwestern part of Arkansas is mostly mountainous terrain, split in two by the valley of the Arkansas River. This region is in some ways similar to the West. It was, in fact, one of the most isolated, frontier-like regions of the United States and only began to become prosperous in the 1970s. People in the capital city of Little Rock, located almost in the center of the state, look more toward wealthier Texas and Oklahoma for their style of dress and attitudes.

The Land

Arkansas is situated in the south-central part of the United States. It is bounded on the east by the Mississippi River, on the north by the state of Missouri, on the west by Oklahoma and a small section of Texas, and on the south by Louisiana.

The state has five natural regions. In the north is the Ozark plateau, tree-covered highlands that extend south from Missouri. The Boston Mountains of the southern Ozarks overlook the Arkansas River Valley. And to the south of the river valley lie the Ouachita Mountains. The two other regions consist of plains. The whole eastern section of the state is Mississippi Flood Plain, stretching from the southeast corner of Missouri down to Louisiana. The flood plain continues through Louisiana to the Gulf Coast.

To the south of the Ouachita Mountains lies the Gulf Coastal Plain. It is slightly higher than the flood plain to the east, and it is highly forested. As its name suggests, it too extends south to the Gulf of Mexico.

All the rivers of Arkansas flow to the south and east and are part of the huge Mississippi River system. The Arkansas River itself cuts the state almost in half, running diagonally from the northwest to the southeast.

Arkansas has a generally mild climate. In the southeast the summers are long, hot, and humid; and the winters are short. The northwest highlands are cooler in both summer and winter. The crop growing season varies from 240 days a year in the south to 180 days in the northwest. The annual rainfall is adequate for growing many kinds of crops. It ranges from 100 centimeters (40 inches) to 150 centimeters (60 inches). The mild climate plus the low cost of living in the state, compared with other southern states has attracted vacationers and older people looking for a pleasant place to retire to.

The People

Arkansas was originally home to a number of Indian tribes, including the Caddo, the Osage, and the Quapaw (also called Arkansas). In the early 1800s the Choctaw and Cherokee from the east were also granted the right to live in the territory. But as white settlers entered the territory, the Indians were gradually forced west into Oklahoma, which was then Indian Territory (see OKLAHOMA).

The first Europeans to visit Arkansas were Spaniards; Hernando de Soto and his party of adventurers paid a visit in 1541–42 in search of gold. Later the state was visited by the French, who built the first permanent settlement. And in the early 1800s settlers came from the states east of the Mississippi and from the north.

Population growth in the eastern plains came from the cotton-growing areas of the old South. In the north and west the settlers arrived from Missouri and other areas to the north. The cotton plantations used slave labor, and when the Civil War approached, the slave-owners drove the state into Confederacy. At the end of the war the state found itself with a large, free black population. Today it makes up about 15 per cent of the total. Most black people live in the counties of the Mississippi Valley plains area.

Among the states, Arkansas ranks 48th in terms of income per person. This statistic reflects in part the fact that the state has proportionately one of the highest rural populations of any state. It also indicates that Arkansas, until recently, has had little manufacturing industry.

The Economy

Prior to the Civil War, eastern Arkansas had many cotton plantations of more than 400 hectares (1,000 acres). After the war the plantations were gradually broken up into smaller units. Today the state has about 60,000 farms, many of them commercial enterprises worked by tenants. Cotton is no longer the primary crop, although a great deal of it is still grown in the northeastern part of the state, in the region between the Saint Francis River and the Mississippi. Arkansas has become the leading state in the production of rice. The second most valuable crop is soybeans. Corn is grown in most of the state's counties.

In the western highlands farmers grow hay, oats, wheat, and fruit. The Arkansas River Valley has many dairy farms. Livestock include cattle, poultry, pigs, and turkeys.

Mineral production has become a significant part of the state's economy. Arkansas is the chief source in the United States of bauxite (aluminium ore). The mines are in the center

Walter Rawlings/Robert Harding Picture Library

A tractor mechanically hoes cotton in Arkansas; soybeans and rice have replaced it as the main crop.

of the state, mostly in Saline and Pulaski counties. Petroleum is extracted from fields along the mid-southern border. Coal is mined in the west-central part of the state, and diamonds have been found near Murfreesboro in the southwestern section. Other economically valuable minerals are natural gas, stone, sand, and gravel.

A fishing industry prospers along the Mississippi River. The major catch is buffalo fish. Other commercially valuable catches are mussels, catfish, carp, and turtles. Lake fishing attracts many tourists each year, particularly in the western part of the state.

Industry was late in coming to Arkansas. The economic rebirth of the state began in 1955 when Governor Orval Faubus established the Arkansas Industrial Development Corporation and named Winthrop Rockefeller to head it. Within ten years Rockefeller had helped bring to the state more than 600 new manufacturing plants, creating 90,000 new jobs. This economic change encouraged natives of Arkansas to remain in the state instead of going elsewhere for work. It also brought in many outsiders. For the first time in decades the population actually began to increase. Rural areas were also revitalized by the incoming industries. So successful was Rockefeller that he was later elected as governor for two terms, in 1966 and 1968.

Food processing is the state's major industry. Other leading industries include lumbering and the manufacture of pulp, paper, and

The state capitol building at Little Rock—capital and largest city of Arkansas.

paperboard; electrical machinery, chemicals, metals, and glass products.

Little Rock, the capital, is also the industrial and commercial center. Fort Smith is the second largest city and the business capital of western Arkansas. North Little Rock, across the Arkansas River from the capital, is the third largest city; it shares in Little Rock's economic activities. Pine Bluff, the fourth largest city, is a lumbering center. The state's chief tourist attraction, and probably best known city, is Hot Springs, a noted health resort. Arkansas has more mineral springs than any other state: other resorts are located at Eureka Springs and Mammoth Spring. To the south, the city of El Dorado is the oil capital of the state.

Education

A system of common (free) schools was established by the state legislature in 1843, but the modern system of public education was not set up until 1868, when the state received a new constitution.

The largest institution of higher learning is the University of Arkansas, which has its main campus at Fayetteville. There are branch campuses at Little Rock, Pine Bluff, and Monticello.

History of Arkansas

What is now Arkansas was part of the Louisiana Purchase of 1803, a vast tract of land stretching from the Mississippi River to the Rocky Mountains, but excluding Texas. The Arkansas Territory was separated from the Missouri Territory in 1819, and the western boundary was established by a treaty with the Cherokee Indians in 1828.

The first permanent white settlement was built by the French in 1686. France ceded the region to Spain in 1762 but took it back in 1800. Three years later it was sold to the United States. In 1836 Arkansas was admitted to the Union as the 25th state.

After the Civil War Arkansas had a "Reconstruction government" run by northerners, until it was readmitted to the Union in 1868.

Aluminium ore was discovered in 1887; natural gas was found in 1901, diamonds in 1906, and oil in 1921. But the state remained basically rural and poor until industrialization began after World War II.

Arkansas gained international notoriety in 1957, when Governor Orval Faubus defied a court order to integrate Little Rock's schools by calling out the National Guard to keep black students out. President Eisenhower, however, took over the Guard and forced the integration.

FACTS AND FIGURES

AREA: 137,754 square kilometers (53,187 square miles)
POPULATION: 2,349,000 (1984)
MOUNTAINS: Ozark Range (Boston Mountains); Ouachita Mountains. Highest peak: Magazine Mountain, 860 meters (2,823 feet).
RIVERS: Arkansas, St. Francis, Ouachita, White, Red.
CITIES: Little Rock (158,461); Fort Smith (71,626); North Little Rock (64,288) Pine Bluff (56,636); Fayetteville (36,608); Hot Springs (35,781); El Dorado (25,270).

ARKANSAS RIVER, in the United States, is the longest tributary of the Mississippi-Missouri system. From central Colorado near the Tennessee Pass on the Continental Divide, it flows south and east for 2,334 kilometers (1,450 miles) through Kansas and Oklahoma before it joins the Mississippi River in southeastern Arkansas. The area it drains, nearly 41 million hectares (157,900 square miles), is almost as large as the state of California.

During its course, the Arkansas drops 3,472

meters (11,400 feet) and passes through many different kinds of country. On its short trip through the Rocky Mountains it flows down nearly 2,130 meters (7,000 feet). This fall has cut a narrow canyon about 427 meters (1,400 feet) deep, known as the Royal Gorge. As the river crosses the cattle and wheat country of the Great Plains it drops another 1,200 meters (4,000 feet).

Below Fort Smith, Arkansas, the river becomes navigable. Here it flows through a broad, flat, cotton-farming valley. At Little Rock, Arkansas, the river reaches the great flood plain of the Mississippi River, a land of swamps and bayous (marshy tributaries), and joins the Mississippi about 64 kilometers (40 miles) northeast of Arkansas City.

ARKWRIGHT, Sir Richard (1732–92). Sir Richard Arkwright was born in the English seaport town of Preston in Lancashire. At the age of ten he became an apprentice in a barber's shop. While he was there he discovered a way of dyeing hair so that the color did not fade in the weather. He also made wigs and sold them in nearby towns and villages.

Arkwright watched the cotton weavers working in their homes. Although they used cotton thread from side to side of the loom, he

The Bettmann Archive

Arkwright's spinning frame had two sets of rollers to pull and twist cotton into a continuous strong thread.

noticed that they wove it in and out of Irish linen threads stretching from the top of the loom to the bottom. When he asked the reason for this, they said that they could not spin cotton thread which was fine enough or strong enough to use for the warp (which ran from end to end of the cloth).

He began to puzzle out how to spin a better thread and gradually worked out the idea for his water-frame, so called because it was worked by water power. His first machine was patented in 1769 and was made with the help of a local watchmaker. It had two pairs of rollers and the top roller of each pair was covered with leather while the bottom one was of steel, with grooves to hold the cotton. There were spindles to twist the thread as it went between the two sets of rollers but one pair turned faster than the other so that it drew the cotton out in a fine but strong thread.

Two years later, Arkwright built his first spinning mill in Nottingham, England, to try out his invention and in time he improved the machine so much that it made the county of Lancashire the center of the world's cotton trade.

Arkwright's factories were well organized and a good example to others, but his attempts to make spinning simpler using machinery were not at all popular at first. It took him a long time to persuade manufacturers that the cost would not ruin them, and the weavers that machines would not put them out of work. His opponents fought in every way they could, even destroying one of his factories. In his early days his own wife had smashed his models because she thought he was wasting his time. In later life he was recognized as a great inventor and managed then to get the education for himself that he never had as a boy.

ARMADA, SPANISH. The Armada was the fleet of Spanish ships that King Philip II of Spain sent to attack England in 1588 during the reign of Queen Elizabeth I. One hundred and thirty ships set sail, but only 67 returned to Spain, and after this one attempt Spain never again tried to invade England.

King Philip had several reasons for wanting

Mansell Collection

The first encounter between the Armada and the English fleet. The English used the wind to retain the advantage.

to conquer England. One was that England was a Protestant country, and Philip wanted to make all Europe become Roman Catholic under the control of the Pope. He was angry when in 1587 the English executed Mary Queen of Scots, who was his aunt and a leading Roman Catholic. Another reason was that Philip owned the Netherlands and he was afraid that his possessions there would never be safe while England was strong. A third reason was that British sailors had been attacking the Spaniards and their treasure-ships all over the world, and Philip was determined to have his revenge.

In 1587 the Spanish fleet was almost ready to start when Sir Francis Drake of England made a daring raid into the harbor at Cadiz, and destroyed the Spanish ships there and many of their stores. In this way he "singed the King of Spain's beard", and Philip had to start building up his fleet all over again. Philip suffered further bad luck when the fleet commander died. The Duke of Medina-Sidonia, who was chosen to command the Armada instead, knew little about naval warfare.

At last in 1588 the great fleet set sail. Of the 130 ships some were great galleons "very stately built and so high they were like castles". About 8,000 sailors and more than 19,000 soldiers manned the ships. In addition there were mules and horses and enough wine and ship's biscuit to last half a year.

However, the Armada had hardly left Lisbon when it was damaged by a storm and had to put back into harbor at Corunna. In the end it was July instead of May when the fleet began its journey up the English Channel.

The plan was that the Armada should fight its way up the Channel to reach the coast of Flanders, where a Spanish army commanded by the Duke of Parma was already waiting. The Armada was to bring this army across the Channel to land on the shores of southeast England.

The Battle

The vast Armada sailed up the Channel in a crescent formation, 11 kilometers (7 miles) long. On 20 July it appeared off Plymouth, and the English fleet, numbering 197 ships, sailed only just in time to avoid being trapped in the harbor by the Spaniards. The English Lord High Admiral, Lord Howard of Effingham, was commander-in-chief. Sir Francis Drake,

Mary Evans Picture Library

The Armada was chased from Calais by English fireships and fought by the English off the coast of Flanders. The Spanish suffered losses and limped home via the north of Scotland.

who had been in command of the fleet at Plymouth, was vice-admiral (see DRAKE, SIR FRANCIS); his lieutenants were Sir John Hawkins and Sir Martin Frobisher (see HAWKINS, SIR JOHN). These commanders, the most famous seamen of the age, intended to prevent the Armada from reaching the Spanish army that was based at Dunkirk. They planned to use the wind to help them. The wind was expected to be blowing from the southwest, and if the English could get to windward of their enemy (that is, on the side from which the wind was blowing) they could prevent the Spaniards from turning back, and drive them up the Channel and past Dunkirk. To reach the enemy, the English could sail straight before the wind, but if the Spaniards wished to turn and tackle the English they would have the more difficult task of sailing against the wind. (At that time ships could scarcely sail to windward at all, but the English ships were better able to do so than the large, clumsy Spanish galleons.)

The English plan succeeded well. The ships

worked round to windward of the Spaniards and began firing on them at long range. The Spanish admiral would have liked to close with and board the English ships, when the great number of his soldiers would have been an advantage to him, but the English gave him no chance to do this. Instead they hovered behind the Spanish fleet for almost a week keeping up their attacks. The English ships were manned by skillful sailors and carried many guns, which had a longer range than the Spanish ones. The Spaniards, though they fought bravely, were no match for the English either in seamanship or gunnery.

At last the Spanish fleet anchored off Calais, in northern France. The English determined to drive them out into the open sea again by using fireships. The next night six ships were filled with pitch, set on fire, and sent drifting down on the tide towards the enemy. In a panic the Spaniards cut their cables and put out to sea.

Next morning Drake chased them in a confused mass towards the coast of Flanders and in one day's fighting caused enormous damage. He might have captured 16 Spanish ships, but luckily for the Spaniards a squall of wind and rain stopped the battle for a time. Moreover, the English ships were running short of ammunition.

During the night, the sea became more stormy as a northwesterly gale sprang up, and next day the Spaniards were trapped between the shore and the English ships. A little longer and they would have been destroyed, but just in time for them the wind changed back again to the southwest and they were able to sail northward and escape into the North Sea. Lord Howard and Drake followed the remains of the Armada as far as the Firth of Forth in Scotland, but when they got there they turned back, because they had no supplies left.

The End of the Armada

The Spaniards' troubles were not over—indeed, the worst was yet to come. They decided to sail round the British Isles. But they met gales all the way round Scotland and the wild coast of Ireland, and their ships, which had already received a hammering from the English gunners, were completely shattered. Some ships sank in the Atlantic, and the shores of western Ireland were strewn with wrecks. Many hundreds of men who lived through the storms were killed by the Irish and by the soldiers of the English garrisons in Ireland.

King Philip's hopes were shattered like his ships, and only half his Armada managed to reach home in the autumn.

The joy in England after the victory was unbounded. The Queen drove in state to St. Paul's Cathedral to offer thanks, and ordered a medal to be struck in memory of the great triumph. Upon it were (in Latin) the words, "God blew, and they were scattered", signifying England's confidence that God was on their side.

ARMADILLO. Armadillos are small, pig-like mammals related to sloths and anteaters. The name armadillo is Spanish and means "little armored one". The armadillo has a bony covering made up of solid plates and flexible bands, jointed in such a way as to form a protective shield. The three-banded armadillos (*Tolypeutes*) are the only ones that can roll themselves up into a ball.

There are 20 species, found in South and Central America, with one species, the nine-banded armadillo (*Dasypus*), also found in the southern United States.

Leonard Lee Rue III/Bruce Coleman

The nine-banded armadillo gets its name from the nine bands of movable armor around its middle.

The largest species is the giant armadillo (*Priodontes giganteus*) which grows to 1.5 meters (5 feet). The smallest one is the tiny pink fairy armadillo (*Chlamyphorus truncatus*) 16 centimeters (6.5 inches). This animal has a dense coat of soft hair on its sides and underparts. When frightened it uses the vertical plates on its back to plug the entrance to its burrow.

Armadillos are mainly active at night. They live mainly in burrows and can dig at great speed with their strong, curved claws. They feed on insects such as termites, as well as roots, worms, small reptiles and anything else they can find. They can run surprisingly fast on their short legs and are also good swimmers. Before they get into the water they swallow air, which helps them to float.

ARMENIA. The Armenian Soviet Socialist Republic is the smallest republic of the Soviet Union, tucked in roughly half-way between the Black Sea and the Caspian Sea, and within the Caucasus Mountain region. It is bordered by Turkey to the west, and a narrow strip runs through another Soviet republic, Azerbaijan, to the south where it reaches Iran. The republic was formed out of a larger region known as Armenia, which was once a kingdom rivaling even the Roman Empire, and home to a people with their own alphabet, language and distinctive culture.

The geography of the area is mostly mountainous, with about 90 per cent of the land higher than 915 meters (3,000 feet). The highest mountain is Mt. Aragats at 4,090 meters (13,418 feet). The northeastern plateau, which includes the second largest city, Leninakan, is prone to earthquakes. The other major geographical features are Lake Sevan to the east, which covers an area of 945 kilometers (587 miles); and the Razdan River, which flows from this lake and provides hydroelectric power for the capital, Yerevan, and its industries.

The climate of this area is dry, a situation that normally creates problems for farmers growing crops. Fortunately, Armenian farmers can rely on the many streams which provide suitable irrigation—a system of feeding water to crops. These crops include cotton, tobacco, silk, sugar-beet, and grapes—Armenia is well known for the wines and brandies made from these grapes. Most of the grapes and other fruits, including peaches, pomegranates, and apricots, are grown in the fertile Aras River region to the southwest.

Although agriculture is still important to the region, and roughly half the population of 3 million are involved with it, the main economic feature of this area today is the growth of towns and the increase in the number and variety of factories. Yerevan has over 1 million inhabitants and is the major industrial center of the republic. It produces machinery, processed food, synthetic rubber, chemicals, and silk textiles.

The Armenian People

During the Roman period, in the 1st century BC, Armenia was established as a kingdom under the rule of King Tigranes II. He conquered other bordering lands and developed an empire that was never again matched in the country's history.

As long ago as AD 300 the Armenian kingdom adopted Christianity as its religion and today most Armenians are still traditionally Christian. A monk, St. Mesrop, is believed to have originated the Armenian alphabet about that time, and the development of a distinctive Armenian culture, especially in literature, sculpture, and architecture began then. The history of this region has been one largely of its people fighting to preserve their centuries-old culture against foreign invasion and oppression.

Armenia suffered from invasions of Arab forces, beginning in the 7th century; but during the reign of the kings from the Bagratid family, between the 9th and 11th centuries, the country became a leading cultural center. Invasions in the following centuries by Turks and Mongols, however, caused a decline. After the invasion of the Egyptians in the 14th century, Armenia lost its last king.

Although Armenia no longer existed as a kingdom, its people continued to try to pre-

Echmiadzin Cathedral in Armenia is the center of the Armenian Catholic Church. It dates from the second century AD.

John Massey Stewart

serve their own culture and tradition against domination by Turkey in the east and Russia in the west, particularly in the 19th century.

It was in the late 19th and early 20th centuries that Armenia suffered its worst casualties from Turkish aggression. During World War I, the Turks, who looked on Armenians as a danger to their country, deported over 1 million Armenians away from the Turkish border across to Syria and Palestine. In what is now generally regarded as the first modern instance of genocide (when an entire population or nation is deliberately wiped out) around 600,000 Armenians lost their lives.

Many of the Armenians who survived, continued to live in Middle East countries, or emigrated to Europe and the United States to settle as Armenian communities, maintaining their cultural traditions. But the majority were absorbed into the Soviet Union in 1936 when Armenia became a republic of the USSR.

ARMOR. Any covering used to protect a person, a vehicle, or a ship might be called armor. Before gunpowder was invented, most battles were fought hand-to-hand between individual soldiers, so everything possible was done to protect a warrior from his opponent's weapons.

The first armor was made from hard leather. Later this was made stronger with rings or flaps made of some harder substance such as bone or metal, with fabric in between.

After bronze and iron were discovered, it was possible to make more elaborate armor. During the Trojan War, in about 1200 BC, the Greeks wore helmets, breastplates, and leggings of bronze (an alloy, or mixture, of copper and tin). About 1,000 years later, however, the Romans made their helmets of iron since it was stronger. Both Greek and Roman armor was easy to move about in. The pieces were shaped to fit snugly on the body. Warriors in ancient times also carried shields, for additional protection. Greek shields were round whereas Roman ones were oblong and curved to protect the front and sides of the body.

Although leather and quilted or padded fabric made reasonably tough armor, metal armor was the strongest. The secret was to make armor that was strong but light and flexible, so that the warrior could move freely.

Chain Mail

The metal workers in Europe and Asia gradually became more skillful and by the 11th century chain armor, or mail, was being worn. Mail was made of small links of iron interlocked, or knitted, together and overlapping.

(1) Greek armor, 500 BC. (2) Roman, AD 100. (3) 9th century. (4) Norman, 1066. (5) 13th century.

Some warriors wore a complete suit of mail, while others wore just a coat of mail. This garment was rather like a long shirt reaching from the neck to the knees, or lower, and with sleeves down to the elbows or wrists. The armored warrior also wore mail mittens on the hands, and a hanging flag, or coif, to protect his head and neck. This kind of armor could be rolled into a bundle, tied to the saddle and slipped on, usually over a padded tunic, or gambeson, when the enemy approached. It was the kind worn by the Normans, and was also favored by the Arabs and Indians.

The coat of mail could turn aside the point of a dagger or ward off a sword or spear thrust, but it was not much use against the battle-axe. A heavy blow could cut through the mail.

Plate Armor

For more protection against such weapons, armorers began to make plates of steel. These covered the most vulnerable parts of the body, the rest being covered by mail. By 1400 mounted warriors, or knights, were wearing a complete suit of overlapping metal plates.

Special care was taken to protect the head. A helmet with a visor (face guard) which could be lifted was sometimes worn. Other kinds of helmet had to be taken off completely if the wearer wanted to have a drink or to talk. All closed helmets had slits so that the wearer could see and breathe.

Dressed like this, a knight could not tell if he was fighting friend or foe. So he had an emblem or device fixed on his helmet to help other knights to recognize him. Sometimes he carried a banner (flag) on his lance. This was the beginning of what is called heraldry (see HERALDRY).

The various parts of a suit of armor had special names. For example, the *gorget* was worn at the neck, the *couter* at the elbow, *gauntlets* on the hands, and *greaves* on the legs.

Armorers had to measure a knight very carefully when they made him a metal suit. The suit was heavy. A complete suit of mail weighed about 23 kilograms (50 pounds); while full plate armor weighed up to 27 kilograms (60 pounds). Those who wanted to become knights had to learn at 14 to vault on a horse while wearing full armor. Knights often needed help in getting into their full fighting or jousting armor.

Only the wealthier fighters could afford a complete suit of plate armor, their poorer followers having to be content with some sort of padded covering, although they might also be able to afford a metal helmet. It was important for a leader to be well protected, for the fate of the battle often depended on whether he could overcome the opposing leader in single combat. Horses also had to be covered, and at the end of the Middle Ages they, too, wore armor.

(6) 13th century. (7) 14th century. (8) 15th century. (9) 16th century. (10) 17th century.

Horse armor was often quilted fabric, combined with specially shaped metal pieces. In India, war elephants were also armored.

Changing Styles of Armor

In the 15th and 16th centuries armorers tried to turn out suits which looked smart, just as the tailors did. Some of their fluted armor is the most beautiful ever made, but in their efforts to keep up with the fashion they added so many decorations and ornaments that the armor was often not much use in battle.

Different styles of armor were worn in Europe, Africa, Arabia, India, China, and Japan. Some was made of metal scales or plates fastened to a leather garment. Other armor was made by lacing together metal plates, while the most massive plate armor was usually fastened by rivets. The North American Indians wore wooden slats, while the Polynesians of the Pacific islands wore armor of wickerwork, bone and coconut fiber.

By the 17th century, it was only in tournaments (see TOURNAMENT) that complete suits of armor were being used. This was because firearms had been invented, and no body-armour could withstand a bullet from a gun. The age of chivalry was over, and the enemy no longer gave a knight time to dress up and mount his horse; he might suddenly attack from behind instead. The knight could no longer ride into battle, relying on the weight of his armor to smash through the enemy lines. So full armor was rapidly discarded from this time.

In the 17th century a soldier on horseback wore much the same as a pikeman on foot—helmet, breastplate, backplate, and some protection for the thighs. Officers had only a little more armor than their men. The musketeer was the first to do without armor altogether, for he had enough to carry without it. Eventually, all infantry soldiers became musketeers. By the 18th century few soldiers even wore a helmet, although some body-armor was still worn by heavy cavalry during the 18th and 19th centuries.

Today, body armor is seen only on ceremonial occasions, as for example when the British Household Cavalry are on ceremonial duty. The infantry helmet was brought back into use by Germany in the 19th century and other nations followed suit in World War I. Metal helmets were necessary to protect soldiers' heads, and have been worn since World War I by most armies.

Modern combat troops may wear protective vests and jackets, while the police and important people whose lives may be threatened, sometimes wear bulletproof vests. Nowadays, fiberglass and other synthetic materials are just as strong as steel, and less cumbersome to wear.

Armor-plated Ships and Vehicles

It was not until the middle of the 19th century that people had to think about protecting ships with armor. The old wooden men-of-war were not easily sunk by solid cannon balls. However, they did not stand up so well to shells which exploded, and so iron plates began to be used as a protection against these. The appearance of the first steam-propelled armored "ironclads" changed naval warfare. (See NAVY.)

As soon as ships became armored, a race started between inventors who were making better guns and other inventors who were improving armor plate. If one country built a ship which was unsinkable, another was sure to invent a gun that could sink any ship afloat.

The first effective armor plate was of wrought iron, and later a layer of steel was put behind it. This was effective until the invention of armor-piercing shells and, later, guided missiles. In the 20th century armor is made by mixing steel and other metals, and rolling it out in plates. During both World Wars, warships were plated with thick armor of toughened steel. Modern ships, however, tend to be more thinly armored than those of World War II. On land, today's tanks have extensive armor for protection against gunfire and missiles. (See TANK.)

See also ARMY; WAR AND WARFARE; WEAPONS.

ARMY. An army is the military force of a country. It is made up of soldiers whose job it is to defend their country against attack from enemies. An army may sometimes include air and naval forces, but these are usually separate organizations. (See AIR FORCE; NAVY.)

In wartime, the army's main task is to fight on land, often working in close partnership with air and naval forces. In peacetime, the army may be called on to carry out other jobs: to put down serious riots, for example, or to help with emergency relief after a natural disaster such as an earthquake. In every army the fighting troops are backed up by other men and women in essential support services (catering, medical, communications, transportation, and so on).

Throughout history the foot soldiers, or infantry, have done most of the heavy fighting. In the past the cavalry, or mounted troops, were used for swift raids and battering charges. Before the invention of rapid-firing rifles and machine-guns drove cavalry from the battlefield, mounted troops often turned the tide of battle. Today, the role of the cavalry has been taken over by the armored units, whose "mounts" are tanks.

Infantry and cavalry usually fought hand-to-hand. Before the invention of gunpowder all missile weapons were in the hands of the artillery. In ancient times, the artillery consisted of huge catapults and slings, which hurled stones and flaming tar at the enemy. Cannon first appeared in the 1300s, but for a long time they were so clumsy that they were of little use. They were fired once at the enemy ranks and then dragged off the battlefield. Wheeled guns pulled by horses made a great difference. They began to be used in the 1600s.

An army also needed engineers to build roads and bridges. The Romans relied greatly on their engineers, whose skill helped the Roman armies to defeat most of their enemies. Engineers were especially useful in a siege. When a walled town or castle was besieged, the army engineers dug tunnels to undermine the walls, mounted the heavy catapults or (later) cannon to bombard the walls, and built ramps and towers with which to storm the fortifications. (See SIEGE.)

Because fighting was generally hand-to-hand, armor was worn as protection (see ARMOR). Even steel armor could be penetrated by a bullet from a gun, and so body armor was of little protection when guns were commonly used after the 1700s. However, modern soldiers still wear metal helmets and protective vests, and they ride in armored vehicles.

Armies of the Ancient World

In prehistoric times, groups of warring hunters no doubt fought with stones and clubs. They learned the value of working together, for a team is much stronger than an unorganized collection of individuals. The empires of ancient Assyria and Egypt were won by large, well-organized armies. The Egyptian pharaoh Ramses II raised a militia (part-time army) of over 400,000 men, who could be summoned from the fields in time of war. The Persians, too, were successful in war. They depended mainly on cavalry armed with bows and javelins (throwing spears).

Mansell Collection/Athens Museum

This carved figure of a Greek foot soldier shows the long spear and round shield he carried.

The Spartans subjected their soldiers to extraordinarily tough discipline. After battle each soldier had to show his shield, for losing it was a disgrace. The Greeks used two kinds of infantry. The heavy infantry were called *hoplites*. They carried pikes (spears) up to 6 meters (20 feet) in length and marched forward in a close formation called the *phalanx*. The phalanx presented a bristling wall of spear points. The Greeks also had lightly armed infantry, who made skirmishing raids.

These troops were armed with spears and javelins. The remainder of the army consisted of auxiliaries (often non-Greeks), armed with bows and slings.

The Roman army relied mainly on infantry. The Roman foot soldier's main weapon was a short sword. The army was organized into regiments called legions, numbering betweeen 4,000 and 6,000 men. The excellent Roman roads made it possible for the legions to march long distances in a short time. (See ROME, ANCIENT.)

Armies in the Middle Ages

During the latter period of the Roman Empire the Roman army was hard pressed to fight off attacks by barbarian invaders. Many of these barbarians were skilled horsemen from central Asia. With the introduction of the stirrup (which made the rider more difficult to unseat) and the use of heavy war horses, the mounted warrior came into his own. From around AD 400 cavalry, rather than infantry, dominated the battlefields of Europe.

During the Middle Ages, peasants were expected to serve their feudal lords in time of war (see FEUDALISM). This custom developed from the *fyrd* of Anglo-Saxon days. The *fyrd* was made up of men owning land, all of whom were sworn to fight for their king. In addition, the king had a personal bodyguard.

The Normans, who conquered England in 1066, had professional soldiers who were mounted knights wearing armor. Many knights were paid soldiers, or mercenaries, and would travel anywhere to fight for whoever would pay them. Each feudal lord also raised his own private army, from his peasants and freemen. Often these soldiers wore their lord's colors and heraldic devices (see HERALDRY). During the Crusades, great armies sailed from Europe to the Holy Land to fight the armies of Islam (see CRUSADES).

In the 13th century Genghis Khan and his Mongol warriors swept across Asia and into eastern Europe. The Mongols were superb horsemen and bowmen. They used signal flags to send orders quickly across the battlefield and traveled so swiftly that they astonished their enemies who were slow by comparison.

However, as the armor worn by European cavalry grew heavier, mounted knights became less effective as "shock weapons". The longbow and crossbow proved deadly weapons against charging knights. Equally effective was the long pike, in the hands of disciplined

Mary Evans Picture Library

The arquebus, the first weapon to be fired from the shoulder, was invented in Spain in the 15th century.

infantry. The English archers defeated the French knights at the battles of Crécy (1346) and Agincourt (1415). Later, in the 1500s, the Spanish armies used pikemen, swordsmen, and musketeers firing arquebuses (the arquebus was the first practical gunpowder musket). The day of the charging knight was over, and the first modern armies began to appear.

The First Modern Armies

The Thirty Years' War (1618–48) saw the beginning of modern armies. Gustavus Adolphus (1594–1632), king of Sweden, set up a system of compulsory military service. He used recruits alongside trained professional soldiers. He improved weapons and used infantry, cavalry, and artillery together in battle.

England did not have a regular army until the Civil War (1642–52). Oliver Cromwell formed the New Model Army to fight for Parliament against King Charles I. Nicknamed the "Ironsides", Cromwell's troops were properly paid, housed, and dressed in uniform. With the restoration of the monarchy in 1660, Charles II came to the throne and the New Model Army was disbanded. One of its regiments is still in existence, however, as the Coldstream Guards.

Throughout the 1700s England's great rival was France. The French army had officers whose sole responsibility was to feed, transport, and house the soldiers. Other officers were full-time military engineers. This was the beginning of the science of military logistics (maintaining supplies of people and equipment). Even so, a soldier's life was a tough one. He could expect to be flogged and ill-treated, and to receive little thanks from his country. For the army was generally disliked, and the civilian population distrusted the notion of a standing army (that is, a full-time professional one).

In the 1700s battles between European armies were fought according to "rules". The opposing forces marched in lines, with bands playing and flags flying. After every musket volley, the soldiers had to stop firing and reload.

Armies usually stayed in camp throughout the winter, for bad weather made it almost impossible to campaign. The troops wore brightly colored uniforms and stood in massed ranks or formations. They were trained to aim, not at an individual on the enemy's side, but at the massed colors of the enemy's formation. Uniforms helped soldiers to recognize friends and allies amid the smoke and confusion of battle.

The formal marching drill of the 1700s can still be seen today, in modern form, at parades such as Trooping the Colour to celebrate the sovereign's birthday. Visitors to London can enjoy this splendid spectacle every year; and they can also see the Changing of the Guard ceremony which takes place at Buckingham Palace every day.

National Armies, New Weapons

During the French Revolution (1789–99), the armies of France grew to an enormous size. The French improved their artillery by assembling lightweight guns in batteries, or groups, for massed firing. Napoleon Bonaparte forged the French army into a mighty force, commanded as a single unit.

During the 1800s, new and more powerful weapons appeared. The railroad and the telegraph speeded up transportation and communications. As early as the American Civil

Soldiers of the English Civil War. Some armor was still worn in the 17th century, but its use was declining.

Mansell Collection

War (1861–65), armies operated in widely separated areas, supplied by rail and keeping in touch by telegraph.

Before the Civil War, the United States had only a small regular army. It was unprepared for the War of 1812 with Britain, poorly trained and badly led. At the start of the Civil War, the army numbered 16,000 men. More than 2 million men eventually served the Union, with about 1 million fighting for the Confederacy. Both sides used the draft (conscription) to compel men to serve.

During the 1800s almost every nation formed its own regular army. Rules were made for the management of these forces, with reforms to improve life for the soldier. There were advances in technology too: bigger guns, stronger armor plate, motor-driven transportation, aircraft, and tanks. Soldiers needed to be specially trained to use the new equipment,

and engineers, signalers, medical and transportation experts, and other specialists became increasingly important.

Women as well as men were by then serving in the army. Individual women had often gone on active service, either alone or with their husbands. During the Crimean War (1854–56) the English nurse Florence Nightingale took her band of nurses to care for the sick and wounded. From this beginning grew the army nursing service, which was quickly adopted by other armies.

Changes in Uniform

The British army wore red coats from the 1600s. During the North American wars of the 1700s, the British found their red coats gave them away too easily. The "rules" of European warfare were ineffective against Indians and American patriots, who knew the countryside and wore clothing which blended into the background.

Uniforms became very fanciful after the Napoleonic Wars. Cavalry wore plumed helmets and metal breastplates, for example. But in the United States, more practical clothing was worn by both sides in the Civil War of the 1860s, the Union armies wearing blue, the Confederates gray. The British gave up their red uniforms during the South African War against the Boers (1899–1902), and uniforms of khaki or dust color were adopted for all the troops. The Germans chose "field-gray" (gray-green), but many French soldiers were still wearing blue coats and red trousers at the outbreak of Word War I.

Today, soldiers of one country tend to dress similarly to those of another. Combat dress is often mottled, for camouflage (see CAMOU-FLAGE). Special clothing is worn for snow or jungle operations. The more colorful parade uniforms are kept for special occasions.

Training and Tradition

Throughout history, the soldier has been trained to obey orders. But the good soldier also uses personal initiative. On entering the army, all newcomers receive a basic training course, during which they learn army ways. Later, as their special skills and interests become known, they may learn a particular job and join one of the army's specialist branches.

The newcomer to the army quickly realizes that great value is placed on history and tradition. Each army unit is proud of its past achievements and famous battles are remembered. The British Yorkshire Light Infantry, for example, fought at the Battle of Minden (Germany) in 1759, during the Seven Years' War. The regiment, then known as the 51st Foot, helped to defeat the French. As they advanced across the German countryside, the soldiers plucked wild roses from the hedgerows and put them in their hats. Ever since then, the soldiers of the regiment, along with others who fought at Minden, have worn roses on the anniversary of the battle.

All army units like to build up a team spirit or *esprit de corps*, as it is called. This helps everyone to live and work together, and to act as an effective military unit in time of war.

Armies in the 20th Century

The armies of World War I fought in dense formations, usually dug into defensive trenches. Artillery and machine guns took a dreadful toll on both sides, and casualties were high. (See WORLD WAR I.) During the 1920s and 1930s new tactics were developed to make full use of the speed and power of the airplane and the tank. In World War II the German army achieved surprise by its *blitzkrieg* ("lightning war") tactics. In *blitzkrieg* warfare, motorized infantry, tanks, and artillery raced across country, while overhead fighter and bomber aircraft provided support for them. Landing-craft ferried armies across rivers, lakes, and seas.

During World War II the largest armies ever seen were assembled by China, Russia, Japan, Germany, Britain and her allies, and the United States. During the war the United States army reached a peak strength of 8 million men and women, in both ground and air forces. In 1944 the Allies landed enormous armies in France, in the largest sea-borne invasion ever mounted. (See WORLD WAR II.)

At that time many army tactics were introduced that are still in use today. Air support played a vital part. Most armies had airborne assault troops, who were soldiers carried by air. Sometimes they were dropped by parachute; sometimes they landed in gliders towed to the battle zone by other aircraft. World War II armies also perfected amphibious warfare. Troops were carried ashore in special landing-craft, and tanks "swam" ashore under their own power.

There were many advances in weapons, chiefly in aircraft and artillery, including rockets and guided missiles. The war was finally ended by the dropping of the atomic bomb, which unleashed a destructive force far greater than that of any army upon Hiroshima, Japan.

Even though the modern army has highly complicated weapons (radar-guided rockets, quick-firing guns, armored helicopters), it has

For protection against gas and other chemical weapons, modern soldiers must wear special clothing.

Frank Spooner

been shown that powerful arms do not always bring victory. During World War II, resistance fighters used guerrilla tactics very successfully. Small bands of fighters would attack suddenly, and disappear into the countryside. In the Vietnam War, the United States faced a determined guerrilla enemy, whose forces in the end proved victorious.

Today's infantryman travels light and at speed. He carries a self-loading rifle or sub-machine-gun, and rides in an armored personnel carrier, equipped with anti-tank weapons. He has special clothing to protect him from biological (germ) and chemical (gas) weapons. The soldier's face-mask allows him to breathe safely in the thick of smoke or gas. The "tin hat" worn by soldiers in the two World Wars has been replaced by a molded helmet.

Communications are vital to the modern army. Units keep in touch with headquarters by radio, and signals can be sent by satellite right across the world in seconds. If necessary, today's infantry can operate as fast-moving independent groups. For their armored vehicles carry not only radio and weapons, but also cooking equipment, food and water, and medical supplies.

Organization of the Army

Most of the world's armies are organized on roughly similar lines, although there are some differences, often in the ways in which armies are controlled by governments.

In the United States and Britain, as in most other democratic countries, the army is under civilian control. The army takes its orders from the government of the day, and its day-to-day affairs are looked after by civil servants. (See CIVIL SERVICE.)

The President of the United States is the Commander-in-Chief of the United States army (as well as of the other armed forces). Reporting to the President is the Secretary of Defense, a member of the government. Under the Secretary of Defense serves the Secretary of the Army, head of the Department of the

Army. He is responsible for all army affairs, and his principal military adviser is the Chief of Staff, the senior officer in the army.

In the British army, too, the senior officer is the Chief of Staff, who also works closely with the heads of the navy and air force. The Chief of Staff advises the Defence Minister, the member of the government with special responsibility for the armed services. Final authority over the army rests with the Prime Minister and the government of the day. Canada and Australia have similar systems, though in Canada the army is part of the country's combined defense forces.

In other countries, the military may be a branch of the government or even form the government itself. Military rule has been common in parts of Africa and in South America.

Jenny Matthews/Format

Irregular forces, or guerrillas, can be as effective as regular troops. These women soldiers are Nicaraguan.

Each person in the army belongs to a basic branch (such as the infantry or artillery), or to a special branch, sometimes called a corps. For example, members of the Signals Corps work with communications. The Adjutant General's Corps deals with records and orders. The Ordnance Corps deals with ammunition. The Quartermaster Corps looks after food and clothing. The army has many specialists, including doctors, dentists, chaplains, nurses, military police, bomb disposal experts, drivers, and scientists.

An army is made up of regulars—or professional full-time soldiers. Conscription, or the draft, is used in wartime to "call up" people in order to build up the army's strength. Conscript soldiers serve in many of the world's armies. Britain, however, has an all-professional army, as does the United States. The United States draft laws were allowed to expire in 1973.

As well as regular soldiers, the army needs a reserve of part-time soldiers. These are people who may be called on in time of war or some other emergency. In Britain, the reserve is known as the Territorial and Army Reserve. In the United States, besides the National Guard and Army Reserve, each state has its own National Guard unit, which may be called into federal service.

Units and Ranks

A "regiment" is the traditional army unit. For example, the whole of the British Army's artillery is known as the Royal Regiment of Artillery (but is split into several smaller regiments). The name "regiment" is now used mainly for historical reasons. Many British regiments were named after the parts of the country from which their recruits were drawn. Thus, there are units with names such as the Durham Light Infantry, the South Wales Borderers, and the Gordon Highlanders. Each regiment is proud of its traditions, and most have colors (flags), decorated with the names of battles in which the regiment fought. Nowadays, regiments have been amalgamated (grouped together) to form larger fighting units, called brigades or battle groups.

In the modern army, the division is the standard fighting formation. It is quite self-contained. In other words, it contains infantry, tanks, artillery, engineers, signalers, doctors, and supply troops. A division may contain from 7,000 to 20,000 soldiers.

Each division is divided into brigades (usually from three to five brigades in each division). In turn, each brigade is divided into battalions, and each battalion is divided into companies. Within each company, the soldiers are organized into platoons, each platoon being made up of squads. In this way, the army has a chain of command, so that orders may be passed swiftly and accurately.

Top left: British soldiers of the Parachute Regiment check their equipment before a training drop. **Top right:** Canadian soldiers race away from the helicopter which has just landed them. **Right:** Tactical guided weapons are among the most powerful weapons of the modern army. These are Soviet troops training with their missiles. **Below left:** Engineers of the West German Bundeswehr building a bridge. **Below right:** Soldiers of the United States Army equipped for wintry conditions and wearing white camouflage clothing. In the background is an armored personnel carrier.

Top left: Crown copyright. Top right: courtesy, Canadian Department of National Defense. Right: Tass. Below left: courtesy, Bundeswehr. Below right: courtesy, U.S. Army

The higher, or commissioned, ranks in the army are held by officers. Next come warrant officers and non-commissioned officers. Ordinary soldiers are called privates. Many officers are trained at military academies, such as Sandhurst (Britain) and West Point (United States). In wartime, officers are also commissioned in the field of battle.

The most senior rank of all is General of the Army (United States) or Field Marshal (Britain). In the United States army, the rank of General of the Army is a special one created by Congress for a particular person. Next, in order of rank, come General, Lieutenant-General, Major-General, Brigadier (or Brigadier-General), Colonel, Lieutenant-Colonel, Major, Captain, Lieutenant (or First Lieutenant) and Second Lieutenant. Warrant officers come between commissioned and non-commissioned officers. The non-commissioned officers include Sergeant-Major, Sergeant (with various grades) and Corporal.

In the army, rank is shown by the wearing of special symbols on the uniform. Non-commissioned officers usually wear chevrons (stripes) on their sleeves. Commissioned officers wear shoulder badges of various kinds. A general usually wears stars.

A division is usually commanded by a general. A colonel commands a regiment or brigade (about 4,000 people). A lieutenant-colonel leads a battalion; a captain is in charge of a company; and a lieutenant commands a platoon (roughly 40 people). The smallest unit (a squad of 10 people, or a section, even smaller) is under the command of a sergeant or corporal.

Special women's corps were first formed during World War I. The women took over jobs (such as driving) previously done by men, thus releasing more troops for the front-line fighting. During World War II women served not only as signalers, decoders, drivers, clerks, cooks, and nurses, but also on anti-aircraft gun sites. Most of the world's armies have women serving alongside men, doing many of the same tasks. In some armies, women are trained to use the same weapons, and serve in combat units.

Special Army Forces

A typical modern army division is a mixture of infantry, armored vehicles, and artillery, supported by specialist units (such as engineers and communications experts).

There are also airborne divisions, normally including paratroops. Airborne units, men and vehicles, can be packed into aircraft and flown long distances. If there are no suitable landing strips, the division can drop by parachute. Forces such as these can be flown in a few hours to a trouble spot anywhere in the world. Air mobile divisions were developed by the United States army during the Vietnam War. Helicopters give these divisions rapid movement and the immediate power of rockets, cannons, and machine-guns fired from the air.

Commandos (named after the Boer raiders of the South African War) and Rangers are highly trained and tough troops. They are equally at home in helicopters or naval ships, and are trained to land in enemy territory, often in small groups. Other highly trained soldiers belong to special operations units, such as the United States Green Berets and the British Special Air Service (SAS). These units are trained for operations behind enemy lines, carrying out sabotage raids or gathering information. They are also occasionally used to tackle terrorists. Marines are special troops who are particularly expert in seaborne operations. See (MARINES.)

The modern army has more powerful weapons than ever before. Yet it still relies greatly on the skill, training, and discipline of its men and women.

See also WAR AND WARFARE; WEAPONS.

ARNOLD, Benedict (1741–1801) was an American general of great ability who betrayed his country during the American Revolution.

Arnold was born in Norwich, Connecticut, the son of a well-to-do family. When the revolution began, he volunteered for the revolutionary army and became a colonel. He joined Ethan Allen in the attack on Fort Ticonderoga (see ALLEN, ETHAN). During the winter of

Benedict Arnold at first fought well for the American Revolution but later joined the British.

1775–76 he led an unsuccessful attack on Quebec. For his bravery he was promoted to brigadier-general. In October 1776 he assembled a fleet on Lake Champlain and caused heavy damage to a larger British fleet.

Early in 1777, Congress promoted to major-general five officers who ranked under him. When Arnold wanted to leave the army, George Washington talked him out of it. After his success in a battle at Ridgefield, Connecticut, Congress gave him his promotion.

Later in 1777 Arnold went to New York, where he prevented a British army from moving down the Mohawk Valley. Later he was wounded in the colonial victory at Saratoga.

After the British left Philadelphia, Washington placed him in command of the city. Some of his enemies accused him of using his job for private profit and he was court-martialed, although he was let off with a reprimand. Even so, this incident was the turning point in his career. His loyalties began to change. During 1779 Arnold began writing to Sir Henry Clinton, the British commander-in-chief, and gave him many valuable military secrets.

When Washington made him the commander of West Point, an important base on the Hudson River, Arnold made a deal with Clinton. He offered to let the British take West Point for a large sum of money and a rank in the British army. Major John André, one of Clinton's officers, went to West Point to make final plans. On his return journey, André was captured and hanged as a spy. Hearing of André's capture, Arnold fled to New York. He served with the British until the end of the war. He spent his last years in Canada and England.

See also AMERICAN REVOLUTION.

ARNOLD, Thomas (1795–1842) and Matthew (1822–88).

Thomas Arnold made his name as an educationist. He was headmaster of Rugby School in Warwickshire, England, for 14 years, during which time he completely changed the life there. His ideas have been copied in English schools ever since. His son Matthew is most famous as a poet and a critic of literature, but he too was interested in English schools, particularly those giving primary education.

National Portrait Gallery, London

Left: Thomas Arnold. **Right:** his son, Matthew.

Thomas Arnold was born at East Cowes on the Isle of Wight, England, and educated at Winchester School and Oxford University. He was ordained as a clergyman and began teaching privately in 1819. He became headmaster of Rugby in December 1827 after spending many years studying and teaching privately. When he took over the school he set out to make it a "Christian community" which would teach its boys to be "Christian gentlemen". In those days boarding schools were rough, lawless, and often cruel and the boys often spent their time bullying, drinking, and gambling. Arnold, however, trusted his boys and made the Sixth Form—his "prefects"—responsible for much of the good order and running of the school. He appointed masters whom the boys could respect and admire. He raised the standard of work, encouraged manly games and sports, and put an end to bullying. The novel *Tom Brown's Schooldays*, which was written by an old pupil of Arnold's, Thomas Hughes, describes the life at Rugby in those days and the evils Arnold had to fight.

Matthew Arnold, Thomas's eldest son, was born at Laleham, Middlesex (now in Surrey), where his father was a private tutor. He was educated at Rugby, where he won the school prize for poetry when he was 18, and at Oxford University, where he won the Newdigate prize for poetry. Two years after this, in 1845, he gained a Fellowship at Oriel College in Oxford, but then, after trying political life for a time and also spending a short period as a master at Rugby, he became in 1851 an inspector of schools. He visited schools all over Europe as well as at home and through his work helped to bring about the beginnings of the free education which England has today. He died suddenly on a trip to Liverpool.

Among the most famous of Matthew Arnold's poems are "The Scholar Gipsy" and "Sohrab and Rustum". This latter poem, a long dramatic work, tells the tragic story of how a father kills his own son by mistake in single combat. Another is "The Forsaken Merman". In this poem, the merman married a mortal wife, but at last she left him and his children to return to her old home on land. The merman searched for her in vain and had to go back without her to the sea.

> Where great whales come sailing by,
> Sail and sail, with shut eye,
> Round the world for ever and aye. . .

ARROWHEAD. An arrowhead is a sharp-pointed piece of stone, bone, or metal that is fastened to the end of a slender stick. This stick is called an arrow-shaft and is shot from a bow. A bow and arrow is a weapon made up of a bow, a bowstring, an arrow-shaft, and an arrowhead.

Arrowheads, and therefore bows and arrows, have been used by people in many different lands. Ancient arrowheads have been found in Europe, Africa, Egypt, China, and the USSR, and in North and South America. The oldest arrowheads were found in Morocco, North Africa. The African pygmies and some South American Indians tip their arrowheads with poison when hunting. The Chinese devised hollow arrowheads with openings through which the wind rushed, in order to produce a whistling sound. The English long-bowmen used iron arrowheads with a short socket which fitted on to the shaft. Most arrowheads found now are those used by the North American Indians for hunting animals and birds, and for warfare.

Arrowheads were most commonly made from flint, a kind of stone that chips easily. This type is commonly found in some parts of the world. But other kinds of rocks, such as quartzite, volcanic glass, jasper, and slate, were also used. Some arrowheads were made from bone, wood, horn, shell, copper, and iron.

The first step in making a flint arrowhead was to knock chips or flakes off a flint stone with a larger *hammerstone*, to produce so-called *blanks*. Further tiny chips were removed from the blank with a bone chipping tool, to shape the arrowhead and sharpen the edges.

Arrowheads made from bone, horn, or shell were not chipped or flaked. They were cut out of a blank piece of material by means of a sharp, stone knife that looked like an arrowhead. The stone knife was usually larger than an arrowhead, sometimes had beveled or sloping edges, and usually had a wooden handle.

Copper arrowheads were beaten into the correct shape by heating a piece of copper slightly, then placing it on a stone anvil and beating it with a hammerstone. Copper arrowheads usually had the same shapes as those made from stone. No flaking was necessary as the thin edge of the copper was sufficiently sharp. Iron arrowheads were forged by heating a small thin piece of iron and then cutting and beating it into the right shape with tools of iron.

Arrowheads were made in various sizes and

shapes, but the tip was always sharp and pointed. The base, the end that was fastened to the arrow-shaft, was flat, pointed, or rounded. The lower edges of the blade were either straight or curved inwards (notched). Some arrowheads were triangular while others were oval or willow-leaf shaped.

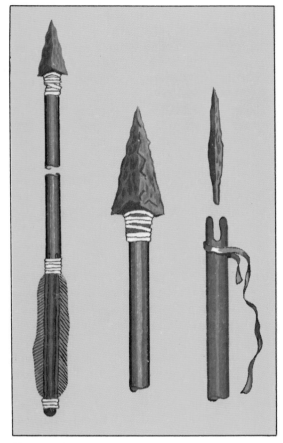

The arrowhead slips into a slot at the end of its shaft and the two are bound together with gut or sinew.

The arrowhead was fastened to the arrow-shaft in a number of ways. One of the best methods was to cut a slit in one end of the arrow-shaft. The base of the arrowhead was inserted into this and was held tightly there by wrapping gut or sinew thread over the slit. Sometimes glue, made from pine pitch or animal hooves, was used to hold it tight.

It is difficult by looking at an arrowhead to tell how old it is or, in the United States, what group of Indians made it. It would take an expert to identify any particular arrowhead, and even he might not be able to do so. The age and type of an arrowhead dug up by an archeologist can be determined because he has many other objects to help him—things such as pottery, spearheads, bone awls and needles, houses, stone-axes, and skeletons. (See ARCHAEOLOGY.)

People in North America can still find arrowheads today in fields, near sand dunes, along beaches of lakes and rivers, and near Indian mounds or ancient villages. The best place to look is in a field just after plowing or a rain storm.

One particular arrowhead, the Folsom point, is found only in the United States. No one knows for certain whether this was a point used with a bow and arrow or with a spear. It is of an unusual style and can easily be recognized by a fluting or groove that runs lengthwise on the faces of the point. The base of this point has projections downward which look like rabbit ears. The Folsom point was first found near Folsom, New Mexico, around the bones of buffalo. It is considered to be one of the oldest points in the West, being between 10,000 and 25,000 years old. Similar points have also been found in many other parts of North America.

ARROWROOT is an easily digested starch used mainly in the preparation of food for invalids and children. Unfortunately, when it is produced, it is often mixed with potato flour, rice flour and even common white flour.

Early explorers to South America gave the plant *Maranta arundinacea* its common name because they confused it with another plant that the Indians used to treat wounds made by poisoned arrows. Later they learned from the Indians that the plant could provide a delicate flour. Another explanation of the name comes from the Amerindian word for flour-root, *araruta*.

To extract the flour, the roots of year-old plants are peeled, then grated in water that has been left to stand in the sun. When the water has evaporated, a fine, white powder remains. It is very light and crackles when rubbed between the fingers; in cooking it swells considerably.

The finest arrowroot comes from the West Indies, but other kinds are cultivated.

ARSENIC is a chemical element that exists in both yellow and gray crystalline forms. In nature it is found on its own near deposits of silver or antimony, or in the compounds realgar and orpiment (sulfides of arsenic), in arsenic oxide, and as a constituent of certain

Mary Evans Picture Library

The poisonous salts of arsenic were used in Victorian times in making the flypapers sold by street sellers.

metallic sulfides (notably arsenopyrite, a sulfide of iron). Gray arsenic, which is more stable than the softer yellow form, sublimes when heated, that is, it turns directly from a solid to a vapor without passing through the liquid state, and goes straight from a vapor to a crystalline solid upon cooling.

Compounds of arsenic were known as early as the 4th century BC, but it was not discovered to be a chemical element until 1649. The compounds of arsenic are mostly poisonous. Among the most important commercially are arsenious oxide (white arsenic), used in pesticides and in the manufacture of glass and the preserving of animal hides, and arsenic pentoxide, which supplies a major ingredient in the production of insecticides, herbicides and weedkillers, and metal adhesives. Arsine, a colorless, poisonous gas composed of arsenic and hydrogen, is used as a doping agent for semiconductors and as a military poison gas. Arsenic acid, lead arsenate, and calcium arsenate are all important in agriculture in sterilizing soils and controlling pests.

Arsenic poisoning usually results from swallowing or breathing in arsenic compounds used in the manufacture of weedkillers, pesticides, paints and wallpaper, and ceramics. Arsenic poisoning can result from taking one large dose or a series of small doses. Many people have been murdered using arsenic.

ART. Originally the word art meant "skill" or "ability"—as in the skill of a craftsman. So we talk about the "art of gardening". But "art" also describes the many ways in which people try to express their ideas and feelings by creating something. The most important arts are usually agreed to be architecture, sculpture, painting, literature, and music. (There are articles on each.) The many others include such activities as ceramics (pottery), furniture, tapestry, metalwork, photography, filmmaking, theater, and graphic arts such as printing, stenciling, etching, and engraving. In each case, the artist tries to express a general truth about life. Artists have been trying to do this since the days of the early Stone Age cave painters.

When looking at paintings, it often helps to know a little about the background. Look at the two pictures shown here. Over 400 years of history separates them. In his study of the Virgin and Child, Leonardo da Vinci (1452–1519) has drawn figures which look quite natural. He has tried to show that the relationship between Mary and Jesus is warm and tender. Pablo Picasso's (1881–1973) painting, on the other hand, is full of anger. The woman's face is distorted by grief. It was painted during the Spanish Civil War (1936–39), and the artist wanted those who looked at the painting to be affected by the emotions it portrays.

ARTESIAN WELL.
Usually when a well is dug, water is found far below the ground. This water must then be brought to the surface of the earth with a pump or with a bucket on a long rope. But sometimes the water in a well bubbles up naturally above the surface of the earth. This is called an artesian, or flowing, well.

Artesian wells can be found only where there is water stored underground at great pressure. Such pressure is built up when a layer of loose rock, gravel, or sand is sandwiched between two layers of solid rock. The loose gravel or sand has spaces or pores to hold the water. Because the water cannot pass through the solid rock, it is held in the middle layer.

These three layers must not lie flat, or horizontal, because no rain or snow could trickle through the upper layer of rock down to the sand or gravel. It would be like pouring water over a pipe that was lying flat. No water would enter the pipe. But if the pipe were tilted upward, water could be poured into the open end. The same thing is true of the two layers of rock and the loose, or porous, middle layer. If these are slanted to form the slope of a hill or the U-shaped sides of a valley, water can easily enter the middle layer at its top end.

To drill an artesian well, a hole is bored through the upper layer of solid rock into the layer that holds the water. The hole may be drilled at any point down the slope of the hill

Above: Detail from *The Virgin and Child with St. Anne and John the Baptist,* a drawing by Leonardo da Vinci. The artist has tried to make his figures look life-like.
Right: In *The Weeping Woman,* Picasso does not paint the woman's face in a realistic way. The emotional message is more important.

SOME ARTICLES TO READ ON ART

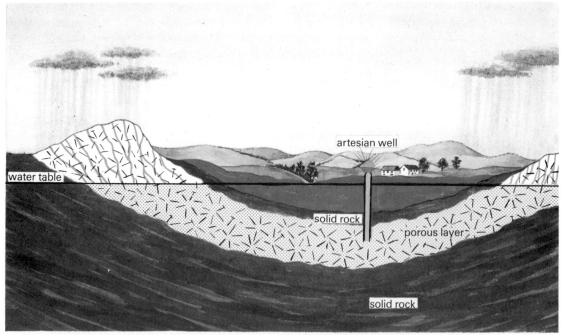

water table

artesian well

solid rock

porous layer

solid rock

Water gushes out of an artesian well because it is stored under pressure in the rock.

or in the bottom of the valley. Because of the pressure of the water that is in the middle layer lying uphill from this new opening, water will gush out of the hole. The height to which the gushing water rises depends on the amount of pressure that forces it out. That is, it depends on how much water lies uphill from the hole.

Not all water from artesian wells has to be drilled for by man. A crack in the top layer of rock may allow the water to flow out. Such a natural "well" is called an artesian spring.

The point where water enters the porous layer may be as much as several hundred miles away from the opening where the water gushes out. Silver Springs in Florida, a famous natural spring, is an example of this. This spring is produced from rain that enters the underground water-storage layer at places as far away as the state of Georgia. Thus, artesian wells are found even in desert regions. This is possible because the water for these desert wells may come from mountains above, where it may rain often.

Because artesian wells are often very deep,

their water is usually pure enough for drinking. Part of the water supply in London, England, and Paris, France, comes from artesian wells, as do the supplies in Denver, St. Louis, and Louisville in the United States.

Artesian water is used in many parts of the world for irrigating farm lands. In the Great Artesian basin of Queensland in Australia more than 2,500 wells have been sunk, some of them thousands of meters deep. In North Africa is the Sahara Basin, in which water comes from the Atlas Mountains and flows in underground streams through beds of sand. A very large artesian basin is the Dakota basin in the United States. It extends under the states of South Dakota, Colorado, Nebraska, and Kansas.

In Europe the use of a boring-tool or drill for well drilling was first begun in Artois, a province in France. There, at the town of Lillers, the first modern artesian well was drilled in 1126. The Romans called the province Artesium and artesian wells were named after it.

Most of the modern methods of well drilling

came after the great success of the famous artesian well at Grenelle, near Paris, France. This well, which was finished in 1841, took eight years to produce. But artesian wells were used long before modern times. The Chinese and Egyptians probably knew how to drill such wells in ancient times. Wells from artesian springs are mentioned in the Bible.

ARTHRITIS AND RHEUMATIC DISEASES.

"Arthritis" is a vague term that generally means problems with the body's joints, aches, pains, and stiffness. "Rheumatism" is another, even vaguer, term often used for aches and pains that might be in joints, muscles, or other parts of the body.

Many people—including some doctors—tend to use these words in an imprecise way. This is partly because arthritic and rheumatic illnesses are not very well understood, despite much medical research over the years.

There are many kinds of arthritis. Most involve deterioration of cartilage. This is the smooth, shiny, gristly material that covers the ends of bones in a joint. When the cartilage is healthy the bones move smoothly. When the cartilage is worn out or diseased it becomes rough, knobbly, cracked, and thickened. This usually causes stiffness, redness, and swelling, and pain when the joint is moved (see BONE, JOINT AND LIGAMENT; SKELETON).

Osteoarthritis

The most common type of arthritis is *osteoarthritis*. Here it is thought that the cartilage simply becomes worn out through old age or through being used too much. The disease affects mainly large, weight-bearing joints such as the hip, knees, and vertebrae (the bones in the back). The knee cartilages of football players and others who play physical sports sometimes suffer from this type of arthritis.

A few people have osteoarthritis even though they are quite young. Perhaps there is a problem with their body chemistry that stops the cartilage being kept healthy, or

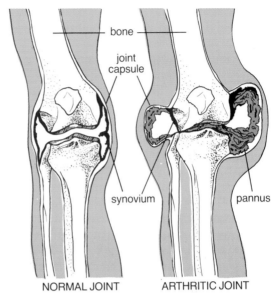

NORMAL JOINT   ARTHRITIC JOINT

A normal joint is surrounded by a healthy synovium lining that keeps the joint moistened and the bones in position. The lining deteriorates in arthritis, thickening and swelling occurs, and bones may fuse.

they may have injured or strained the joint in the past.

Osteoarthritis can usually be treated with *anti-inflammatory* drugs such as aspirin. In general it does not shorten a person's life or make the person feel ill. If a patient is disabled, however, he or she may be able to have an operation to replace the arthritic joint with an artificial one (see BIOENGINEERING).

There are well over a hundred other types of arthritis, mostly very rare. Juvenile arthritis (Still's disease) affects children, although up to three-quarters recover completely. Gout is another type of arthritis.

Rheumatoid Arthritis

About one person in thirty, mostly young adults and older people, develop *rheumatoid arthritis*. This is a different and often more serious disease than osteoarthritis. The person feels ill, and joints, usually the fingers, swell and become red and painful. Other joints that are affected include the wrists, shoulders, ankles, knees, and elbows.

Rheumatoid arthritis usually becomes chronic; that is, it continues for many years with periods of improvement called *re-*

missions. Eventually the hands may become deformed and moving about is difficult. Some drugs help this disease by making the joints less painful. However, like other forms of arthritis, there is no cure.

Rheumatoid arthritis is what is called an *auto-immune* disease. This means the body's immune system, which is designed for fighting infections and healing wounds, goes wrong and begins to attack its own tissues. (See IMMUNITY.)

Rheumatic Fever

This disease is so called because of the swollen, painful joints (rheumatism) and the high body temperature, or fever, that it causes. Actually, the whole body may be affected by this illness. The heart is often more seriously damaged than the joints.

Rheumatic fever is not caused directly by bacteria, but it is believed that bacteria are partly responsible for it. It may be a form of allergy to the streptococcal bacteria responsible for most sore throats (see ALLERGY). Nowadays it is a rare complaint.

About ten days after a sore throat or tonsillitis, the sufferer, who is usually a child, gets a fever and pains in several joints. The painful joints may be swollen and the skin over them warm and red. As one joint gets better another one becomes affected. There may also be a skin rash on the body, arms, and legs.

The usual treatment takes the form of pain-killing drugs. The attack may last anything from two weeks to several months. The sick child may not complain about chest pains, although often the heart is also inflamed. The main risk lies in the heart valves becoming affected, when they may be permanently damaged (see HEART, HUMAN).

Rheumatic fever is now much less common that is used to be. But it may still be a serious disease and cause heart problems later in life. Antibiotic drugs help to limit the damage, and anyone who has had the illness should always tell the doctor or dentist so that the necessary precautions can be taken.

A type of nervous disease called St. Vitus's Dance may also result from rheumatic fever.

A child with this disease constantly moves his hands and feet or face.

ARTHROPODS are small crawling animals that make up the largest grouping in the animal kingdom. Over 900,000 species have been described, representing about 75 per cent of all animals.

The word arthropod comes from the Greek meaning jointed feet. It really describes the jointed legs which may serve the animal for walking, swimming, or the collection and handling of food.

The other common feature is a hard outer skeleton that forms a waterproof covering in insects and spiders and a thick shell in crabs and lobsters.

Arthropods live in most habitats. Crustaceans mainly live in the sea and fresh water, but most insects, spiders, and centipedes live on land.

The success of arthropods is partly due to their small size, which allows them to live in small spaces in the soil or among the vegetation. These spaces are unavailable to larger animals. Insects have the power of flight and have well-developed sense organs. Spiders, scorpions, and centipedes have well-developed poison glands for defense and for paralyzing their prey.

SOME OTHER ARTICLES TO READ ON ARTHROPODS

ANT	HORSESHOE CRAB
BEE	INSECT
BEETLE	LOBSTER
BUG	LOCUST
BUTTERFLY	MITE
CENTIPEDE AND	MOTH
MILLIPEDE	SCORPION
CRAB	SHRIMP AND
CRAYFISH OR CRAWFISH	PRAWN
CRUSTACEAN	SPIDER
FLEA	TERMITE
FLY	TICK
GRASSHOPPER	WASP

ARTHUR, KING. King Arthur and his Knights of the Round Table are the heroes of a series or collection of medieval stories. Although the stories are well known, no one knows who King Arthur really was. Today most writers of history believe that Arthur was a great chief of one of the tribes in Britain, sometime after AD 500. He may have been part Roman and part British, for the Romans had ruled England and Wales for nearly 400 years. Arthur seems to have led a large army against the Saxon invaders. Nennius, an early Welsh historian who lived about the 8th century, is the first writer to mention him, but he also features in a very old Welsh story, written down, long after it was invented, in a collection of tales called the *Mabinogion*.

The Saxons against whom Arthur fought came mostly from the Scandinavian countries and Germany. One group after another sailed across the North Sea to England. They attacked the native Britons, looted the countryside, and finally settled down to live in England. Many native Britons were killed by the Saxons, but many married them. Large groups of the Britons, or Celts, fled to the western parts of Britain, to what are now called Wales and Cornwall (a southwestern county of England). Others crossed the English Channel and settled in Brittany, a province of France.

In Wales, Cornwall, and Brittany, Arthur was remembered and admired. Stories about him were passed on from one generation to another. Each story was more wonderful than the last. Finally, Arthur became one of the greatest heroes who ever lived. He killed horrible monsters; had great magical powers; and became a great and good king, looked up to by many brave knights who rode out from his castle to do good deeds.

The place where Arthur's castle is supposed to have stood remains a mystery. There are about six different sites in England that claim to be the location of Camelot, his home. Many of the stories say that Arthur lived in Cornwall or Wales. But most historians believe that he could not have been in Cornwall. This is because the Saxons he was fighting were all on the eastern coast of England. Probably the stories about Arthur were carried into Cornwall by the Britons who fled there. Later these Britons came to believe that the Arthur stories had happened in Cornwall itself.

It does not really matter today who Arthur was or where he lived. The important thing is the long tradition of King Arthur stories that are found in England, in France, and even in Germany.

How the Legends Grew

For 400 years after Nennius mentioned Arthur, nothing else was written down about him. But in the 12th century, stories about King Arthur became quite common. The earliest stories were written in Latin. But soon both English and French poets were using stories about Arthur in their poetry. Layamon, a 12th-century English poet, told about Arthur in a poem called *Brut*. Robert Wace and Chrétien de Troyes, who were French, also wrote poems about Arthur. A German writer, Wolfram von Eschenbach, wrote a poem called *Parzival*, which was about one of King Arthur's knights. The tales written by these authors were combined with Christian traditions concerning the death of Jesus. The core of this tradition was the Quest (search) for the Holy Grail, the cup that Jesus had used at the Last Supper and in which his blood was collected when he died.

In the 15th century the English writer Sir Thomas Malory wrote down a large group of Arthurian stories in a book called *Morte d'Arthur* ("Death of Arthur"). Although the title is French, the book itself is written in English. It appeared in 1485 and was one of the first English books ever to be printed. Another work dating from the 15th century is a long poem called *Sir Gawain and the Greene Knight*, featuring yet another of Arthur's brave knights, Sir Gawain.

In the 19th century many people became very interested in the Middle Ages. A group of famous English poets were inspired by Malory's book to write the Arthurian stories again in their own way. Probably the best known of these is *The Idylls of the King* by Alfred, Lord Tennyson. Others are *Tristram and Iseult* by Matthew Arnold, *Tristram of Lyonesse* by Algernon Charles Swinburne, and *Defence of Guenevere* by William Morris. The German composer, Richard Wagner, wrote operas on heroes from Arthurian legend, including *Par-

Observer Magazine, photo Dave Newell Smith

Archeologists at work on the hill fort of South Cadbury, Somerset, thought to be King Arthur's Camelot.

sifal (Parzival), *Tristram and Isolde*, and *Lohengrin* (a story centered on the son of Parsifal).

Many books for children have been written about King Arthur. Among these is Sidney Lanier's *The Boy's King Arthur*. Howard Pyle has written and illustrated four books for young people about King Arthur: *King Arthur and His Knights*, *The Champions of the Round Table*, *Sir Launcelot and His Companions*, and *The Grail and the Passing of Arthur*. Best-known in Britain is the tetralogy (group of four novels) by Terence Hanbury White, carrying the general title *The Once and Future King*.

The Story of King Arthur

According to legend, Arthur became king of the Britons when he was only a boy. He was the son of King Uther Pendragon of Britain. When King Uther died, all the knights went to church to pray that God would help them find a new king. As they left the church, they saw a huge stone in the churchyard. An anvil was on top of the stone, and a sword was stuck fast in the anvil. Golden letters on the sword said that whoever could pull out the sword would be king. All the knights tried to pull it out, but no one could move it.

Months later, the knights were having a tournament. But Sir Kay, one of the knights, forgot to bring his sword. So he sent Arthur, his squire, home to get it. When Arthur could not find it, he pulled out the sword in the anvil instead and brought it to Sir Kay. At first the knights did not want to have a king who was only a boy. But Arthur had pulled out the sword and so he became king.

Later Arthur married Guinevere, the daughter of the king of Carmalide. He had helped her father to defeat the Irish. Arthur and Guinevere lived in a castle at Camelot, where the bravest knights also stayed.

All the knights had places around the Round Table, which had been made by Merlin, the magician, Arthur's tutor and adviser. Because the table was round, there was no head and no foot and all the knights were equal. The most famous knights were Sir Lancelot, Sir Gawain, Sir Tristram, Sir Galahad, and Sir Percivale. The knights rode out from Camelot on horseback to their many adventures. They killed wicked knights and saved many

Mansell Collection

This picture from a medieval manuscript shows the lake from which a hand appears clutching the magic sword Excalibur. It was given to King Arthur who used it wisely. Upon his death it was returned to the lake.

beautiful ladies. Sir Lancelot was the strongest knight of all. No one was able to defeat him. Sir Galahad, his son, was the purest knight. He was allowed to see the Holy Grail.

King Arthur was killed by his nephew, Sir Modred, who rebelled against him. The two armies met at a place called Camlan, and Modred was defeated. Arthur killed Modred himself. But as Modred was dying, he struck Arthur over the head with his sword. Arthur knew that he was dying too. He gave his magic sword, called Excalibur, to Sir Bedivere. Arthur had been given this sword by the Lady of the Lake and promised to return it when he died. He told Sir Bedivere to throw the sword in the lake beside the battlefield. Sir Bedivere did not want to throw the beautiful sword away, so he hid it. But Arthur sent him back again and again. The third time Sir Bedivere threw the sword as far as he could into the lake. A hand came out of the water, caught the sword, and waved it three times in the air. Then the sword disappeared under the water. After this, three fairy queens in black hoods came for Arthur in a boat. They carried him away to the magic island of Avalon, from where it was said that one day he would return.

ARTICHOKE. Artichokes are vegetables that have a very delicate flavor. There are two main kinds, the globe or French artichoke (*Cynaria scolymus*), and the Jerusalem artichoke (*Helianthus tuberosus*). Both plants are members of the sunflower family.

The globe artichoke comes from the warm lands around the Mediterranean Sea. It is now

The tender leaves of the unopened globe artichoke bud and the fleshy heart are the parts that are eaten.

grown for food in other parts of Europe and in the United States. Plants may live for many years, but gardeners often replant with new shoots every four years or so. The globe artichoke looks like a large thistle, with long, prickly, gray-green leaves. It bears large white or blue flowers, and it is the buds of the flowers that are eaten. The buds are picked when still tightly closed, before the flowers have opened. When cooked (boiled, for instance), the tender leaves have a delicate, nutty flavor.

The Jerusalem artichoke can grow to a height of 4 meters (13 feet) and has large yellow flowers. It produces underground tubers (like potatoes), and these tubers can be either eaten raw or boiled in much the same way as potatoes. The Jerusalem artichoke is also known as the girasole. It grows wild in North America, where, because it spreads easily, it can become a troublesome weed.

ARTICLE. The adjectives *a, an* and *the* are called by the special name "articles": *A* is in fact a shortened form of *an*, which in Old English meant *one*. Like all adjectives, *a, an* and *the* provide us with information about the nouns before which they are placed. When we use the articles in a sentence, they still mean *one*, but it is the way that they are used that is more important. For instance, "I bought *one* book" makes it clear that only one book was bought and not two or three, but "I bought *a* book" only tells us that what was bought was a book and not something else. Because *a* and *an* provide us with limited information (*a* book could be any book), they are called the indefinite articles.

A is used before words beginning with a consonant sound and *an* before words beginning with a vowel sound. It is correct, and much easier, to say "an orange, an article, an empty bottle", but "a pear, a ship, a ripe apple". *An* is also used before words beginning with a silent *h*: "an hour, an honest man".

The is called the definite article because it gives more information. It points out a particular person or object. "I bought *the* book" tells us that not only was one book bought, but that it was one particular book. Compare other examples, for instance, "I saw *a* dog" with "I saw *the* dog". "*The* dog" is one particular dog described by the definite article.

The is used with both singular and plural nouns, for example, "the man, the men". The plural of *a* or *an* is *some*: "a man" but "some men".

ARTICLES OF CONFEDERATION. The Articles of Confederation were the first constitution, or rules of government, of the United States of America. They were drawn up during the American Revolution, when the 13 American colonies broke away from British rule (see AMERICAN REVOLUTION).

The colonies shared a common desire for independence, but they were not sure how they wished to govern themselves. Each new state was anxious to preserve its own rights and freedoms and to look after its own affairs. They agreed that "confederation", or a form of union was necessary, but they did not want to give up their rights to any central government.

The Second Continental Congress met in May 1775, less than a month after the first fighting between the Americans and the British. A committee of delegates drew up the Articles of Confederation. It was a first attempt to write a new constitution, to create a united nation from the 13 "free and independent" states.

Agreement was not easy and Congress was so busy fighting the war that it took some time to settle the differences. The Articles were adopted at York, Pennsylvania, in November 1777. Even then there were still more arguments over land boundaries. Finally, the Articles went into effect in March 1781.

The Articles planned for a Congress, or parliament, with delegates from every state. Each state would have just one vote. The Congress was not to be an all-powerful central government; its powers were very limited. It was to take charge of certain foreign affairs; declare war and make peace; regulate the coinage; raise an army and navy; provide post offices and post roads; and have authority over the Indian tribes. It could not raise money through taxes, nor enforce its own orders through a national court.

The Congress found it difficult to get very much done, and it was often impossible to reach the necessary agreement among the states. So in 1787 a new Constitutional Convention met at Philadelphia. Its task was to improve on the Articles of Confederation, and the result was the present United States Constitution. This took effect on 4 March 1789 (see CONSTITUTION OF THE UNITED STATES).

ARTIFICIAL INTELLIGENCE see COMPUTER; ROBOT.

ARTIFICIAL LIMB. Someone who loses part or all of an arm or leg through accident or disease, can have an artificial limb, or "prosthesis", fitted in its place. Today, a person who is lacking a limb can be fitted with an artificial limb that looks and works like the missing one, and will be taught and encouraged to use the replacement as if it were real. The aim is to help the person lead as normal a life as possible without needing assistance from others.

Earliest Artificial Limbs

Amputation, or the removal of a limb, is one of the oldest surgical techniques known, dating back to late Neanderthal man some 45,000 years ago. It is uncertain when or where the first artificial limbs were made, but the earliest reference is found in the *Rig-Veda*, a book of Sanskrit hymns, about 1500 BC. The oldest artificial limb ever found dates from Roman times, about 300 BC. This was a leg made from thin strips of bronze fixed to a wooden core with bronze nails.

During the Middle Ages, only the "peg leg", as worn by some pirates, was available. For knights, these had elaborate armored coverings, and were often strapped to the horse because they were too heavy for the wearer. Also during this time, many ingenious artificial arms and hands were constructed to enable a warrior to hold a sword or lance.

In the 16th century, the great French military surgeon Ambroise Paré improved surgi-

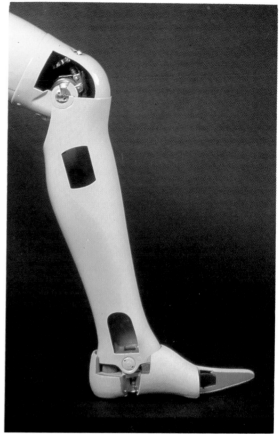

James Stevenson/Science Photo Library

An artificial prosthetic leg constructed of very light and strong materials and finished with a life-like skin.

cal techniques and the treatment of wounds. He founded prosthetics as a modern science, working out the preferred way to amputate limbs, and employed craftsmen to make appliances for his patients.

Modern Prosthetics

Medical researchers and bioengineers (see BIOENGINEERING), are continually developing new and improved types of artificial limbs. Today, a carefully designed artificial leg will allow the wearer to stride at normal walking speed in comfort and safety, and without too much effort and with little or no limp. An artificial arm and hand will enable its owner to operate in most occupations, including riding and driving. Spare limbs are usually provided so that servicing and adjustment can be carried out without inconvenience.

The design of prostheses is based on the detailed study of the structure of the skeleton. Normal walking is accomplished by the long bones rotating about the joints, actuated by the muscles and controlled by the central nervous system (see SKELETON).

In the modern artificial leg, the long bone structure is replaced by very light and exceedingly strong carbon fiber composite tubing. Ankle mechanisms are manufactured from very light and strong aluminum alloys of the kind used for aircraft, with the natural movements controlled by rubber springs. Artificial feet have carbon fiber reinforced structures encased in tough polyurethane foam plastic and molded with natural-looking toes, and are manufactured in standard shoe sizes.

The knee must be able to carry the full weight of the person without collapsing or buckling. A device is fitted to control the swing of the knee and make the leg move in a natural manner. The knee is surrounded with a very soft, flexible, plastic foam shaped to match exactly the natural leg, and is finished with a life-like silicone skin which water or any other substance cannot penetrate.

Modern artificial arms are manufactured in a similar way. One type of artificial arm is known as a "cosmetic arm": it looks like a natural arm and can be fitted with a natural-looking cosmetic glove. Movements of the fingers and the elbow joints are controlled by miniature electric motors powered by rechargeable batteries. Electronic sensors pick up the minute electrical signals that occur as the muscles contract in the shoulder or the remaining part of the arm. These signals are amplified and sent to "servo motors" controlling the wrist and fingers. By moving certain muscles, the wearer can control the force and speed of the fingers' grasp. With practice, the person is able to master such delicate movements as pouring a drink.

"Robust" working arms, the other type of artificial arm, are very strong and are still worn by some amputees. They can be fitted with devices such as hammers, screwdrivers, and hooks. They are powered by moving the opposite shoulder, using a steel cable and body harness, the cable passing around the body to the other shoulder.

ARTIFICIAL SATELLITE see SATELLITE.

ASBESTOS. Asbestos is the name given to a group of minerals which are found in veins in rocks. Asbestos usually contains lime, magnesia and, sometimes, iron and it is dug up from great open pits. It is not hard like most minerals, but is made of rather soft, silky fibers, sometimes more than 60 centimeters (2 feet) long.

Crown copyright

Gloves and a protective helmet made from asbestos protect this man from the flames of a crashed aircraft.

Because it is made of fibers, asbestos can be woven and made up like wool and cotton; no other mineral can be spun into yarn or thread, woven into cloth, or pressed together like felt. Asbestos can stand a temperature of up to 2500°C (4500°F).

People have used asbestos for hundreds of years. In ancient temples the wicks of torches were made of it so that they would not burn away as cotton wicks do, but it was only in the 19th century that asbestos became cheap enough to be used in industry for preventing fire. Nowadays it is used to make parts of an automobile which get very hot such as the lining of the clutch. Other things made from asbestos are insulating jackets for boilers, sheeting for making buildings and roofs fire-resistant, and protective clothing.

Nearly half the asbestos products in the world are made in the United States, but the raw material comes chiefly from other countries: Quebec in Canada, the USSR, China, Italy, and South Africa. A blue form of asbestos is sometimes used as an ornamental stone called "cat's eye".

Health Hazards

Asbestos can be harmful to health. The fine fibers, if inhaled, can produce a lung condition called "asbestosis" or can induce lung cancer. The health hazards have been known since the turn of the century, and the United Kingdom was first, in 1931, to produce regulations that would protect people who work with it. The United States produced similar laws in 1971, and Canada in 1972. It was not until the 1970s and 1980s that people started to take the danger seriously and there have been serious attempts to ban the material altogether. However, in 1985, a report submitted to Britain's Health and Safety Council suggested that the danger was exaggerated and that asbestos was no more harmful than any other hazards of modern life.

ASCENSION see St. Helena.

ASH (*Fraxinus*) are attractive trees of the olive family. All grow in the northern hemisphere. Of the 70 species, about 20 come from North America.

Ash leaves are compound—made up of several leaflets. The seed has a wing on one side, forming a fruit. When caught by the wind, these fruits whirl like propellers and are carried long distances.

The white ash (*Fraxinus americana*) is the most common and largest species of North America, growing about 25 meters (80 feet) tall. Other North American species include the green ash (*Fraxinus pennsylvanica*) and the Oregon ash (*Fraxinus latifolia*). These trees all have long, straight trunks. They are fast-growing and valued for timber and as shade trees.

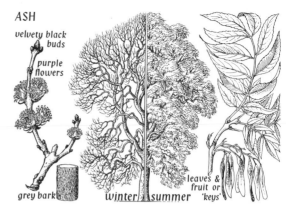

ASH — velvety black buds — purple flowers — grey bark — winter — summer — leaves & fruit or 'keys'

The European ash (*Fraxinus excelsior*) grows to 40 meters (130 feet) and is one of the largest species. The flowering ash (*Fraxinus ornus*) of southern Europe is unusual among the ashes in producing masses of creamy-white, fragrant flowers.

Ash wood is straight-grained, hard, and fairly light, and has a large number of uses. The Greek warrior Achilles is said to have killed Hector with an ash spear in the Trojan War. It is used for tool handles, baseball bats, tennis rackets, skis, and hockey sticks. Because of its good bending qualities, it is also used for boat-building and for some furniture. Since ash is free of odor and taste, staves are often made from its wood to make barrels that contain food.

The mountain ash is not a true ash but in the rose family (see Mountain Ash.)

ASIA is the largest of the continents of the world. It stretches from the Arctic Ocean to the equator, while its eastern shores are washed by the Pacific and its southern ones by the Indian Ocean. In the southeast, Sumatra, Borneo, New Guinea and many smaller islands are all part of Asia. On the west, Asia is joined to Africa only by the narrow isthmus, or neck of land, through which the Suez Canal has been cut.

The western boundary of Asia lies along the Ural mountains and Ural River and includes the area between the Caucasus Mountains and the Black Sea, called Transcaucasia. However, there is much disagreement about this boundary and some people would even

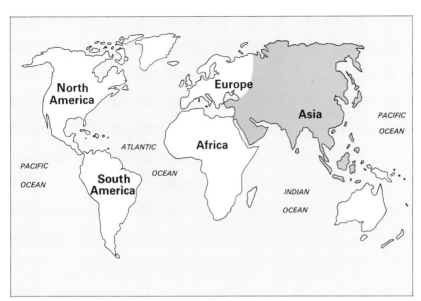

Asia is the world's largest continent. It is, however, part of the even larger land mass of Eurasia.

regard Europe and Asia together as one continent, Eurasia.

Asia is a land of extremes. It has the world's highest mountain peaks, including Mount Everest, and most of the world's longest rivers. Yet it also has the Earth's lowest land surface, the shore of the Dead Sea. It includes one of the world's wettest places (Cherripungi, in India) and some of the driest deserts. Verkhoyansk and Oymyakon in Siberia are two of the coldest places in the world and some of the hottest temperatures on the Earth's surface have been recorded near Aden, in the Arabian Peninsula. Asia has some of the world's most densely populated lands (Macao, Hong Kong, Java, Japan, and parts of China and India), whereas some parts of it have scarcely any people at all. Some of its people live lives that have changed hardly at all for centuries. Others have seen their country alter beyond recognition due to the arrival of Western culture and industrial methods in a very short space of time. Many of these people were civilized and living in well-governed cities, with skilled workmen and learned scholars, at the time when people in parts of Europe still dressed in skins and made tools and weapons of stone.

Today, Asia is the home of about 60 per cent of the world's population. Most of these people are still peasant farmers living in small villages. Almost 90 per cent of Asia's people live in the eastern and southern parts of the continent which contain some of the most thickly populated regions in the world. This densely populated zone runs in a crescent from Pakistan to northern China and Japan. The customs, religions, and culture of these areas have had a considerable influence on people living in other parts of Asia. Agriculture remains the most important activity throughout eastern and southern Asia. Most of the people regard the family as extremely important and family bonds are close.

Only in Japan has industrialization reached and even surpassed the high levels of western countries, although in many other Asian countries new industries are changing the face of the land and the lives of the people. In place of the traditional village life, more people are moving into the towns and cities to find work in factories. Most Asians are still poor, however, and great efforts are being made to raise their standard of living.

Asia has always had a high birth rate, but for centuries this was balanced by a high mortality (death) rate, caused by disease, famine, and natural disasters. Modern scientific advances have greatly reduced the death rate, with the result that Asia has had to face a

Traditional "beehive" houses in Syria. Their thick walls are made of sun-baked mud.

population crisis, with too many mouths to feed and not enough food. Governments in many Asian countries are trying to persuade people to have smaller families. (Traditionally, a father wanted many sons to help farm his land.) Efforts have been made to improve farming methods and many Asian farmers are now able to produce more and better crops than before, thanks to the use of fertilizers, insecticides, and cheap, modern machinery.

Asia is divided into at least three distinct parts. The north is a land of dark forests and windswept plains, where the winters are bitterly cold and the life hard. In the south and east there are warmer, often hot, lands where the ancient civilizations of India, Mesopotamia, and China grew up.

These southern and eastern areas are separated both from the northern lands and from Europe by a wide barrier land, with great mountain ranges and desert or semi-desert areas. These lands are so difficult to cross that they have kept the people of the north and west apart from those who live in the south and east.

The Monsoon Lands

The southern and eastern parts of Asia are among the most crowded in the world and they contain more than half the world's total population. Nevertheless, there are many moun-

tain and forest areas where few people live. Most of the inhabitants are to be found in the river valleys and the marshy lands near the coast. In the summer months all these areas have heavy rains, brought by winds from the oceans, but the cooler winter months have little rain. Because the year is thus divided into two such different seasons, these lands are said to have monsoon climates; *monsoon* is the Arab word for season (see MONSOON).

FACTS ABOUT ASIA

AREA: 44,614,399 square kilometers (17,225,709 square miles) including the Asiatic part of the USSR, which is about 17,301,089 square kilometers (6,680,002 square miles).
POPULATION (estimated): 2,665,412,000 (1981).
NATURAL RESOURCES: Tea, rice, sugar-cane, and spices; coal, iron, copper, tin, tungsten, graphite, petroleum, rubber, and pottery clay; furs, cotton, wool, silk, hemp, and jute.
FEATURES OF SPECIAL INTEREST: The continent contains the two largest nations in the world (China and India); 20 of the highest peaks in the world, the highest being Mount Everest (8,848 meters) [29,030 feet]; the third largest lake in the world (Aral Sea, about 65,000 square kilometers [25,000 square miles]); and three of the longest rivers in the world (Ob, Yangtze, and Amur).

Many great rivers flow out from the mountains of Tibet. The Indus, Ganges, and Brahmaputra rivers run down to India and Pakistan, the Irrawaddy to Burma, the

Asia is the home of three of the world's most important religions. **Top:** A vast crowd of Muslim worshippers gather at the Badshahi mosque in Lahore, Pakistan. **Bottom left:** Young Buddhist monks in their saffron robes in a temple in Sri Lanka. **Bottom right:** Hindu pilgrims bathing in the Ganges River at Varanasi.

ZEFA

A mosaic pattern of terraced paddy (rice) fields in western Japan is split by a modern railroad.

Mekong to Indochina, and the Changjiang and Huanghe flow through China. In summer, the heavy rains and the melting snows on the mountains cause great floods in the lower valleys, and most of the rivers have deltas (see DELTA). These hot, muddy lands suit the rice plant, and it is on rice that most of the people live. Where there is too little rain or too little heat for rice, they grow other grain crops such as millet and wheat.

In the 1500s Europeans began visiting these monsoon lands. They came to trade, as well as to explore. At first they sought spices, then they encouraged the growth of cotton, tea, and sugar and in later years much forest land was cleared and planted with rubber trees. Some Europeans settled as planters. Some of the early explorers hoped to find gold and precious stones, but the really valuable mineral today is petroleum.

In Bangladesh, India, and Pakistan most of the people live on the hot plains across which flow the Indus, Ganges, and Brahmaputra rivers. The land is irrigated with water from these rivers. By using this method, some districts can harvest cool-land crops such as wheat and barley in winter, as well as hot-land crops such as rice, cotton, and sugar-cane in the summer. The large cities of the Plain are Lahore, Delhi, Cawnpore, and Varanasi, while its ports are Karachi and Calcutta. The mills of Bombay on the west coast obtain their cotton from the much drier and higher Deccan in the southern part of India, where tea is also grown. In the tropical climate of Sri Lanka (Ceylon) rice, tea, rubber, coconuts, and spices are grown.

Paul Popper

A golden winged messenger of the Indian god Vishnu stands at this Buddhist temple in Bangkok, Thailand.

Further to the east lies Burma, whose dense forests provide teak, a wood which is very hard, while the rich delta of the Irrawaddy River produces large amounts of rice. Eastwards again, the lands of Thailand and Southeast Asia (Cambodia, Laos, and Vietnam) also produce teak and rice. To the south, the Malay Peninsula is one of the chief suppliers of tin and natural rubber.

The East Indies include the large islands of Sumatra, Java, and Borneo and many hundreds of smaller islands. All these lie well within the tropics, while the Philippines lie farther to the north. Spices are still grown on many of the islands, but more important crops are rubber, sugar, tea, coffee, and fiber for making rope. Borneo and Sumatra have a lot of oil, too. Many countries in Southeast Asia were colonized, mainly by Britain, France, and Holland, but became independent after the end of World War II.

Much of China is mountainous and its climate is cooler than that of India and Indochina. A large part of its population of about 1,043,100,000 (1985) lives in the valleys of two rivers, the Changjiang and the Huanghe, or else on the plain between the two. Many of the people are farmers, cultivating the land with great skill and care. Their chief crops are rice, tea, beans, millet, and cotton. The Chinese developed crafts such as pottery, weaving, and wood carving many centuries ago, but it is only since 1949 that industrialization on a large scale has taken place with the development of heavy industries, such as coal, and iron and steel. New factories and improved communications have helped China emerge as one of the most important and powerful nations in the modern world.

Japan is very mountainous and the people are crowded together on a few narrow coastal plains. The country was completely closed to Europeans until the 19th century. However, Japan rapidly became westernized, building up strong armed forces and setting up modern factories producing goods which were sold to many countries. By 1939 Japan had created a great empire, but was defeated in its attempt to gain control of all eastern Asia during World War II. Since 1945 Japan has become a prosperous trading nation with modern industries and a strong economy rivaling those of Western Europe and the United States.

The Barrier Lands

The densely populated lands of southern and eastern Asia are separated from northern Asia and Europe by the thinly peopled and much drier barrier lands. These stretch for over 8,000 kilometers (4,970 miles) from the shores of the Mediterranean almost to the Pacific, and in some places they are more than 1,600 kilometers (990 miles) wide. In the southwest they include Arabia, Asia Minor (that is, most of Turkey), Iraq, and Iran; in the center are Tibet (part of China) and the Chinese province of Xinjiang (Sinkiang); while farther to the northwest lies Mongolia. These barrier lands are thinly peopled for two reasons—many of them are desert lands while others are mountainous or high plateau areas. These geographical features have made communications difficult.

China is forging ahead on a program of industrialization—as these steelworkers show.

Marc Riboud/Magnum

The mountain chains begin in Asia Minor with the Taurus Mountains, which almost join the Caucasus range in Armenia. They separate to form a loop round the plain of Persia. They come together again in the Hindu Kush and the Pamirs, the meeting place of Afghanistan, the USSR, China, India, and Pakistan. The Pamirs are sometimes called the "Roof of the World" because of the great height of the land; at one point the mountains rise over 7,000 meters (23,000 feet) above sea-level. To the east, the high ranges spread out across eastern Asia like the ribs of a fan. The southernmost rib is formed by the Himalayas, the highest range in the world. Other ranges farther to the north include the Kun Lun, the Tien Shan, and the Altai Mountains.

The high passes through the mountains are often blocked with snow, but it is not just the mountains which make it difficult to enter China, Pakistan, and India from the north and west. The fact that only one railroad passes through to China and none to India or Pakistan shows just how difficult it is. The mountain ranges enclose high, dry, and barren plateaus, such as that of Tibet. To the north of the mountain belt, in Russian Turkestan, are the cold deserts of Kara Kum (the black sands) and Kyzil Kum (the red sands), while still farther to the northeast is the great Gobi Desert.

All the deserts and desert plateaus are called cold deserts, because they are swept by cold blizzards in the winter; but they are all very hot and dry in the summer.

The lowlands to the southwest are often desert, too, but of a different kind. From the Red Sea to India, through Arabia, southern Iran, and to the Thar Desert, lies one great belt of hot desert; these are indeed among the hottest and driest lands in the world. They have not always been so, however. The southern part of Arabia, now mostly desert, was once fertile—its name, Aden, may be the same as Eden. Today all its former irrigation canals and storage tanks are dry and the land has become mere sand and rock. Much the same has happened to the Sahara Desert in Africa, which long ago grew wheat and barley but is now arid desert only.

All these desert lands have few inhabitants, are difficult to cross, and are therefore part of the great barrier between the lands of the south and east on one side and those of the north and west on the other.

Great areas of the barrier lands have no people at all. One part of Arabia is called the Empty Quarter for this reason, and in northern Tibet there are districts that no one ever visits. The high snow-clad ranges are just as empty of people.

Picturepoint

Caroline Humphrey

Left: A village school, high in the mountains of Nepal. **Right:** These Mongol horsemen move their herds from pasture to pasture in the traditional way, although the herds are now owned by co-operatives.

Some of these deserted lands are crossed by trading caravans, traveling along routes which have been used for hundreds of years. On camel and horseback the merchants pass to and fro, watering their animals at occasional wells or at rivers that flow down from the snowy peaks. From China they carry tea and rice, and from the west they take metal cooking pots, tools, weapons, and cloths. They exchange these for sheepskins, wool, and camel hair of the nomadic tribes, whose flocks feed on the scanty, scattered pastures.

Where these trading routes cross, or two or three of them meet, caravan cities have grown up. Here the traders rest and refresh themselves and their animals, and then perhaps exchange their tea and wool for such things as carpets and leather goods made by the craftsmen of the towns.

The main routes run from east to west, but other traders come to the cities over the high mountain passes from India, bringing their goods on yaks. These animals are rather like buffaloes; their thick, shaggy coats enable them to withstand the blinding snowstorms and intense cold, while their short legs and sure feet help them to make their way over stony and icy tracks where any other beast would perish. Other merchants bring furs and grain from the grassy plains in the north to trade with the nomadic inhabitants of the desert.

Such caravan cities as Samarkand, Kashgar, Tashkent, and Bukhara have been famous for centuries. Their craftsmen weave carpets and rugs of bright colors, in patterns that have been copied by generation after generation. Their ancient palaces and mosques are often built of sun-dried bricks, but they have a beautiful outer covering of glazed tiles with brilliantly colored designs.

These cities have grown up in what are really oases. In summer the snows melt on the mountains and the rivers flow down steep, rocky valleys to the lower country. Channels have been cut to lead the water through the streets and out of the cities. The gardens,

ZEFA

An Arab mosque ruin dominates this market scene at Bukhara, in the Uzbek Soviet Socialist Republic.

which are watered by similar channels, often have splendid orchards. Where there is a good supply of water, such crops as tobacco and cotton can be grown. In the caravan cities of the Russian lands, in particular, far bigger areas are now watered in this way than used to be the case, and many of them have been linked together by railroads.

The Plains and Forests of the North

In times gone by, the caravan cities were sometimes raided by Tatar horsemen. These people used to wander on the flat, grassy areas called steppes (see STEPPES), to the north of the barrier, where the vast land of Siberia begins. Here they used to graze big herds of horses, sheep, and camels on the spring and summer pastures, driving them south to the sheltered mountain valleys when the pasture became too dry in summer, or was covered with snow, as happened in winter. Sour milk and especially mares' milk, together with the flesh of their animals, provided most of their food. Their clothing was generally of sheepskin, and their homes were round tents covered with woolen or camel-hair felt.

Today the great expanses of flat, open country have been made into farms where modern machinery and methods help farmers to grow a lot of wheat, just as in the prairie lands of the United States and Canada. The number of cattle is increasing, too, to provide milk and butter and cheese, and there are branch railroad lines to take the farmers' produce to the main Trans-Siberian line. Factories are growing up in the older towns, such as Omsk, Tomsk, and Irkutsk, and new industrial towns have been built near the Karaganda and Kuznetsk coalfields.

North of the steppes, trees begin to appear and gradually the traveler finds himself in the swampy *taiga*, the world's greatest forest land (see TAIGA). All the trees are conifers—pines, larches, and firs. The first Russian settlers here used to trap the forest animals for their fur; the most valuable of these was the sable. Today the chief product is timber, of which there is an enormous supply. However, it is difficult to get it to market. This is because all the rivers which flow north to the Arctic Ocean are frozen for many months of the year, and although a few ports have been built on the shores of the Arctic, even icebreakers can reach them only during a few weeks in the summer.

All along the Arctic shores stretch barren plains, once more without trees, known as the tundra (see TUNDRA). These tundra plains are frozen and covered with snow for half the year, and even in summer only the top 30 centimeters (12 inches) or so of the soil thaws in the sun. However, the summer days are long and there are many flowering plants which make the boggy land bright for a few weeks. Then the air is full of insects, and great flocks of wild geese and ducks nest in the marshes. The few people who live up here depend on fish from the rivers and upon the reindeer which they breed. During the worst of the winter months they take shelter in the fringes of the forests.

All these lands to the north of the great barrier—the steppes, the *taiga*, and the tundra—were added to the Russian Empire in the time of the tsars, and now they are part of the USSR.

History of Asia

The earliest beginnings of all world civilizations have been traced to Asia. When Europe and the Americas were still inhabited by primitive peoples, high forms of civilization existed in Asia. Many of these have long since disappeared and have been followed by new cultures. Chinese civilization, however, has lasted for more than 5,000 years. The earliest written history of the Chinese people begins about 3,000 years ago, and their legendary history may be traced back well beyond that.

In South Asia there is evidence of some civilization in the northern borderlands as far back as 5,000 to 7,000 years ago. After that period, Bronze Age farming villages existed between 4000 to 3000BC. Two groups of people appeared then in South Asia. The city builders lived on the Indus Plain, and the farming people (the Indo-Aryans) lived on the Upper Ganges Plain between 1500 and 1000 BC.

The early civilizations of Asia were widely separated from each other and from European civilizations. Until modern times, when steamships, trains, and other means of fast transportation appeared, the peoples of Asia were kept apart from the Western world by oceans to the east and by mountains, deserts, and forests to the west. Only the desert peoples of southwest Asia were in contact with the Europeans. The Arabian, Persian, and Turkish peoples served as middlemen in a limited trade of spices, ivories, and other products from Asia. By the 1st century AD a small amount of trade between Rome and China had developed. Silk from Cathay, as China was called, was carried westward across Central Asia to Europe. There were two main trade routes: the Overland, or Silk, Route and the Sea Route through the Straits of Malacca (between the Malay Peninsula and the island of Sumatra). In time the Silk Route was blocked by fierce nomadic tribes, and the Sea Route was cut off by Muslim forces as the religion of Islam spread throughout southwest Asia. Cathay, the land of silk, remained only as a legend to Europeans.

The Crusades of the Middle Ages brought European pilgrims and armies into southwest Asia. When the Crusaders returned to Europe, they took along a knowledge of the area. (See CRUSADES.) Before the Crusades were ended, the great Mongol warrior Genghis Khan overpowered most of Asia and united the greater part of it. Communications between east Asia and Europe became easier and safer. (See GENGHIS KHAN.) Such journeys as those undertaken by Marco Polo and accounts of the great wealth and civilization of China caused widespread interest among Europeans. The unknown lands of spices, ivories, and silks were viewed as lands of great wealth and ancient learning. (See POLO, MARCO.)

China, however, had little interest in Europe. The Chinese believed their country to be the center of the world. The Europeans were looked upon as barbarians. China was willing to sell its products in exchange for gold or silver, but it was not prepared to buy European products.

As long as the old Overland and Sea Routes were the only ways to travel to the countries of Asia, the Chinese were able to avoid European influence. The routes were long, difficult, and dangerous. But at the close of the 15th century the Portuguese sailed around Africa into the Indian Ocean and began trading with India.

Once the ocean routes to East Asia were found, the possibility of the Chinese living in isolation was gone forever. Merchants, missionaries, adventurers, and a few scholars and diplomats poured into Asia. Where the European powers found Asian countries that were militarily weak, poorly organized, or divided, they soon carved out colonial empires. All of southeast Asia except Thailand, almost all of south Asia, and much of southwest Asia were soon under European control.

Asian colonies were profitable for the Europeans during the 17th, 18th, and 19th centuries. Raw materials produced in the colonies were taken to Europe to be manufactured. A large part of the finished goods were resold to the colonies. As a result, the Western nations developed rapidly, and the countries of Asia lagged behind. The few nations that did not fall completely under foreign control—China, Japan, Korea, and Thailand—were forced to open their countries for trade. The shame of being dominated by the Western countries caused great bitterness in the peoples that had so long been proud of their ancient and great civilizations.

With trade came the spread of Western ideas. Japan, in the late 19th century, was the first nation in Asia to adopt Western industrial methods. In the 20th century, Western ideas and learning began to spread throughout Asia. Trouble spread with them because, again and again, Asian peoples had to decide whether to accept Western ideas or to keep their old traditions. Some of them turned against their native ways, yet others refused to have anything to do with Western ways. Eventually people began to see that many of the ideas of the West could be adapted to meet certain needs of the East. In the colonies of the

European countries ideas of nationalism and self-rule began to develop. The desire to be independent spread rapidly after World War I, and after World War II most of the colonies in Asia, one after another, gained independence. (See articles on individual countries.)

ASIA MINOR is the name given to the main (Asiatic) part of the country of Turkey. This was the Roman name, but it is also known as Anatolia.

Anatolia is a large peninsula at the very western edge of Asia. To the north is the Black Sea and to the west is the Aegean Sea. The Mediterranean Sea and the Arab states of Syria and Iraq lie to the south, and on the eastern side are the USSR and Iran.

The Hutchison Library

Many peoples settled Asia Minor. Some remain nomadic, particularly in the east, as these Yuruks.

In the early part of the 20th century, Anatolia was a very poor area of Turkey, even though it was so large. Since then, however, there have been many improvements. The city of Ankara in Anatolia was made the capital of the new Turkey. Fine railroads, airports and roads have been built, and old roads have been improved. You can read more about modern Anatolia in the article TURKEY.

The story of Asia Minor is full of invasions, for the way between the continents of Asia and Europe has always been across Asia Minor. It is like a gateway between the two continents. The first people who came to power in Asia Minor were the Hittites (see HITTITES). From about 1750 BC they expanded their empire to include Mesopotamia. After them the Phrygians enjoyed a period of power. They belonged to the same people as the Trojans, who fought a long war against the Greeks (see TROJAN WAR). After the Phrygians the Lydians, who came from Asia Minor, were the dominant force. About this time, too, Greek colonists founded several cities along the Aegean coastline. The last king of the Lydians was Croesus, who was famous for his extreme wealth (see CROESUS). In 546 BC the Persians defeated the Phrygians and Lydians and claimed the Greek colonies.

The Persians held Asia Minor until the region was conquered by Alexander the Great in 334 BC (see ALEXANDER THE GREAT). Alexander's empire did not last long. From 301 to about 100 BC Asia Minor was split up into a number of states. Then the Romans arrived and one by one the states were defeated and added to the Roman empire. The Romans unified Asia Minor but governed it through provinces. The richest province was Asia. Its name gradually came to be given to the whole of the peninsula. It was called Asia Minor, meaning Asia the Smaller, so that it would not be confused with the continent of Asia.

In AD 395 the Roman empire was divided into eastern and western sections. Asia Minor became an important part of the eastern, or Byzantine, section (see BYZANTINE EMPIRE). The empire was ruled from Constantinople (now Istanbul). The Byzantine empire was under attack almost continuously. Turks from the plains of Asia settled in central Asia Minor. Coastal areas came under the control of the Christian Crusaders and became trading outposts for merchants of Genoa and Venice (see CRUSADES). The fall of Constantinople to the Muslim Turks in 1453 marked the end of the Byzantine empire and the beginning of the Ottoman, or Turkish, empire. This empire lasted until World War I, in which Turkey, fighting on the same side as Germany, was defeated.

After the war Mustafa Kemal, better known as Atatürk, proclaimed Turkey a republic. He carried out many reforms to make Turkey a modern, efficient country (see ATATÜRK).

ASIMOV, Isaac (born 1920), is a Russian-born United States scientist and author, especially noted for his numerous science fiction novels and short stories, and for his many books about science for the ordinary reader. Asimov was born at Petrovichi, in the Soviet Union, and traveled with his parents to the United States when he was three years old. He grew up in Brooklyn, New York, and graduated in biochemistry from Columbia University in 1939. He took his doctorate in the subject from the same university in 1947 and joined the staff of Boston University, holding a teaching post there until 1958 and an honorary position thereafter.

Asimov began contributing short stories to science fiction magazines in 1939 and published his first book, *Pebble in the Sky*, in 1950. His set of three books, *Foundation*, *Foundation and Empire*, and *Second Foundation*, appeared in 1951–53 and won science fiction's prestigious Hugo Award. This series of books, which was extended in 1982 with the publication of *Foundation's Edge*, charts the progress of a society set up to salvage the remnants of human civilization destroyed by the disintegration of the great galactic empire. The society's destiny has been mapped out in advance by the predictions of its founder Hari Selden through the science of psycho-history, the statistical examination of how a population will react to changes, and particularly to crises.

Psycho-history is one of Asimov's most interesting inventions. But Asimov is perhaps better known for his stories about robots. In his set of short stories, *I, Robot*, published in 1950, he first introduced his so-called Laws of Robotics. These set out the moral principles governing the relationship between humans and machines. For example, the First Law states that it is impossible for a robot to carry out or allow any action that will bring harm to a human.

Asimov has written over 300 books. His science fiction writings include *The Stars like Dust*, *The Caves of Steel*, and *Earth is Room Enough*. Asimov's most popular science books include *Inside the Atom*, *Life and Energy*, *Our World in Space*, and *Views of the Universe*.

ASPARAGUS, a member of the lily family of plants, is a vegetable. About 150 species of asparagus are grown in the temperate parts of the world, but just one (*Asparagus officinalis*) is usually eaten.

Asparagus grows best in loose, rich, sandy soil. In gardens the seeds are sown early in the spring, though the plants may be started at any time of the year in greenhouses. Asparagus plants must be from two to four years old before they are ready for cutting. After that they continue to grow and produce new shoots annually for 15 to 20 years.

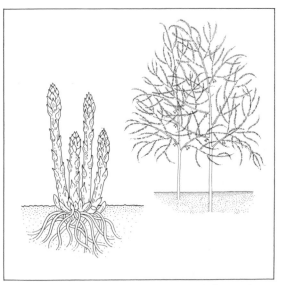

Young asparagus shoots, or spears, ready for cutting. Asparagus plants must be cut down every autumn.

The young stems of asparagus plants are used as food. They are cut when the leaves of the plant are small buds and the stems or spears are tender and less than 25 centimeters (10 inches) high. The young spears are cut each day for six to eight weeks. After that time the stems begin to get tough and woody as they branch and start to blossom. Each autumn the old stalks of the garden variety are cut down.

If left to grow, the plants reach heights of 1.2 meters (4 feet). Most asparagus leaves are tiny and fern-like; the flowers are small and yellowish, and the fruits are red berries.

The asparagus fern (*Asparagus plumosus*) is grown for its delicate foliage. Wild varieties of asparagus grow in Europe and Asia, especially along the seacoasts, and in some parts of the United States.

Asparagus has been a popular food since Greek and Roman times. It is most often cooked in water and eaten hot, but it is also used to make soup or chilled and served in salads.

ASPEN. This beautiful tree is sometimes called the trembling poplar, because its rounded leaves hang on such slender stalks that they quiver in the slightest breeze. The flowers hang in long catkins.

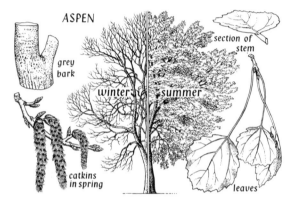

The quaking aspen (*Populus tremuloides*) is a common and widely distributed North American tree. It reaches 30 meters (100 feet). It has yellowish-green or whitish bark. The leaves are lustrous green above and pale silvery below. This aspen has a narrow, rounded crown of slender branches. It grows abundantly on the mountain slopes, painting them a golden yellow as the leaves change color in the autumn. In some places, the bark is scarred where deer have rubbed their horns against it.

The bigtooth grows somewhat larger. It is the aspen (*Populus grandidentata*) found in southeastern Canada and the eastern United States. The leaves are larger than those of the quaking aspen, rounded and coarse-toothed. The bark is greenish, smooth and thin, becoming dark brown. The European aspen (*Populus tremula*) has gray-brown bark. In Britain it is common in damp woods and on heathland. In northern Europe it forms large stands.

The light, fluffy seeds of aspen are carried long distances by the wind. Aspen are often the first trees to spring up in areas that have been burned.

The soft, white wood is used for making pulpwood for high-quality paper, and also for matchsticks. In Scandinavia herring casks and clogs are made from it.

ASPHALT. The blackish substance known as asphalt is a natural or manufactured mixture of bitumen with crushed minerals such as sand, limestone and granite. When heated, asphalt becomes plastic and can be molded by pressure to any shape or form. Its melting point is between 32° and 37° centigrade (90°–100° Fahrenheit). As a result of temperature and the presence of impurities, asphalt may be found in forms ranging from liquids to solids. Bitumen, a tar-like substance from which asphalt is made, is a combination of carbon and hydrogen. It therefore belongs to the larger group of compounds called hydrocarbons.

There are two types of asphalt: natural asphalt and petroleum asphalt. Natural asphalt comes from deposits that are found in the Earth's crust. These deposits are left when petroleum partially evaporates from oil-bearing rocks. Petroleum asphalt is manufactured from crude oil by petroleum-refining processes.

Natural asphalts have been formed for millions of years by oil being forced to the Earth's surface through sand beds and porous rock formations. The purest asphalt was trapped in the rocks where it was protected. It later oozed out as almost pure liquid asphalt.

In its natural state asphalt is a limestone rock which has been soaked with bitumen. It is obtained from mines at Val de Travers in Switzerland, Seyssel in France and in various places in the United States and other countries.

The most famous natural asphalt deposit is the asphalt lake in Trinidad, in the West Indies, which was discovered in 1595 by Sir Walter Raleigh. When he was writing about it afterwards he said that it was "most excellent goode" for making the seams of his ships waterproof. The lake is about 87 meters (285 feet) deep in the center and covers an area of over 40 hectares (100 acres). Chunks are dug up with pickaxes and, although large quantities are removed during working hours, the lake fills up again each night. Light railroads run across the surface but they have to be continually moved, otherwise they would sink.

The material from this lake is a true asphalt. It is refined, or purified, in Trinidad, poured into barrels and then sent all over the world. It is then known as *épuré* and when combined with other materials can be used for waterproofing such things as protective paints and storage batteries. It is also used with natural rock asphalt. The lake was an important source of paving asphalt as early as 1876 when the streets of Washington, DC, were paved with Trinidad asphalt.

Volunteers removing fossils of extinct animals trapped in asphalt at the La Brea pits near Los Angeles.

Deposits like those near Los Angeles, called the La Brea Pits, are famous for the fossils of prehistoric animals, such as the saber-toothed tiger, that have been found in them. Many springs of asphalt are found in Iraq, some of them being very ancient.

Refined asphalt is fluxed (mixed) with 30 per cent to 45 per cent of petroleum asphalt to make an asphalt cement. Asphalt cement is the name for modern paving asphalt. It is used to hold sand and stone tightly together and to prevent water from entering the pavement. It has rubber-like qualities that cause it to bend under great pressure.

Because it is waterproof, asphalt is used to make roofing materials. The shingles or long rolls are made of felt that has been soaked in asphalt and covered with stone chips. Building walls below the ground level are covered with asphalt to keep water out and to keep the interior walls from becoming damp. Ceilings in tunnels and the floors of some bridges are also waterproofed with asphalt.

Manufactured asphalt is usually a mixture of bitumen and limestone, which is very similar to the natural rock asphalt. It is used both in road surfacing and in building construction for waterproofing roofs, forming dampcourses, damp-proofing basements and lining water towers and reservoirs.

Asphalt for road work usually has only about one-twelfth bitumen added to the finely crushed minerals and the broken stones. The materials are heated separately to between 325°C and 350°C (617°F and 662°F) and are thoroughly mixed together by machine. The mixture is spread on the road base and after being pressed by rollers is ready for use as soon as it has cooled. Because it is pressed like this it is called rolled asphalt. Experiments in surfacing roads with asphalt were made in England as early as 1872.

For building work and for certain streets and pavements the type of asphalt used is called mastic asphalt. Mastic asphalt is made in heated mechanical mixers and when hot and plastic is applied to the surface required with wooden hand tools.

ASPHODEL is the name for several plants of the lily family. They are mainly native to the Mediterranean region. Typical plants (*Asphodelus*) have spikes of white or pale yellow flowers that shoot up from a dense clump of grayish-green leaves.

The largest plant *Asphodelus ramosus* grows to 1.2 meters (4 feet) high and has sword-shaped leaves. Its white flowers bloom

NHPA/G. J. Cambridge

European bog asphodel grows in wet places. The two kinds of North American bog asphodel are much rarer.

in May. The European bog asphodel (*Narthecium ossifragum*) grows on moors and wet heaths. It has narrow leaves and small yellow flowers. Two kinds of bog asphodel are found in the United States, one in the pine barrens of New Jersey and Delaware, and one along the north Pacific coast of California and Oregon.

Asphodels grow well in ordinary garden soil in sunny or half-shady places. They are used as border plants in gardens and sometimes are grown with wild or woodland flowers.

In Greek mythology, meadows of asphodel were associated with the land of the dead. The flowers were often used to decorate graves.

ASS. An ass can easily be distinguished from a horse because it is smaller and has long ears, narrow feet, a tufted tail, and a mane that stands up. The bray of an ass is harsher than the horse's gentle neigh, while its body is usually gray, always with black stripes down each shoulder and another along its back. Sometimes, however, an ass is brown or nearly black all over, and very occasionally it may be piebald.

Wild asses are fast, well-built animals that live in the open plains and deserts of Africa and Asia. There are two species. The African wild ass (*Equus asinus*) is thought to be the ancestor of the domesticated animal. The Asiatic wild ass (*Equus hemonius*) is better known by the local names of its different races, for example, the onager found in Iran and Turkestan and the large kiang of Mongolia and Tibet. Wild asses are now rare in the wild because of hunting.

People began to use the ass long before they domesticated the horse. The Egyptians caught and tamed wild asses more than 4,500 years ago. The ass is the same animal as the donkey but it was only called this at the end of the eighteenth century. In Mexico and the southwestern United States the ass is known by the Spanish name, *burro*. The ass is a very strong and hardy animal. It is particularly useful in mountains where it can keep a better footing than a horse. R. L. Stevenson gives a fine description of the surefooted but stubborn ass in his *Travels with a Donkey*.

W. Suschitzky

A wild ass from North Africa with its foal.

The male ass is called a jack or jackass. It is often mated with a female horse, a mare, to produce the sturdy mule used for farm work and as a baggage animal for carrying equipment on expeditions.

ASSAM is situated in the distant northeast corner of India. It is almost cut off from the main Indian continent by the country of Bangladesh to the west, and only a narrow stretch of land running along the Himalayan foothills joins Assam to India.

Picking tea on a plantation in Assam, northeast India. Tea is exported around the world from Assam.

Geographically, Assam consists of lowland plains and valleys split down the middle by the Brahmaputra River. This river flows on through to Bangladesh where it joins the mighty Ganges River (see GANGES, RIVER) continuing as one river to the Bay of Bengal. Rice is grown on either side of the river in fields which are flooded every summer by the rain-bearing monsoon winds, particularly in June (see MONSOON). These rains make Assam the wettest area of India, and one of the wettest places in the world. It is also an area with frequent earthquakes.

Beyond the rice fields, the land climbs higher to hill areas and this is where the tea plantations are found. Assam tea is well known throughout the world and over half of India's tea exports come from this area. Beyond these hills lie vast forests which are used for the timber industry. Some areas of the forest have been made wildlife sanctuaries and parks, where you can see the very rare one-horned Indian rhinoceros, as well as tigers, swamp deer, and herds of elephants.

There are just under 20 million people in Assam and only 10 per cent live in towns. The vast majority inhabit rural areas, and in the outlying hill regions there are still many primitive tribes living a remote existence, unchanged by the modern world.

The Nagas, an important tribe, have at times sought independence, but an attempt in 1961 to give them their own homeland failed. About 100 different languages are spoken in Assam, more than in any other area of the same size elsewhere in the world.

ASSASSINATION is a form of murder which is violent, treacherous, and sudden. The term is usually applied to the killing of rulers or people well known in public life. Usually their murderers believe that they are right to kill because of some harm which their victims have done, or which the murderers imagine they have done. The motive is often political or religious. The assassins of Julius Caesar said that they had killed him for the good of the Roman state because they thought he wanted to be king, but most of them were jealous of Caesar's fame and power.

In medieval times there was in Persia and Syria a secret order of assassins belonging to a Muslim sect. They kept the land in a state of terror for nearly two centuries by killing their enemies as a sacred religious duty. The head of this order was always known as the Old Man of the Mountain. He kept his followers loyal and persuaded them to kill by providing them with the drug hashish which gave them wonderful visions of paradise. They were known as Hashishins, from which the word "assassin" comes.

Dictators have often used assassination as a means of getting rid of their opponents. The Russian Communist, Leon Trotsky, was murdered in 1940, almost certainly by order of Stalin, his bitter enemy. In recent times, terrorists seeking to overthrow governments have also resorted to assassination. Every country has its list of murdered rulers, statesmen and officers. Henry IV of France was assassinated in 1610 by a religious opponent. Abraham Lincoln, president of the United States, was shot in a theater at Washington in 1865. It was thought that his murderer wanted to avenge the defeat of the Southern

AFTER THE EXPLOSION OF THE SECOND BOMB

THE ASSASSINATION OF THE LATE CZAR OF RUSSIA — SCENE OF THE EXPLOSIONS BESIDE THE CATHERINE CANAL

SKETCHES FROM OPPOSITE SIDES OF THE ROAD

Mary Evans Picture Library

Newspaper illustrations showing the assassination of Tsar Alexander II of Russia in 1881 at St. Petersburg.

States in the American Civil War, but it may be that he was part of a conspiracy among members of the government. The Austrian archduke, Francis Ferdinand, the heir to the throne of the Austro-Hungarian Empire, was killed in 1914 and this brought to a head the disputes between the countries of central Europe and resulted in the outbreak of World War I.

Among modern victims of assassination were Dr. Engelbert Dolfuss, the Austrian chancellor, 1934; Mahatma Gandhi, in India, 1948; John F. Kennedy, president of the United States, 1963; his brother Robert F. Kennedy, and the black American leader, Martin Luther King, Jr., both in 1968; the former Beatle, John Lennon, in 1980; Anwar el-Sadat, president of Egypt, in 1981; Indira Gandhi, prime minister of India, in 1984; and Olaf Palme, prime minister of Sweden, in 1986.

ASSOCIATION FOOTBALL see SOCCER.

ASTARTE. In ancient times, Astarte was a goddess of fertility, or fruitfulness. She was worshipped by the Phoenicians, who lived along the eastern shore of the Mediterranean Sea. They built temples to her at the cities of Tyre and Sidon and on the island of Cyprus.

Astarte was believed to control the moon and the life and growth of all plants and animals. People thought she helped new crops to grow and animals and human babies to be born.

Gazelles, doves, and turtles were sacred to her, and the planet Venus was her special star.

Other tribes of Semitic people living near the Phoenicians also worshipped Astarte. The Assyrians and Babylonians called her Ishtar and in the Bible she is called Ashtoreth. Many statues of her have been dug up in Palestine. The Bible tells how King Solomon built a temple for her in Jerusalem, but King Josiah had it torn down (II Kings 23:13). After the Greeks took Cyprus from the Phoenicians, they identified Astarte with their goddesses Aphrodite and Artemis. Astarte has been likened also to the Roman goddesses Diana and Juno, and the Egyptian goddesses Isis and Hathor.

ASTER is a flowering plant of the daisy or *Compositae* family. It is so common in the United States that it has been suggested as the national flower. More than 175 species grow in North America. The flower also grows in parts of Europe, Asia, and South America.

NHPA/N. A. Callow

These little alpine asters belong to one of the largest of the plant families. The word aster means star.

The aster is related to the daisy. It gets its name from the Greek word for star. The blossoms may be from one-half to two inches in diameter. They vary in color from white through pink, red, and blue. All have flat yellow centers surrounded by many narrow petals.

Most asters are perennial (grow year after year). They bloom in late summer and early autumn. Asters are popular garden flowers because they bloom after other flowers are gone, have few diseases and insect enemies and last well after cutting. Some common types are the purple New England aster (*Aster novae-anglia*) known in Britain as the Michaelmas daisy, and the smooth blue aster (*Aster laevis*). The China, or garden aster (*Callistephus cinensis*) is related to the true asters and is an annual grown from seed each year. Its showy flower heads grow to 13 centimeters (5 inches) across.

All species of aster need rich soil and sunlight to grow well, but they cannot stand much hot weather.

ASTEROID. In 1801 the Italian astronomer Giuseppe Piazzi discovered a new object in the Solar System orbiting the Sun out beyond the planet Mars. At first, people thought that it was a new planet between Mars and Jupiter. But over the next few years several more such objects were sighted, all of them much smaller than a planet. Astronomers now refer to them as asteroids, minor planets, or planetoids.

Ceres, the asteroid that Piazzi discovered in 1801, is the largest known of these objects. It has a diameter of about 1,020 kilometers (640 miles). But most asteroids are very small. Pallas, the next in size to Ceres, is only 585 kilometers (365 miles) across. Of the 2,000 asteroids so far known, there are probably only 250 with a diameter of 100 kilometers (60 miles) or more.

Astronomers think that there are millions of asteroids in the Solar System, ranging in size from a small planetary moon to a tiny object the size of a boulder. Experts who have analyzed light reflected from asteroids believe that most of them are made of stony material mixed with metals such as iron and nickel. Asteroids found farther out from the Sun may be made of rock and ice.

The great majority of asteroids travel around the Sun between the orbits of Mars and Jupiter. Astronomers used to think that they were the remains of a planet that blew up, but it is now thought that no planet ever formed between Mars and Jupiter because the very

Julian Baum/Science Photo Library

An asteroid (bottom right) is a tiny, rocky world devoid of life, orbiting the bright Sun (center). This remarkably realistic view is, however, only an artist's impression.

strong gravitational influence of Jupiter, the largest planet in the Solar System, would have pulled apart any planetary material that might have begun to collect there.

Asteroid Groups

Although most asteroids orbit between Mars and Jupiter, there is a small group whose orbits bring them closer to the Sun. A group known as the Apollo Group come close to the Earth. They include Apollo (from which the group takes its name), Icarus, and Eros. Two other groups are trapped in Jupiter's orbit around the Sun. One group precedes the huge planet and the other follows it by the same distance. These asteroids are called the Trojans, because many of them have names taken from characters in the Trojan War, such as Achilles, Hector, Agamemnon, and Patroclus. About 40 Trojan asteroids are now known.

ASTOR FAMILY. The Astor family is one of the most prominent and wealthy families in the United States. The family fortune began with the fur trade and real estate (land) investments in the late 1700s. Each head of the family has added to the fortune.

John Jacob Astor (1763–1848) founded the American house of Astor and the family fortune. The son of a butcher, he was born in Waldorf, near Heidelberg, Germany. When he

was about 17 years old, Astor went to London, where he spent three years working in his brother's piano and flute factory. In 1783 he set sail for the United States. His talks with a fur trader during the voyage led to his great interest in furs. He spent many of the following years organizing the trade in the area west of the Great Lakes. In 1811 he founded a trading post, Astoria, the oldest white settlement in Oregon. During the War of 1812, the British took over the settlement, and Astor's dreams of a great fur empire headed by his American Fur Company suffered a setback, but by shrewdness and hard work, he had already made a large fortune. He added to it by making large loans to the United States government and by investing heavily in New York City real estate. When Astor died, leaving a fortune of about $30,000,000, he was the wealthiest man in America. He left $400,000 for the founding of the Astor Library. It was combined in 1895 with the Lenox Library and the Tilden Trust to form the New York Public Library.

William Backhouse Astor (1792–1875) was a son and heir of John Jacob Astor. He was known as the "Landlord of New York" because he continued his father's policy of buying real estate in the city and erecting buildings. By doing this he added to the family fortune.

John Jacob Astor III (1822–90) was the elder son of William B. Astor. During the Civil War he served as a colonel on General George B. McClellan's staff. Both he and his wife contributed large sums of money to charities and to the Astor Library.

William Waldorf Astor (1848–1919) was the son and heir of John Jacob Astor III. He became a member of the New York Assembly in 1877. From 1882 to 1885 he was United States minister to Italy. He moved to London in 1890 and nine years later became a British subject. He was made a baron in 1916 and a viscount a year later. William Waldorf built the Waldorf section of the hotel that later was named the Waldorf-Astoria.

When Viscount Astor died, his eldest son, **Waldorf Astor** (1879–1952), became viscount. He married Nancy Langhorne of Vir-

John Jacob Astor I (1763-1848)

William Backhouse Astor (1792-1875)　　　　　　John Jacob Astor II (?)

John Jacob Astor III (1822-1890)　　　　　　William Astor (1830-1892)

William Waldorf Astor (1848-1919)　　　　John Jacob Astor IV (1864-1912)
1st Viscount

　　　　　　　　　　　　　　　　　　Vincent Astor (1891-1959)

Waldorf Astor (1879-1952)
2nd Viscount　m　Nancy Witcher　　　John Jacob Astor (1886-1971)
Langhorne (1879-1964)　　　　　Baron

William Waldorf Astor (1907-1966)
3rd Viscount

Family tree of the Astors. John Jacob Astor made a fortune by fur trading in the United States.

ginia, who was the first woman to become a member of the British House of Commons. The 2nd Viscount Astor was actively interested in politics and social reform. From 1910 to 1919, he was a member of the House of Commons. He owned *The Observer* newspaper. His eldest son, **William Waldorf Astor** (1907–66), became the 3rd Viscount Astor when his father died.

Nancy Witcher Astor (1879–1964) was born in Danville, Virginia, the daughter of Chiswell Dabney Langhorne. When she was 18 years old, she married Robert Gould Shaw, whom she divorced in 1903. Three years later she married Waldorf Astor and became a naturalized British subject. In 1919, when her husband became a member of the House of Lords, he had to give up his seat in the House of Commons. His wife then became Unionist candidate in his place, and in 1919 was elected as the member for Plymouth. She was re-elected many times before she retired in 1945.

In her parliamentary work, Lady Astor was concerned with affairs affecting family life and the welfare of women and children. She supported pensions for widows, government care of orphans, higher education for children, and police positions for women. In 1923 she persuaded Parliament to pass the Intoxicating

BBC Hulton Picture Library

Nancy Astor in 1919 with her children (left to right) Phyllis, John Jacob, Robert Shaw, Michael, David, William Waldorf.

Liquor Act, prohibiting the sale of alcoholic beverages to persons under the age of 18.

Lady Astor, an energetic and witty woman, won for herself a respected position in English life. She was the mother of six children, and the hostess of Cliveden, the famed Astor country house. Her book, *My Two Countries*, was published in 1923.

John Jacob Astor IV (1864–1912) was the only son of William Astor (1830–92), the younger brother of John Jacob Astor III. He invented a bicycle brake and other mechanical devices. He built the Astoria section of the

Waldorf-Astoria Hotel. During the Spanish-American War he took part in the Battle of Santiago. He died in the sinking of the *Titanic*.

John Jacob Astor (1886–1971), younger brother of Waldorf Astor, was born in the United States but lived most of his life in England. He served in the British Army during World War I, and in the City of London Home Guard during World War II. In 1922 he became director of *The Times* newspaper. From 1922 to 1945 he was a member of Parliament and in 1956 he was made a baron.

Vincent Astor (1891–1959) was the elder son and heir of John Jacob Astor IV. He served in World Wars I and II. Large portions of the Astor property were sold at his order.

ASTROLOGY is the study of the effect of the stars and planets on human life. Astrologers claim that they can predict future events by observing and charting the movements of heavenly bodies. Because there is no scientific evidence to support it, astrology is sometimes called a false science. Many centuries ago astrology was closely connected with astronomy. Today they are totally different studies and should not be confused. (See ASTRONOMY.)

To foretell the events of a person's life by the stars the astrologer first draws a map called a horoscope. On the map he marks the heavenly bodies in the positions they occupied at the time of the person's birth. He divides the map into 12 equal parts called "houses", representing the 12 months of the year. In the 12 houses the stars are grouped into constellations. The names of the 12 constellations correspond to the names of the 12 signs of the zodiac (see ZODIAC). By studying the positions of the Sun, Moon and planets in relation to these houses and constellations the astrologer makes his forecast.

Modern astrologers believe that they can tell a person's fortune by working out the influences the Sun, Moon, and planets have in his or her life. If at the time of someone's birth a planet is in its own "house", its influence is supposed to be strong and beneficial; if it is far away from its own "house", its influence is weak and may be unlucky. In popular news-

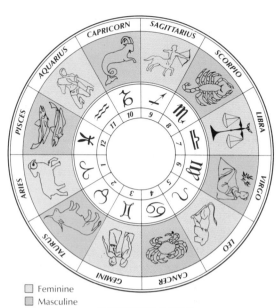

□ Feminine
■ Masculine

SIGNS OF THE ZODIAC

SIGNS	DATES		ELEMENTS HOUSES		RULING PLANETS	
ARIES	March 21–April 19	1	Fire	♂	Mars	
TAURUS	April 20–May 20	2	Earth	♀	Venus	
GEMINI	May 21–June 21	3	Air	☿	Mercury	
CANCER	June 22–July 22	4	Water	☽	Moon	
LEO	July 23–Aug. 22	5	Fire	☉	Sun	
VIRGO	Aug. 23–Sept. 22	6	Earth	☿	Mercury	
LIBRA	Sept. 23–Oct. 23	7	Air	♀	Venus	
SCORPIO	Oct. 24–Nov. 21	8	Water	♂ E	Mars Pluto	
SAGITTARIUS	Nov. 22–Dec. 21	9	Fire	♃	Jupiter	
CAPRICORN	Dec. 22–Jan. 19	10	Earth	♄	Saturn	
AQUARIUS	Jan. 20–Feb. 18	11	Air	⛢ ♄	Uranus Saturn	
PISCES	Feb. 19–March 20	12	Water	♃ ♆	Jupiter Neptune	

papers, astrologers write very general and vague horoscopes, which are supposed to hold good for everyone born under the same sign of the zodiac.

The earliest people saw the sky as a great dome, lit at night by stars and the Moon and during the day by the Sun. They did not know what these lights were, but they knew that the sunshine and rain that made the crops grow came from the sky. They therefore worshipped the heavenly bodies as gods. Their priests believed that they could foretell the will of these gods if they watched the sky carefully.

In ancient times one of the duties of priests was to watch the Sun, Moon, stars, and planets. From their observations they made important astronomical discoveries. By the 6th century BC the Babylonians had invented a calendar and had made charts showing how the planets moved among the stars. They knew how to forecast eclipses of the Sun and Moon. They also knew when to plant the crops. Because they were successful in these predictions, the astronomer-priests believed they could foretell all kinds of events, such as plagues, wars, and the success of their armies in battles. This kind of forecasting has no true foundation. The astronomers or priests who practiced it became known as astrologers.

From Babylonia the study of astrology spread to Greece, Egypt, India and elsewhere in Asia and Europe. In the year AD 1066 a brilliant comet appeared in the sky. People were afraid of it and astrologers predicted many important events, including the death of a king. A few months later Duke William of Normandy conquered England after King Harold was killed at the Battle of Hastings. (See HASTINGS, BATTLE OF.) Many people thought that the comet caused these changes, but later it was discovered that the comet, now called Halley, returns every 76 years without mishap.

At first astrologers foretold only events important to the country or its ruler, but later they began to forecast events for individual people. Until about 300 years ago almost every ruler in Asia and Europe had an official astrologer. Some famous early astronomers also practiced astrology. The Greek astronomer Ptolemy, living in Egypt in the 2nd century AD, was also an astrologer. In the 16th and 17th centuries, the Danish astronomer Tycho Brahe lectured on astrology, and Johannes Kepler was court astrologer to the Austrian emperor. (See BRAHE, TYCHO; KEPLER, JOHANNES; PTOLEMY.)

ASTRONAUT. Astronauts are people who travel in space. The word "astronaut" means "star traveler". The Russians call such people "cosmonauts". A Soviet cosmonaut, Yuri Gagarin, was the first person to journey into space, traveling once around the Earth on 12 April 1961 in an orbit that lasted about 90 minutes. The first American astronaut to circle the Earth was John Glenn, who made a three-orbit journey in February 1962.

The early space missions were dangerous, for no one knew at the time how human beings would withstand the stresses of space flight. Today manned space flight has become almost routine. Astronauts regularly fly into space and are able to remain there for months at a time without suffering permanent harm. But dangers still exist. Several Soviet and United States spacemen have died over the years. One of the worst disasters was in 1986, when seven United States astronauts died as their space shuttle *Challenger* exploded shortly after liftoff.

The early manned spacecraft, such as *Mercury*, *Gemini*, and *Apollo* in the United States and *Vostok* in the Soviet Union, were small and had cramped crew quarters. Also they could be used only once. The Russians use relatively small "once-only" craft called *Soyuz* to ferry their cosmonauts to and from orbit. In orbit, however, the cosmonauts find more roomy accommodation in a space station known as *Salyut*. American astronauts now travel into space in the space shuttle. They fly in a delta-winged orbiter, which looks much like an airliner, and inside they can travel in "shirt-sleeve" comfort for most of the time. The orbiter can land back on Earth much like an aircraft. Unlike earlier spacecraft, it is intended to be reused.

Selection and Training

The first astronauts were usually test pilots, highly experienced flyers, who were trained to react swiftly in emergencies. This was necessary since they were taking hazardous steps into the unknown. Today, space is more familiar so astronauts need not be expert pilots. The space shuttle, for example, has two kinds

Edward White (1920–67) became the first US astronaut to walk in space, in 1965. This picture of him was taken during the flight of Gemini 4 by fellow astronaut James McDivitt. The visor of White's helmet was gold coated to protect him from the unfiltered rays of the Sun. In one hand he held a self-propulsion device. White was tethered to his ship by an umbilical, which kept him supplied with oxygen. Space-walking was developed to allow astronauts to work outside the spacecraft and move from one spacecraft to another. Space walks by US and Soviet astronauts led to improvements in spacesuit design on the later Apollo and Soyuz missions.

Courtesy, NASA

of astronaut, pilot-astronauts and scientist-astronauts. The pilots fly the craft, while the scientists look after the scientific experiments.

Each kind of astronaut needs different training for their different jobs. The pilots spend a great deal of their training in "simulators" practicing shuttle takeoffs and landings. The simulator is a computer-controlled dummy spacecraft, with controls and instruments that behave just like the real thing. Projectors show the pilot a picture on a screen similar to the view he would actually see during a real flight.

The scientist-astronauts are not involved in flying the shuttle. But they need to know how it works. They are concerned mainly with the payload or cargo the shuttle will carry, and they rehearse the different operations; for example, to launch and check a satellite in orbit and work experimental equipment.

Both kinds of astronaut undergo similar intensive training to prepare themselves for space flight. They prepare their bodies for the fierce accelerations on takeoff by training in a centrifuge—a capsule on the end of a long arm that is driven around in a circle at high speeds and produces high accelerations by centrifugal force. (See CENTRIFUGAL FORCE.) Astronauts practice for the weightlessness they will experience in orbit in two ways. They can actually become weightless for a few minutes inside an aircraft that flies up to a great height and then dives down with an acceleration equal to that due to gravity. They can also become almost weightless by being submerged in weighted suits in a water tank.

Living in Orbit

It is weightlessness that causes most problems in orbit. Things that we take for granted on Earth—walking, eating, drinking, sleeping—cannot be done in the same way in orbit where there is no gravity. (See GRAVITY.) Astronauts float and move by pushing or pulling themselves around. They cannot sit down to a meal at an ordinary table, for chairs, table, knives and forks, plates and food would gradually drift all over the place. In space, everything is firmly anchored down. When they sit down, the astronauts slip their feet into footholds. Food cans or packs, trays, and forks are held in place by suckers, magnets, or sticky strips. Crumbly foods are banned because the crumbs would float about and get everywhere! Drinking from a glass is also impossible, because under zero gravity liquids cannot be poured from or into containers. Instead, they have to be squirted into the mouth. Many foods are dehydrated (that is, prepared by having the water content removed) and have to be made fit to eat by having the water squirted back into them inside their special pouches. To sleep, the astronaut zips himself into a sleeping bag fixed to the spacecraft wall.

Weightlessness always affects the human body, especially the body fluids. For the first few days of a flight many astronauts experience "space sickness" until their bodies adjust to the strange new environment. Astronauts staying in space for many weeks experience more serious effects. For example, their bones lose calcium, and their muscles (used to battling against gravity) quickly start to waste away. The reason for the calcium loss is not yet known, but probably can be corrected by a suitable diet. To prevent the muscles wasting away, the astronauts must take regular exercise, on bicycle machines or treadmills.

Personal hygiene also presents problems in weightless conditions. Washing in a bowl of water would send cascades of water droplets into the air. So short-stay astronauts must make do with a rub-down with a wet towel. The long-stay cosmonauts on Salyut, however, enjoy the occasional luxury of a shower. Going to the lavatory in space could be unpleasant, since without gravity, getting rid of the body wastes is a problem. Space lavatories are fitted with suction devices, and are flushed effectively with air (instead of water).

Inside the spacecraft the astronauts are kept alive by the life-support system. This supplies them with air to breathe in, removes the carbon dioxide they breathe out, and also filters out any odors. It also keeps the air at a comfortable temperature, humidity, and pressure. From time to time the astronauts

Courtesy, NASA

On 20 July 1969 US astronauts from Apollo 11 became the first people to set foot on the Moon. This picture shows Edwin Aldrin. Reflected in his visor are the lunar module and his photographer, Neil Armstrong.

may need to venture outside their craft to work in space. This is known as EVA ("extra-vehicular activity"). Then they must take their "atmosphere" with them, by wearing a spacesuit.

The spacesuit is a many-layered garment: it has an inner water-cooled suit, a pressure suit and an outer insulated suit and helmet which protects the astronaut from dangerous radiation and the showers of minute particles that are found in space. The astronauts may get air and cooling water through a flexible tube (called "the umbilical"), connected to the main life-support system on the spacecraft. Or the spacesuit may be self-contained, with its own life-support system: the shuttle spacesuit is like this.

For moving about in orbit, shuttle astronauts can use a manned maneuvering unit (MMU), equipped with gas jets which can fire in different directions. Wearing this, an astronaut can float free in space to repair satellites in orbit and, in the more distant future, perhaps to work on a great space engineering enterprise such as a huge solar power plant or space port. This could happen early in the 21st century. By then astronauts may be embarking once again on longer voyages of discovery—back to the Moon and perhaps to the planet Mars.

See also SPACE EXPLORATION.

ASTRONOMY is the study of the planets, the stars, and the many other objects in the Universe beyond the Earth. The things of interest to astronomers include the Sun, the Moon, the planets, the stars, nebulae, and galaxies. All these are studied carefully with the aim of finding out as much as possible about them. What are they like and how did they come to exist? How indeed did the entire Universe come into existence? These are some of the questions astronomers are trying to answer. They hope that eventually all the facts that have been discovered will fit together like a jigsaw puzzle to give us an overall picture of the kind of Universe we live in.

In 1969 two American astronauts became the first men to land on the Moon and the first people to be able to explore an object in space. In the 1970s, the Moon was visited a number of times. Scientific experiments were done there and rock samples brought back to Earth. By the end of the 1980s, the planets from Mercury out to Neptune had been studied by unmanned space probes. We now owe a vast amount of our present knowledge and understanding of the solar system to these spacecraft, but for things farther away astronomers still have to rely on the telescope as their most important tool.

Our eyes are sensitive to light, but the visible light they see is only a small part of what is called the electromagnetic spectrum. The full spectrum includes a whole range of radiation that is similar to light, but is mostly invisible. Radio waves, ultraviolet and infra-red radiation, X-rays and gamma rays are all part of the spectrum. The strongest radiation given out by our Sun lies in the visible part of the spectrum. But many of the other objects in space give out strong radiation in other parts of the spectrum. Astronomers came to realize how much they can learn from "invisible astronomy" as well as from optical astronomy. Radio astronomy was the first kind of invisible astronomy to be done. Now, every part of the spectrum is used to study the sky. Most of the radiation outside the bands of visible light and radio waves gets absorbed in the Earth's atmosphere. Infra-red telescopes have to be put on very high mountains and in deserts to avoid the water vapor in the atmosphere that cuts out infra-red radiation. In the 1980s, an Infra-red Radiation Artificial Satellite (IRAS) made valuable observations in Earth orbit well above the atmosphere. Ultraviolet, X-ray and gamma-ray telescopes always have to be put on board orbiting satellites, because these radiations are completely blocked by the atmosphere.

It is quite common for astronomers to specialize in one branch of astronomy. Some are skilled at using a particular type of telescope to study one region of the spectrum. Others make a special study of one kind of object, such as the Sun or galaxies, and might use optical or radio telescopes to learn as much as possible. There are also astrophysicists or theoretical astronomers who make no observations at all. Their job is to use the laws of physics to work out explanations for the things observational astronomers see.

The kinds of telescopes and equipment professional astronomers need in order to make important new discoveries are now so expensive that usually only governments can afford to buy them. Many countries have national observatories. Astronomy is also studied at universities, and some of these have their own observatories, too.

A big telescope is not necessary to enjoy

astronomy, which is a fascinating hobby for millions of people throughout the world. Some amateur astronomers make useful discoveries and observations, even with small telescopes. Some amateur astronomers specialize in observing the Moon or Sun very closely or

Courtesy, The Hale Observatory

The open star cluster of the Pleiades is one of the most beautiful sights in the sky. Light from the cluster, which is 400 light-years from the Solar System, is scattered by surrounding clouds of gas and dust.

in looking for new comets or supernovae (exploding stars). Most just enjoy looking at the beautiful and interesting sights in the sky.

Astronomy and Astrology

Thousands of years ago, before there were any clocks or calendars, people used to tell the time of year, as well as the time of day or night, by watching the Sun and the stars. It was important for them to know the time of year so that they could sow their crops and reap their harvests at the right seasons. People who could tell the time of year by "reading the sky"

gained a high position among the members of these early communities, because food supplies depended on their advice. These early astronomers were often priests of primitive religions, and many religious myths and legends grew up about the Sun, Moon, stars and planets, which were even worshipped as gods by many peoples.

By watching the sky carefully, astronomers of this early period found that the stars and planets seemed to move round the Earth in quite regular ways, and so, from knowledge of what had happened before, they eventually learned to foretell the future movements. Because the coming of the seasons and other events like the rising of the Nile in Egypt (which happened at just the same time every year) could be foretold from the stars, many peoples believed that all kinds of future events could be foretold in the same way. It was thought, for example, that the whole future life of a newborn child could be foretold from the position of the Sun, Moon and planets at the time of its birth. There is no evidence for this. Apart from the tides, which are controlled by the position of the Sun and Moon, the heavenly bodies, as they are called, have nothing at all to do with everyday events on Earth. The false science of seeing into the future by watching the heavens is known as astrology. It was mixed up with astronomy and religion for thousands of years. (See ASTROLOGY.)

An important feature of the stars that the ancient peoples noticed is that they appear to be grouped into patterns. We now call these patterns "constellations". We also know that the stars that make up each constellation are not connected with each other at all. Constellations are the result of what we call "line-of-sight" effects. To identify constellations people started giving them names. Many of these names were given by Babylonian astrologer-astronomers who lived about 5,000 years ago. But most of the names we use today are taken from Greek astronomers. There are 88 constellations, and astronomers usually refer to them by Latin forms of their names.

Of course the first astronomers did not know

Mansell Collection

Medieval astronomers gained their view of the Universe from the ancient Greeks. This view was changed by Copernicus who showed that the solar system is sun centered.

why things happened in the sky. They only knew *what* happened, and they had to make use of this knowledge as best they could. For example, they knew that certain constellations disappear from view for part of the year and later reappear. These stars always reappear at the same time of year and they rise again in the same part of the sky.

The Babylonians, the ancient Egyptians, and the Mayas and Incas in America all built temples for watching the stars. Some of these temples were built in such a way that as a particular star came into the sky again after a disappearance it could be seen through a narrow slit specially made in the temple wall. The first appearance of the star through the slit announced the time for planting crops.

Ancient Astronomy

The greatest astronomers of the ancient world were the Greeks. The store of astronomical knowledge that had been built up by the Babylonian and Egyptian astronomers from the 7th century BC was passed on to the Greeks, and many strange beliefs were passed on as well. Besides the rising and setting of the so-called "fixed" stars—the heavenly bodies that did not appear to change their positions in relation to each other—the Greeks recognized five bright "wandering" objects that move against the background of the fixed stars. The Greek word, *planetes* means "wanderer", and we now know that these objects, the planets, are dark bodies that shine by reflected light. The Earth is one of these. The Greeks knew five planets—Mercury, Venus, Mars, Jupiter, and Saturn.

The early Greek astronomer Thales of Miletus (*c.* 624–*c.* 546 BC) knew how to forecast eclipses (see ECLIPSE), but he did not understand how eclipses happen. He believed that the Earth was flat and that it floated on water. Pythagoras of Samos, who lived in the 6th century BC, was, like many other astronomers, also famous as a mathematician. He believed that the Earth was round and fixed at the center of the universe with the Sun, stars and planets moving round it. Aristarchus of Samos, an astronomer of the 3rd century BC, was one of the first people to say that the Earth goes round the Sun, not the Sun round the Earth, but at that time hardly anyone believed him. He invented a way of finding the distance from the Earth to the Sun, but it was not very successful. He thought that the Sun is only 20 times as far away as the Moon, but it is really about 400 times as far.

One of the greatest Greek astronomers was Hipparchus, who lived in the 2nd century BC. He invented the kind of mathematics known as trigonometry, which he used to work out the positions of stars in the sky. He made a catalogue of about 850 stars, divided into six classes of brightness, or magnitudes. Hipparchus' classes of brightness form the basis of the system used by astronomers today. Stars of the first magnitude are the brightest in the sky. Stars of the sixth magnitude are the faintest visible with the unaided eye.

The last great Greek astronomer, Claudius Ptolemaeus (Ptolemy), lived at Alexandria in Egypt in the 2nd century AD. He believed, like Pythagoras, that the Earth was fixed at the center of the universe, with the stars going round it in circles. It was obvious to Ptolemy that the Sun and planets did not simply circle round the Earth—occasionally the planets seemed to backtrack on themselves—but he believed that they moved in "epicycles". (An epicycle is the kind of curve you get if you trace out a circle whose center is itself moving round a bigger circle.) Ptolemy wrote down his ideas in a book known as *The Great Treatise*.

Practically the only astronomers between

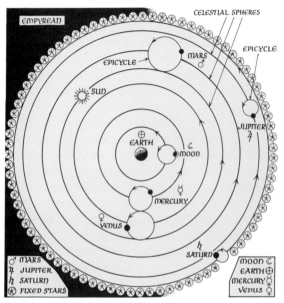

Ptolemy's theory of the Universe (2nd century AD).

the 2nd and the 14th centuries were Arabs, who learned from Ptolemy's work and made a few discoveries of their own. They produced an influential translation of Ptolemy's work called the *Almagest*. The Arabs gave names to the brightest stars that we still use today. They carried on the Greek traditions in astronomy and passed their knowledge on to Europe, mostly through the Moors, who occupied Spain from the 8th to the 15th centuries.

Copernicus, Tycho Brahe, and Kepler

Modern astronomy begins with Nicolaus Copernicus (1473–1543), who was born in Poland. In his major work on astronomy called "Concerning the Revolutions of the Celestial Spheres", Copernicus came to the conclusion that the Earth goes round the Sun, and that it turns on its own axis, or revolves, once every 24 hours. He also said that all the planets went round the Sun in circles, which was much better than Ptolemy's scheme of epicycles, but

still not quite right. For a while Copernicus' suggestion was not generally accepted. Even in the 17th century, people still believed in Ptolemy's theory, which they mixed up with their religious beliefs.

Copernicus' theory of the Solar System, with some alterations, is the one still used today. We call it the heliocentric (sun-centered) theory. The alterations to it were brought about mainly by the combined work of two men, Tycho Brahe (1546–1601), a Danish nobleman, and Johannes Kepler (1571–1630), a German, who worked with Brahe for a time.

Tycho, who was a clever instrument maker, made more accurate observations of the movements of the planets than had ever been made before. Kepler worked out from Tycho's observations a new and improved scheme for the Solar System. Kepler's scheme is contained in three laws. He announced the first two in 1609 and the third in 1618. The first law says that the planets move round the Sun not in circles but in slightly oval paths called "ellipses". The second law tells how the speed of a planet varies at certain points in its orbit, going fast when it is near the Sun and slower when it is farther away. The third law tells how long a planet takes to go round an orbit of any particular size.

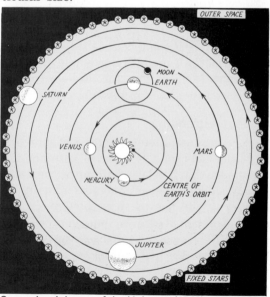

Copernicus' theory of the Universe (1543).

Discoveries of the Telescope

Tycho Brahe and all astronomers before him lived before the invention of the telescope and therefore had to look at the stars with the unaided eye. It is not quite certain who invented the telescope, but it was first used in astronomy by the famous Italian scientist Galileo Galilei (1564–1642), who made a telescope in 1609. He at once made a great many important discoveries, including sunspots, the mountains and "seas" on the Moon, and four of the moons of Jupiter. He found that Venus,

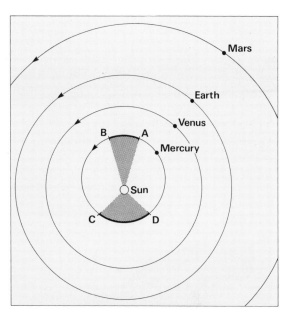

At the start of the 17th century Kepler's laws showed that planets follow elliptical paths round the Sun; that the further they are away from it the longer their journeys take; and that planets travel fastest when nearest to the Sun and slowest when furthest away.

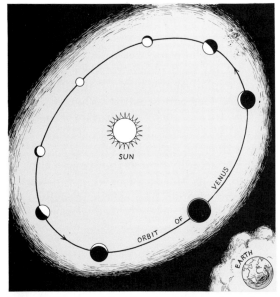

When Galileo found that the planet Venus showed phases like the Moon, he realized that it went around the Sun, not the Earth. Therefore, Copernicus was right, and the Earth could not be the center of the Universe.

like the Moon, goes through phases, or apparent changes in its shape. This could only happen if Venus were orbiting the Sun, not the Earth, and convinced Galileo that Copernicus had been right.

Following Galileo's discoveries, many people began making telescopes and using them to look at the stars. These telescopes had glass lenses and so were called "refracting" telescopes because the light was refracted, or bent, by the glass. It was not long before Sir Isaac Newton, the great English mathematician, invented a telescope with a curved mirror instead of lenses. This is called a "reflecting" telescope. Most of the big optical telescopes used by astronomers in modern observatories are reflecting telescopes. Telescopes have to be very large in order to see faint and faraway stars. The world's largest reflecting telescope is in the Soviet Union at Zelenchukskaya in the Caucasus, and has a mirror 6 meters (20 feet) across. (There is more about the equipment used by astronomers in the articles OBSERVATORY and TELESCOPE.)

The Law of Gravitation

Newton's work on the reflecting telescope was very important to the study of astronomy. But his discovery of the law of gravitation was even more significant. Gravitation, or gravity, is the force of attraction which acts between any two objects—stars, planets, aircraft, people, apples, raindrops, and atoms included. Newton's law of gravitation gave a complete explanation of Kepler's three laws for the planets, and also explained some discrepancies between the laws and observed facts. It explained also why objects fall to the ground when they are dropped instead of remaining in mid-air. (See ACCELERATION; GRAVITY.)

Newton's law has twice led to the discovery of a new planet. As was explained earlier, Mercury, Venus, Mars, Jupiter, and Saturn, as well as our own planet Earth, have been known since ancient times. The seventh planet, Uranus, was discovered through telescopic observations in 1781 by Sir William Herschel, a German-born astronomer and pioneer of telescope-making who worked in England. Later it was found that Uranus was

Science Museum, London

A copy of the first reflecting telescope invented by Sir Isaac Newton, shown to the Royal Society in 1671.

not moving quite as Newton's law said it should. The only explanation was that there must be another planet out beyond Uranus which was affecting its behavior. John Couch Adams, an Englishman, and Urbain Leverrier, a Frenchman, each without knowing what the other was doing, worked out where the new planet would have to be in order to produce the right effect on Uranus. In 1846 the German astronomer Johann Galle looked through a telescope at the part of the sky pointed out by Adams and Leverrier and found Neptune, the eighth planet.

Neptune in its turn was later found to be moving not quite in agreement with Newton's

law. Again a new planet turned out to be responsible. This was Pluto, the ninth planet, discovered by the American astronomer Clyde Tombaugh in 1930. Few astronomers believe that there are any more planets in our solar system beyond Pluto. However, there may be planets orbiting other stars. Light emitted from a nearby star known as Barnard's Star "wobbles", and this could be due to the effect of a large planet in orbit around it.

There was one disagreement with Newton's law for which no explanation could be found. The planet Mercury was found to be moving in a way slightly different from that predicted by the law. Leverrier suggested that there might be another planet between Mercury and the Sun, but no such planet could be seen. The correct explanation was given in 1915, when the great German scientist Albert Einstein put forward his law of gravitation. Einstein's law, which is part of his "Theory of Relativity", showed that the light rays reflected from Mercury were actually bent as they passed close to the Sun. Thus Mercury looked as if it was in a different position from where it really was. Einstein proved that the Sun attracts light rays like this because energy, such as light, is equivalent to mass.

The Camera and the Spectroscope

After the invention of the telescope, astronomers began to take more interest in the stars as objects, which, being so much more distant than the planets, are far harder to study. The study of the stars by astronomers was much helped by the invention of two instruments which were first used in astronomy in the 19th century. These were the camera and the spectroscope.

The first astronomical photographs were taken by John W. Draper, an American, who photographed the Moon in 1840. The first star to be photographed was the bright star Vega, which was photographed at the Harvard observatory in the United States in 1850. Nowadays nearly all astronomers take photographs of the stars instead of just looking at them through telescopes. They use special cameras fixed to the telescopes and generally take the photographs on glass plates instead of on films. Photography is convenient for several reasons. One important reason is that plates can be exposed for several hours, so that the light from very faint stars has time to collect on the plates and the stars appear in the photographs, even though they cannot be seen by the eye. Special instruments, such as the charged couple device, are now used to intensify the image, so that photographs can be taken in a shorter time.

The other important astronomical instrument is the spectroscope. Ever since Newton's time, it has been known that a beam of light passing through a glass prism could be split into the rainbow of colors that make up its spectrum. The spectroscope, which was invented early in the 19th century, was used to split up the visible light from stars and other objects. Sir William Herschel and the German scientist J. W. Ritter examined the spectrum of the Sun and discovered infra-red and ultraviolet radiation. The first man to look at the spectra of the Sun and stars properly was the German scientist Joseph von Fraunhofer (1787–1826). He used a telescope and a prism. Fraunhofer's work laid the foundations of the science of spectroscopy, by which astronomers have been able to detect the chemical elements present in the stars, planets, and other objects. Spectroscopes have also helped to work out the motion of stars and galaxies. (See DOPPLER EFFECT; SPECTRUM.)

There are other instruments besides the camera and the spectroscope that are used by astronomers. A particularly useful one is the photoelectric cell, which is used to find out how bright the stars are. It was first used for this purpose by the English astronomer G. M. Minchin in 1891. It is often used with a spectroscope to compare the brightness of light of different colors.

The Sun and Stars

The information that astronomers have gained by means of the camera and the spectroscope has completely revolutionized our understanding of the Universe. It turns out that our Sun is just an ordinary star. Like most stars it consists almost entirely of the lightest of all gases, hydrogen. There is a small proportion of helium and traces of many other chemical elements such as sodium, iron, and chromium. The Sun's surface is at a temperature of about 6000°C (11,000°F). Some stars are hotter than the Sun and some cooler. The color of a star shows how hot it is. The hottest are white, the coolest red. Our yellow Sun comes somewhere in between.

In the 1920s, the English astronomer, Sir Arthur Eddington (1882–1944) realized that the source of energy that keeps the Sun and stars going is nuclear energy. Before that time, nobody had thought of a source of energy that could have fueled the Sun even for as long as the known age of the Earth. Soon the details were worked out of the nuclear processes that turn the hydrogen in stars into helium, with the release of tremendous quantities of energy.

Now astrophysicists can work out all the stages in the life of a typical star. Some of the different kinds of stars that are observed can be recognized as stars of different ages. Some large stars end their lives in a violent explosion called a supernova. The Crab Nebula, in the constellation of Taurus, is the remains of a supernova that went off in 1054.

Nebulae and Galaxies

In 1770 the French astronomer Charles Messier published a list of small misty patches that he could see in the sky from his observatory in Paris. Messier was interested in comets. He made his list so that he would not confuse these permanent fuzzy objects with the comets he was searching for. Eventually, his catalogue contained 108 objects. Astronomers today still use the names M1, M2, M3 and so on, for the objects in Messier's list.

Messier did not know what his misty patches of light were. To him they were all *nebulae*. The word *nebula* (plural *nebulae*) is Latin for "cloud". Later it was discovered that there are several different kinds of nebulae. Bigger and better telescopes showed that some are clusters of stars and that some looked like spirals. Others were proved to be real glowing clouds of gas. Today the term nebula is generally used only for clouds of gas or dust in space.

All the stars we can see in the night are part of a giant family containing many thousands of millions of stars altogether. This collection of stars is called the Galaxy and our Sun belongs to it. The Galaxy is disk-shaped with a bulge in the middle. Because we are inside the disk we can see many of the distant stars as a broad band of faint light circling the sky called the Milky Way. Even a small telescope or binoculars turned on the Milky Way will reveal dense clouds of stars.

Some of the stars in the Galaxy belong to tight groups called clusters. There are two kinds of star cluster. Open clusters are loosely grouped containing between a hundred and several thousands stars. The Pleiades are an example. Globular clusters are dense balls of closely packed stars containing up to a million. The Galaxy also contains numerous clouds of gas and dust. Some of these are well known and have familiar names such as the Trifid Nebula and the Lagoon Nebula.

It is not easy to work out what our Galaxy would look like from outside. Sir William Herschel was one of the first people to try to guess. A picture has gradually been built up, however, and radio astronomy has been particularly useful in this work. Radio waves from the gas between the stars can be detected even where dust clouds block out the light. From this we have learned that our Galaxy is almost certainly spiral in shape, with trails of stars and gas forming "arms".

In the 1920s it was found that some of the so-called nebulae are actually other galaxies, vast collections of stars similar to our own Galaxy but far out in space beyond the Milky Way. What is more, as the American astronomer Edwin Hubble (1889–1953) discovered, the galaxies are all moving away from us and each other. The Universe is expanding and the farther away a galaxy is, the faster it is receding. As far as telescopes can probe, the Universe contains galaxies. Some are spirals, but others are elliptical with no arms. A few strangely

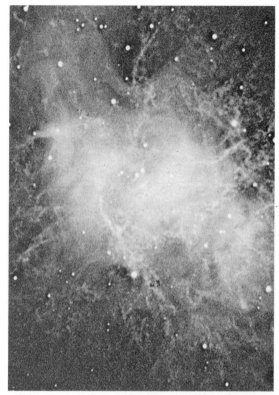

Courtesy, Mount Wilson and Palomar Observatories

The Crab Nebula, in the constellation Taurus, is the remains of a star that exploded in 1054. The Crab emits X-rays, and experts think a new star is forming in it.

shaped galaxies look as if explosions have taken place inside them. Even galaxies are often found in clusters.

Since the 1960s astronomers have discovered a number of extraordinary things in the vastness of outer space. A class of rare objects called quasars are extremely remote structures the size of a solar system putting out the same amount of energy as a small galaxy. Astronomers generally believe that quasars lie on the very fringes of the observable Universe and are moving away from us at enormous speeds. Other strange objects are neutron stars, tiny very dense bodies only a few kilometers across that lie at the heart of a supernova remnant. Some neutron stars "blink" and are called pulsars. A third type of object is the strangest of all. It is called a black hole. It cannot be seen but is so massive that not even light can escape from it, and it sucks in nearby matter.

The Size of the Universe

How do you measure the distance to the Sun and stars? Astronomers have had to think up ingenious ways of solving this difficult problem. Edmond Halley, the English astronomer famous for predicting the orbit of the comet that now bears his name, devised a method of finding the Sun's distance by observing the planet Venus when it goes directly between the Earth and the Sun. This event is called a transit. Transits are rare, only happening twice in over a hundred years. Astronomers watching a transit from different places on the Earth see the planet Venus take different paths across the Sun. This is an effect of parallax. You can see parallax for yourself just by moving your head about. When you do, nearby things change their positions against the background of objects farther away. The distance to the nearer things can be judged by how big that change in position is. To see parallax between the planets and stars, an observer needs to travel a long distance. Astronomers used the Earth's motion in space as a way of changing position. This is far enough to find the distances of the planets and a few of the nearer stars. In six months the Earth has moved by 300 million kilometers (200 million miles), the diameter of its orbit around the Sun. Distances within the solar system can now be found very accurately by means of radar, but star-distance finding still depends on parallax and other indirect measurements. The distance from the Earth to the Sun is about 148 million kilometers (93 million miles). This is called an astronomical unit.

After the Sun, the next nearest star is over four light years away. A light year is a convenient measurement for astronomical distances. It is the distance light travels in a year, nearly 10 million million kilometers (6 million million miles).

Another important way of finding distances in space is by looking at stars whose natural light output is known. How faint these stars look tells us how far away they are. The American astronomer Henrietta Leavitt (1868–1921) found that certain stars called Cepheid variables could be used for distance finding. Cepheid variables can be identified in some of the nearer galaxies, and thus it became possible to judge how far away the galaxies are. One of the nearest to us, the Andromeda galaxy, is over 2 million light years away.

Then it was found from the spectra of galaxies that they are moving away and the farther away they are the faster they are going. Perhaps that rule holds good as far out as galaxies where we can no longer pick out individual stars. If so, then we can guess how far away these distant galaxies are just from how fast they are traveling, and that can be found fairly easily from their spectra. The most distant objects that can be detected are probably around 15 thousand million light years away!

Astronomers deal with the largest of all things—the Universe as a whole. They are also concerned with some of the smallest since the nuclei of hydrogen atoms are the source of energy in the Sun and stars. Many of the things astronomers observe in space could never be made to happen in a laboratory on Earth. Astronomy teaches us things about the world of physical science that we could not discover in other ways.

ASUNCIÓN,

ASUNCIÓN, a port on the east bank of the River Paraguay, is Paraguay's capital and largest city.

With about one-sixth of Paraguay's population, Asunción is the economic, social, and cultural center of the country. Most of the country's industries are in or near the city. The major industry is the processing of products from the rich farming area surrounding the city. There are also textile mills and shoe factories.

The river system that links Asunción with the Atlantic Ocean has been important throughout the history of Paraguay. Asunción is a shipping point and junction for air routes. Nearly all goods entering or leaving Paraguay pass through the city.

Asunción was founded in 1537 by Spanish explorers seeking a new route to Peru. Because it was founded on Assumption Day, the city was originally named *Nuestra Señora de la Asunción* (Our Lady of the Assumption).

As a colonial city, Asunción became the most important Spanish center in the southern part of South America. In the 17th century it lost this position to Buenos Aires, Argentina. When Paraguay declared its independence from Spain in 1811, Asunción became the capital of the new republic (see PARAGUAY).

In the older part, along the river, the buildings are much as they were in colonial times. They are mainly pastel-colored houses with red Spanish-tile roofs. Modern buildings are found in the center of the city. The National University of Paraguay was founded in Asunción in 1889. The population is 457,210 (1982).

ATATÜRK (1881–1938).

Mustafa Kemal transformed Turkey from a backward feudal society into a modern democratic republic. As the first president of the republic, he introduced many reforms, and in 1933 he took the name Atatürk, meaning "father of the Turks".

Kemal was born in Salonika, Greece. He attended a military staff college in Istanbul and then embarked on a brilliant army career. He fought in the Italo-Turkish War of 1911–12 and the Balkan Wars of 1912–13. Although he opposed Turkey's alliance with Germany in World War I, he successfully defended Gallipoli against the Allied attack.

After the war, the Turkish government agreed to give up nearly all its European territories and to hand over Izmir and Gallipoli to its deadly enemy Greece. In protest Kemal set up a rival government at Ankara and called on Turks to resist this shameful surrender. He took command of the Turkish armed forces in a war against Greece, won a great victory, and proclaimed the end of the Ottoman empire. By the Treaty of Lausanne in 1923 Turkey was allowed to keep all purely Turkish lands. The frontiers then agreed have remained virtually unchanged.

In 1922 Kemal became the first president of the Turkish republic, a position he held until his death in 1938. He abolished the sultanate and caliphate in 1924, and during the next ten years carried through a series of social, legal, and political reforms. The most startling change was that the Muslim faith was no longer to be the official state religion. Kemal abolished religious education and changed the day of rest from the Muslim Friday to Sunday. He forbade women to wear the veil and men to wear the fez or turban. Instead he urged everyone to wear Western clothes.

Kemal Atatürk (seated front right) in 1923, the year when the frontiers of modern Turkey were established.

Kemal introduced a new criminal and civil code of justice. He replaced the Arabic alphabet with the Roman alphabet used throughout the West. He instituted the metric system of weights and measures. He much improved the position of women. They became equal with men socially and politically, and polygamy (one man having more than one wife) was forbidden. In 1934 women became entitled to vote, and the following year 17 women became deputies in the assembly, or parliament.

ATHENA see PALLAS ATHENE.

ATHENS.

Looking at Athens today, it is hard to imagine that this city, the capital of Greece, was once the cultural center of the world, nearly 2,500 years ago. Although the city is still dotted with ancient and beautiful buildings, monuments and statues, modern Athens, with its noisy and polluting traffic, busy port of Piraeus, bustling streets with stores and offices, and a population of just over

3 million, is like any other major city of the Western world.

Athens is situated in the southern part of the mainland of Greece in a region called Attica. About 9.5 kilometers (6 miles) southwest of the city is the Saronic Gulf, an inlet of the Aegean Sea. Athens is built on a plain. To the north and east are mountains. In places the plain is broken by limestone ridges and crags. The Acropolis, which still dominates the city today, is one of these ridges and stands 156 meters (512 feet) high.

Ancient Athens

Athens probably began as a fortress built on the Acropolis ridge. By the middle of the 6th century BC it had become the greatest city on the mainland of Greece. It was a strong outpost against the invading Persians, who were finally driven out of Europe in 479 BC. After that, Athens became the head of a new league of states to prevent another invasion from Asia. Gradually this league became the great Athenian Empire.

When safety was assured, the money given by other states to help defend the empire was used to transform Athens into the hub of Western civilization. Pericles, who became leader of Athens in the middle of the 5th century BC, was the man responsible for this transformation. Under his guidance the magnificent temples, statues, and monuments that still stand on the Acropolis today, were built.

Ancient Athens stretched for about a mile around the Acropolis. At its base was located the Agora, or market-place, a natural meeting place for the inhabitants. Extremely narrow streets went in all directions from the Agora, and one winding road led up to the rock of the Acropolis. At the top of the path was an all-marble gateway, through which could be seen a colossal bronze statue of Athena, the goddess of wisdom, after whom the city was named.

High on the right stood the Parthenon, great temple of Athena. Here was another statue of the goddess, made of gold and ivory and surrounded by all-marble columns. Athena shared with a mythical king of Greece another

ZEFA

Modern Athens lies in a plain, with mountains to the north and east. These include Mount Hymettus.

temple near the Parthenon, whose Porch of the Maidens was supported by six women expertly carved in stone. To the south was the graceful little temple of victory.

On the southern slope of the Acropolis was the open-air theater. The seats were cut out of the rock and ran two-thirds of the way round the circular space in the middle. This space was called the orchestra, meaning "a place for dancing", where the chorus performed. The stage was just beyond the orchestra, in full view of the 30,000 spectators. Competitions were held to choose the best dramatic chorus— a very important part of Greek plays—and the leader of the winning chorus was given a tripod which he placed on a shrine in the Street of Tripods near by.

All this is what would have been seen by anyone who visited Athens in the days of its glory. As well as plays, Athens became noted for its literature, philosophy, education and science. However, over the following centuries Athens' power crumbled, first against Sparta, next Macedonia, and then in the 2nd century BC Athens fell under Roman rule—though it continued to play an important cultural role. When the Roman Empire collapsed in the wake of the Byzantine Empire, based in Con-

ZEFA

The famous ancient Acropolis, with the imposing columns of the Parthenon.

stantinople, Athens was relegated to a provincial town. The bronze statue of Athena was carried off to Constantinople and destroyed by a mob in 1203. The Turks eventually took over this empire and, in 1458, conquered Athens, and the Parthenon became a Muslim mosque. The Turks ruled Athens, and Greece, for four centuries. During this time, most of the ancient monuments were destroyed by fires and bombardments which the city suffered.

Modern Athens

Greece won independence in 1832, and Athens has been growing rapidly ever since. Many of the ancient buildings and monuments that had fallen into ruin under the Turks are being restored, and many new buildings have been built.

The modern city has spread north and east towards the port, Piraeus, about 8 kilometers (5 miles) away. The center of the city is a triangular area between Constitution and Concord Squares. Venizelos Avenue and Stadium Street, the main avenues, run parallel to each other and connect these squares. In this area are the main stores, hotels, restaurants, the National Library, the Academy of Athens, and the University of Athens. Near the center of the city is the old palace that now houses parliament. The Royal Palace, once home to the now exiled royal family, is to the southeast. Not far away is the stadium, which was restored to hold the first modern Olympic Games in 1896. Away from these large squares and broad avenues, however, you can still walk down old, narrow streets with their markets of local produce.

Together with its port, Piraeus, Athens is the industrial and maritime center of Greece. Millions of tourists flock to the thousands of Greek islands from Piraeus, as well as visit this ancient cradle of Western civilization. Apart from tourism, the other main industries centered round Athens are textiles, carpets, chemicals, leather products, pottery, furniture, and wines and other beverages.

ATHLETICS. The oldest and most widely played of all games have been those in which people have shown their ability to run, jump, or throw objects. Such activities have been popular in all ages and throughout the world. Some nations or groups of people have developed exceptional ability in particular events of track and field athletics. The Ethiopians and Kenyans, for example, have shown outstanding abilities as long-distance runners, the Finns as javelin throwers, and West Indians as sprinters.

Running seems to have been organized as early as 3800 BC, in ancient Egypt. But the most famous athletics event in ancient times was the Olympic Games in Greece (see OLYMPIC GAMES). The Olympics were not only sporting contests but were also great artistic and cultural festivals, maintaining the Greek ideal of perfection of mind and body. Athletes prepared for ten months before the games and spent the last month at Olympia itself, just as athletes today train intensely for major championships.

Athletics Organizations

The governing body of world athletics, the International Amateur Athletic Federation (IAAF), has 174 nations affiliated to it, more than any other international organization, sporting or otherwise. Formed from a meeting held in 1912, it aims to "establish friendly and loyal co-operation between all members for the benefit of amateur athletics throughout the world". Its rules govern international competition for men and women in all events.

The modern Olympic Games, begun in 1896 and held every four years, have long been the sport's main attraction, and the athletics events in the Olympics are recognized by the IAAF as world championships. In recent years the number of athletics competitions has grown considerably. Separate world championships are now additionally held between Olympic Games, as well as smaller championships confined to a continent or an area. A national federation administers athletics within each country, encouraging the sport in schools, colleges, and clubs. National championships form the main competition at home. Teams are chosen from these and other major competitions to compete against other individual countries, or in such events as the European Championships, the Pan-American Games, the Commonwealth Games, and the Asian or African championships. Each of these championships provides a full program of athletic events. In addition, some branches of the sport, such as cross-country running, walking, and road running, also have their own major championships.

The IAAF and its member federations, while keeping many of the important aspects of the old "amateur" traditions, have realized that they must change their approach as the sport changes. Thus it provides for the needs not only of club and school athletes but also of the practically full-time top sportsmen and women who compete at the highest level.

At least as popular as the major championships are the big international meetings to which top athletes are specially invited. These provide opportunities for sponsorship and advertising, and attract considerable numbers of spectators and television viewers.

The three main divisions of track and field athletics are the running events, the walks, and the field events (jumps and throws).

Track Events

Running events range from sprints to long-distance runs. They may be contested on indoor or outdoor tracks, on the roads, or across country. Sprinting events are those distances up to 400 meters, in which the athlete runs at almost full speed for the entire race. The standard distances are 100, 200, and 400 meters, the last being one lap of an outdoor track. Indoors, smaller tracks are used, most commonly of 200 meters with banked turns. Indoor sprints are run over distances as short as 50 meters. A sprinter needs a fast start, good acceleration, and the power to maintain a high leg-speed.

The standard middle-distance races are over 800 and 1,500 meters and the classic old-fashioned distance of 1 mile. The most famous target in athletics used to be to run a mile in less than four minutes. Since the British athlete Roger Bannister first achieved that feat, at Oxford on 6 May 1954, such a time has become commonplace (see BANNISTER, SIR ROGER). This indicates the relentless improvement in world-class standards. It took 70 years for the world record to improve from 4 minutes 10 seconds to 4 minutes. But it was only a further 21 years before New Zealander John Walker became the first to run the mile in less than 3 minutes 50 seconds in 1975. The middle-distance runner must combine speed and endurance with good tactical sense. His or her training must develop all these aspects.

Long-distance races range from 5,000 and 10,000 meters, on the track, to the marathon and even longer distances on road courses. Men have raced over such distances throughout the sport's history, but women's distance running has been recognized only in very recent years. It was not until 1969 that women first raced at 1,500 meters in international competition. The 3,000 meters followed in 1974 and the marathon in the late 1970s. Recognized running events for women are now the same as for men, except for the steeple-

UPI, Ed Lacey and CPNA

The excitement of different athletic events lies in the variety of skills needed by the competitors.

chase. Only men run the 3,000 meters over 28 hurdle jumps and 7 water jumps.

Distance running has become enormously popular all over the world. There was a great boom in marathon running from the mid-1970s, first in the United States and then in other countries. The marathon was included in the 1896 Olympic Games to commemorate the legendary run by Pheidippides from Marathon to Athens with news of the Greek victory over the Persians in 490 BC. The distance of 42,195 meters (26 miles, 385 yards) was that used at the 1908 Olympic Games, and it became standard from 1924. Such events as the London and New York marathons attract fields of well over 10,000 runners each year. (See MARATHON RACE.)

The remaining flat-racing events are the relay races. These involve teams of runners. Each member of the team runs part of the race. A baton is held by the runner which must be passed on to the next team member before he can run his leg (or portion).

The standard hurdles events are run over ten flights of hurdles. For men the hurdles are 106.7 centimeters (42 inches) high in the 110 meters race and 91.4 centimeters (36 inches) in the 400 meters; and for women 84 centimeters (33 inches) at 100 meters and 76.2 centimeters (30 inches) at 400 meters. The hurdles events are so called because ordinary sheep hurdles were originally used as obstacles.

In walking races unbroken contact must be maintained with the ground and each leg must be straightened at least momentarily. Olympic walks are contested on road courses over 20 and 50 kilometers for men and 10 kilometers for women.

Field Events

High jump techniques have changed over the years from a rather clumsy scissors-style jump, through the Eastern cut-off, Western roll, and straddle to the flop, which is used nowadays by nearly all the world's best jumpers. In the flop, the jumper twists after take-off to go over the bar backwards.

The use of fiberglass poles has dramatically improved performances in the pole vault. The world record has improved by more than a meter (36 inches) in 25 years since these poles replaced the former metal or bamboo ones. The vaulter needs good sprinting speed as he goes down the runway, grasping the pole in both hands, before planting it in a V-shaped box beneath the crossbar. As well as speed he needs strength and gymnastic ability to "ride" the pole and push his body vertically upwards and over the bar, while the pole falls back. In both high jumping and pole vaulting the competitor is permitted three attempts to clear each height. The long and triple jumps demand great sprinting speed and explosive power in lifting the body up and out from the 10-centimeter (4-inch) take-off board. The triple jump consists of three phases: the hop in which the jumper lands on his take-off foot, the step to land on the other foot, and the jump.

The shot-put evolved from throwing or heaving heavy stones. Experts at the event are the biggest and strongest of all athletes. They "put" a metal ball from the shoulder with one hand from a circle 2.1 meters (7 feet) in diameter. Men use a 7.26 kilogram (16 pound) shot, and women one of 4 kilograms (8 pounds 11 ounces). A 7.26 kilogram (16 pound) metal ball is also used in the hammer-throwing event, in which only men compete. The ball, or head, is attached to a handle by a length of wire to make up the hammer. It is thrown from a circle 2.1 meters (7 feet) in diameter partially surrounded by a protective cage. The hammer event originated with throwing sledge-hammers in British country sports.

The discus weighs 2 kilograms (4 pounds 6 ounces) for men and 1 kilogram (2 pounds 3 ounces) for women, and a slightly larger circle of 2.5 meters (8 feet 2 inches) is used. Discus throwers must use speed and strength to give momentum to the discus as they rotate in the circle. They release it at such an angle as to give it the best flight path. Throwing the javelin obviously originated from spear throwing. The men's javelin weighs 800 grams (28 ounces) and the women's weighs 600 grams (21 ounces). The competitor throws the javelin

WORLD ATHLETICS RECORDS

World records at a selection of events show the progress that has taken place this century in world-class standards.

MEN

EVENT	1925	1950	1975	1985
100 metres	10.2 sec.	10.1 sec.	9.9 sec.	9.9 sec.
400 metres	47.1 sec.	45.8 sec.	43.86 sec.	43.86 sec.
1500 metres	3 min. 52.6 sec.	3 min. 43 sec.	3 min. 32.16 sec.	3 min. 29.46 sec.
1 mile	4 min. 10.4 sec.	4 min. 01.3 sec.	3 min. 49.4 sec.	3 min. 46.32 sec.
10,000 metres	30 min. 06.1 sec.	29 min. 02.6 sec.	27 min. 30.80 sec.	27 min. 13.81 sec.
Marathon	2 hours 29 min. 01.8 sec.	2 hours 25 min. 39 sec.	2 hours 8 min. 33.6 sec.	2 hours 7 min. 12 sec.
400 m hurdles	53.5 sec.	50.6 sec.	47.82 sec.	47.02 sec.
High jump	2.03 metres	2.11 metres	2.30 metres	2.41 metres
Long jump	7.89 metres	8.13 metres	8.90 metres	8.90 metres
Shot putt (7.26 kg)	15.54 metres	17.95 metres	21.82 metres (4 kg)	22.62 metres
Javelin (800 g)	68.55 metres	78.70 metres	94.08 (600 g)	104.80 metres

Note: In the shot and javelin events, lighter shots and javelins are thrown nowadays than formerly, so no direct comparison of records is possible

Note: A dash indicates that there was no official world record for the distance at this time

WOMEN

EVENT	1925	1950	1975	1985
100 metres	12.2 sec.	11.5 sec.	10.9 sec.	10.76 sec.
400 metres	60.5 sec.	56.7 sec.	49.9 sec.	47.60 sec.
1500 metres	—	4 min. 37.8 sec.	4 min. 01.38 sec.	3 min. 52.47 sec.
1 mile	—	5 min. 15.3 sec.	4 min. 28.5 sec.	4 min. 16.71 sec.
10,000 metres	—	—	34 min. 01.4 sec.	30 min. 59.42 sec.
Marathon	—	—	2 hours 38 min. 19 sec.	2 hours 21.06 sec.
400 m hurdles	—	—	56.51 sec.	53.55 sec.
High jump	1.52 metres	1.71 metres	1.95 metres	2.07 metres
Long jump	5.54 metres	6.25 metres	6.84 metres	7.44 metres
Shot putt	11.57 metres	15.02 metres	21.60 metres	22.53 metres
Javelin	27.30 metres	53.41 metres	67.22 metres	75.40 metres

Mike King/Allsport Photographic

Willy Banks of the USA does the triple jump, an event sometimes called the hop, step (skip), and jump.

with a whiplash arm action from behind a line after a controlled run up.

Multi-event competitions

The greatest all-round athletes are generally considered to be those who succeed in the toughest of all athletics tests, the decathlon (for men) and the heptathlon (for women). These events are contested over two days, with performances achieved in each event scored on international scoring tables to give a combined total. Men contest the ten events of the decathlon—on the first day: 100 meters, long jump, shot, high jump, and 400 meters; and on the second day: 110 meters hurdles, discus, pole vault, javelin, and 1,500 meters. The women's heptathlon comprises seven events: the 100 meters hurdles, shot, high jump, and 200 meters on the first day; and the long jump, javelin, and 800 meters on the second day. To succeed, therefore, athletes need to combine speed, strength, skill and endurance.

Coaching

To achieve success in any track or field event natural ability is not enough. Experts who know how the body works and how performances can be improved help athletes enormously. Methods of developing speed, strength, and the necessary skills vary according to the event that an athlete chooses. The advice and encouragement of trained coaches are vital at all levels of athletic activity. All the main athletics nations have developed national coaching schemes. Particularly notable has been the success of East Germany, where scientists have studied all aspects of sporting activity. Coaching there has been based on these scientific studies. This coaching and a burning desire to succeed in athletics has brought great success in international competitions.

ATLANTA is the capital of Georgia and a commercial center for the South. It is among rolling hills at the southern end of the Blue Ridge Mountains, about 320 kilometers (200 miles) from the Atlantic Ocean. It is 320 meters (1,050 feet) above sea-level, higher than any city of its size east of Denver, Colorado. This altitude, and its nearness to the ocean, makes its climate fairly even, without extremes of heat and cold. Near by is the Chattahoochee River, from which Atlanta draws its water supply.

Atlanta was built up along old Indian trails and cow paths. One of these trails became the city's main artery, Peachtree Street.

Atlanta is the transportation center of the south-east. It has one of the busiest airports in the United States. Many leading businesses have branches there for manufacturing, warehousing, and distributing their products.

Into Atlanta pour the raw materials of the South, which are soon shipped out as manufactured goods. Some of the important products are cotton goods, clothes, chemicals and fertilizers, food products, furniture, paper and paper products, confectionery, books and newspapers, and iron and steel products.

Livestock, grain, tobacco, and other farm products add to the city's wealth. Most of the work of the federal government in the southeastern states is centered in Atlanta.

In 1836 the government of Georgia decided to build a railroad from the Tennessee line to the southwestern bank of the Chattahoochee River. Soon a trading center called Terminus grew up. In 1845 it was renamed Atlanta and in 1847 it officially became a city. In 1868 Atlanta became the capital. It was the setting for much of the film *Gone With the Wind*.

Atlanta's population is 425,022 (1980).

ATLANTIC OCEAN. At first only the sea near West Africa was called the Atlantic, probably after the legendary island of Atlantis. Later the name was given to the whole ocean between Europe and Africa on the east and North and South America on the west. It is the second largest ocean, over 16,000 kilometers (10,000 miles) long and between 2,900 kilometers (1,800 miles) and 8,500 kilometers (5,280 miles) wide. (The largest ocean is the Pacific.) Before there were regular shipping services, the Atlantic isolated America from Europe, but today it is crossed by the world's most important trade routes.

In the Atlantic the warm, surface water near the equator usually flows towards the North and South Poles. Deep down, however, there is a slow movement of cold water in the opposite direction. In the north Atlantic there is a great clockwise movement of water. Some water flowing north forms the Gulf Stream which reduces the cold of Greenland and Iceland and then turns east to warm the British Isles and Norway. The Labrador Current, sweeping down from Greenland, brings cold water and dangerous icebergs. (You may have read how in 1912 the great liner "Titanic" struck an iceberg on its maiden voyage from England to America, sinking with nearly three-quarters of those on board.) When the Labrador Current meets the warm Gulf Stream, much fog is formed near Newfoundland. In the south Atlantic the currents flow in a generally counterclockwise direction, resulting in the cold north-flowing Benguela

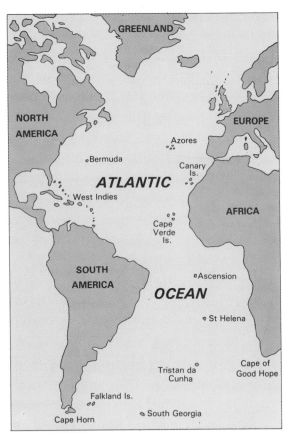

Europe and Africa are divided from the continents of North and South America by the Atlantic Ocean.

Current along the coast of southwestern Africa and the warm south-flowing Brazil Current off South America.

Because of the ocean currents, places that are the same distance from the North Pole sometimes have very different temperatures. Labrador is no further north than the British Isles, but it has long, cold winters and the average temperature is well below zero. Greenland, covered in perpetual snow, is in the same latitude as Norway, where at least the summers are warm and sunny.

In the western mid-Atlantic lies a quiet area called the Sargasso Sea. It varies in size but is over 1,500 kilometers (900 miles) broad and to this calmer area have drifted masses of seaweed, especially a type known as *Sargassum*. The sea was first reported by Christopher Columbus and later, legends (quite untrue) grew up of doomed ships, trapped in the weed until they sank. The Sargasso Sea is the only spawning ground of the European and North American eel.

A great variety of living creatures are found in the Atlantic: from mammals such as whales and seals, through fish to small invertebrate creatures. Most live near the ocean surface where there is most light, and many, notably the commercially caught species of fish, live on the continental shelf.

By taking depth soundings, oceanographers have been able to map much of the ocean floor (see OCEAN AND OCEANOGRAPHY). Near the coast, where the water is shallow, the ocean floor is known as the continental shelf. It slopes gradually to a depth of more than 180 meters (600 feet), then is broken by great valleys thousands of meters deep.

The bottom of the Atlantic is quite unlike the land in shape. In some places it is a monotonous, level plain, but in others it rises in great mountains and ridges. The most important ridge is the mid-oceanic ridge, along which new ocean floor is being produced and spreads out continually in either direction (see EARTH). It runs roughly north and south down the middle of the ocean. It comes above the surface to form islands such as the Azores, Ascension, and Tristan da Cunha, but most of it lies more than 1.5 kilometers (5,000 feet) beneath the surface. The deepest canyon, or valley, is 8 kilometers (5 miles) below the surface.

ATLANTIS was an imaginary island in the Atlantic Ocean. From the time of ancient Greece, stories were told about the beautiful lost land of Atlantis.

The Greek philosopher Plato tells us that Atlantis was really several islands, one inside another. In the center was one island with a ring of water around it; then came a ring of land, then another ring of water round that, and so on. Altogether there were nine rings of land and nine of water. Atlantis had been given to the sea-god Poseidon (Neptune), and he lived there with his beloved Cleito. They had ten sons, five sets of twins. In Plato's story, one of the sons, called Atlas, became king of the central island, while the other nine

each ruled over one of the nine outside rings of land. From them the kings and peoples of Atlantis were descended.

The country flourished and grew rich, for there was copper, timber and many fruits on the islands. The people dug canals through the rings of land so that ships could sail through to the central island, and they also built bridges from one island to another.

The city of Atlantis was built of red and black stone, which was dug up in the island, and the roofs of the houses were of red copper which shone in the sun. The central island, with its two gorgeous temples, was rich beyond all dreams. One temple was surrounded by a golden wall. The other had silver walls, golden pinnacles, and a roof of ivory, copper, gold and silver. There was also a great statue of Neptune driving six winged-horses. Near the temples were baths of hot and cold springs.

Atlantis was a powerful kingdom whose people had conquered many countries. They were finally defeated by the Greeks. The legend tells how the people of Atlantis refused to worship the Greek gods. As a punishment Atlantis was shaken by terrible earthquakes and swallowed up by the sea.

A new theory claims that Atlantis was in the Aegean Sea, north of Crete, on the present-day island of Santorini which was overwhelmed by a violent volcanic eruption about 1500 BC. It is possible that Atlantis was a great Bronze Age state, like nearby Crete. (See GREECE, ANCIENT.)

ATLAS. An atlas is a book of maps, or collection of maps, but behind this familiar word lies a very old story. According to a tale told by the ancient Greeks, Atlas was one of a race of giants called Titans, who once ruled the Earth (see Titans). They were conquered by Zeus and the other gods, who became the rulers of the world in their turn, and Atlas was condemned by Zeus to stand beyond the western horizon of the Earth and there hold up the heavens on his shoulders.

Map books came to be given the name "atlas" in the late 16th century because many of them had a picture at the beginning of the

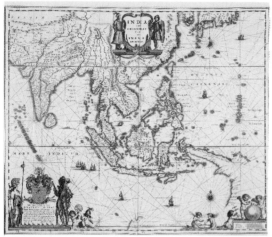

Michael Holford

A map of southeastern Asia produced by the great Dutch cartographer Willem Blaeu in 1635. He was among the first to produce atlases that were superior to those of Ptolemy. This map was one of the earliest to depict Australia.

giant Atlas. A fine Italian collection of maps, known as the Lafréri Atlas, was produced between 1556 and 1575. The great Flemish map maker Mercator published his atlas in 1585 and during the next century the Dutch, who were great sailors and traders, produced many fine atlases.

See also MAPS AND MAP MAKING.

ATLAS MOUNTAINS.

These are not one mountain range but a series of ranges stretching some 2,400 kilometers (1,500 miles) across northwest Africa, through Morocco, Algeria, and Tunisia. To the north the mountains face the Mediterranean Sea and Atlantic Ocean, to the south they overlook the vast Sahara Desert. They are named after the giant Atlas, from Greek mythology (see ATLAS).

The highest range of the Atlas Mountains is found in Morocco and is called the Great Atlas. There are several peaks over 3,500 meters (11,000 feet)—high enough to be snow covered. The highest of all the Atlas Mountains is Toubkal, at 4,185 meters (13,730 feet).

Lower down the slopes that face the Mediterranean, it is hot and dry in summer, and cold and wet in winter.

Forests of pine, oak, cedar, and juniper cover these slopes. The oak forests are a major source of cork. Towards the Sahara the climate and vegetation is more desert-like with only shrubs and short grasses growing in the southern regions.

Most of the inhabitants of the Atlas Mountains are Berbers and Arabs. Most Berbers are farmers who grow grains, olives, figs, and grapes in the valleys. Many of the Arabs are nomads. They tend flocks of sheep and goats. The Atlas Mountains are a rich source of phosphates. They also contain iron ore, manganese, and other minerals, which are being mined much more today than in the past.

ATMOSPHERE.

This name is used for the layers of air or gas surrounding the Earth or a planet. The Earth's atmosphere causes a pressure on our bodies; but we do not notice it because the outside pressure of air is balanced by the inside pressure of the air within us. We are inclined to think that air is weightless, but at sea-level a cubic meter (1.3 cubic yards) of air has a mass of 1.225 kilograms (2 pounds 11 ounces). The atmosphere surrounding the Earth gives us protection. It helps to maintain a fairly even temperature by protecting us from the cold of outer space at night, and by softening the glare of the sun by day.

Information about the atmosphere around and above us has been obtained from observations at ground level and as the result of ascents by balloons, by aircraft, and more recently, by rockets and orbiting artificial satellites. (See SATELLITE.) The brilliant lights of the aurora borealis and australis which are caused by streams of electrically charged particles from the sun entering the upper atmosphere, show that some atmosphere exists as high as 500 kilometers (300 miles). (See the article NORTHERN AND SOUTHERN LIGHTS.)

The Regions of the Atmosphere

Scientists divide the atmosphere into several regions, or layers, although the boundaries between these layers are not always very clear.

The lowest part of the atmosphere, in which we live, is the *troposphere*. The troposphere contains almost 75 per cent of the mass of the atmosphere. It is the layer in which weather as

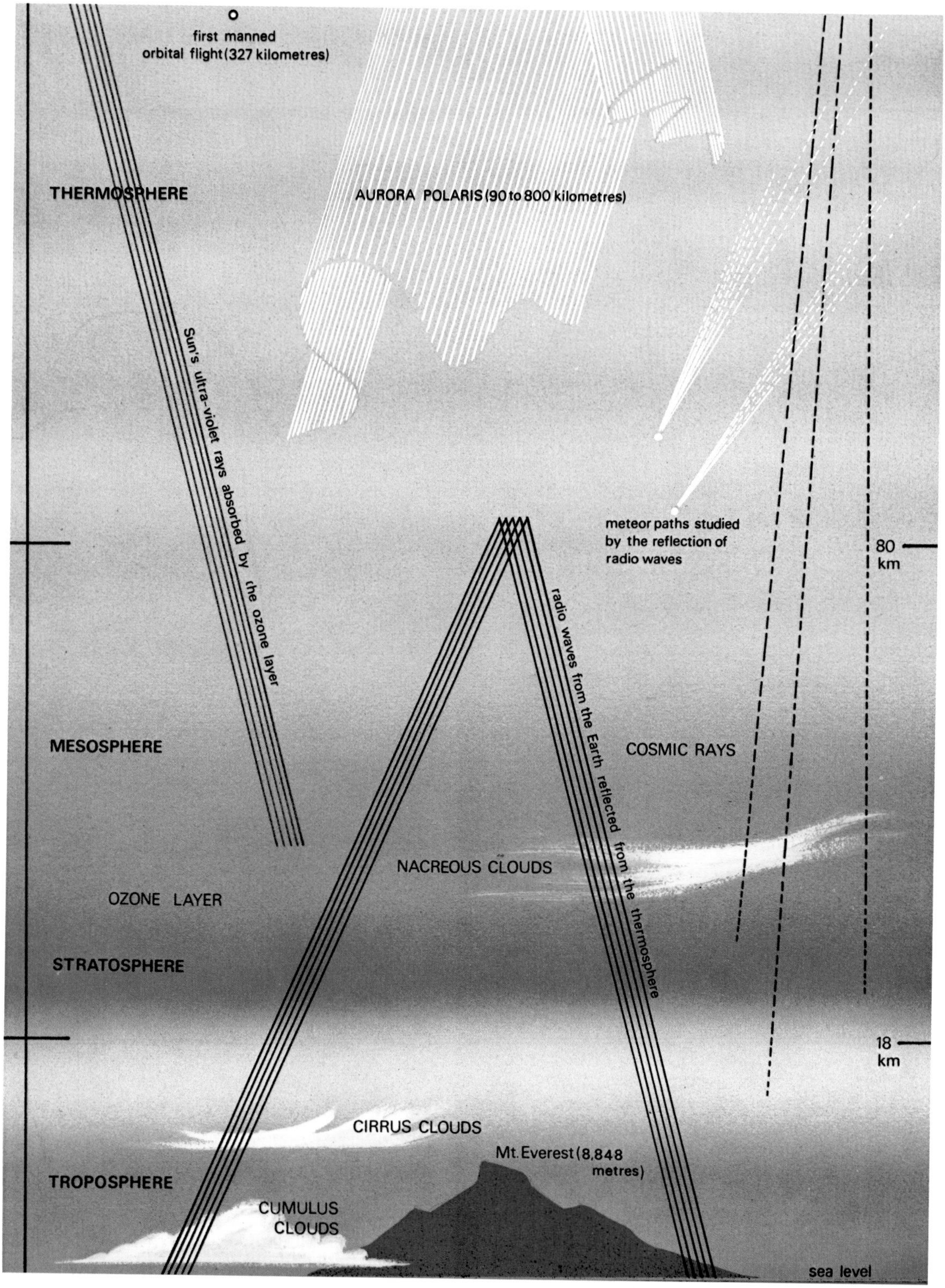

first manned
orbital flight (327 kilometres)

THERMOSPHERE

AURORA POLARIS (90 to 800 kilometres)

Sun's ultra-violet rays absorbed by the ozone layer

MESOSPHERE

meteor paths studied
by the reflection of
radio waves

radio waves from the Earth reflected from the thermosphere

COSMIC RAYS

80
km

OZONE LAYER

NACREOUS CLOUDS

STRATOSPHERE

18
km

CIRRUS CLOUDS

Mt. Everest (8,848
metres)

TROPOSPHERE

CUMULUS
CLOUDS

sea level

The atmosphere is divided into layers: troposphere, stratosphere, etc., each having different properties.

we know it exists and in which nearly all clouds form. As we go up in the troposphere, both the pressure and temperature decrease. At the top of Mount Everest, which is about 8 kilometers (5 miles) above sea-level, the air pressure is only about 30 per cent of the pressure at sea-level and climbers must carry oxygen to help them breathe. The height of the troposphere varies from above 8 kilometers (5 miles) in most latitudes to about 18 kilometers (11 miles) above the Equator. The temperature in the upper layers is −55°C (−67°F), or roughly that of the South Pole in winter.

Above the troposphere is the *stratosphere*. The air becomes thinner still with increasing height and above 30 kilometers (18 miles) the atmospheric pressure is only 1 per cent of the pressure at sea-level. The thin air offers little resistance and so the lower layers of the stratosphere are ideal for jet aircraft traffic. Higher up there is not enough air for the engines to give forward thrust. The cabin of the aircraft must be pressurized so that the air inside is close to normal sea-level pressure. Steady stratospheric winds blow at speeds of up to 300 kilometers (180 miles) per hour and airliners regularly take advantage of these. Occasional nacreous (mother-of-pearl) clouds are seen at heights of between 19 and 28 kilometers (12 and 17 miles), but otherwise the sky is clear.

Above 28 kilometers (17 miles) the temperature rises, reaching 10°C at 50 kilometers (50°F at 30 miles), but from here upward it begins to fall once more. This layer, above 50 kilometers (30 miles), is called the *mesosphere* and it extends to about 80 kilometers (50 miles) above sea-level. Above this lies the *thermosphere*, where the temperature once more increases with altitude. This top layer, which extends from a height of about 80 kilometers to about 500 kilometers (50 to 300 miles) is also known as the *ionosphere*. It contains very little air and the molecules (particles) of gas are widely scattered. But the temperature of each molecule is very high, reaching 395°C at 180 kilometers (740°F at 110 miles) and 700°C at 320 kilometers (1300°F at 200 miles). For comparison, metals glow with a dull-red heat at 700°C (1300°F).

The ionosphere is important chiefly for its effects on radio communications. The particles in it are ionized, or made electrically conductive, by the sun's radiation. This causes the layers in which the particles are most densely clustered to act as reflectors of radio waves. The two chief reflecting layers are at heights of about 110 and 240 kilometers (70 and 150 miles), and their action is explained in the article Radio. Much further out are the Van Allen radiation belts of charged particles, "trapped" in the Earth's magnetic field (see Earth, The).

Far out in space there is nothing but darkness, yet on the Earth we see a clear blue sky. This is because the molecules and particles in the atmosphere scatter more of the blue light than any other color as the sunlight passes through. Nearer the Earth's surface dust particles in the atmosphere reflect all the sun's rays and so the sky sometimes has a white hazy appearance.

The gases forming the atmospheres of the other planets in the solar system are believed to contain very little oxygen and are therefore unlikely to be able to support intelligent life. The moon and Mercury have no atmosphere, and that of Mars is very thin and is made up mostly of carbon dioxide and nitrogen. The immensely dense atmosphere of Venus is more complex; it consists mainly of carbon dioxide, in which float clouds of sulfur dioxide, sulfuric acid, and liquid and solid sulfur. Venus's atmosphere on the surface is nearly 100 times the sea-level pressure of Earth's atmosphere. The atmosphere of Jupiter and the other giant planets beyond it is composed mostly of ammonia and methane. Stars, which are very dense balls of exceedingly hot hydrogen continually being turned into helium, and then into other elements, by nuclear fusion, also have atmospheres around them consisting of hydrogen that is less dense.

ATOLL. A type of reef found in the open ocean, sometimes thousands of kilometers from land, especially in the Pacific and Indian Oceans. Like the reefs found nearer continental coastlines, atolls are actually made up of coral—

Fringing reef

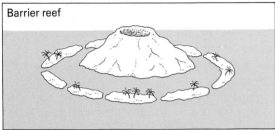

Barrier reef

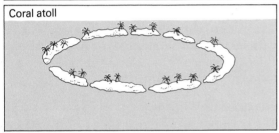

Coral atoll

Atolls form in three stages. First, coral forms a fringing reef round an island. As the island sinks a barrier reef results. An atoll is left when the island is submerged.

millions of skeletons of dead sea-creatures related to anemones, that have collected on the seabed for millions of years. (See CORAL REEF.)

Atolls are circular or horseshoe-shaped with a shallow lagoon, or lake, in the center. They originate as ordinary coral reefs fringing a subsiding volcanic island. As the island sinks, the coral grows upwards to stay near the light. Eventually the island disappears leaving only a ring of coral. Because parts of the atoll are submerged and other parts are above water, the atoll looks like a chain of islands, with channels running in between. These channels are narrow and dangerous to cross, but once through them the atoll provides a relatively safe haven from open ocean storms.

Despite their remoteness and the dangers of ocean storms, many of the atoll islands have been inhabited for centuries by seafaring peoples including Polynesians (see POLYNESIANS), Micronesians and Maldivians (see MALDIVES). The isolation of these atolls also means that many have become the last reserves for rare wildlife including bird colonies. However, this isolation also made ideal sites for testing nuclear weapons, in the past. The largest atoll islands, Kwajalein and Christmas, are in the central Pacific and have become strategic military bases for the United States.

ATOM. Suppose a piece of iron were being divided up into smaller and smaller fragments. Could the dividing up go on for ever or would there be a point when some very small particle could be divided no further? Early scientists thought and argued about this question. A Greek philosopher called Democritus, about the year 400BC, taught that all substances are built up from grains which cannot be subdivided. He used the Greek word *atomos* to describe these grains; *atomos* means "indivisible" and gives us our word *atom*. Democritus taught that all matter is built up of atoms or tiny bits of elements. (An element is a substance made up of atoms which are all alike but different from the atoms of any other element.)

Even the Greeks at this time realized that the atom was very small and they could not obtain just one separate atom of an element. More than 2,000 years passed before any

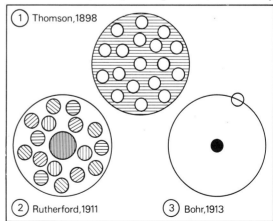

① Thomson, 1898

② Rutherford, 1911

③ Bohr, 1913

Atoms are too small to be seen. Early models of their structure were made on the basis of experimentation.

important advance was made in man's knowledge of atoms.

Early Ideas about Atoms

In 1807 John Dalton, a British chemist and mathematician from the English county of Lancashire, produced his famous atomic theory. He restated what the Greeks had said earlier and added to their writings his own ideas. He stated that:

(1) Everything is made up of extremely small components called atoms which are indivisible and can be neither made nor destroyed.

(2) Atoms of the same element are alike in every respect and atoms of different elements differ in shape, size, weight (mass) and general behavior.

(3) Simple whole numbers of atoms of one element combine with simple whole numbers of atoms of another element to form compounds. For example, two atoms of hydrogen combine with one atom of oxygen to form a group of atoms which is the smallest possible bit of water.

Dalton's atomic theory has been altered as a result of later discoveries. For instance, it is now known that atoms are themselves arrangements of smaller objects called elementary particles and some rearrangements of the outer part of the atom occurs in all chemical reactions. Even the center part can be changed, and one atom can be converted into another.

An atom is very tiny: it is only 1 millionth of a millimeter across and the heaviest atom weighs only 0.000 000 000 000 000 000 004 grams. Because these numbers are so awkward to use, atoms have their own mass scale. Nowadays the standard is taken from a particular atom of carbon which is given the "relative atomic mass" of exactly 12. On this scale, hydrogen, the lightest atom, has a relative atomic mass of about 1 and oxygen of about 16. The heaviest atom found in nature is the atom of uranium with a relative atomic mass of about 238.

Amedeo Avogadro, an Italian count who worked at the same time as Dalton, came to the conclusion that atoms of gaseous elements do not usually exist alone but are with few exceptions joined in pairs. These pairs of atoms are called the molecules of the element; for example, the oxygen molecule contains two atoms. Free atoms are usually very active and look for other atoms to which they are electrically attracted so that they can link up. When different atoms join together, they make a compound. The atoms of carbon have a very great attraction for each other and long chains of carbon atoms can be linked together. This is the simple basis on which many artificial fibers like nylon and Dacron have been made. These have proved to be very strong because the atoms link together so firmly. On the other hand the atom of neon is so inactive that it does not combine with any other atom or with one of its own kind: its molecule contains only one atom.

When atoms of different elements combine to form a molecule of a new compound the result is often remarkably different from the original elements; for example, an atom of the soft metal sodium, which reacts explosively with water, and an atom of the poisonous gas chlorine combine to form a molecule of common salt. (See MOLECULE.)

Electrons

Towards the end of the 19th century some remarkable discoveries were made as a result of passing an electric current through gases. The lightning flash and the electric spark are examples of electricity passing through a gas. High voltages are necessary to produce these effects. If, however, a tube has some air withdrawn from it by an air pump, electricity will pass through it almost silently, giving rise to beautiful colored effects. As more and more air is withdrawn, the colored effects change until eventually they disappear. The tube is then dark except for a greenish glow on the glass at the anode end, that is, the end to which the electricity is flowing. This glow is due to cathode rays, a stream of particles which are shot out from the cathode (the plate from which the electricity flows) at great speed. The British scientist, J. J. Thomson was the first to study these particles in 1897. He called them *electrons* and discovered that they carry a negative electrical charge. It was also found that as these electrons moved in one direction so another stream of different par-

HYDROGEN
atomic number 1

PROTIUM
1 proton

DEUTERIUM
1 proton, 1 neutron

TRITIUM
1 proton, 2 neutrons

Hydrogen has three isotopes. Unlike the isotopes of most other elements these three each have special names. Protium makes up more than 99.98 per cent of natural hydrogen in its compounds, for example, water. Deuterium makes up less than 0.02 per cent of hydrogen found in water. Tritium is the only radioactive isotope and is found in extremely tiny amounts in the hydrogen in water. The relative atomic mass of natural hydrogen is 1.00797 which takes into account the masses of the isotopes of which it is composed.

ticles moved in the opposite direction, down the tube. This showed that the atom could be split; it was possible to remove electrons from the atoms to which they belong.

Just before the discovery of the electron, the German physicist Wilhelm Roentgen had observed that penetrating rays were coming from the anode of a discharge tube and, soon after, the French scientist Henri Becquerel found that similar rays were given off by some substances. Two years later, in Paris, France, Pierre and Marie Curie isolated a previously unknown element which gave off many rays of different types. They called this element radium and its emission of rays is called radio-activity. Roentgen's rays we now call X-rays, and those given off by radium and other radio-active materials are called alpha, beta, and gamma rays. It was clear that atoms were not the simple solid objects they had seemed to be. (See RADIOACTIVITY; X-RAY.)

Inside the Atom

From 1897 onwards, scientists in many countries carried out large numbers of experiments to try to discover more about the structure of the atom. Ernest Rutherford, a New Zealand scientist working in Britain, and Niels Bohr, a Danish scientist, suggested that although atoms of different elements differ in mass they are nevertheless built in the same way. They said that the atom consisted of a central body, or *nucleus*, with electrons revolving round it. Each central nucleus had a positive electrical charge which was balanced by the negative electrons so that the whole atom was electrically neutral. The nucleus is very small in comparison

with the whole atom. If we could enlarge an atom to the size of a football stadium, the nucleus would look like a small pile of peas in the middle.

Nearly all the mass of the atom is concentrated in the tiny nucleus. The nucleus is composed principally of two sorts of particle: the

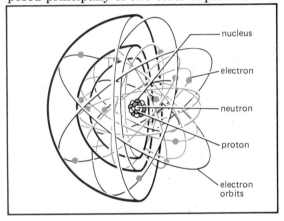

An atom consists of a nucleus made up of protons and neutrons around which tiny particles called electrons travel in elliptical orbits. This phosphorus atom has a nucleus formed by 15 positively charged protons and 15 neutrons, which carry no charge. The 15 negatively charged electrons orbiting the nucleus make the atom electrically neutral. The electrons in the phosphorus atom orbit within three "shells"—two in the inner one, eight in the middle one, and five in the outer one.

proton which carries a positive electric charge and the *neutron* which is electrically neutral and has a mass slightly bigger than that of the proton. Protons, produced by stripping the electrons (see ELECTRON) from hydrogen atoms, can be accelerated to high speeds and fired at a target made of certain light elements. They get through the opposition put up by the massed proton charges in the target nuclei and disturb these nuclei so

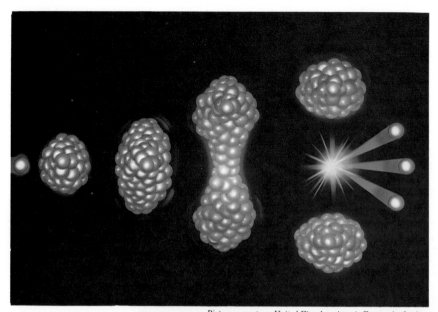

Left: The splitting of an atom is called "fission". This picture shows what happens when a neutron strikes a uranium atom. The atom splits into two roughly equal pieces, and at the same time produces two or three "free" neutrons. These neutrons can in turn strike other uranium atoms. As neutrons strike uranium atoms, heat is released. Each time this happens, more neutrons and more heat are released. A "chain reaction" has begun.

Pictures, courtesy, United Kingdom Atomic Energy Authority

Right: This picture shows how plutonium can be formed as part of a chain reaction. Only a tiny part of natural uranium is made up of the isotope uranium-235. The rest is uranium-238. As a chain reaction needs only one free neutron to keep it going, there are many "spare" neutrons. Some are absorbed inside the reactor. Others are absorbed by the uranium-238, to create a new element not found in nature: plutonium. The plutonium produced in this way can itself be used as fuel in a so-called "fast reactor".

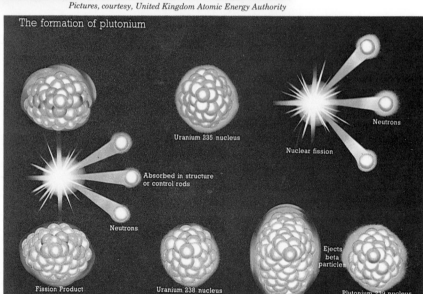

The formation of plutonium

Uranium 235 nucleus

Neutrons

Nuclear fission

Absorbed in structure or control rods

Neutrons

Fission Product

Uranium 238 nucleus

U238 + neutron

Ejects beta particles

Plutonium 239 nucleus

that neutrons are thrown out. Another way to generate neutrons is to use the radiation from natural radioactive materials as "projectiles". These neutrons, having no electric charge, can then be used to penetrate the nuclei of other atoms, which they enter quite easily. (See also NEUTRON; PROTON.)

In its simplest form, the hydrogen atom is made up of one central proton and one orbiting electron. There are, however, other forms of hydrogen, called *isotopes* of hydrogen, where the nucleus consists of a proton plus one or two neutrons. These are given the special names of deuterium (for hydrogen atoms containing a proton and a neutron) and tritium (for those containing a proton and two neutrons). All elements can be found or made in several isotopes and it is more common to identify the isotope of interest by giving the name of the element and the number of *nucleons* (protons

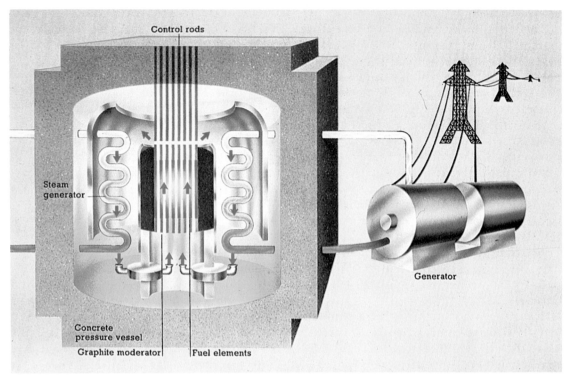

Control rods

Steam
generator

Generator

Concrete
pressure vessel

Graphite moderator | Fuel elements

Courtesy, United Kingdom Atomic Energy Authority

Scientists have harnessed the power of the atom to make the electricity we use every day. The advanced gas-cooled reactor is one of several types of nuclear reactor used for this purpose. Uranium is sealed in rods clustered together in the core. Free neutrons bombard the uranium nuclei causing the core to heat up. Control rods can be raised or lowered into the reactor to regulate the power output. A moderator (graphite, water, or heavy water) is used to slow down the neutrons. Gas flows around the core to remove the heat for use in powering a steam generator, which turns turbines that produce the electricity. A thick concrete shield around the reactor keeps in the dangerous radioactivity that is produced as a result of the reaction in the core.

and neutrons) in the nucleus. This is called the mass number of the element.

The electrons in the atom are arranged in a series of "shells" which are filled from the inside. The innermost shell is complete with a pair of electrons. But as we move outwards, we find that complete shells contain 8 electrons or multiples of 8. When the outer shell is complete (as in the family of six "noble gases", made up of helium, neon, argon, krypton, xenon, and radon), the atom is very stable and has no urge to link up with other atoms. If it is incomplete, the atom will readily join with other atoms to form molecules so as to complete the electron shell or compensate for the extra or missing electrons. For example, an atom of sodium with one electron in the outer shell links readily with a chlorine atom which has one electron missing to form common salt.

But a magnesium atom with two electrons in the outer shell links up with two atoms of chlorine. The number of missing or extra electrons determines the *valence* of the element. The valence is the property of an element that determines the number of other atoms with which an atom of the element can combine. (In Britain, valence is also referred to as "valency".)

An electron can jump from an inner to an outer shell if there is room as a result of, for example, a collision with another atom. When it falls back, a pulse of light is emitted. The light's wavelength (color) is determined by the difference in energy of the electrons in the two shells. This is why we can identify elements, even in the stars, by the pattern of light colors they emit when the atoms are excited.

Using the Atom's Power

Because all nuclei are made of the same "building blocks", it seems natural that one kind of nucleus could be changed into another. This can be done by adding one or more protons or neutrons to a nucleus, or by knocking one or more nucleons out of it. Transmutation, or changing, of an element was first achieved by Rutherford in 1919.

As study of the atom progressed, machines called particle accelerators or cyclotrons (see PARTICLE ACCELERATOR) were developed to "smash" atoms. By bombarding nuclei with high-speed projectile particles, the nucleus of one element can be split to form the nuclei of two lighter elements. At the same time, vast energy is released. Scientists first controlled this energy in 1942 (see NUCLEAR ENERGY).

Nuclear power offered almost limitless sources of energy. It also gave the world a terrible new weapon, the atomic bomb. The first atomic bomb was tested in 1945. Later, the even more destructive hydrogen or "thermonuclear" bomb was developed.

The chief use for nuclear power is in generating stations to make electricity. Nuclear-powered ships and submarines can travel thousands of kilometers without the need to refuel. Tiny nuclear power plants operate "pacemaker" devices inside the body to control the heartbeat of people with heart disease.

Radioactive materials also have valuable uses in medicine and industry. Radiation can produce changes in substances it hits. The radioactive sources must normally give off low-energy rather than high-energy rays to avoid damage to living tissue. However, gamma radiation can penetrate deep inside the body to kill cancer cells. Gamma rays are also used in the sterilization of medical equipment; the radiation kills any bacteria.

Radioactive isotopes can be heated, cooled, melted, converted into glass, or combined with other chemicals, without their radioactivity being affected. So they are widely used as "tracers", that is, as "labels" to follow the movement of materials, even inside the human body. Because radiation can penetrate matter, it can be used to examine metal parts for tiny cracks. And since all animals and plants absorb an isotope called carbon-14, ancient remains can be dated by examining the amount of carbon-14 left in them. (See also ARCHEOLOGY; RADIATION.)

ATTILA (c.406–53) was king of the Huns, a nomadic people who roamed central Europe. Attila was a great warrior, but showed no mercy to his enemies. The Christians of the time nicknamed him "the scourge of God".

During the first eight years under Attila's leadership, the Huns conquered the other barbarian tribes in central Europe. He was feared in all the lands that lie between the River Rhine and the Caspian Sea.

In 451 his tribes pushed further west, destroying most of the cities in the area that has become Belgium. They then went on into what is now France and attacked Orleans. But at Châlons-sur-Marne, near Orleans, the Huns were met by the combined armies of the Roman general Aetius and the Visigoth king Theodoric. Although Theodoric was killed in the fierce fighting, Attila's hordes were defeated and forced to retreat.

The next year Attila invaded Italy and sacked many of the cities. He would have destroyed Rome itself if Pope Leo I had not pleaded with him. In 453 he married the beautiful Ildico. But on his wedding day, after a huge feast, he suddenly died.

ATTLEE, Clement Richard, 1st Earl of Walthamstow (1883–1967). Clement Attlee was the leader of the Labour party in the British House of Commons for 20 years from 1935 until 1955, and he was prime minister while the Labour government was in office from 1945 to 1951.

Attlee was born in Putney, London, and was educated at Oxford University. At first he worked as a lawyer. But when he saw the poverty and unhappiness of the people of the East End of London, he gave up law. He devoted himself to social work, spending much of his time in charge of a settlement, or club run for the welfare of the local people. He joined the Fabian

BBC Hulton Picture Library

Clement Attlee had been in the British parliament for 23 years when he became prime minister in 1945.

quietly-spoken, Attlee was a strong leader. The Labour government brought in many important reforms. The National Health Service was created; new pensions and national insurance programs were set up; and key industries—such as the railroads, coal, gas, electricity, steel, and airlines—were nationalized, that is, brought into public ownership. Burma, Ceylon (now Sri Lanka), India, and Pakistan were granted independence.

In 1951 the Conservative party came to power. Attlee was leader of the Labour opposition until his retirement in 1955, when he received an earldom.

ATTORNEY see LAWYER.

AUBERGINE, also called eggplant, is a member of the nightshade family, *Solanaceae*. The

Society (a group formed to spread socialist ideas) in 1907 and the Labour party shortly afterwards. He thought that the state, not just private people, should make life better for those in need. He believed that there should be sweeping political changes. For a while he was a lecturer in social science at the London School of Economics. After serving as an officer in World War I, he became the first Labour mayor of the London Borough of Stepney.

Attlee was elected the member of parliament for Limehouse, in east London, in 1922, and 13 years later he was elected leader of the Labour party. During World War II, when members of several political parties joined together in the government (this is called a "coalition" government), Attlee held several important posts. From 1942 to 1945 he was deputy prime minister under Winston Churchill.

Attlee became prime minister in 1945 after the Labour party had overwhelmingly won the general election. This was the first time Labour had won an overall majority in the House of Commons. Although rather shy and

NHPA/J. B. Free

The aubergine, or eggplant, is a starchy vegetable related to the potato, which grows in warm climates.

Courtesy, New Zealand High Commission

Auckland stands on a neck of land between Waitemata and Manukau harbours.

eggplant (*Solanum melongena*) is closely related to the potato. It has long been grown for its large, fleshy fruit. It is believed to be a native of southern and eastern Asia. The plant grows in tropical climates to a height of 1 meter (3 feet).

The fruit, or berry, sometimes reaches 30 centimeters (12 inches) in length and 20 centimeters (8 inches) in width. It is egg- or pear-shaped, shiny, and usually dark purple. It can also be yellow, white, or striped. The fruit hangs among downy, grayish-green leaves. The flowers are purple. The plant is cultivated in the United States for market chiefly in Florida, New Jersey, and Texas. It grows only in warm weather. The seeds are planted in a hothouse in early spring, and the plants ripen in about four months.

The eggplant has few vitamins or calories, but it is popular for its flavor. It is important in Mediterranean cooking in such dishes as the Greek moussaka and Italian eggplant parmigiana.

AUCKLAND in the North Island is the largest city and seaport of New Zealand. It lies on the isthmus, or narrow neck of land, that connects the North Auckland peninsula with the rest of the North Island. To the north the city looks over the deep and sheltered Waitemata harbor, and the extinct volcano Rangitoto, 260 meters (853 feet) high, in the Hauraki Gulf beyond.

The chief shopping and business thoroughfare is Queen Street. The suburbs spread around the harbor and up the slopes of cone-shaped hills found in the area, such as Mount Eden, Mount Albert, and One Tree Hill, which were once volcanoes.

Auckland's parks and public gardens include the Domain, which is an area of gardens and sports fields and contains the War Memorial Museum, which has the finest collection of Maori art in the world. The City Art Gallery contains paintings by Frances Hodgkins (1869–1947) and other New Zealand artists. Auckland has a university and numerous schools and colleges.

Ferries run across the Waitemata harbor to the north shore, but the chief road link is a four-lane bridge, 1,020 meters (1,115 yards) long. On the north shore is the suburb of Devonport and the chief base of the Royal New Zealand Navy.

Auckland is the chief industrial center of New Zealand. Industries include vehicle assembly, engineering, meat freezing, sugar refining, and the production of chemicals, foodstuffs, beer, clothing, leather, plastics, bricks, and cement. About one-third of New Zealand's exports and nearly half the imports (which include petroleum, fertilizers, iron and steel, and wheat) pass through Auckland. International air services use Mangere airport, 22 kilometers (14 miles) south of the city.

The population of the city proper is 143,800 (1984). The total urban area, however, has a population of about 800,000, which is about one-fifth that of all New Zealand. The regions of Central Auckland and South Auckland lie to the north and south of the city.

In 1840 Auckland was chosen for the capital of New Zealand by the first British governor, Captain William Hobson. It remained the capital until 1865, when Wellington, which has been the capital town ever since, was substituted because of its more central position on the island.

Peter Mitchell/Camera Press

The poet W. H. Auden in later life.

AUDEN, W. H. (1907–73).

Wystan Hugh Auden, one of the leading poets writing in English in the 20th century, was born in York, England, and studied at Christ Church, Oxford, before spending a year in Germany. During the 1930s he belonged to a group of poets, including Stephen Spender, C. Day Lewis, and Louis MacNeice, who wanted to bring poetry back to everyday life. Their poetry was simple and direct, using ordinary language, and made many references to the way people lived and worked, and to machines. Auden and his friends were encouraged by the ideas of socialism and the brotherhood of man and wrote much about the social problems and politics of the time. He was very interested in the writings of Karl Marx and in psychoanalysis. During the 1930s Auden published *Poems, The Dance of Death* and *Look, Stranger.*

When civil war broke out in Spain, Auden went to serve with an ambulance unit and wrote some fine poems about his experiences. He also traveled to China, reporting and writing poems about the war with Japan. In 1939 he went to live in the United States and in 1946 became an American citizen. He returned often to England to teach and later to live.

Auden also turned his attention towards religion, psychology and the problems of human existence. He wrote much humorous verse and his serious poems, though sometimes bitter and ironic, are often cheerful and light in tone.

Besides poetry, Auden's works include travel books, poetic dramas (the best of these is *The Ascent of F6*, written with Christopher Isherwood), and critical essays about other writers. He also collaborated with the composers, Benjamin Britten and Igor Stravinsky. For example, he wrote the libretto (words) for Stravinsky's opera *The Rake's Progress*.

AUDUBON, John James (1785–1851).

John James Audubon is probably the world's best-known ornithologist, or student of birds. Audubon's drawings were different from any that were ever done before because he drew from live or freshly killed birds instead of from dusty museum specimens. He also had the birds in natural positions and put plants and other living creatures in the paintings to make them look more authentic.

The son of a French naval officer, Audubon was born in Les Cayes, Haiti, in 1785. He went to France when he was about nine years old. He was sent to school to study mathematics and geography so that he too could be a sea captain. But he was not a good student because he spent all of his time outdoors collecting specimens, watching birds and animals, and drawing birds.

When he was 17 his father sent him to the United States to manage his estate near Philadelphia, Pennsylvania. There he found new birds and animals, and continued his collecting and painting. He became friends with the English family on the next estate. Later he married the daughter, Lucy Bakewell.

Audubon tried to make a living in business first in New York and then in Kentucky. Each of these failed because Audubon spent more time wandering in the woods, collecting and painting, than he did working.

By 1826 he had painted several hundred life-sized pictures of birds. He had to go to London to get them published. There he sold 200 subscriptions to his *Birds of America*. This is often called the elephant folio, because each page is over 1 meter (3 feet) long and 0.6 meter (2 feet) wide. Altogether there were 435 pages with life-sized drawings of 1,055 birds. The pages were engraved and then colored by

Peter Green—ARDEA

The ornithologist John James Audubon painted birds in their natural settings. These barn owls are preparing to eat a chipmunk.

hand. The four volumes cost $1,000. Today they are very valuable and are owned mostly by large libraries and museums.

While Audubon was in England he published the *Ornithological Biography*, in five volumes. The books describe the birds in the elephant folio, and tell of Audubon's experiences in the United States. Later a seven-volume *Birds of America* was published in the United States. His last book was a two-volume book of mammals called *Quadrupeds of North America*. After he died, three of Audubon's journals and some of his more important letters were published.

In 1905, 54 years after Audubon died, the National Audubon Society was formed to try to protect the birds that were being rapidly destroyed. Today the Audubon Society works to save all animals and plants. It knows that all living things depend on one another (see ECOLOGY).

AUGUSTINE OF CANTERBURY, Saint.

The story is told of how Pope Gregory the Great, when he was a deacon, saw a group of children up for sale as slaves in the market place in Rome. They were fair-haired with blue eyes and were very different from the dark Mediterranean children. When he asked who they were and where they came from he was told that they were heathens, Angles from an island called Britain. Gregory replied that they should not be called Angles, but angels.

Years later, when Gregory became Pope, he still remembered these fair-haired children and decided to send missionaries to re-establish Christianity in England. The British Christians had been driven north and west by the pagan Angles and Saxons. Gregory chose a Benedictine abbot, Augustine, to lead the missionaries. When they reached France, Augustine's followers heard such terrible stories of the wildness of the Angles that they turned back. Augustine returned to Rome but was persuaded by Gregory to set out once more. He and his followers landed on the Isle of Thanet, in Kent, in AD597.

Ethelbert, who was the King of Kent, was himself a heathen, although his wife, Bertha, was a Christian. Ethelbert allowed the missionaries to stay and to preach in St. Martin's church in Canterbury. Led by Augustine, and with a silver cross, they marched to the town barefoot chanting litanies, which are a kind of prayer. The people flocked to hear Augustine preach, and by Christmas Ethelbert himself and thousands of his subjects had been converted.

Augustine became the first Archbishop of Canterbury and sent his missionaries throughout southern England. Later they built the monastery of Saint Peter and Saint Paul and founded Christ Church, Canterbury. This was built on the site of the present cathedral but was burned down in 1067. Augustine died some time between AD604 and 605 and was made a saint soon afterwards. He was finally buried in Christ Church, which was still being built at the time of his death. On his tomb were written these words:

> Here rests the Lord Augustine, first Archbishop of Canterbury, who being formerly sent hither by the blessed Gregory, Bishop of the City of Rome, and by God's assistance supported with miracles, reduced King Ethelbert and his nation from the worship of idols to the faith of Christ . . .

A stone cross was erected to mark the spot near Minster in the Isle of Thanet where Augustine and his missionaries landed.

AUGUSTINE OF HIPPO, Saint (354–430).

Saint Augustine was an early Christian philosopher and writer. He was born in Numidia (now Algeria), in North Africa. Although his mother was a Christian, Augustine was not baptized as a child. For a while he led a rather wild life and tried many different religions and philosophies. After great mental and moral struggles Augustine finally turned to Christ through reading the letters of St. Paul in a garden in Milan, Italy. He was baptized by St. Ambrose in AD387, when he was 33 years old.

Augustine returned to Africa where he was

Alinari/EPA, Inc.

Saint Augustine of Hippo, painted by the Italian artist Sandro Botticelli in 1480.

ordained a priest, and, in AD 396, he was made Bishop of Hippo in North Africa. It was not an easy time to be a bishop, because the barbarians were sweeping over the Roman Empire and people could not understand why God allowed this to happen. To help them understand, Augustine wrote a book called *The City of God*. In the book he explained his belief that, although the Roman Empire might come to an end, the Church would remain and God's purpose would finally be fulfilled.

It was not only Augustine's learning that made him great but also his understanding of the inward struggle that everyone has against evil. In his *Confessions*, the book about his early life, he explains how he could never have overcome this evil by himself but had been able to do so only with God's help.

Augustine's ideas were very important to the Christian Church—more so, many people think, than those of anyone else after St. Paul. His ideas are all based on his own experiences of God which he reveals most fully in the prayers he wrote in his *Confessions*. Here is one of the most famous examples of his writing; "Thou hast made us for Thyself and our hearts are restless until they find rest in Thee."

AUGUSTUS CAESAR (63 BC-AD 14) was the

first and probably the greatest emperor of Rome. During Augustus' reign the power of the city and the empire grew to heights unknown before, and he made many wise laws. He made Rome more beautiful by the great buildings he put up, and he encouraged the arts, especially poets and other writers. One famous writer who admired Augustus was Virgil whose great poem called the *Aeneid* was written partly to glorify Rome.

Augustus never called himself "emperor", because he understood the Roman people well and knew that they hated dictators. Instead he preferred to be known as the "first citizen", or, in Latin, *Princeps*.

Before the period of peace and prosperity, Augustus had to struggle to obtain and preserve power. He fought several battles and was responsible for many deaths.

Caius Octavius, as Augustus was first

Mansell Collection

Augustus survived danger and difficulty to become a wise ruler. He was the first emperor of Rome.

called, was born in Rome in 63 BC. (He was later called Octavian.) He was a young man of 19 when his great-uncle Julius Caesar was murdered in 44 BC (see JULIUS CAESAR). As soon as he heard the news, he hurried back to Italy from Greece where he had been studying. When he landed in Italy he found that Caesar had adopted him in his will and had made him his heir. However, Caesar's friend Mark Antony (see ANTONY, MARK) had already taken most of Caesar's private property for himself. Octavian immediately joined the party which was against Mark Antony, and fought a war against him. Octavian defeated him at Mutina in 43 BC. The Senate (a kind of parliament) appointed him consul and recognized him as Caesar's adopted son to be known as Caius Julius Caesar Octavianus, or Octavian. He and Antony became friends for a time. It was agreed that these two and a man named Lepidus should rule the Roman world for the next five years. This was called the Second Triumvirate, or "rule of three men".

Octavian and Antony had many enemies in Rome, including the group of senators who had murdered Julius Caesar. These they murdered, killing more than 2,000 people in a reign of terror. Brutus and Cassius, who had planned Caesar's murder, were finally defeated in battle at Philippi in 42 BC. Octavian became ruler of the western provinces, while Antony received the eastern provinces.

However, peace did not come to Rome yet, for Octavian and Antony quarreled again. One reason was that Antony had married Octavian's sister Octavia and then left her for Cleopatra, queen of Egypt. In a sea battle near Actium, on the coast of Greece, Octavian's ships defeated the fleet belonging to Antony and Cleopatra. The next year, in 30 BC, both Antony and Cleopatra committed suicide.

At last Octavian was the sole ruler of Rome, for Lepidus was not a strong character and had already been given a post which kept him out of the affairs of government. However, Octavian was very anxious not to let the Roman people think he wished to be a dictator, so he gave up his title and declared that the republic was restored. The Senate knew by now that he was the best man to rule, so in 27 BC they made him the commander of the army and navy for ten years, and every year they elected him as a consul. They honored him with the title of Augustus, which means majestic. Octavian made it seem that Rome was still a free republic which chose its own ruler, yet he really had all the power in his hands.

During the 40 years from this time until his death, Augustus introduced many reforms to improve the government of Rome and its empire. For example, he set up a strong police force to keep order and protect the citizens, and put an end to the many gangs of bandits which had grown up during the civil war. He made laws to prevent people indulging in luxury and extravagance, and to encourage family life. He established an efficient postal system. He made new settlements of people in ancient towns to keep them from falling into decay, and built better roads, bridges, and aqueducts. He added Egypt and much of the Balkans to the empire and brought peace to Spain and Gaul. He also carried out schemes for making the city of Rome itself more beautiful. He spent huge sums of money on noble buildings, and claimed that he had found Rome a city of brick but left it a city of marble.

Augustus himself did not live in great state and luxury for he preferred the life of an ordinary citizen.

Perhaps he was not such a remarkable personality as his great-uncle Julius Caesar. He was somewhat cold-blooded and scheming. But Rome prospered under his wise and moderate rule, which is often regarded as the golden age of the Roman empire, at that time vast, well-governed, and peaceful. The phrase "Augustan Age" is used to describe the flowering of literature that took place at that time. It was the age of the poets Virgil, Horace, and Ovid and also of the historian Livy.

AUK refers to some 22 species of mainly black and white seabirds. It includes the great and little auks, auklets, and murres as well as guillemots, razorbills and puffins.

These birds live in the colder parts of the northern hemisphere. After spending the winter at sea, usually in flocks or "rafts" as they are called, they come to breed on land in the summer. They collect together in huge colonies on cliffs—in Canada, Greenland, Iceland, the Farne Islands of Scotland, and Norway.

The auks usually lay only one blotched egg, either in May or June. They place this on the ledge of a cliff, in a crack in a rock. While they are in their colonies, the birds utter a variety of barks, yelps or groans, but at sea they are usually silent. They have a distinct whirring flight but because of their small wings, they cannot make long flights. However, they swim and dive well, and they use their wings to help them through the water. They feed on small fish. On land, they usually sit in an

The little auk is a stout, rather dumpy small bird.

upright position, because their legs are so far back.

The great auk (*Pinguinus impennis*) became extinct (died out) in 1844. This bird stood 75 centimeters (30 inches) high and it had such small wings that it could not fly at all. It used to travel great distances by swimming, but it had a poor chance against its enemies. It nested on low rocky islands in the North Atlantic and laid one pear-shaped egg. During the 17th and 18th centuries it was killed in great numbers by fishermen for food, for bait, and for its feathers. The last known specimens were captured on Eldey Island off the coast of Iceland in June 1844. All that can now be seen are a few skins and eggs in museums.

The little auk or dovekie (*Plautus alle*) is 20 centimeters (8 inches) long with a stout beak. It breeds in immense colonies in arctic Canada, Greenland, Iceland, and other islands and lays its pale blue egg among the rocks.

The six species of auklets breed only in the North Pacific and Bering Sea. During the breeding season auklets grow plumes or other decorative features such as colored bill plates.

The smallest member of the auk family is the least auklet (*Aethia pusilla*) about 15 cen-timeters (6 inches) long. It winters far north in rough waters. (See GUILLEMOT; PUFFIN; RAZORBILL.)

AURORA. The goddess of the dawn was called Eos by the Greeks and Aurora by the Romans. Each morning, when the sun god Apollo set out in his chariot, Aurora in her rose-colored robe opened the gates of the east and pro-ceeded before him.

One day Aurora fell in love with a beautiful mortal called Tithonus. She stole him away from the Earth and persuaded Jupiter, the king of the gods, to make him immortal like herself. She forgot, however, to ask as well for the gift of everlasting youth, and so Tithonus grew old and helpless, yet could not die. One story said that in the end Aurora got so tired of his chattering that she turned him into a grasshopper, which may still be heard chirp-ing away. According to some stories Aurora was the mother of the Trojan hero Memnon. After the Greek warrior Achilles killed Mem-non in battle, Aurora was said to weep tears every morning in the form of dew.

Aurora has given her name to the strange lights that are sometimes seen high in the Earth's atmosphere. You can read about this in the article NORTHERN AND SOUTHERN LIGHTS.

AURORA AUSTRALIS and AURORA BOREALIS see NORTHERN AND SOUTHERN LIGHTS.

AUSTEN, Jane (1775–1817), was one of England's finest novelists and a clever and witty observer of England's genteel society in the early years of the 19th century. The books that she wrote are now very famous, but when she first started writing it was hard for her to get them published. This was because while other authors of her time were writing exciting and thrilling romances, Jane Austen wrote books about the quiet life of a small English country town or village where exciting things did not often happen.

Elizabeth Bennet, the heroine of Jane Austen's book *Pride and Prejudice*, says at one point that she hopes she never laughs at what

Jane Austen in a watercolor by her sister, Cassandra.

is wise or good, but only at foolishness and nonsense. The odd ways in which people behave amuse her and she laughs at them whenever she can. In this way Jane Austen was like her own heroine, gently exposing people's faults. This, among other things, is what makes her books so fascinating to modern readers.

Jane Austen was born at Steventon, Hampshire, in 1775. Her father was a clergyman and she was the youngest of seven children. She lived at Steventon until she was 25 and she often wrote stories and poems to amuse her family. After her father died in 1805 Jane went on living with her mother and her sister Cassandra. She lived successively at Bath, Southampton, Chawton (in Hampshire), and Winchester. She never married, and her days were spent in long hours of sewing and housework, and writing. She died in 1817 at Winchester.

Her most popular novel is *Pride and Prejudice*, begun in 1796, but not published until 1813. It is the intricately woven story of a Hert-fordshire family and the far from smooth relationships that the daughters of the family have with their prospective husbands. Jane Austin's other novels include *Mansfield Park, Emma, Sense and Sensibility, Persuasion* and *Northanger Abbey*. Another novel, *Lady Susan*, was not published during her lifetime and only appeared in 1925, along with a fragment of an incomplete novel called *The Watsons*.

AUSTRALASIA is a geographical term that means "south of Asia". Centuries ago, when parts of the Earth were still largely unexplored, the name Australasia was used in a vague sense to describe certain unknown lands that geographers of the time thought lay somewhere to the south of Asia. Later the name was used to include all the islands of the South Pacific. Today, the term used for those and other islands in the Pacific Ocean is *Oceania*. Australasia is used to refer to Australia, New Zealand, and the island of New Guinea. It is sometimes used to include the Philippines and the Malay island chain. The islands of Oceania and Australasia are described in the article PACIFIC ISLANDS. Australia and New Zealand have separate articles as do other independent countries.

AUSTRALIA lies in the South Pacific Ocean, on the opposite side of the world from Europe. The Commonwealth of Australia occupies both the largest island in the world (although it is not usually counted as an island) and the smallest continent. It covers an area of 7,682,300 square kilometers (2,966,200 square miles).

Along the northeast coast of Australia, for a distance of 2,000 kilometers (1,200 miles), and as much as 160 kilometers (100 miles) out into the Pacific Ocean in some places, is the Great Barrier Reef, which is a chain of wonderfully colored coral reefs, islands and sandbanks, with only a few safe openings for ships. (There is a separate article GREAT BARRIER REEF.) The island of Tasmania, which is part of Australia and about which there is also a separate article, lies off the south coast of the mainland.

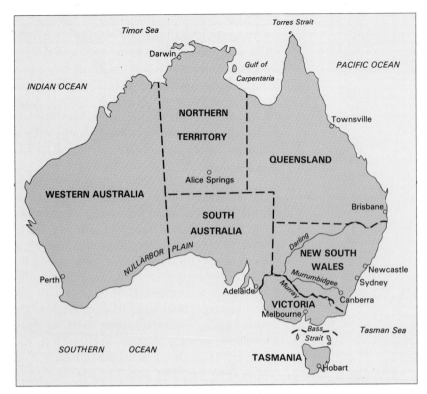

The vast island sub-continent of Australia is largely desert or semidesert. People only live in large numbers away from the center, mainly in the east and in the southwestern tip.

FACTS ABOUT AUSTRALIA

AREA 7,682,300 square kilometers (2,966,200 square miles).

POPULATION: 15,543,600 (1984).

GOVERNMENT: Independent federal state; member of the Commonwealth of Nations.

FEDERAL CAPITAL: Canberra.

FEATURES OF SPECIAL INTEREST: About four-fifths of the continent is a hot, dry desert with few inhabitants. Mount Kosciusko 2,230 meters (7,316 feet) is the highest mountain. The Murray and its tributaries is the principal river system in the country. Great Barrier Reef.

CHIEF PRODUCTS: Wool, meat, wheat, minerals.

LEADING INDUSTRIES: Farming and stock raising, engineering, mining, forestry, textiles and clothing, food processing.

IMPORTANT CITIES: Canberra, Sydney, Melbourne, Adelaide, Brisbane, Perth, Hobart.

EDUCATION: Education from 6 to 15 (16 in Tasmania) is compulsory.

The mainland of Australia has neither very high mountains nor large forests, but all the way down the east coast, from Cape York in the north to Melbourne in the south, lie the beautiful forested slopes of the Eastern Highlands, sometimes called the Great Dividing Range. They form a series of tablelands descending steeply towards the sea and more gradually to the plains inland. (See GREAT DIVIDING RANGE.)

Most of the center of Australia is a plain either with grass, or grass and trees, or desert. The sea once covered much of this area, but now the land is very dry. Fortunately some water is obtained from artesian wells which are driven deep down into the earth (see ARTESIAN WELL). The pressure of the water underground brings it up to the surface.

The western half of Australia is flat and covered with low scrub, but there are barren, rolling hills near the west coast. In this desert region, once used for testing guided missiles fired from Woomera in South Australia, valuable discoveries of minerals, such as nickel and iron ore, have been made. In the far south-western corner the natural vegetation is temperate forest.

Rivers and Lakes

The great river of Australia is the Murray, part of which forms the boundary between the states of New South Wales and Victoria. The

In the center of Australia lies the great red mass of Ayers Rock, a sacred site of the Aborigines.

other main rivers in the southeast are the Darling, Murrumbidgee, and Goulburn, all of which run into the Murray. (See MURRAY AND DARLING RIVER SYSTEM.) Farther inland, only a few rivers have much water and they sometimes dry up altogether before they reach the coast. In Queensland and Western Australia the rivers often flow only short distances from the highlands to the sea, but they may flood severely when there is heavy rainfall.

The lakes are often just beds of salt without any water. Lake Eyre, which lies about 12 meters (39 feet) below sea-level in the south, is over 9,300 square kilometers (3,600 square miles) in area, but it seldom holds any water. Farther to the southwest, however, there are freshwater lakes which are full when the Darling River floods.

The reason why so many Australian lakes and rivers are nearly dry or quite dry for so much of the time is that there is so little rain in most places, while the sun usually evaporates what water there is. Even the great Murray River has dried up at least three times. The mountains in the east break the clouds as they come in from the sea, so that much rain falls near the coast, but farther inland the climate becomes drier and drier, and near Lake Eyre there is not enough rain in a whole year to fill a jam jar left out in the open. In the north the rain falls mainly in the summer and in the south mainly during the winter.

People have chosen to live in places where there is an adequate rainfall. The coastal regions have naturally proved most attractive to European settlers, although the tropical northern coast, which is hot and wet, is more sparsely inhabited. Rainfall, and population density, decrease from the coast into the interior, as does the richness of vegetation. The Australian seasons are exactly the reverse of those in the northern hemisphere. The summer is in December, January, and February and the winter is in June, July, and August. There is plenty of sunshine and the winters are mild, because over a third of the continent lies in the tropics; snow falls only in the Australian Alps in the southeast, and in Tasmania.

Trees and Plants

Over the years settlers have introduced European trees and plants into Australia and these generally grow well. The continent's native trees are mostly green all the year round. The most typical tree is the eucalyptus, or gum tree, of which there are at least 500 different kinds (see EUCALYPTUS). They range from dwarf gums called mallees in the drier regions to the white mountain ash of Victoria and Tasmania, which may reach a height of 90 meters (300 feet). Some of the trees in the southwest are very beautiful with pink, cream, or flame-colored flowers, and many towns use them to line their streets.

The other plant that people think of as especially belonging to Australia is the wattle, or acacia, which is in fact the country's national flower. About 750 kinds of acacia can be found, many of them having yellow, fluffy flowers like mimosa.

The middle of the continent is so dry that plants find it difficult to grow. But if rain does fall thousands of desert flowers quickly spring up from seed that has lain dormant, perhaps for years.

In the northeast, where the tropical plants grow luxuriantly in the moist heat, are found orchids, great ferns, palms, and spectacular flowering trees such as the silky-oak.

Ferns of many kinds grow in the southeast, but the real paradise for people interested in plants is the southwest, for many of its wild flowers are found nowhere else. The most striking ones are the red and green kangaroo paws which seem to have the same shape and "fur" as the paws of the animal.

Australian Mammals

The mammals of Australia are even more interesting than the plants. They are quite unlike any found anywhere else in the world. Most of them carry their young about in pouches in their bodies. They are called marsupials.

(There is a separate article MARSUPIAL.) They range in size from tiny, pouched mice to the large kangaroo. Wallabies, possums (see OPOSSUM), wombats, bandicoots, squirrels, the Tasmanian devil and the Tasmanian wolf, which is very rare or may be extinct, are all marsupials. The favorite of all, however, is the koala which is now specially protected. It feeds only on the leaves and shoots of certain kinds of eucalyptus trees. (See KOALA.)

Australia has another type of mammal not found anywhere else, the egg-laying mammals, or monotremes. These animals have survived from very early times and are like reptiles in some ways. These are just two living species: the duck-billed platypus and the echidna. The platypus is an extraordinary water animal which has a furry coat, a bill and webbed feet like a duck, and lays eggs. The echidna, or spiny anteater, also lays eggs which it hatches in its pouch, but it lives only on land; it has short, sharp spikes in its hair and digs so fast that it seems to vanish into the ground. (See ECHIDNA; PLATYPUS.)

The only other truly Australian mammals are the rats and the bats. The dingo or wild dog, which is a menace to sheep, probably came from Asia originally. Another pest, which eats the grass the sheep feed on, is the rabbit, which was brought from Europe in 1788. It soon overran the whole continent because at that time there were no foxes or stoats to keep it down. However, large numbers of rabbits were killed by a disease called myxomatosis which was spread deliberately by man, and as a result sheep have flourished and the production of wool has been increased by an amount worth many millions of Australian dollars. There are now signs that the rabbits are becoming immune to myxomatosis and new ways of controlling them are being investigated.

Birds, Reptiles, and Insects

Perhaps the most famous Australian bird is the kookaburra or "laughing jackass", which is a kind of kingfisher. Two flightless birds, the emu and the cassowary, are not found anywhere else; nor is the lyrebird (see LYREBIRD), which has wonderful powers of mimicking other sounds. Other birds to be seen are brilliantly colored parrots, cockatoos, honeyeaters, bower-birds, and mound-builders (see MOUND-BUILDER), which hatch their eggs by burying them in warm mounds of rotting leaves. The wedge-tailed eagle is larger than the golden eagle of Europe and Asia. There are also cranes, ibises, herons, ducks, snakebirds, pelicans, and black swans to be found near the lakes and rivers. The birds seen in the towns and cities include sparrows, brought from Britain by the early settlers to make them feel at home.

Snakes are common and include many poisonous ones such as the taipan and tiger snakes. There are also pythons, carpet snakes and tree snakes which are not poisonous. Two kinds of crocodile live in the north and many types of lizard can be found, while there are turtles in some of the freshwater lakes. Australia has a rich insect life with well over 50,000 native species. Added to this are the thousand or so kinds that have been introduced by settlers. Many of these are serious pests such as cockroaches, scale insects, blowflies and cabbage white butterflies.

The People and where they Live

Two hundred years ago the only people in Australia were dark-skinned people who had come from Asia. They were known as Aborigines because they were the original inhabitants. There were about 300,000 of them when Europeans began to settle in the country in the 18th century; but their numbers steadily decreased. There are now about 125,000 Aborigines in Australia. This includes many that are of mixed blood. Traditionally, they lived by hunting and gathering, but many now work on farms and ranches, or in towns. The Aborigines and their way of life is described in the article ABORIGINALS, AUSTRALIAN.

In total, there are only 15,000,000 people living in this huge country and by far the largest number are descended from people who originally came from the United Kingdom, although there have been colonists from Germany and Italy. The urgent need to develop the country rapidly led to a change, and since World War II more than 3,350,000 immigrants have settled in Australia. Although most of the newcomers still came from Great Britain, large numbers came from Greece, Italy, Germany, the Netherlands, and Poland, and from the Baltic States. Others have come from Asia. Because of Australia's policy of helping refugees coming to the country from the politically troubled parts of South-East Asia, there are now more Asians than non-Asians entering the country.

Australia is divided into six states and two territories. The states with the most people living in them are New South Wales and Victoria. Hardly anyone lives in the center of the continent or on many parts of the west coast. The largest towns are nearly all capitals of the various states and territories. Sydney is the capital of New South Wales, Melbourne is the capital of Victoria, and Brisbane is the capital of Queensland, while the capitals of South and Western Australia are Adelaide and Perth; Darwin is the capital of the Northern Territory; Hobart is the capital of Tasmania; and Canberra, in the Australian Capital Territory, is the capital of Australia as a whole. The chief ports are Sydney, Melbourne, Adelaide, Newcastle, Brisbane, and Fremantle. Others, such as Port Hedland in Western Australia, concentrate on the export of minerals. (There are separate articles on the states, the Northern Territory and the capital cities.)

Although Australia is still a great farming country, four-fifths of the people live in the cities and towns. Most people live in single-family, one story houses built of wood or brick with roofs of tile or corrugated iron, and with yards. Some houses have wide verandahs, sun rooms and "sleep-outs", which are outside bedrooms enclosed with fine wire netting and canvas blinds. However, the demand for urban land is so high that many people now live in small town houses or apartments, many of which are located in high-rise buildings, erected by private or government organizations. People who live on farms often have to provide their own electricity, water and sewerage arrangements.

Three views of three Australian state capitals. **Top:** Construction-worker's view of Sydney, capital of New South Wales, from high up the girders of Sydney Harbour Bridge. **Left:** Perth, on the other side of Australia, is the capital of Western Australia. **Above:** Beyond the Yarra River modern skyscrapers dominate the skyline of Melbourne, capital of Victoria.

Northern Territory Tourist Commission

Darwin, Northern Territory, Australia, is a busy seaport and has one of the country's best harbors.

Courtesy, Australian News and Information Bureau

Canberra, Australia's federal capital, seen from Mount Ainslie. The country's government buildings are located here.

Sport, the Arts, and Education

Australians have made a great impact in many sports. Cricket and tennis are the main summer games throughout the country, but while in the winter New South Wales and Queensland play Rugby Union and Rugby League football, the southern states play a game of football unique to Australia that is known as the Australian National Code, or Australian Rules (see AUSTRALIAN RULES FOOTBALL). Australians also enjoy golf, soccer, field hockey, lacrosse, athletics, rowing, swimming, surf-riding, and sailing as well as the more American games of baseball and basketball. Horse racing, shooting, and fishing are all popular and so are winter sports in the mountains.

From early days, writers and artists have been active in Australia. Many have been concerned about whether they should develop purely Australian forms of art or follow European (especially British) models. The "Australian" idea was strong about 1890, with painters such as Arthur Streeton and Tom Roberts and writers such as Henry Lawson and Joseph Furphy. The "Australian" stress later became weaker, although the paintings and literature were about the country and its people. This is true of the work of painters such as Russell Drysdale, Arthur Boyd, and Sidney Nolan and the writers Henry Handel Richardson and Patrick White.

Theater has a long tradition in Australia, dating from the late 18th century, and the country has its own orchestras and ballet companies. Music is well developed and many Australian singers and musicians have become world famous. Sydney Opera House is known all over the world. Australia has also contributed some great names to the world of music and ballet: the singers Nellie Melba and Joan Sutherland and the dancer and choreographer Robert Helpmann, for example. Australian films have recently enjoyed international popularity. Radio has been very important in Australia, especially for people who live far from towns. There are many radio and television stations, some run by the government while others are owned by commercial companies. The Australian Broadcasting Commission owns nearly half the radio and television stations. It has organized orchestras and invites well-known musicians to come and play, conduct, or sing in Australia. Its educational broadcasts are used by schools as well as by children who live so far from any school that they must do correspondence classes at home (sending their work by mail). This is called the School of the Air. There are also radio and television stations that broadcast in the languages of the more recent settlers. These programs are sponsored by the government which is anxious to give immigrants an opportunity to keep in touch with the culture of their previous homeland.

Australian children go to primary schools, as in the United Kingdom and North America. Secondary education is in high schools, technical schools, and agricultural high schools. Most schools are run by the government, but one-fifth of Australian children attend church or independent schools which are given grants by the government. Students can study at any of Australia's 22 universities free; however, overseas students have to pay fees.

The Church of England has more followers than any other church in Australia. More than a quarter of the population is Roman Catholic.

The Importance of Sheep

Although Australian industry is developing fast, farming still provides a valuable export trade. Most of the early settlers were farmers and today about 40 per cent of the money Australia earns from goods sold abroad comes from products such as wool, wheat, meat, fruit, and butter; the most important is wool.

In 1791 there were only 57 sheep in Australia. By the 1980s the country had roughly 135,000,000 and the shearing produced almost 500,000 tonnes of wool yearly. This is almost one-third of all the wool produced in the world.

Australia is the chief wool-producing country of the world largely because of the foresight of the early pioneers who settled in New South Wales, for they realized how suitable the climate and general conditions were for sheep. Then, at the beginning of the 19th century, some merino sheep were brought to Australia. By now the flocks are mostly merinos and these give the fine wool for which the country is famous. Crossbred sheep for wool and meat are also raised, as are breeds for fat lamb and mutton production.

New South Wales still has more sheep than any other state. The sheep farms, or stations as they are called, are fenced off into enormous paddocks, or fields, over which the farmers and their men travel about in cars or on motorcycles. If the sheep relied on rain for their water many of them would die when there was a drought, but some of their water comes from artesian wells that rarely dry up.

When shearing time comes, teams of shearers travel from one sheep station to another. In the shearing sheds the men sort the fleeces into different grades, or qualities, pack them into bales, and then send them off to the towns where buyers from all over the world come to bid for them at the auction sales.

Meat and Milk, Wheat and Fruit

Besides being valuable for their wool, the sheep provide meat for Australia, the United States, the Middle East and other countries. Cattle are even more important for meat, the great cattle areas being Queensland and the Northern Territory. The beasts are often driven or trucked hundreds of kilometers to the nearest port before they are killed and shipped to other countries. In the past, long "droving" journeys on foot, known as "over-landing" the cattle, were part of the cattleman's life.

Cows are kept for milk and butter, too, chiefly on the east coast where there is sufficient rain to make the grass grow richly enough. Australians also keep a lot of pigs.

Wheat is by far the most important crop in Australia, which sends more than 10,000,000 tonnes a year to other countries, particularly to China and to India. Many large storage tanks have been built for the wheat, while modern machinery has been installed for handling it in bulk and loading it into the ships that take it abroad. The other chief grain crops are oats, barley, sorghum, corn, and rice. In Queensland and New South Wales farmers grow sugar-cane, and nowadays more cotton, flax, and tobacco are being cultivated.

The climate is often very good for fruit and vegetables. In the north tropical fruits such as bananas, pineapples, mangos, guavas, and papaws are grown; while farther south there are oranges, lemons, peaches, and apricots as well as the kinds of fruit that are grown in Europe and North America, such as apples, plums, currants, raspberries, and strawberries. Much of this fruit is sent to other countries—either fresh, dried, or in cans. In a good year enough grapes are grown in Australian vineyards to make 14 liters (24 pints) of

A flock of merino sheep in New South Wales being herded by a traditional drover (ranch-hand) on horseback.

wine for every person in the country. Much is exported to other countries.

Australia is by far the driest continent, and the total flow of all its rivers is no more than that of the Danube in central Europe. Rainfall is therefore the most needed thing in Australian farming and great importance is attached to making the best possible use of all water. (See IRRIGATION.) The Snowy Mountains hydroelectric scheme, one of the largest in the world, takes water from the Snowy River through the Eastern Highlands to the Murray and Murrumbidgee rivers in southeast Australia, thus providing a great increase of irrigated land and large quantities of electric power.

Mines, Factories, and Transportation

Mining (especially for iron, coal, and bauxite) is a fast-growing activity, and now makes up about a third of Australia's exports. Gold attracted many settlers to the state of Victoria after it was first discovered there. In the 20th century, however, most of the gold which the country produced was mined in Western Australia. Coal is mined in New South Wales,

Queensland, and Victoria, which is why so many of the factories are in these three states.

Silver, lead, zinc, copper, and tin have long been mined in Australia. Since the 1950s there has been a great increase in mining, especially of bauxite (see BAUXITE) and of rutile. In the 1960s, the export of iron ore mined in the barren Pilbara district of Western Australia began, and valuable finds of nickel and manganese were made. Uranium mines exist in Queensland and the Northern Territory. Australia obtains oil (petroleum) from wells in Queensland, at Barrow Island off the coast of Western Australia and in the Bass Strait off the coast of Victoria, and has rich supplies of natural gas (methane).

Although Australia is often regarded as an agricultural country, more of its people now work in factories than on the land. Not only have old industries expanded but new ones have grown up, so that Australia now makes most things from airplanes to agricultural machinery.

The railroads were responsible for the opening up of much of Australia. Originally, the states had railroad tracks of different gauges

Agent General for South Australia

Gas fields at Moomba, South Australia. Flames from burning unwanted gas light up the surrounding area.

(widths) but now standard-gauge track (143.5 centimeters or 4 feet 8½ inches) ensures that freight is carried rapidly and without delay. Australia has about 900,000 kilometers (560,000 miles) of roads, of which the most striking is Highway One. It runs almost around the continent from Darwin in the northwest to Cairns in the northeast for a distance of 12,334 kilometers (7,664 miles) and links the capitals of all the states on the mainland.

Air passengers within Australia can travel by the government-owned Trans-Australia Airlines or by several privately owned airlines. International services are provided by Qantas Airways. (Qantas stands for Queensland and Northern Territory Aerial Service.) Aircraft are particularly suitable for carrying freight and mail because there are such long distances to travel and the weather is usually good for flying. With so many people living on sheep- or cattle-stations or in small townships which are far away from hospitals and doctors, the Royal Flying Doctor Service is an essential service. People can call up the Flying Doctor when someone is ill and sometimes advice on treatment is given back over the phone or radio. Often an aircraft is sent to fly the patient to hospital and sometimes the doctors and nurses are flown hundreds of kilometers to treat a very sick patient.

Even the smallest settlements in remote country areas (the outback) receive their mail regularly. Telephones are also important in a country where people often live far apart; Australians send more telegrams than anyone else in the world.

Australian Government

To start with, the Australian colonies were governed from London, but by 1900 they had all been allowed to set up their own governments. Although independent of one another, they found they had to co-operate on such matters as armed forces and trade. After several attempts to unite the colonies, the Common-

Courtesy, Australian News and Information Bureau

This massive dragline excavator dwarfs the people near by. The machine strips coal from open-cast mines in Queensland.

wealth of Australia was created on 1 January 1901. At first Melbourne served as the national capital but only until an entirely new city was built. In 1927 enough of the buildings had been completed for the national parliament to move to Canberra, which is now the national capital (see CANBERRA). The national parliament makes laws on matters such as defense, trade and relations with other countries, customs duties and the immigration of people from abroad. The individual colonies became "states" in 1901 and have gone on looking after their own schools, law courts, roads and railroads, health, agriculture, and industry.

The Commonwealth of Australia is part of the Commonwealth (see COMMONWEALTH, THE) and has the same sovereign as Britain, represented in Canberra by the governor-general. Australia was the first country in the Commonwealth to have one of its own citizens as governor-general, Sir Isaac Isaacs (who held office from 1931 to 1936).

There are two houses in the national parliament. The House of Representatives has 148 seats which are shared by the six states according to their population, while the Northern Territory and the Australian Capital Territory each have one representative. The Northern Territory Representative may vote only on questions relating to his Territory. The Australian Capital Territory member has full voting rights. The Senate has 76 members – 12 from each state, whatever its size, so as to safeguard the interests of the smaller states – and two members each from the Northern Territory and the Australian Capital Territory. There are three main political parties – the Labor Party, the Liberal Party and the National Party. When a new parliament is chosen in a general election, everybody over 18 is required to vote except Aboriginals, who may vote but do not have to.

Australia is a realm, or independent member, of the Commonwealth of Nations. It has its own ambassadors to major foreign countries and high commissioners in Britain and other Commonwealth countries. In the latter part of the 20th century it has greatly increased its trade with countries in Asia and plays a leading role in Pacific affairs. Australia administers a number of overseas territories. These are Norfolk Island in the Pacific Ocean; the Ashmore and Cartier Islands in the Timor Sea; the Cocos Keeling Islands, Christmas Island and the Heard and McDonald Islands in the Indian Ocean; and the Australian Antarctic Territory.

Prime Ministers of the Commonwealth of Australia

	In office from	To
Sir Edmund Barton	1 Jan 1901	24 Sept 1903
Alfred Deakin	24 Sept 1903	27 April 1904
John C. Watson	27 April 1904	18 Aug 1904
Sir George Reid	18 Aug 1904	5 July 1905
Alfred Deakin	5 July 1905	13 Nov 1908
Andrew Fisher	13 Nov 1908	2 June 1909
Alfred Deakin	2 June 1909	29 April 1910
Andrew Fisher	29 April 1910	24 June 1913
Sir Joseph Cook	24 June 1913	17 Sept 1914
Andrew Fisher	17 Sept 1914	27 Oct 1915
William M. Hughes	27 Oct 1915	9 Feb 1923
Stanley M. Bruce, later Viscount Bruce of Melbourne	9 Feb 1923	22 Oct 1929
James H. Scullin	22 Oct 1929	6 Jan 1932
Joseph A. Lyons	6 Jan 1932	7 April 1939
Sir Earle Page	7 April 1939	26 April 1939
Robert Menzies	26 April 1939	29 Aug 1941
Arthur Fadden	29 Aug 1941	7 Oct 1941
John Curtin	7 Oct 1941	6 July 1945
Francis M. Forde	6 July 1945	13 July 1945
Joseph B. Chifley	13 July 1945	19 Dec 1949
Sir Robert Menzies	19 Dec 1949	26 Jan 1966
Harold Holt	26 Jan 1966	19 Dec 1967
John McEwen	19 Dec 1967	10 Jan 1968
John G. Gorton	10 Jan 1968	10 Mar 1971
William McMahon	10 Mar 1971	5 Dec 1972
Gough Whitlam	5 Dec 1972	11 Nov 1975
Malcolm Fraser	11 Nov 1975	11 Mar 1983
Robert Hawke	11 Mar 1983	

There are also separate articles on the following aspects of Australia: AUSTRALIAN HISTORY; AUSTRALIAN LITERATURE; AUSTRALIAN RULES FOOTBALL.

AUSTRALIAN HISTORY. Human beings have lived in Australia for tens of thousands of years, not as long as they have lived in Africa and Europe but longer than they have lived in either North or South America.

Historians are not sure when the first Aboriginals arrived because prehistoric sites are difficult to find in Australia. Much of the early evidence lies buried beneath layers of sediment and has not been exposed by earth movements or erosion as it has been in, for example, Africa. However, the archeological evidence available at present suggests that Aboriginal migrants crossed from Southeast Asia about 40,000 years ago. There may have been one or several waves of migration.

At the time these migrants arrived, the level of the sea was much lower than it is today. A series of ice ages had frozen vast areas of the world's oceans around the North and South Poles. Since so much water was taken up to make ice, areas of land were exposed that are today covered by sea. (See ICE AGE.) Although there was never a land-bridge between Australia and Asia, it is probable that the Aboriginals were able to walk most of the way to Australia, completing their journey by canoe or raft. Evidence of these early settlers has been found at an archeological site at Upper Swan in south-western Australia.

Before the arrival of the Europeans most of the Aboriginals lived in the fertile areas of Australia which lie along the coast and rivers and around lakes. Very few of them moved to the arid zones of the centre. Settlement of Tasmania was via a land-bridge created by the drop in the sea-level. Australia's native dog, the dingo, was brought to Australia by Aboriginals about 6000BC. By then sea-levels had risen and Tasmania was separated from mainland Australia. Consequently the dingo never reached the island state of Tasmania.

The First Outside Contacts

When Europeans first reached Australia in the 16th century, there were about 300,000 Aboriginals living there. They were divided into approximately 600 tribal groups and spoke some 250 different languages. Like all human beings until about 10,000 years ago, the Aboriginals lived entirely by gathering plant food and hunting animals and insects. Those near the coast or with rivers within their tribal land also caught fish. Their weapons and tools were privately owned, but the land, their food, and all other property belonged to the whole tribe. They had no kings or chiefs, and they were not organized to defend themselves against invaders. There is a separate article on ABORIGINALS, AUSTRALIAN.

The first outsiders to visit Australia were probably Macassans from Indonesia, who came every year to the Gulf of Carpentaria, northern Australia, in search of trepang, or sea slugs. Many historians agree that the first European visitors were Portuguese sailors, who between 1516 and 1536 examined and mapped eastern Australia. In 1606 Luis de Torres, a Spanish captain, sailed his ship between Australia and New Guinea through the strait which now bears his name.

In the same year Willem Jansz, a Dutch captain, discovered and mapped part of the northern coast of Australia, though he thought that it was part of New Guinea. The Dutch found that the best way to sail to the East Indies (now Indonesia and Malaysia) was by a route which took them south of Australia. As a result, from 1611 onwards many Dutch ships visited Australia. The first Dutch captain to land in western Australia was Dirck Hartog, in 1616. Many others followed, and the country came to be called New Holland. Anthony Van Diemen, the Dutch governor-general of the East Indies, was interested in the new continent, and when the Dutch explorer Abel Tasman discovered the southern coast of what is now Tasmania, he named it Van Diemen's Land. But the Dutch saw no hope of trade with the Aboriginals and founded no settlements in Australia.

British Settlement

The first Englishman to write about Australia was William Dampier. He visited Australia twice, the first time in 1688 as one of the crew of a pirate ship, and the second time in 1699 as captain of a ship of the British navy. On neither voyage did Dampier carry out much exploration, but in 1697, after his first visit to Australia, he published his journal under the title *A New Voyage Round the World*. Although Dampier described the Australian Aboriginals as "the miserablest People in the World" and said that the west coast of New Holland was a waterless series of sand-hills lying behind dangerous reefs, his book aroused British interest in Australia.

More than 70 years after Dampier's book

Captain Cook claimed the entire eastern coast of Australia in the name of the English king in 1770.

was published, one of Britain's greatest explorers, James Cook, set sail for the Pacific Ocean in a tiny ship, the *Endeavour*. He visited Tahiti, mapped the coast of New Zealand, then sailed west. In April 1770 he sighted the eastern coast of Australia at Point Hicks, in what is now the state of Victoria. He sailed northward along the coast right up to the tip of Cape York Peninsula, passing through Torres Strait on 22 August. On that day he took possession in the name of the king of England of the whole of the eastern coast of Australia, giving it the name New South Wales. (See COOK, JAMES.)

With Cook in the *Endeavour* was a scientist, Joseph Banks, whose main interest was botany. During the eight days the ship was anchored in Botany Bay, so called because of the many unfamiliar plants there, Banks made many observations on the country, its people, its animals, and its plants. When his books, and Cook's reports, were published after the *Endeavour* returned to England, people came to realize that New South Wales, unlike the northern and western coasts of Australia, was a fertile land and suitable for

European settlement. At that time no one considered any rights the Aboriginals might have to their own lands.

In 1783 a long war between Britain and France came to an end. Britain had won Canada from France, but its 13 colonies along the Atlantic coast of North America had become independent. As a result the British government faced two problems. The more important was where to establish a naval base to help defend British trade in the eastern seas. The less important was to find a place to which to deport British convicts, who until 1776 had been sent to Britain's American colonies.

In Britain at that time laws were so severe that the penalty for stealing goods of, or above, the value of a shilling (5 pence or about 10 cents) could be death. Many judges, however, instead of ordering that a convicted person be hanged, sentenced him or her to transportation to a penal colony for a term ranging from seven years to life. Since the beginning of the war with America in 1776, those convicts sentenced to transportation had been kept in unused ships in English rivers and ports. Their numbers there were growing daily.

The British prime minister William Pitt finally decided to solve both his problems at once. A settlement at Botany Bay in New South Wales would provide both a naval supply base for the Indian and Pacific oceans and a suitably distant prison to which to send convicts. In 1787 the First Fleet, commanded by Captain Arthur Phillip of the British navy, set sail from England. It carried, as well as its naval crews, 213 marines and some 788 convicts, male and female. By 20 January 1788 the whole fleet had reached Botany Bay. Phillip rapidly decided that Botany Bay was not a good place for a settlement. Nearby Port Jackson, he found, had safe anchorages for his ships and fresh water for the colonists. He named the bay where the settlement was to be established Sydney Cove, and on 26 January a party was landed and the British flag raised. Australians still celebrate 26 January as Australia Day.

Founding the Australian Colonies

For the first two years of its settlement, Sydney was always on the brink of starvation. Few of the convicts knew anything about farming, and the colony depended for food on ships from England. Gradually farms began to produce food. James Ruse, one of the few convicts who was a farmer, was by 1791 able to produce enough food to support himself and his family. Quite early in Australia's history wool became a major source of the country's wealth. While John Macarthur, in England, persuaded merchants that Australian wool was of good quality, his wife Elizabeth Macarthur managed the Australian estate on which merino sheep produced the wool. Lachlan Macquarie, as governor from 1809 to 1821, did much to improve conditions. He carried out important building projects and introduced land reforms.

Tasmania was first settled by the British out of fear of the French. Soon after the French navigator Nicolas Baudin had visited Sydney, Governor King in 1803 sent Lieutenant John Bowen to found the settlement of Hobart. Tasmania became a separate colony in 1825. Western Australia was first settled for the same reason. In 1826 Major Edmund Lockyer founded a settlement at Albany, and in 1829 Captain James Stirling founded a settlement at Perth and claimed the whole of "New Holland" for Britain. Western Australia is the only Australian state that was never part of New South Wales.

In the southeastern corner of the continent overlanders from Sydney and sheepmen from Tasmania converged to settle the Port Phillip District, which later became Victoria. In 1834 Edward Henty took up land at Portland, and in 1835 John Batman and John Pascoe Fawkner led parties which settled in the Melbourne area. Victoria was not separated from New South Wales until 1851, after gold had been discovered in the colony.

Quite soon after New South Wales was established, its governors began to seek places to send convicts who committed crimes after arriving in Australia. Tasmania was the first of these convict stations. The Queensland area near Brisbane, first explored by Lieutenant Henry Miller and John Oxley in 1824, was established as a convict station by Captain Patrick Logan in 1826. Queensland was separated from New South Wales in 1859.

Mary Evans Picture Library

When gold was discovered in 1851 immigrants swelled Australia's population from 740,000 to over one million inhabitants.

Settlers flooded to Australia in the late 19th century as minerals were discovered and new industries were established.

Mary Evans Picture Library

South Australia was settled in a quite different way. Edward Gibbon Wakefield, an Englishman who had never been to Australia, published a theory on the best way to set up colonies. He argued that land should be sold to wealthy settlers and the money used to bring out laborers from Britain (see WAKE-FIELD, EDWARD GIBBON). South Australia was begun on these principles. In 1836 the new "Province of South Australia" was carved out of New South Wales and a settlement established by Surveyor William Light and Governor John Hindmarsh.

Towards a United Australia

The early settlers in Australia knew very little of the continent they had taken over from the Aboriginals. The person who mapped most of Australia's coast was Matthew Flinders. With George Bass in 1798 he established that Tasmania was an island separated from the mainland by Bass Strait. In the period 1801–03 he sailed right around Australia, completing the map of the entire coastline. (See FLINDERS, MATTHEW.)

Among those who explored inland Australia were Gregory Blaxland, William Lawson, and William Charles Wentworth. They discovered a way across the rugged Blue Mountains in the Great Dividing Range that separates coastal New South Wales from the inland region. Also notable were Charles Sturt, who traced the course of some of Australia's inland rivers, and John McDouall Stuart, who crossed the continent from south to north. (There are separate entries on WENTWORTH, WILLIAM, and STURT, CHARLES.)

Until the discovery of gold, Australia's population remained small. In 1851 gold was discovered in New South Wales and Victoria, and in the next ten years the population jumped by 740,000 to 1,100,000 as people from all over the world flocked to the gold-fields. In the next 30 years this figure tripled, as new industries were established. Links by rail and sea between the six separate colonies were formed and people began to see themselves as Australians rather than as New South Welshmen, Tasmanians, Victorians, and so on. In 1901 Australia became one nation, the Commonwealth of Australia, with Edmund Barton as the new nation's first prime minister. At first Melbourne served as the national capital, but only while an entirely new city was built. In 1927 enough of the buildings had been completed for the national parliament to move to Canberra, the present capital. In 1931 all British control ceased and Australia became an independent member of the Commonwealth.

Australia Since Federation

In 1901 Australia's population was just over 3 million. Today it is more than 15 million. Much of this growth can be accounted for by the arrival of immigrants who were attracted by the jobs in Australia's new industries.

In the years between Federation and World War I, manufacturing and mining began to be developed. The mining of coal and lead, and the manufacture of food, drinks, clothing, and steel became important in this period. As a Dominion of the British Empire, Australia automatically entered World War I when Britain declared war on Germany, and Australian soldiers fought with distinction at Gallipoli, in the Middle East, and in France.

Between World War I and World War II Australia's industries grew rapidly. When war

BBC Hulton Picture Library

Australia entered World War I with Britain, and its forces fought in all main campaigns.

broke out in 1939, Australia again entered the fight at the same time as Britain, though she was now an independent member of the Commonwealth. But while Australian troops initially supported the British in the Middle East, Greece, and Crete, in the latter part of the war they mainly fought alongside United States troops in the war in the Pacific.

After World War II Australia began a major campaign to attract migrants from all over the world. This campaign lasted until the 1970s and changed the country from a mainly British community to a multi-cultural society. In this period, too, Australia began to try to improve the life of the first Australians – the Aborigi-

nals. Australian troops supported American troops in the Korean War (1950–53) and the Vietnam War (1965–73). During the 1980s, although it was by then a major industrial country, Australia still relied largely on agricultural and mineral products to earn money overseas.

AUSTRALIAN LITERATURE is the body of literary work produced in English in Australia.

Early Years

Australian literature began simply as an extension of English literature. In the early years of settlement, writers of British or Australian origin modeled their novels and poems on British examples. But as an Australian sense of nationhood developed, writers began to capture the special experience of their extraordinary continent. They wrote about their new surroundings, emphasizing what was different (from Britain), and sometimes hostile. Their books were read by other settlers as well as by people in Britain who were planning to emigrate to Australia and wished to find out more about the country. One such early novel was *Tales of the Colonies* (1843), by Charles Rowcroft. Other accounts were the journals of Watkin Tench describing vividly the early years of the colony, and *Quintus Servinton*

Mary Evans Picture Library

The life of the transported convicts was a popular theme of early 19th-century Australian writers.

Books about the settler's life in Australia provided prospective immigrants with useful information.

Mary Evans Picture Library

(1830–31) by Henry Savery, which describes the harsh convict system at work.

The contemporary Australian poet Peter Porter has written that "Nature—real Australian nature—quickly became, and still remains, the main protagonist of Australian literature." The pioneer writers described an exotic world—the landscape, the drought and desert, the bush fires, the animals and flowers. They also wrote of the trials and tribulations of pioneer life, the conditions in the goldfields, the convicts, and the Aborigines. Marcus Clarke's novel, *For the Term of his Natural Life* (1874), one of the great Australian novels of this period, is an attack on the brutal conditions in the penal colony in Tasmania.

Henry Kingsley, brother of the more famous English writer Charles Kingsley, spent some years in the province of Victoria between 1853 and 1858. On his return to England he published two books about Australian life: *The Recollections of Geoffrey Hamlyn* (1859) and *The Hillyars and the Burtons* (1865). These are both about British immigrants to the country. One family returns to Britain, and the other stays on in Australia and achieves a much higher social position in Australian society, where class barriers were much less rigid, than it could possibly have reached back in Britain. Another distinguished novel of this period is Catherine Spence's *Clara Morrison* (1854), which is about Adelaide in the 1850s.

The early Australian children's books were often about adventures in the bush. The dangers tended to be exaggerated, and the local people depicted as far fiercer and more savage than they actually were. Typical of this genre were William Howitt's *A Boy's Adventures in the Wilds of Australia* (1854), which was even translated into German, and Richard Rowe's *The Boy in the Bush* (1865). Later, Aborigines were more sympathetically portrayed by children's writers, and their culture was taken more seriously. Mrs. K. Langloh Parker collected their legends in *Australian Legendary Tales* (1896), and an Aboriginal girl was the heroine in Mrs. Aeneas Gunn's *The Little Black Princess* (1905).

The Middle Years (1880–1940)

In the latter years of the 19th century, Australian writers turned to new themes. These included the growing communities in the rural areas, whose struggles were dealt with sympathetically. Three noted women writers of this period led this trend: Ada Cambridge, "Tasma" (Jessie Catherine Couvreur), and Mrs. Campbell Praed.

A landmark was the publication of a journal, *The Bulletin* in 1880. *The Bulletin* influenced the development of Australian literature, and was the first to publish many writers of the period. Some of the short stories to appear in it were about rural life. *The Bulletin* also published the early "bush ballads", a specifically Australian ballad form, which developed from local bush rhymes that poets heard on their travels. The first bush ballads were Adam Lindsay Gordon's *Bush Ballads and Galloping Rhymes* (1870). Other ballad writers were Will Ogilvie, Henry Lawson, E. G. Dyson, and, perhaps the best known of all, A. B. "Banjo" Paterson. Steele Rudd's sketches of Queensland farm life, which are still read today, also first appeared in installments in *The Bulletin*.

Children's literature of this middle period developed a distinctive Australian style. Books about family life were the most popular form. One book still read today is *Seven Little Australians* (1894) by Ethel Turner. The author warns the reader not to expect to find anything about model children in her tale: "Not one of the seven is really good, for the very excellent reason that Australian children never are." The mother of the seven children is dead, and their father, Captain Woolcot of Sydney, has no understanding of children. The novel is about the children's various escapades. It was a great success in Australia and in England, was also published in America, and was translated into several foreign languages.

Books for children also included stories about animals, real and make-believe, and their adventures. One such book, which has been described as Australia's only real classic book for children, is *The Magic Pudding* (1918), written and illustrated by Norman Lindsay. It is about Bunyip Bluegum, a koala bear who lives in a tree house with his Uncle Wattleberry, whose huge whiskers cannot fit into the house. The author, a well-known cartoonist of the period, apparently wrote the book to take his mind off the horrors of the First World War, in which many of his friends were being killed.

Two milestones in the development of Australian literature of this middle period are Miles Franklin's *My Brilliant Career* (1901), a fictional autobiography which draws on the heroism and strong pioneer spirit of the time, and Joseph Furphy's *Such is Life* (1903), a picture of country life in the 1880s. Both books rapidly became Australian classics, and *My Brilliant Career* was made into a successful film in the 1970s. A book dealing with related themes is the trilogy, *The Fortunes of Richard Mahony* (1917–29) by Henry Handel Richardson (whose real name was Ethel Florence Lindsay Robertson). It is a study of the fluctuating fortunes among immigrants to the growing Australian cities of the late 19th century. Richardson also wrote a book about student life in Europe, called *Maurice Guest* (1908), which enjoyed renewed success many years later. Other writers who concentrated on inner-city life were Louis Stone and Edward Dyson. Mrs. Aeneas Gunn's *We of the Never Never* (1908), explores the relationship of a white man to the Aborigines. This was also the theme of *Coonardoo* (1929) by Katharine Prichard, and *Capricornia* (1938) by Xavier Herbert.

Modern Australian Literature

In the last fifty years or so, many new literary magazines have appeared. There is also a much larger reading public than ever before. New themes have been taken up in Australian literature in books about new immigrant groups including Greeks, Lebanese and Jews, and in others dealing with the subject of the Far East.

The most famous of all modern Australian novelists is Patrick White (born 1912), who has written mostly about Australia, although his books also deal with much wider universal themes. White reflects in his life (if not his writing) certain mixed feelings towards Europe, which is characteristic of many Australian writers. His great-grandfather went to Australia from England in 1826, but the family kept up its links with England, where White was actually born and educated. After a number of visits to Australia, White finally settled there in 1948, and he became a bitter critic of the country's intellectual culture. He wrote about the great Australian outback in one of his most famous novels, *Voss* (1957). In another novel, *The Tree of Man* (1950), he described life on a poor small farm in the 1930s. White won the Nobel Prize for Literature in 1973.

The other major Australian novelist of this period was Christina Stead (1902–83), who spent most of her adult life in Great Britain.

Only one of her novels, *Poor Men of Sydney* (1934), was set entirely in Australia. Other well-known writers include Ruth Park, Martin Boyd, Shirley Hazzard, Randolph Stow, Hal Porter, Eleanor Dark, Kylie Tennant, Xavier Herbert, C. J. Koch, David Malouf, and Thomas Keneally. Keneally has written on various themes, among them the Australian convict settlement, World War I, and the Jewish Holocaust (in *Schindler's Ark*, 1983, for which he was awarded the prestigious Booker Prize of that year). Colin Johnson, an Aboriginal writer, established his reputation with *Wild Cat Falling* (1965). Well-known Australian poets are Judith Wright, David Campbell, Peter Porter, Bruce Dawe, James McAuley, and Robert D. Fitzgerald.

In children's literature, the best post-war writers are H. F. Brinsmead, Nan Chancy, Reginald Ottley, and Ivan Southall, who is considered one of the best writers for children of his generation in the English-speaking world. His books are full of excitement and adventure, and at the same time realistic. *Hills End* (1962), his first novel, is about young people in a storm and flood. *Ash Road* (1965) has as its theme a forest fire, and *To the Wild Sky* (1967), an air crash. His later works, for example, *Bread and Honey* (1970), are more concerned with relationships between different types of personalities, and with young love. They paint a very realistic picture of Australian society in the 1930s.

AUSTRALIAN RULES FOOTBALL is a winter game played only in Australia. It is a spectacular and exciting code of football which draws huge crowds mainly in the southern states. It is widely played and supported in Victoria, Western Australia, South Australia, and Tasmania. New South Wales, Australia's most populous state, follows Rugby League football enthusiastically but even there the Australian game is widely played. Queenslanders, too, generally prefer Rugby League but Australian Rules is played throughout the state from Brisbane, the capital, to Cairns in the far north.

How the Game is Played

Australian Rules football is played on an oval arena which measures in major competitions from 135 to 185 meters (150 to 200 yards) long and from 110 to 155 meters (120 to 170 yards) wide. The preferred size is 165 by 135 meters (180 by 150 yards). The game is played with an oval ball weighing between 450 and 500 grams (16 and 17½ ounces). At each end of the ground stand two goal posts 6.4 meters (7 yards) apart and not less than 6 meters (6½ yards) high. Two more posts known as behind posts stand on either side, 6.4 meters (7 yards) from each goal post. The line between the goal posts is called the goal line, and the lines between the behind posts and the goal posts are called the behind lines.

The game is played between two teams of 18 players over four 25-minute quarters (plus any time the umpires add on). The winning team is the one that scores the greater number of points. A goal is scored when the ball is kicked untouched by any player other than the kicker between the goal posts. A goal scores six points. A behind is scored when the ball is kicked or forced between the goal and behind posts. A behind is also scored when the ball passes between the goal posts but is touched by another player. A behind scores one point.

After a goal, the ball is returned to the center. Play resumes when one of the two field umpires bounces the ball in the center circle. After a behind, the ball is kicked back into play by any player from the opposing team (usually the full back), who must kick the ball from inside what is known as the 10 meter (10 yard) square.

Teams comprise six forwards, three center-line players, six backmen, and three followers known as ruckman, ruck-rover, and rover. The ruckman is almost always the tallest player in the team. His main job is to hit the ball to his rover at center bounces and boundary throw-ins. Center bounces are made after every goal and also when the umpires decide there is a stalemate in play and there has been no clear infringement by either the player with the ball or the player making a tackle. When the ball crosses what is known as the boundary line, which circles the playing arena, play

Australian Rules football is a mixture of soccer and rugby. It probably started in the gold-fields of Victoria, in the 1850s.

Steve Powell/Allsport Photographic

ceases until a boundary umpire sends the ball back into the playing area by means of an overhead throw of about 15 meters (15 yards).

The ball is moved by either hand or foot, but goals must be kicked. At senior level, players consistently kick the ball distances of up to 65 meters (70 yards), while a handpass may cover 30 meters (30 yards). Players may run as far as they like provided they touch the ball on the ground every 15 meters (15 yards), either by bending down or bouncing the ball while running. There is no offside rule and the ball may be moved forward, backward, or sideways.

The field umpires penalize breaches of the rules with a free kick to the opposing team. More serious breaches of the rules and laws of the game, such as striking and kicking, may be reported. The charges are heard by an independent tribunal which has the power to suspend players from any number of matches. There is no order-off rule in Australia's major competition, the Victorian Football League.

When the ball is gathered in general play, a player must dispose of it before being tackled. If he marks (catches) the ball after it has been kicked more than 10 meters (10 yards) by any other player, and not touched on the way, he is entitled to take a deliberate kick without being tackled. The opposing team may have a player stand on the spot where the mark was

taken. Marking the ball is probably the most spectacular feature of Australian Rules football. It is a thrilling sight when several giant players leap to seize a high, dropping ball. It requires great athletic ability and courage.

The ball may be passed to another player only by kicking or handballing. Handball, once a defensive means of disposing of the ball before a player is tackled, is now a vital attacking tactic. The ball may never be thrown. To make a handball pass, a player holds the ball firmly in one hand and strikes it with the clenched fist of the other hand. The player receiving a handballed pass must play on: he is not allowed to take a deliberate, unimpeded kick as he is after a mark.

The Victorian Football League (VFL)

Australian Rules football is played to varying standards in all states and territories of the country. Each state organizes competitions which have considerable local following. But of all these competitions the Victorian Football League attracts the most interest nationally. Huge crowds attend football matches in Melbourne. The 1970 grand final, played at the Melbourne Cricket Ground, drew a record crowd of 121,696. Ground changes have since reduced its capacity to 100,000, but the world-famous football and cricket stadium is always filled to capacity on the final day (the last Saturday in September). The match is watched on television by several million Australians and in many countries throughout the world.

The football season in Victoria occupies nearly seven months. The 12 teams in the VFL play each other twice (22 rounds), with the leading five then contesting a finals program spread over four weeks. Of the VFL's 12 clubs 10 are based in Melbourne, one in Geelong—Victoria's second largest city 75 kilometers (45 miles) from Melbourne—and one (since 1982) in Sydney (even though the city is in New South Wales). Games in the domestic competitions are usually played on Saturday afternoons, but may be played on Sundays or week nights under lights. Teams representing Victoria, South Australia, and Western Australia meet in interstate matches each year.

History

Australian Rules football is believed to have had its origins in the Victorian goldfields in 1853, when local sportsmen mixed rules and procedures from both rugby and gaelic football, with a few new ideas of their own. The major initiative in organizing the game is believed to have come in 1858. It is credited to T. W. Wills, who returned to Australia after studying at Rugby School in England, where he had excelled at cricket and rugby. He considered that rugby was not well suited to Victorian conditions, particularly the hard playing fields, and he also favored a faster game which flowed more freely.

Formal rules were drafted in 1859. The popularity of the game and its development throughout Victoria resulted in the formation of the Victorian Football Association (VFA) in 1877, "to have the entire control and management of all inter-colonial and other matches". The first interstate games were played in Adelaide in 1877 and Melbourne in 1878. The Victorian Football League was born during 1896 when six of the stronger clubs in the VFA (Collingwood, Essendon, Fitzroy, Geelong, Melbourne, and South Melbourne) broke

away as a group and invited St. Kilda and Carlton to join them in the new competition. Payments to players were approved by the governing body in 1911 and the popularity of the game grew to such an extent that 59,479 people saw Fitzroy win the 1913 grand final, a record crowd for any Australian sporting event at that time. The VFL competition expanded to 12 clubs when Footscray, Hawthorn, and North Melbourne were admitted for the 1925 season.

AUSTRIA lies in central Europe, at the boundary of Eastern and Western Europe. To the north of Austria are Germany and Czechoslovakia, and to the south Italy and

Yugoslavia, while the country touches Liechtenstein and Switzerland to the west and Hungary to the east. Its present size is nothing compared to its size in the days of the much larger Austro-Hungarian Empire, which ended in 1918. (See AUSTRIAN EMPIRE.) The capital and by far the largest city is Vienna, on which there is a separate article.

Austria is mostly mountainous, the eastern end of the Alps stretches right through the country. (See ALPS.) This makes much of the country inaccessible; however, there is a chain of valleys across the middle which makes traveling easier. Many Austrians inhabit the lower levels of these valleys.

The geography of Austria is dominated by these mountains, capped by snowy peaks. Below are steep cliffs, fantastic-looking masses of rock, dense forests, and chains of

ZEFA

The City Hall (*Rathaus*) of Vienna is a fine 19th-century Gothic landmark of the Austrian capital.

mountain lakes. The great Achensee lake, in the western province of Tyrol, lies 929 meters (3,050 feet) above sea-level, and the next-door province of Salzburg has 20 similar lakes. Among European countries, only Switzerland has such spectacular ravines, waterfalls, and glaciers, while the meadowlands and farms of northern Austria have no equal for their natural beauty.

The meadowlands are dotted about the gently sloping foothills of the Alps, and here, too, is much beautiful wooded country sloping down to the River Danube. This river flows eastwards through northern Austria on its way to the Black Sea. (See DANUBE RIVER.)

Austrian Customs and Culture

The official language of Austria is German, but there are hundreds of local dialects and the nine provinces maintain their own traditional customs, cuisine and dress. Felt hats, often adorned with feathers or brushes of hair from the chamois (mountain goat), together with bright-buttoned waistcoats and leather shorts

called *Lederhosen* are a common sight in Austria. Austrian women sometimes wear their regional costumes which usually include colorful embroidered blouses and bodices, with full skirts gathered at the waist.

Nearly half the people live in small villages which, with their backcloth of alpine scenery, their ornate woodwork, and hand-painted murals, depicting religious scenes, are extremely eye-catching. The houses are normally built of brick, with overhanging wooden roofs, and balconies outside the second-story windows. Sometimes, as in the Tyrol, there is a third story of wood, while some of the modern houses are made entirely of timber. Most Austrians are Roman Catholics, which explains why their homes are decorated with bright paintings of the Virgin Mary or some favorite saint. There are often shrines beside the road, too.

Many of the finest composers in the world, including Haydn, Mozart, Schubert and the two Johann Strausses (father and son), were Austrians. The life of Vienna has also attracted other composers who were not of Austrian birth, such as Beethoven and Richard Strauss. There have been many great writers of books, plays and poetry. Austrian universities are famous and for a century and a half Vienna has been one of the world's great centers for science and medicine, as well as for art and music.

Farming, Mining, and Manufacturing

Although there are about 500,000 of the inhabitants of Austria at work on small farms, the soil is not rich enough to make farming very profitable. Nevertheless, with the help of fertilizers the land produces good crops of rye, oats, barley, wheat, potatoes, turnips, and sugar beet. Austrian wine is world famous and comes from vineyards between the Alps and the Danube. In recent years cattle breeding for meat and for milk has increased.

Millions of tourists, particularly from Germany and other European countries, come to Austria in summer to walk in the lovely alpine scenery, and to ski in the mountains in winter. It is a major source of revenue for the country.

Courtesy, Austrian State Tourist Department

Pictorial Press

Left: Austrians dancing in their national costumes. **Right:** Typical Tyrolean building with murals and eaves.

Another valuable industry comes from its forests of spruce and pine. Timber, together with the sawmills and factories dealing with wood, provides many jobs for Austrians. Other important industries today are chemicals, clothing, leather goods, and musical instruments. Iron and steel are made at Linz and Donawitz where the Linz-Donawitz blast furnace process, used in many steel mills, was invented. Lignite (brown coal), iron ore, lead, zinc, copper, magnesite (used to make magnesium), graphite, and petroleum are all to be found in Austria. Water from the mountain lakes and streams yields electric power.

Among the most important towns of Austria are Innsbruck, set in the beautiful Tyrol mountains; Salzburg, the birthplace of Mozart and famed also for its castle and music festivals; and the industrial cities of Graz and Linz.

Vienna is an important center for industry, trade and communications. It is also the headquarters of several United Nations and other international agencies.

Austria After the Empire

When the Austro-Hungarian Empire (see AUSTRIAN EMPIRE) collapsed in 1918, three-quarters of its territory went to Czechoslovakia, Italy, Poland, Hungary, Romania, and Yugoslavia, and Austria itself was left in a powerless state. Prices rose so much that Austrian money became worthless and the nation bankrupt. Many people died of starvation in the desperate winter of 1920–21, and for several years the Austrians relied on loans from other countries.

At this time most of the German-speaking population of the broken up Austro-Hungarian Empire wanted to unite with Germany, but the Austrian government stood against this. The rise of Hitler (who was born in Austria), and Nazism in the 1930s, stirred up calls for an *Anschluss*, or link-up, between the two countries, and eventually, after an earlier attempted coup, revolt, and assassination of the Austrian chancellor, Dollfuss, Hitler and his troops invaded Austria and made it part of Germany in 1938.

So it was that Austria came into World War II on the side of Germany. The country suffered badly from the war, and some of it was turned into a wasteland when, towards the end of the war, the western Allies invaded from one side and the Russians from the other. An estimated 160,000 Austrians died in the war.

After Germany had been defeated in 1945, Austria was separated from it again. Austrians suffered difficult post-war years as their country was divided into four zones occupied by troops of the United States, Great Britain, France, and the USSR. Gradually, however, the country recovered from the effects of the war and in 1955 it was at last agreed that all foreign troops should be withdrawn. Austria became an independent republic with its boundaries of 1938 reinstated. The Austrian parliament also passed a law proclaiming Austria's permanent future neutrality.

FACTS ABOUT AUSTRIA

AREA: 83,855 square kilometers (32,376 square miles)
POPULATION: 7,554,000 (1987)
GOVERNMENT: Republic with a federal structure.
CAPITAL: Vienna, which has a fifth of the country's population.
GEOGRAPHICAL FEATURES: The country includes much of the mountainous territory of the eastern Alps as well as parts of the Pannonian plains.
CHIEF EXPORTS: Iron ore, steel, timber and wood pulp, manufactured goods, machinery.
IMPORTANT TOWNS: Vienna, Graz, Linz, Salzburg, Innsbruck, Klagenfurt, Bregenz, Eisenstadt.
EDUCATION: Children must attend school between the ages of 6 and 15.

AUSTRIAN EMPIRE. Nowadays Austria is a comparatively small country but for hundreds of years the Austrian empire covered most of the central part of Europe.

The Habsburg family held lands for 400 years which from 1806 to 1867 were known as the Austrian Empire.

A map of Europe just before 1914 showed almost the whole of central Europe as one single state called Austria-Hungary. In 1815, when it was even larger, the same state existed and was then called the Austrian Empire. For hundreds of years before that, all these lands were the same color on the map and were called the lands of the House of Habsburg—that is, lands that belonged to the Habsburg family. (Habsburg was the name of the family castle in Switzerland.)

Now this great state is in fragments. One bit is Austria; another is Czechoslovakia; a third is Hungary; and parts of it are in Italy, Romania, Yugoslavia, and Poland.

How the Empire Grew

Although people have puzzled a great deal about why this huge empire fell to pieces, the explanation is not really difficult. It began as a collection of lands which belonged to the family of the Habsburgs. The inhabitants of the empire had nothing in common except for the fact that they were all ruled over by the Habsburgs. However, when people began to be interested in their own special nations, the peoples of the Austrian empire realized that they were not "Austrians" at all but Germans, or Czechs, or Croats, or Magyars (Hungarians). The Germans began to want to rule themselves, the Magyars wanted to rule themselves, and so on. The history of the Austrian empire is really the story of a single family, the Habsburgs; it is not the history of a single people such as the English or the French.

The original "Austria" was just a small duchy (this means "land ruled by a duke") by the River Danube, with Vienna as its capital. The first of the Habsburg family to rule it was Rudolf; in 1273 he was elected Holy Roman Emperor and was also made Duke of Austria, which meant that his position as emperor was stronger. (There were many separate states in the Holy Roman Empire with their own rulers, and these rulers elected the emperor, see HOLY ROMAN EMPIRE.)

In 1438 another Habsburg, Albert II, was elected Holy Roman Emperor. In 1440 Frederick III was elected. From this time until the Holy Roman Empire came to an end in 1806, every emperor except two was a member of the Habsburg family. During the whole of this period of nearly 400 years, Austria was a private possession belonging to the Habsburg family and there was still no "Austrian Empire".

The Habsburgs were always seeking new lands in order to make themselves stronger. One of the ways in which they gained new possessions was by marrying princesses who inherited their father's kingdoms, which then became Habsburg property. Spain, Bohemia, Hungary, the Netherlands, and parts of Italy were gradually added to the family lands, and the family also owned parts of Germany.

The Habsburgs were very keen Roman Catholics and were often at war with the Protestants in the German states. In 1618 the Protestants of Bohemia rebelled against their rulers and asked the German Protestants to help them. This was the beginning of the Thirty Years' War, which at first was between the Habsburg emperor and the German Protestants. Later Sweden and France came in on the German side. In 1648 peace was made without either side being victorious. (See THIRTY YEARS' WAR.)

Trying to Make a United Empire

In 1740 Maria Theresa, became ruler of the lands of the Habsburgs. Though other princes claimed that some or all of the lands belonged to them, Maria Theresa managed to hold on to nearly all of them after two long wars. However, she had to give up the state of Silesia to Frederick the Great of Prussia.

Maria Theresa was the first Habsburg ruler who tried to rule the lands as one empire instead of as a collection of single kingdoms and states. She needed a very strong army and she only obtained this by recruiting soldiers from all the different states.

Her son, Joseph II, went on with the work of trying to unite all the Habsburg lands. He tried to get rid of the differences between the various states and to rule them all from Vienna with the same laws. This, however, did not please the states themselves, and there was a rebellion in Hungary. All the same, the separate lands went on being run as a single organization.

Joseph's nephew Francis II was the last of the Holy Roman Emperors. By his time, the Holy Roman Emperor did not have any real power at all, and so in 1804 Francis decided to change his title and call himself Emperor of Austria. Two years later the Holy Roman Empire came to an end because of the conquests of Napoleon (see NAPOLEON I).

From now on, the lands that Francis ruled were the Austrian empire. He lost many lands during the wars with Napoleon, but got most of them back when the wars ended. He gave up the southern Netherlands, but took Venice instead.

Changes and Revolutions

The chancellor, or foreign minister, of Austria from 1809 was Metternich. Since the French Revolution, new ideas had been developing in Europe which Metternich thought were very dangerous to the Austrian empire. The idea of freedom for the people was one of these; another was the idea of nationalism, or the belief that the people of one nationality should govern themselves and not be ruled by another nation. It is not difficult to understand why Metternich thought this idea was so dangerous when one remembers that the Austrian empire ruled people of several different nations. He tried hard to keep these ideas out of Austria, and for more than 30 years succeeded, until in 1848 there were revolutions in every part of the Austrian empire. The Austrian army managed to put an end to them all, except in Hungary where they had to ask for help from the tsar of Russia.

Francis Joseph, whose reign lasted until 1916, became emperor during the revolutions, and all the time he tried to keep the peoples of his empire quiet without letting them break up the empire. Because of two defeats by foreign armies, however, he had to give up his lands in Italy and Germany.

In 1867 he came to an agreement with the Hungarians. They were to have their own parliament and government, while in exchange they agreed to one army for the whole empire. Then the name of the whole state was changed to Austria-Hungary.

The German-speaking Austrians and the

Hungarians ruled the empire, but the other races and groups then became discontented and demanded states of their own.

On 28 June 1914, Francis Ferdinand, the heir to the Habsburg throne, was murdered by a Serbian assassin. The Austrian government blamed Serbia, and a war began which turned into World War I.

The Austrian armies were defeated and in 1918 the various peoples of the empire broke away and became independent. All that was left was Austria, and it threw off the rule of its emperor and became a republic. Early in 1919 the emperor Charles left his country, and the empire of the Habsburgs had come to an end, although the Habsburg family still exists.

AUTOBIOGRAPHY see BIOGRAPHY AND AUTOBIOGRAPHY.

AUTOGYRO see HELICOPTER.

AUTOMOBILE see MOTOR VEHICLE.

AVALANCHE. When great masses of ice, snow, rocks or soil crash down the side of a mountain, the result is an avalanche. People who live at the foot of steep, snow-covered mountains are always in danger from sudden avalanches, which hurtle down with tremendous force and a roar like thunder. Everything in their path is swept away—people, buildings, trees and animals. They may travel at 90 meters per second (over 200 miles an hour). The level of a narrow valley may be raised hundreds of feet by the material from a single slide.

Avalanches may occur for different reasons and at different times of the year. The commonest type is rather like a landslip, and it happens in the spring. The melting snow makes the slopes slippery and thousands of tonnes of snow, rocks and soil are carried down by their own weight. This leaves an ugly scar on the face of the mountain. In some places a very small movement, or even a sound, is enough to start loose snow crashing down. Alpine guides often tell climbers to be absolutely silent when they are near such dangerous spots.

The ice avalanche occurs only in the summer. The heat causes great blocks of ice to break away from the end of a glacier and these thunder down into the valley. This often happens on the steep slopes of the Jungfrau in Switzerland.

Powder avalanches are usually caused by strong winter winds which take hold of the dry, powdery snow on steep mountains and whirl it downwards. They are so violent that trees are

Frank Lane Picture Agency

Avalanches can be controlled by triggering them off artificially. This avalanche took place in Colorado, USA, and was set off by an explosive charge dropped by helicopter. In this way the avalanche was released before it became too large to be managed and at a time when there was no danger of anyone being injured.

uprooted and carried down like matchsticks. But often the avalanche itself causes the wind, and then it is the wind that does the damage to houses. In one instance, an avalanche stopped about 200 meters (200 yards) away from a group of 30 small buildings, but the buildings were destroyed by the wind.

In places where people live, trees are sometimes planted close together to stop large masses of snow collecting. Sometimes men start small avalanches deliberately by firing a gun. This is to loosen the snow mass and make it fall before it becomes too big.

See also LANDSLIP.

AVERAGES see STATISTICS.

AVIATION, HISTORY OF. Men were inspired to fly by watching the birds with envy and curiosity. From early times every race had its myths of flight. Most of those who actually tried to fly were tower-jumpers, wearing crude wings. In the 15th century AD, Leonardo da Vinci gave serious scientific thought to the problems of mechanical flight. Only slowly was it realized that a man's muscles were incapable of supporting his weight in the air.

Rather unexpectedly, *aerostation*, or floating flight, appeared before winged flight. In 1783 the French brothers Joseph and Étienne Montgolfier invented the hot-air balloon, which was raised by lighting a fire underneath to fill it and hanging a brazier in its neck to keep the air hot during the flight. You can read more about the history of hot-air ballooning in the article BALLOON. This article deals with the history of winged mechanical flight.

The First Airplanes

The scientific foundations of aviation, or heavier-than-air flight, were laid between 1799 and 1809 by an English baronet, Sir George Cayley, who went on with his experiments until 1853. Cayley realized that the lift essential for successful flight must come from the action of air upon a flat, inclined (sloping) surface, like that of a kite. He built excellent models and full-size gliders, but only once sent

Authenticated News

German scientist Otto Lilienthal built and flew several gliders, including this biplane, in the early 1890s.

up a man—his coachman—in one of the full-size machines (1853). Inspired by Cayley, W. S. Henson, another Englishman, designed a monoplane which he called an aerial steam carriage (1842–43). Although only unsuccessful models of it were built, it was a brilliantly prophetic idea.

During the second half of the 19th century, many talented men in Britain and France designed all kinds of flying machines and made many successful models powered by steam, clockwork, elastic, and compressed air. One or two full-size airplanes were built and

Courtesy, The Aeronautic Archives of the Institute of Aerospace Sciences

Orville and Wilbur Wright's modified No. 3 glider flew at Kill Devil Hill, North Carolina, in 1902.

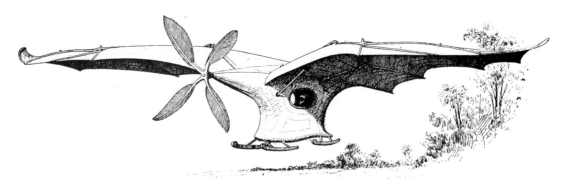

The *Oiseau* (Bird) was a heavier-than-air flying machine designed in the 1890s by Clément Ader of France.

tested but they could not fly. In 1890, however, the French inventor Clement Ader just managed to leave the ground for a few seconds in his steam-driven machine.

Meanwhile many inventors had tried to fit engines to balloons to make them dirigible (that is, capable of being propelled in any direction), and in 1852 the French engineer Henri Giffard made the first airship—steam driven—which could travel in calm weather under its own power, but only just. In 1884 two other Frenchmen, Charles Renard and A. C. Krebs, built a more workable airship driven by an electric motor and batteries, but aircraft of this kind were not really promising until the Lebaudy airship of 1903 and the Zeppelins of 1906 onwards. (See AIRSHIP.)

The German Otto Lilienthal was the first to make and fly successful gliders (1891–96). Supporting himself by his arms, he controlled the balance by swinging his body in the required direction. Lilienthal was killed while gliding in 1896. The American brothers Wilbur and Orville Wright, inspired by Lilienthal and encouraged by Octave Chanute (a follower of Lilienthal), decided in 1899 to master gliding before attempting powered flight. They flew three biplane gliders from the sand-hills near Kitty Hawk, North Carolina, and by 1902 had developed a fully practical biplane glider. It could be balanced and controlled in every direction, by combining the actions of warping (twisting) the wings and turning the rudder for lateral (sideways) control, and by using a

device called an elevator for up and down movements. All flight control today has developed from this 1902 Wright glider.

The Wrights next completed an entirely new biplane, with a 12-horsepower engine and two propellers—all designed and built by them— and made the world's first true powered, sustained and controlled flights on 17 December 1903, the best lasting for 59 seconds. By 1905, with their third "Flyer" (as they called their aircraft), they had the world's first practical airplane, which could be banked, turned, circled and flown easily for half an hour at a time.

News of the Wright gliders soon reached Europe and encouraged the French pioneers in their determination to fly. But progress was slow, and it was not until 1906 that the Brazilian Alberto Santos-Dumont, who lived in Paris, managed to make the first wavering flights of a few seconds in Europe. Not until Wilbur Wright came to Europe in 1908 did the Europeans learn to fly properly. Wilbur showed them the correct way to control and maneuver an airplane by his brilliant flying near Le Mans in France and in Rome. These flights attracted worldwide attention. One lasted 2 hours 20 minutes.

By 1909 the Europeans were catching up with the Wrights, and a number of excellent machines were flown at the first great air meeting at Reims, France, in August. These included the Antoinette and Bleriot monoplanes; a Bleriot monoplane had just been the first to cross the English Channel (25 July)

On 25 July 1909 Frenchman Louis Blériot prepared for the first airplane flight across the English Channel.

Mary Evans Picture Library

and had shown the world what aircraft could do. Among the biplanes, as well as the Wright machines, were the slow and steady Voisin and the two most popular of all, the American Curtiss and the new Henri Farman, which was French. The airplane was now accepted as the world's new vehicle; the best machines had a speed of some 60–70 kilometers (35–45 miles) per hour, they could carry a passenger, and they could stay up for two hours.

Many of these early designs appear very strange today. By 1910 designers realized that the most stable arrangement was a "tractor" engine in front of the wings, with the control surfaces at the tail. From then on, most planes developed along these lines.

The monoplane was very successful before World War I, although its fragile wings needed to be supported above and below by bracing wires. A series of accidents, caused by insufficient bracing, led to a decline in the monoplane's popularity. Tractor biplanes became the most widely used type and held this position for 25 years. Their two sets of wings, with struts in between, made a strong, box-like structure that was best suited to the wood and fabric materials of the period. Notable early designs were the Breguet in France and the Avro in Britain.

Aircraft in War

Between 1910 and 1914 civil airplanes were used mainly for sport, exhibitions of flying, and training. The military possibilites were soon seen and special military and naval air organizations formed. At this time, military airplanes were intended chiefly for reconnaissance, or scouting. However, there were many experiments in dropping bombs from airplanes and in arming them with machine guns. In North Africa during the war with Turkey of 1911–12, the Italians used airplanes for reconnaissance and bombing.

From the start of World War I in 1914, both sides soon found the value of aircraft for reconnaissance. Various forms of armament were tried and occasional dogfights took place between opposing airmen. However, it was some time before the vital importance of air fighting was understood. The Germans were the first to achieve this when they introduced the E.1 monoplane fighter designed by the Dutchman Anthony Fokker. The E.1 had a fixed machine-gun with an interrupter gear which allowed the gun to fire straight ahead through the tractor propeller without hitting the blades. The E.1 thus had an important advantage over Allied aircraft and it lost this only gradually as the Allies produced special-

Both spectators and aircraft makers enjoyed the novelty of the first air show, held at Reims in August 1909.

ized fighters, including pushers such as the British de Havilland D.H.2 and Farnborough F.E.2B, and tractors such as the French Nieuport 17 and British Sopwith Pup.

The struggle for command of the air continued throughout the war. Both sides produced more and better fighters. Amongst the most successful were the German Fokker D.VII biplane and the D.VIII monoplane, the British Farnborough S.E.5 and Bristol Fighter and French Spad 13 biplanes. These aircraft were mainly single-seaters, usually with two fixed machine-guns. They had maximum speeds of about 225 kilometers (140 miles) per hour and engines of up to about 300 horsepower. Designed chiefly for air fighting, they were also useful for ground attack and could thus play a part in the trench warfare which was the usual method of land fighting throughout World War I.

Reconnaissance, photography, and spotting for the artillery (that is, correcting the aim of the guns by signaling the fall of the shells) remained, however, the main air activities. These were usually performed by larger two-seater aircraft such as the French Breguet 14, German LVG and British RE8. Aircraft of this kind were also used for bombing, as also were larger multi-engined aircraft specially developed for the purpose, such as the Russian four-engined Sikorsky Ilia Mourometz biplane of 1913, the first successful large airplane. By 1918 there were four-engined bombers weighing 13 tonnes. However, most bombers—such as the German Gotha and the British Handley Page 0/400—were smaller, weighing 4.5 to 7 tonnes. They had cruising speeds of 100 to 110 kilometers (60 to 66 miles) per hour and the largest could carry 2,000 kilograms (4,410 pounds) of bombs for about 650 kilometers (400 miles).

The Germans used their Zeppelin airships

widely for bombing until these craft with their highly inflammable hydrogen gas proved too easy to shoot down in flames. They then developed larger bomber aircraft. The British recognized the possibilities of the bomber for attacking enemy factories, and formed special bomber forces for this purpose. In 1918 the Royal Air Force was formed as the first separate air service, ranking equally with the army and navy, to be set up by any major country.

Britain also played a leading part in the development of naval aircraft. Like the Germans, who used their Zeppelins, the Allies used airships—the simplest were the non-rigid "blimps"—for reconnaissance over the sea. However, the most important British effort was the large multi-engined flying boat, the first of which was developed from the American Curtiss designs. Britain also led the way in the development of ship-based aircraft and during the war produced (although too late for active service) the flush-deck aircraft carrier on which wheeled aircraft could take off and land.

Although the great wartime increases in engine power and aircraft size gave additional speed, load and distance, there was little advance in aircraft design in 1914–18. Almost all aircraft were still wire-braced tractor biplanes built mainly of wood, covered with linen fabric. In Germany, however, monoplanes which obtained part of their strength from coverings of wood or aluminum alloy, were developed and used in some numbers. These included the Fokker monoplanes with wooden wings and steel-tube fuselage and the all-metal corrugated-skin designs of Hugo Junkers. Also under development were the even more advanced, smooth stressed-skin, metal airplanes of Claudius Dornier and Adolf Rohrbach, which later set the fashion for the monoplanes of the 1930s.

Civil Aviation

In the years immediately following World War I, aircraft design seemed to make very little progress. By the Treaty of Versailles, Germany was forbidden to buy military aircraft and on the Allied side there was little money

Quadrant Picture Library/APL

Quadrant Picture Library/APL

Courtesy, The Boeing Company

Quadrant Picture Library/APL

Between the World Wars many civil aircraft went into operation. This illustration shows, from the top, (1) the Handley Page HP 42; (2) the Junkers Ju 52; (3) the Boeing 247; and (4) the Douglas DC2.

to spare for what many people still considered to be expensive playthings. Air forces were cut down to a fraction of their previous size and had to make do with machines left over from the war.

Some wartime pilots went into business as air-taxi operators, while others scratched a living giving 10-minute "joy-rides". A number of firms began to run regular passenger services, but they all used converted bombers like the de Havilland 4 and 9 and the Vickers Vimy. The Vimy was used for the first nonstop transatlantic flight by Alcock and Brown in 1919 and for the epic England-to-Australia flight by Ross and Keith Smith later the same year. These flights showed the possibilities of air travel, but for many years the regular commercial services only ran within Europe. In the United States the Post Office set up an air-mail service, flown by military pilots using converted de Havillands. In 1929 private companies took over the service and began carrying passengers.

As the airlines became established, they looked for safe, reliable aircraft to carry their passengers in reasonable comfort. Fokker had returned to Holland after the war and produced a series of high-wing wood and steel tube monoplane transports. Junkers continued his all-metal designs, the most famous of which was the Ju 52 of 1932. This was a three-engined transport which remained in civil and military service until well after World War II. Metal construction was adapted more and more, but many designers clung to the traditional biplane layout. In Britain this formula reached its conclusion in the stately Handley Page HP 42, a four-engined biplane introduced in 1930 which could carry up to 38 passengers for 480 kilometers (300 miles) at 160 kilometers (100 miles) per hour.

The method of making the fuselage, or body, as a smooth tapering tube of aluminum alloy had been tried in Britain, and was used in flying boats made by Dornier and Rohrbach. However, it was Boeing in the United States who in 1933 first took full advantage of this method of construction to produce their model 247, a twin-engined low-wing monoplane. The

247D could carry ten passengers for 1,200 kilometers (750 miles) at 300 kilometers (200 miles) per hour. It was the forerunner of all modern airliners, although it was overshadowed by the faster Lockheeds and the larger Douglas DC-2s that followed. These new airliners included many other improvements; they had wing flaps to reduce their landing speed, retractable undercarriages to reduce air resistance at cruising speed, variable-pitch propellers to improve the efficiency of their engines and superchargers to give better performance at height.

Wide World

In 1927 Charles Lindbergh made the first flight across the Atlantic from New York City to Paris, France. His aircraft was named the Spirit of St. Louis.

The new monoplanes could carry greater loads over longer distances, but as their weight increased, they needed larger airfields and hard runways instead of grass surfaces. Flying boats needed no runways and many of the long routes to Africa, the Far East, and across the Pacific were flown by large flying boats.

Many record-breaking flights by military aircraft and light airplanes like the British de Havilland Moth of 1925 pioneered new air routes and helped develop the reliability of aircraft. A small band of adventurous pilots, some of them women, performed remarkable feats of daring and endurance. Among the most famous flights of this kind was that of the young American, Charles Lindbergh, who flew

The history of aviation during the period between the two World Wars featured many adventurous pilots, both men and women. Among the most famous of the ladies who took to the air was the English pilot Amy Johnson. In 1930 she became the first woman to fly from England to Australia alone. She also flew solo to South Africa and Japan.

BBC Hulton Picture Library

non-stop from New York to Paris in 1927 in a small Ryan monoplane. The competition of the Schneider Trophy races and the England-to-Australia race of 1934 encouraged the development of new high-performance aircraft.

World War II (1939–45)

Although the United States, thanks to such notable designers as John K. Northrop, was first with the large-scale use of all-metal monoplanes, other countries soon followed. By 1939 most front-line fighters and bombers were clean-looking monoplanes with enclosed cockpits and retractable undercarriages. In 1933, Russia produced the Polikarpov I-16, one of the first effective monoplane fighters, and tested it during the Spanish Civil War (1936–39). However, it was the British and the Germans, with types like the Hawker Hurricane, Supermarine Spitfire and Messerschmitt 109, who produced the most efficient fighters, with top speeds of up to 560 kilometers (350 miles) per hour. The British pioneered the use of very heavy armament by fitting eight machine-guns in their fighters and four-gun power-operated turrets in heavy bombers like the Avro Lancaster.

The Germans concentrated on aircraft to support their armies, and to begin with favored the dive bomber (which had been first developed by the United States navy in the late 1920s). They also led in employing troop-carrying aircraft and gliders and in the use of parachute troops. The Russians also used most of their air forces in direct support of their armies and pioneered the use of anti-tank rockets.

The British, joined in due course by the Americans, paid more attention to the strategic bombing of the enemy's cities, industries, and transportation. The Royal Air Force, using its heavy bombers and the fast, unarmed de Havilland Mosquitos, concentrated on night bombing while the Americans attacked by day, using vast formations of Boeing B-17s, escorted by long-range fighters. Throughout the war, radar (which was developed separately by the British and the Germans) played a vital part in the aerial battles, by enabling fighters and bombers to find their targets at night and in bad weather. At sea, flying boats and long-range shore-based aircraft helped defeat the German U-boats.

In the Far East, the Japanese had built powerful air forces and concentrated on a carrier-based naval air arm, which was used with devastating effect on the United States naval base at Pearl Harbor in 1941. The war in the Pacific was marked by a series of great naval battles in which carrier-borne aircraft played an important role. Finally, long-range, land-based Boeing B-29 bombers attacked Japan itself, delivering the atomic bombs on Hiroshima and Nagasaki, which brought the war to an end.

Post-War Progress

World War II brought about increases in the size and power of aircraft. By 1945 fighters

Quadrant Picture Library

The X-15 was a supersonic rocket-powered aircraft of the 1960s. It set world speed and altitude records.

such as the North American Mustang could fly at around 720 kilometers (450 miles) per hour and, carrying external "drop-tanks" of fuel, travel non-stop for 3,000 kilometers (1,900 miles). Bombers carried bomb loads of 10 tonnes and reconnaissance aircraft could climb to an altitude of well over 12,000 meters (39,500 feet).

Both Germany and Britain developed jet engines, but the Germans flew the first successful jet aircraft (the Heinkel 178) in 1939, and their Messerschmitt 262 jet fighter went into service before the British Gloster Meteor. Germany also pioneered the use of pilotless bombers and built the first long-range missile, the V2, which had a range of about 300 kilometers (200 miles). After the war, a number of German scientists and engineers went to the Soviet Union or the United States and helped build up their space research programs, using the V2 as a starting point.

The first rocket aircraft, the Heinkel 196 of

1938, led to the first (and so far the only) operational rocket fighter, the Messerschmitt, which was used in 1944. After the war, the United States built a series of rocket-powered research aircraft which were air-launched from high-flying aircraft. Of these, the Bell X-1 was in 1947 the first manned aircraft to travel faster than the speed of sound. The North American X-15 first flew in 1959 and in its later flights exceeded six times the speed of sound and reached heights above 80 kilometers (50 miles).

Near the speed of sound, air can no longer flow easily around the wings and fuselage of an aircraft. The X-1 used thin, straight wings, but German research during World War II had shown that the best solution was to use swept-back or triangular (delta) wings. The Russian MiG-15 and the United States F-86 Sabre and B-47, all of which first flew in 1947, set the fashion for a new generation of swept-wing fighters and bombers. The early swept-wing fighters like the F-86 and the Hawker Hunter only reached supersonic speeds in a dive, but later types such as the British Aircraft Corporation Lightning could reach 2,400 kilometers (1,500 miles) per hour in level flight and climb to 18,000 meters (59,000 feet). Bombers remained subsonic (flying at speeds below the speed of sound) for much longer. Bombers such as the Avro Vulcan and the Boeing B-52, carrying stand-off nuclear weapons, remained in service into the 1970s. Supersonic types such as the United States Convair B-58 Hustler, the French Dassault Mirage IV and the Russian Tu-22, rivaled the fastest fighters for speed.

The most successful modern military aircraft are multirole types that can combine the duties of strike, interception, and reconnaissance. Among the most successful of such aircraft have been the Russian MiG-21, the Dassault Mirage III, and the McDonnell F-4 Phantom of the United States.

Civil air transportation has developed rapidly and is now the most important method of long-distance passenger travel. Until the late 1950s most airliners were piston-engined, following the pattern of the successful American monoplanes of the 1930s. Then larger, four-engined types like the Douglas DC-4, DC-6 and DC-7 and the Lockheed Constellation series, were introduced.

During the 1950s a number of turbo-prop airliners came into service. These included the British Vickers Viscount, one of the few foreign aircraft to be widely used in the United States. The greatest change in civil aviation, however, came with the introduction of jet airliners, which set new standards of speed and comfort for air travelers. The first was the British de Havilland Comet, followed by the American Boeing 707, and the Douglas DC-8.

Short- and medium-range routes were taken over by smaller jets, such as the BAC One-Eleven, the Hawker Siddeley Trident and the Boeing 737. Many of these aircraft had their engines mounted at the rear of the fuselage, an idea first tried in the French Caravelle.

The huge Boeing 747 "jumbo jet" weighs over 300 tonnes (330 US tons) and can carry up to 500 passengers. The Lockheed C-5A Galaxy is a military transport, equally huge, which is designed to load heavy vehicles and bulky equipment through doors at the front and rear. The SST, or supersonic transport, offers even quicker journeys to air travelers. The BAC/Sud Aviation Concorde is a joint Anglo-French project, introduced in 1976, and carrying 128 passengers at twice the speed of sound. Its rival is the slightly faster, but smaller, Russian Tu-144.

Helicopters are now used throughout the world. They can land in places which conventional aircraft cannot reach and are invaluable for rescue duties. Early helicopters had a very limited lifting capacity but the Russians developed huge machines, like the Mi-10 weighing 40 tonnes (44 US tons). The even larger Mi-12 weighs 200 tonnes (220 US tons) and can carry a load of 40 tonnes.

Rivaling the helicopter in its ability to land in confined areas and on rough surfaces is the Vertical Take-Off and Landing (VTOL) air-

These six aircraft were among the earliest postwar civil aircraft. They are, from the top, the Fairchild Amphibian; the Boeing Clipper; the Douglas DC-3; the Douglas DC-6; the Lockheed Constellation; and the De Havilland Comet.

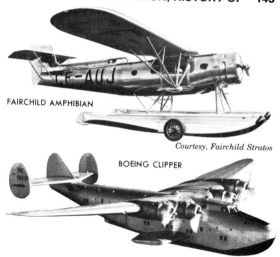

FAIRCHILD AMPHIBIAN

Courtesy, Fairchild Stratos

BOEING CLIPPER

Courtesy, The Boeing Company

DOUGLAS DC-3

Courtesy, Trans World Airlines

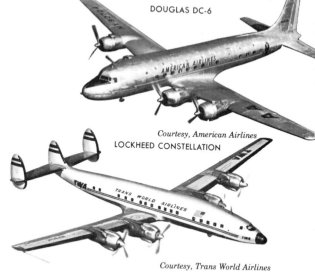

DOUGLAS DC-6

Courtesy, American Airlines

LOCKHEED CONSTELLATION

Courtesy, Trans World Airlines

DE HAVILLAND COMET

Courtesy, BOAC

craft. The world's first operational VTOL aircraft was the British Hawker Siddeley Harrier introduced in 1969. Some conventional aircraft are designed for Short Take-Off and Landing (STOL).

Another development is the variable geometry or "swing-wing" aircraft. The wings can be swept back for high speed flight and spread out for economical cruising and slow landing. The first operational swing-wing aircraft was the General Dynamics F-111. The United States used the knowledge it gained from the flights of such rocket-planes as the X-15 to develop the space shuttle. Unlike earlier spacecraft, which could be used only once, the shuttle was intended to be re-usable. It could re-enter the atmosphere and, using its delta wings, glide down to make a ground landing, like a conventional aircraft.

The space shuttle came into regular service in the 1980s. A mid-air explosion in 1986 destroyed one of the space shuttle vehicles, killing its crew of seven astronauts. This tragic accident held up progress on the shuttle's development for a time. (See ROCKET.)

An exciting development stemming from the use of the space shuttle is the rocket plane. Scientists in Britain and the United States were already working on this project in the 1980s. They hoped that early in the 21st century these would be the craft that could take off and land like an airplane but spend part of the flight in orbit around the Earth. With such a vehicle a flight from London to Sydney might take only 40 minutes.

AVIGNON is a famous ancient French town on the River Rhône in the southeast of the country. Originally a stronghold for local tribes, it became a Roman city, Avennio. But Avignon really came to prominence in the 14th century, when the Pope left Rome because of troubles there, and made Avignon the seat of the Popes from 1309 to 1377.

Their great palace on the Rocher des Doms still towers above the narrow streets, as do the walls which surround the town. The fast-flowing Rhône has washed away most of the famous 12th-century bridge, St. Bénézet. This

bridge has become the subject of a famous folk-song which children all over the world know.

> Sur le pont d'Avignon
>> On the bridge of Avignon
> L'on y danse, l'on y danse,
>> People dance and dance,
> Sur le pont d'Avignon
>> On the bridge of Avignon
> L'on y danse tous en rond.
>> We all go dancing around.

And local people did once dance there, but actually underneath the bridge, on a small river islet. A modern suspension bridge further down the Rhône now takes all the traffic.

Avignon is now the market center of the lower Rhône, and local industries make fabrics, leather, oil, soap, and fine French wines.

AVOCADO is the round, oblong or pear-shaped fruit of the *Persea americana*, a tree

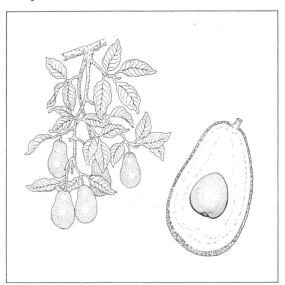

An avocado fruit has an outer skin; an edible pulp, which is full of vitamins; and an inner seed, or stone.

that is native to Mexico and to the areas southward to Colombia in South America. It belongs to the laurel family. The three main varieties of avocados are Mexican, Guatemalan, and West Indian.

In the 16th century, Spanish explorers found the avocado fruit a favorite food among the lowland Indians of tropical America. The Aztec name for the fruit was *ahuacatl*, which the Spanish pronounced *aguacate*. It has become known since as the avocado in English-speaking countries.

Avocados weigh up to 1.8 kilograms (4 pounds). The fruit is sometimes called the alligator pear, probably because the skin usually is tough, but in some varieties it may be as thin as that of an apple. The color ranges from green, maroon, or brown to purplish-black. Beneath the skin is a layer of greenish-yellow pulp that is soft and meaty and has a delicate flavor. In the center is a large seed. The pulp has a large fat content and is high in food value. Avocados are commonly eaten in salads. They are also used as a flavoring for soups or as spreads.

The avocado tree is a thickly leaved evergreen, which occasionally reaches 18 meters (60 feet) high and serves as an excellent shade tree. One tree may produce as many as 3,000 fruits in a season. The trees require a warm climate. In the United States they are cultivated in Florida, California, and Hawaii. The other main center of cultivation is around the Mediterranean, Israel being a top producer.

AVOCET is the name of several species of shorebirds (*Recurvirostra*). The scientific name describes the unusual, long, and upward-curved beak. They live in fresh and salt marshes where they eat small animals such as crustaceans, fishes, and also plant material found at or near the water surface. When feeding, they wade through the shallows with the partly-open bill held just below the surface. The bill is swept from side to side in an arc of about 50 degrees. When they have collected sufficient material they raise the bill to swallow the food. They often feed in a line.

Avocets are attractive-looking birds. During the breeding season the American species (*Recurvirostra americana*) has a pinkish-brown head and neck. It is about 45 centimeters (18 inches) long. It nests in the western United States and winters as far south as Guatemala.

The European avocet (*Recurvirostra avosetta*) has black and white plumage. In Britain it is an uncommon nesting bird and forms the

Eric Hosking
Avocets at the nest. Notice their long, upcurving beaks.

symbol of the Royal Society for the Protection of Birds. In winter large numbers of avocets are found in Africa's Rift Valley region. The Australian avocet (*Recurvirostra novaehollandae*) has a reddish-brown head and neck. Its alarm call is like a puppy's bark followed by a whistle.

AVON is a county in the southwest of England, bordering on Gloucestershire to the north, Wiltshire to the east and Somerset to the south. On the west is the estuary of the River Severn, leading to the Bristol Channel and the Atlantic Ocean. To the east and northeast are the Cotswold Hills and to the southwest are the Mendip Hills. These hills form a roughly semicircular rim of highland facing towards the Bristol Channel. The county lies largely within the enclosed lowland. Avon is 1,346 square kilometers (520 square miles) in area and has a population of 939,800 (1984). The River Avon finds its outlet at Avonmouth on the Severn estuary, and at Clifton, near Bristol, the river has cut through steep cliffs to form the famous Avon Gorge.

Avon is mainly an agricultural county, with many dairy farms. It has a rich wildlife. The island of Steep Holme in the Bristol Channel is a nature reserve and bird sanctuary. It is the only place in Britain where wild peonies grow. Inland, the rare buzzard may be seen over the hills.

The main cities are Bristol and Bath, both

of which have universities. Bath is not far from the Wiltshire border. Its hot springs made it a famous spa and it has a long history. Visitors to Bath admire the fine Georgian buildings (see BATH). On the Avon coast are vacation resorts such as Weston-super-Mare and Clevedon. Weston-super-Mare was originally a small fishing village. It developed into a health resort and vacation town in the 1800s. To the north of the town, at Worlebury Hill, is the site of a large Iron Age fortification.

Around Bristol are many industries (see BRISTOL). Near the port of Avonmouth is a large chemical works, and at Filton is the factory which manufactured the Concorde airliner. Other industries in and around Bristol include engineering, paper-making, and the processing of chocolate and tobacco. Limestone and clay are extracted in the southeast of the county and fuller's earth (which is used in insecticides) is found near Bath.

Avon was formed in 1974 from parts of Somerset and Gloucestershire, together with the county boroughs of Bath and Bristol.

AVON, 1st Earl see EDEN, ANTHONY.

AXOLOTL (*Ambystoma mexicanum*) is the name given to an unusual, tailed amphibian which lives in cold-water lakes around Mexico City in Central America. It is closely related to salamanders and newts, and belongs to a group known as mole salamanders (see SALAMANDER).

The axolotl grows to about 25 centimeters (10 inches) long, although about half of this is tail. It has a broad head with three pairs of feathery gills that are used to obtain oxygen from the water in which the axolotl spends its entire life. The body is rounded, with two pairs of short, weak legs, and the tail has a fin-like fringe running along the top and bottom surfaces.

Most axolotls are dark brown in color and patterned with black speckles, but white ones do exist and are often seen in aquariums.

The axolotl is unusual because it never really grows up. Other adult salamanders lose their gills and live part of their lives on dry land, but axolotls remain in the water for their

The axolotl reproduces as a juvenile and will only grow into an adult in unusual conditions.

entire life. Another strange thing about it is that it can breed as a "youngster". Axolotls have an elaborate courtship display, after which the male releases a small packet containing his sperm. This is then picked up by the female and used to fertilize the eggs inside her body. A string of eggs is laid, each inside a ball of clear yolk, which sticks to water plants. Young axolotls, or larvae, hatch from the eggs after two weeks and look like tiny copies of their parents. The larvae feed on very small water animals and after about six months are large enough to begin breeding themselves.

A Strange Life

The axolotl was once thought of as a unique amphibian because it could breed as a larva, but in 1865 French scientists discovered that it could change into the adult form if it is kept in warm water. Once adult, the axolotl looks very much like a tiger salamander (*Ambystoma tigrinum*) that can live on land as well as in water.

In nature, the remarkable change happens when, for example, the lake in which it lives dries out. As the lake gets shallower, the sun heats up the water which causes the axolotl to change into the adult form. This helps the axolotl survive because the adult can live on land, the larval form cannot.

In the laboratory, axolotls have been made to change body form by putting them in different situations, such as starving them of food and changing the acidity of the water. These "stress" conditions stimulate the axolotl's body to make a chemical called thyroxine, a growth hormone (see HORMONE). Axolotls can be made to change into adults by simply injecting them with high concentrations of this hormone. Some other cold-water salamanders respond to the same treatment. However, there are salamanders such as the European olm (*Proteus anguinus*) that have never developed into the adult form.

AYERS ROCK is a huge, steep-sided outcrop of bare red sandstone in the Northern Territory, Australia. The nearest town, Alice Springs, is about 443 kilometers (275 miles) to the northeast. The rock, the remains of an ancient mountain, measures about 8 kilometers (5 miles) around the base and rises 348 meters (1,142 feet) above the surrounding plain. Its color varies as the light changes, especially at sunrise and sunset.

Ayers Rock was named in 1873 after the then prime minister of South Australia, Sir Henry Ayers. The Australian Aborigines, who have lived in the area for thousands of years, call it Uluru, meaning "great pebble". To them Uluru is sacred and it features in their beliefs about the Creation. Cave-paintings in the rock depicting epic journeys made by their ancestors have a religious importance.

Ayers Rock lies within the Uluru National Park and is a major tourist attraction. In 1985 the Australian government handed over the title deeds to the park to its traditional Aboriginal owners, who then leased it back for 99 years to the Australian National Parks and Wildlife Service. There is a photograph on page 111 of this volume.

AZALEA is one of several species of *Rhododendron* of the heather family. They are native to hilly regions of North America and Asia. Most grow in woods and on rocky banks, as well as in swampy, shady places. The azalea shares the rhododendron's need for peaty soil and dislike of lime. (See RHODODENDRON.) Most azaleas are sweet-smelling and in spring or summer the little bushes are covered with bunches of flowers of all shades of pink, gold, flame, and orange, and also white. Well-

known American kinds include the smooth or sweet azalea (*Rhododendron arborescens*), a fragrant white-flowering shrub that grows to 6 meters (20 feet) high.

The Japanese were growing dwarf azaleas in pots by a secret method 1,000 years ago. The "Indian" azalea was brought back from China by the Dutch in 1680. Many European shrubs have been developed from this, and one of them is the national flower of Belgium. The Common Yellow seen in Britain comes from near the Black Sea.

AZERBAIJAN. Azerbaijan Soviet Socialist Republic is one of the 15 republics of the Union of Soviet Socialist Republics. It is bordered by the Russian Soviet Federated Socialist Republic to the north, by the Georgian and Armenian Soviet Socialist Republics to the west, and by Iran to the south. The Caspian Sea lies on Azerbaijan's east coast. A portion of the Armenian S.S.R. divides Azerbaijan into two parts. The southern part is the Nakhichevan Autonomous Soviet Socialist Republic.

The area has a history that dates back to pre-Christian times. Up to the 19th century it had been dominated at various times by Arabs, Persians, Turks, and Mongols. The part of the region that today makes up the republic was incorporated into the Russian Empire in the early 19th century. It became a union republic in 1936.

The large plain of the River Kura forms the

Novosti Press Agency

Azerbaijan riders in traditional dress compete in this Russian equestrian game of skill and daring.

heart of the republic. The edges of the flat plain are rimmed by rugged mountains. In the north are the southeastern hills of the Great Caucasus range of the Caucasus Mountains. South and west of the plain is the Lesser Caucasus range and the Armenian Highland (see CAUCASUS MOUNTAINS). To the south is the Talysh range of the Elburz Mountains. A narrow lowland runs along the republic's Caspian coast. The mountains shelter the land from northern cold air masses and from moisture-carrying west winds.

The Azerbaijanis belong to a Turkic race. They make up about two-thirds of the republic's total population. The rest of the population mostly consists of Russians and Armenians. By tradition, the Azerbaijanis are Shiite Muslims. Many of their religious customs, however, have been weakened by Soviet government pressure.

Most of the flat grassland is widely used for grazing cattle, sheep, and other livestock. Irrigated fields in the lowlands produce high quality cotton, rice, and alfalfa (lucerne). Winter wheat, grapes, and tobacco are important crops in the valleys and foothills. In the moist climate around Lenkoran, tea, oranges, lemons, figs, and other subtropical crops grow without irrigation.

The republic's major resource is petroleum. At one time the area produced about half of the world's oil. Natural gas and oil from Azerbaijan remains important to the Soviet economy, although the republic's production has been surpassed by that of the Volga-Urals area. Most of the petroleum is refined at Baku, which is the capital and the country's largest city. Exported oil is transported by pipeline to Batumi, Georgian S.S.R., on the Black Sea. Azerbaijan also has important textile, metal refining, and fishing industries.

Azerbaijan, like other Soviet Socialist Republics, is controlled by the Communist party. The Supreme Soviet of Azerbaijan is the chief legislative body. It has some 400 deputies, elected for two-year terms. The chairman of the council of ministers heads the government. The population is more than 6,399,000 (1983).

AZORES. The Azores are a group of nine islands and a few rocks lying out in the Atlantic about 1,290 kilometers (800 miles) from Portugal, to which they belong. They are actually the visible peaks of the massive underwater Mid-Atlantic Ridge (see ATLANTIC OCEAN). This is a region prone to earthquakes, and only 30 years ago a volcanic eruption increased the size of Faial—one of the nine islands.

Most of the islands rise steeply from a rocky, pebbly shore to heights reaching over 2,000 meters (6,500 feet) on Picó. The generally hot climate allows many fruits to grow, and pineapples, particularly, are a major export of the islands.

The central islands include Graciosa, Terceira, Faial, São Jorge and mountainous Picó. Further east lie Flores and the smallest island Corvo. At the western end is São Miguel with the largest population of over 130,000 and the biggest town Ponta Delgada. Below São Miguel is Santa Maria. The total population is around 250,000.

The Azores were uninhabited when the Portuguese discovered them in about 1427. Shortly afterwards they began to settle on the islands, and trade with Portugal became well established. From 1580 to 1640 the Azores were ruled by Spain and were a rendezvous for the treasure fleets on their voyage home from the West Indies. The Azores became an area of sea warfare, as Britain, who was at war with Spain, sent ships to intercept these gold- and silver-laden vessels.

Today the islands are ruled as three districts named after the ports of Angra (on Terceira), Ponta Delgada (on São Miguel) and Horta (on Faial). The Azores also provide an important United States military air base. Population 250,699 (1984).

AZTECS. These were one of the most important peoples of ancient America before the continent was discovered by Christopher Columbus in 1492. They called themselves the Mexica or Tenochca, and they lived in the valley on the central plateau where Mexico City now stands. No one knows exactly where they came from but according to their legends, they left their home on Aztlan, a lake island, somewhere in the north, and probably arrived in the valley of Mexico in the 12th or 13th century.

At the time of their arrival, they were an insignificant and weak tribe who survived by hunting and gathering, fishing, and trading. They settled on a marshy island near the edge of Lake Texcoco, which has now dried up. At first they had to pay money and goods as tribute to their more powerful neighbors to save themselves from being attacked. Gradually, they acquired more possessions by trading. But the main reason that they were successful was their great agricultural system and their schemes for reclaiming land. They obtained more land for farming, first by building small artificial islands, called *chinampas*, in the lake and then by conquering land around them. By 1325 they had started to build a great capital city on their island, calling this city Tenochtitlan (which came from their name *tenochca*, and meant "place of the cachis"). It was connected to the mainland by causeways, or roads raised above the water, and guarded by bridges which could be drawn up if the city were attacked. They extended the area of the city through land reclamation. It is estimated that 150,000 people lived there at one time. The only means of transportation were canoes, which taxied people about the city, and brought food and other goods from the neighboring states.

The Power of the Aztecs

The power of the Aztecs continued to grow. During the reign of their fourth king, Itzcoatl, from 1428 to 1440, they gave up paying the tribute of money and goods to other tribes, and were equal in power to the Texcocans, who had been the most important people in that part of the country before. The Aztecs soon became the leaders of the neighboring peoples and their conquests stretched up to what is now called Guatemala. They were the most densely populated state ever in Middle America.

The Aztecs grew richer and more powerful. By the 16th century, the city of Tenochtitlan had become the most splendid in all Mexico. Canals were made to make traveling between the different parts of the island easier, and houses and palaces were built. There was also a sacred enclosure which contained 25 pyramids. The main one of these, which was not finished until 1485 was the pyramid of Huitzilopochtli, built on a high platform, with steep stairways leading to the flat top where the altar and the idols stood. It was dedicated to the gods of rain and war.

The Aztecs were successful traders. Their chief trade articles were jade and other precious stones, feathers, and cocoa beans. They also managed to get many trade items from their vassals, who were obliged to pay tribute to them. The merchants in Aztec society occupied a special position of privilege: they lived in their own "suburb", and had their own god, Yacetecuhtli.

The Aztecs built great buildings and were able to carve huge pieces of stone with lifelike figures or strange designs. They were also clever at making smaller things, like miniature figures of men and animals carved in jade or crystal, or sacred masks covered with pearls

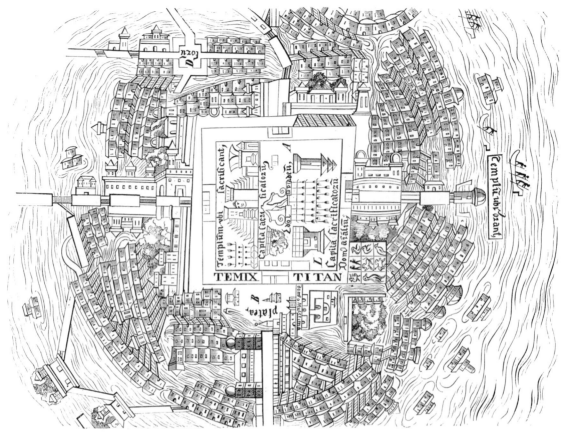

Tenochtitlán (Temixtitlán) was the capital city of the Aztecs and is now the site of Mexico City. This plan of it, published in 1524, was based on one drawn up in 1519–20 by the Spanish conqueror of the Aztecs, Hernán Cortes. Tenochtitlán was a huge city covering 13 square kilometers (5 square miles). It was built on two small islands in a lake and was connected to the mainland by causeways. In 1519 it had about 400,000 inhabitants, mostly traders, craftsmen, soldiers, priests, and administrators. Much trade with the surrounding district was carried on by canoe. The plan shows in the center the huge temple complex where human sacrifices were made to the Aztec gods. Within this area were three large pyramid temples and six smaller ones, accommodation for the priests, and a place where the heads of sacrificial victims could be displayed. There were also a sacred pool, a sacred grove, and open courtyards. To the east of the temple complex lay the *domus animalium*, the zoo kept by the Aztec emperor Montezuma. On the extreme right of the plan lies another large temple complex, which was used for religious ceremonies.

or precious stones. They made brightly colored pottery, and there was a flourishing cotton industry, producing fine clothes that were often decorated with gold, rare furs, and the bright feathers of tropical birds. Their musical instruments were pipes, trumpets, drums and rattles, and they probably sang or recited poetry at their festivals.

The Aztecs had no alphabet, but they kept records of their history in picture-writing (see illustration of Aztec picture-writing). The priests and priestesses ran schools to teach children of rich citizens, and they had hospitals staffed by doctors and surgeons. The Aztec astronomers knew enough to be able to say when eclipses of the sun or moon would happen, and they had an accurate and elaborate calendar which they developed. There were 52-year cycles called *xiuhmolpilli*, and Aztec legend prophesied the end of the world at the close of one of these periods. One of the most famous relics of the Aztecs is a carved calendar stone weighing about 20 tonnes. It was meant to depict the Aztec universe, and

Greenstone mask of the Aztec god Quetzalcoatl, the feathered serpent, wind god, and founder of Aztec kingship.

carved on it was the face of the Aztec sun god Tonatiuh. Another relic was the sacrifice stone, used for human sacrifice.

The Aztecs worshipped many gods whom they feared; many of them they borrowed from their neighbors. They thought that the gods, especially the terrible war god Huitzilopochtli, demanded the sacrifice of human beings. Sometimes thousands were necessary, and the priests would sacrifice prisoners captured in the wars by tearing out their hearts, which the gods were supposed to need as food. In fact, one reason for their military exploits was to have enough prisoners to sacrifice to the gods.

"The White God"

Just as the Aztecs were near the development of a great Mexican empire, under their ruler Montezuma II, their power was broken by the arrival of what they believed to be a "white god" from the East. This "god" was the Spanish captain Hernan Cortes, leading a small army of about 600 men, coming from the island of Cuba. Aztec legend and prophecy told of a white god who would someday return to them from the East and rule over them. Cortes took advantage of this Aztec belief. It helped him in his conquest of the Aztec confederacy, starting in 1519.

The beautiful city of Tenochtitlán, with its gleaming white temples and palaces, dazzled the eyes of the invading Spaniards. They found there shady parks and gardens rich with the rarest plants of the country. They found zoos containing the strange animals of Mexico. There were large, busy markets thriving on a brisk trade in food, clothing, and handicrafts which the Spaniards had never seen before. Tenochtitlan was as large and as beautiful a city as they had ever seen in Europe. They were astounded when they first saw it from the mountain heights surrounding the Valley of Mexico. It was a jewel city in a strikingly beautiful natural setting. It surpassed the wildest dreams of the European soldiers who were coming to conquer it.

The Spaniards were also amazed by the centrally controlled and efficient state organization. State schools trained all boys in the art of warfare; tax collectors collected taxes throughout the kingdom; civil and criminal laws were made and enforced, and wrong doers punished; while merchants traveling in foreign lands acted as government envoys and spies.

The Spaniards under Cortes, after much hard fighting, were finally able to destroy the Aztec power. They then made Mexico into a realm in the empire of Spain. They called the country of the Aztecs, New Spain. But even now, more than four centuries after this conquest, many Indians living in Mexico still speak the Aztecs' language. Modern Mexico and Mexicans are proud of their Aztec ancestry. They have preserved much of the way of living, eating, and dressing of Aztecs. Many Aztec words are still used in Mexico and they form an important addition to the Spanish language. Some of these words, such as *chocolate*, *tomato*, *ocelot*, *coyote*, and *avocado*, have also become part of the English language.

BAAL was any of many gods of the Canaanites and Phoenicians. The word "Baal" means lord. Baals were gods of the Semitic peoples, who lived in ancient times from Arabia to Syria. Some of the Baals were gods of the fields and sheepfolds. Prayers for fertility were offered and the first fruits of the harvest were given to their images. Other Baals were gods of the cities, and temples were built to them in Tyre, Sidon, and Carthage. The Carthaginian conquerors Hannibal and Hasdrubal took the endings of their names from Baal or Bal. Living among the Baal worshippers were the Jews, who worshipped a single God. Often they were attracted to the worship of a Baal. The Bible tells how some Jews prayed to Baalpeor in the desert and were killed by order of Moses. Solomon built a temple to a Baal in Jerusalem. Ahab and Jezebel tried to make Baal-worship the state religion. The prophet Elijah and later prophets, especially Hosea, denounced the ceremonies of Baal worship. Not until much later, in the Persian period, did this Semitic religion disappear.

Baalzebub, or Beelzebub, meaning "Lord of the Flies", is one such god mentioned in the Bible. Beelzebub has appeared in some well-known literary works. John Milton, in his long poem *Paradise Lost*, describes him as an angel fallen from Heaven, next in power to Satan "and next in crime". In the *Pilgrim's Progress*, by John Bunyan, Beelzebub is a devil who lies in wait for the pilgrim Christian on his journey, hoping to kill him with arrows.

BABBAGE, Charles (1792–1871). The British mathematician and inventor Charles Babbage is generally regarded as the father of the computer. He was born at Teignmouth, in the English county of Devon. In 1812, he helped to found the Analytical Society, an organization dedicated to the study of the latest European developments in mathematics. In 1816, Babbage was elected a Fellow of the Royal Society, and was one of the founder-members of the Royal Astronomical Society (1820), and the Royal Statistical Society (1824). In 1827 he was appointed Lucasian Professor of Mathematics in the University of Cambridge. This was a research post, which gave Babbage time to concentrate on his main area of interest, mechanical computation.

Babbage first thought about the possibility of manufacturing a mechanical calculating machine in about 1813. He made a small mechanical calculator that could work to eight places of decimals. In 1823, with the help of government funds, he developed a more advanced calculator that could work to 20 decimal places.

In the 1830s, Babbage developed plans for his so-called "analytical engine", the forerunner of the modern digital computer. This

National Portrait Gallery, London

Above: Charles Babbage, father of the computer. **Left:** This model of the Difference Engine was made in 1832. It was probably the world's first automatic calculator in that it could do a number of calculations without human aid (apart from having its handle turned).
Courtesy, IBM

machine was intended to be able to perform any arithmetical operation (multiplication, addition, subtraction, and division) by accepting instructions input from punched cards. The machine was also to have a "memory unit" for storing numbers, and was to possess many of the other features now found in computers of today. Babbage never built his "analytical engine" because the components he needed could not be made accurately enough. However, he became so absorbed in work on mechanical calculating machines that he spent his family fortune on the necessary research and development.

Babbage worked on other projects in both economics and technology. He helped to found the modern British postal system and invented a kind of speedometer. He wrote several influential books, but his work in the field of mechanical computation was forgotten until his unpublished notebooks came to light in 1937.

BABEL, TOWER OF. The Book of Genesis (chapter 11) in the Bible tells the story of the Tower of Babel. According to this story, after the Flood, when all the people of the Earth spoke the same language, they came to the plain of Shinar in Babylonia. Here they collected bricks and mortar to build a city and a tower whose top would reach to heaven. On seeing this, God knew that men were trying to make themselves equal with him, and he therefore made them speak different lan-

Courtesy, Kunsthistorisches Museum, Vienna; Mansell Collection photo

The building of the Tower of Babel as the Flemish artist Pieter Bruegel imagined it. He painted this in 1563.

guages so that they could not understand one another. As a result, the people were unable to go on with their building and many left Babylonia to settle around the world.

The city was called Babel, a name which comes from two words meaning "the gate of God". Because of the Bible story, the word is used today to mean noisy confusion.

The remains of several great towers built by the Babylonians have been discovered, but it is not known for certain which was supposed to be the Tower of Babel. Some people believe that it was the same kind of building as a ziggurat, which was a great tower built in seven huge steps with the shrine of the god on top.

BABOON. The baboon is a short-tailed monkey; the tail may be a mere stump. There are five species, or kinds; but the related forest-dwelling species, the drill (*Mandrillus leuco-*

Barnaby's

A female baboon with her baby. Baboons live in well organized social groups called troops.

pheus) and the mandrill (*Mandrillus sphinx*), are usually classed as baboons.

The typical baboon has a heavy body and its big head has large cheek pouches and a long, naked muzzle with the nostrils at the tip. Its canine teeth (that is, the pointed ones) are enormous and it has powerful limbs. Baboons go about in troops of up to 200 individuals led by one or more males. Large males are powerful animals and will defend the troop against their main enemies such as leopards and lions. The coat of hair is harsh and in the males may be long around the shoulders, forming a kind of cape, but the face, hands, feet, and behind are hairless. The males are much bigger than the females, which usually have their babies one at a time. The young stays with its mother for several months. At first it is carried in her arms or clings to her, but later rides on her back as she moves about with the band. Baboons breed successfully in zoos.

Baboons live mainly in the grassland and rocky regions of Africa south of the Sahara Desert, and in Arabia; they are seldom found in forests. They will eat almost anything and can be a menace to farm crops, but they prefer roots, peanuts, fruit, insects, and birds' eggs. They tear their food into pieces by hand and can store it in their cheek pouches. They are noisy, with an alarm call like a dog's bark, and they use grunts, squeals and chatterings— each with a distinct meaning—for communicating with one another, as well as signaling with their tails. Baboons are intelligent animals and can be trained.

The largest species is the dark-coated South African chacma (*Papio ursinus*) and the smallest the bright rust-colored Guinea baboon (*Papio papio*). The most striking is the hamadryas or sacred baboon (*Papio hamadryas*), with a long mane of hair and a bright-red, bare behind. It was worshipped by the ancient Egyptians, who also trained it to pick fruit for them.

BABY. A "baby" usually means a young human being, although the word is also used for the young of other animals—for example, a baby cat is a kitten. For humans we tend to use the word "baby" to cover the period of time spent developing in the mother's womb, then during birth, and up to about one year or 18 months old. After this words such as "toddler" and "child" are used. The word "baby" probably comes from "ba-ba", a sound made by many small babies (and their parents).

A loving relationship between mother (or caregiver) and baby is critical for the baby's future development.

The Baby in the Womb

A baby's life begins when it is conceived by its mother and father. As in other mammals, the egg cell, or *ovum*, of the mother is fertilized by a *sperm* cell from the father. The fertilized egg settles in the mother's womb, or *uterus*, and multiplies quickly (see CELL), and the main organs and body parts develop—the brain, heart, intestines, and lungs. At this stage of development, during the first eight weeks after fertilization, the baby is technically known as an *embryo*. It is smaller than a rice grain and looks something like a tadpole.

As the cells in the baby's body continue to multiply and become different, the baby becomes more like a tiny human being. After about 12 weeks, its arms, legs, hands and feet have formed, and the bones of the skeleton are developing. By 16 weeks virtually all of the body parts have formed—even the fingernails and toenails. At this stage the baby is 160 millimeters (7 inches) long. Between eight weeks after fertilization and birth, the technical term for the developing baby is a *fetus*.

While in the womb the baby floats in a pool of liquid that cushions and protects it. Inside the fluid, the baby cannot eat or breathe for itself. It gets its food and the oxygen it needs to live from its mother. The food and oxygen are dissolved in the mother's blood. They pass into the baby's blood inside a special organ called the *placenta* which develops in the wall of the womb. The baby's blood passes from its body along a "lifeline" called the *umbilical cord* to the placenta. Here it absorbs food and oxygen from the mother's blood and then flows back along the umbilical cord to nourish the baby's developing body.

The journey from inside the womb to the outside world is called birth. Most babies are born after about 40 weeks (roughly nine months) in the womb. This is only an average, however, and only 5 per cent of babies are born on the expected day. Around 85 per cent arrive in the two weeks before or the two weeks after the expected day. (See CHILDBIRTH.)

The earlier a baby is born, the smaller and less developed it is, and so it is less able to cope with the sudden changes to life outside the womb. Babies born earlier than 38 weeks may have trouble breathing and feeding, even with modern hospital care. Those born earlier than 28 weeks after fertilization have only a slim chance of surviving. A baby born earlier than usual is called *premature*; one born later than usual is called *postmature*.

Most mothers have only one baby at a time, but sometimes two babies (twins) and, more rarely, triplets, or quadruplets are born. It is very unusual for more than four babies to be born at one time, and if it does happen, the babies are so small that they rarely survive.

Immediately they arrive in the world, new-born babies take their first breath and begin to cry almost at once. They are perfectly formed but tiny human beings and usually weigh between 2 and 4 kilograms (4 pounds 6 ounces and 8 pounds 12 ounces). Premature babies may weigh 900 grams (2 pounds) or even less and have to be kept alive in a special apparatus called an incubator. If they are kept free from germs and are carefully fed, they can live and grow to a normal size.

The Newborn Baby

Newborn babies may seem helpless, but they are not. They can suck strongly to drink milk from their mother's breast. They cry if they are hungry or uncomfortable. They are startled by loud noises and sudden movements, throwing their arms and legs out and grasping with their fingers as if trying to hold on. They can see quite clearly, although they have not yet learned to make sense of all the bright colors and patterns after months in the darkness of the womb. They can hear well and usually recognize the voice of their mother, since they could hear her speaking while in the womb.

However, a newborn baby depends on some-one, usually the mother, for food and warmth and comfort. Like other newborn mammals, human babies feed on milk. Milk from the mother's breast is ideally suited to the baby's needs. But sometimes a mother is unable to feed her baby, perhaps for health reasons. In this case the baby can be fed with specially prepared *formula* milk powder. The powder is mixed with water and the baby sucks it through a rubber teat from a bottle.

Feeding and Teething

As a baby grows, milk alone is not enough. After several months the average baby needs some solid food—that is, not milk. These first solids are usually cereals, mixed vegetables, fruit, or other bland foods. These foods must be mashed into a pulp since the baby may not yet have any teeth with which to chew its food. Changing from milk feeding to eating solid foods is called weaning. Like so many aspects of a baby's growth and development, there is

Carlos Reyes/Andes Press Agency

Mothers register babies for treatment at a refugee camp in drought-stricken Sudan. Most suffer from malnutrition.

no "right" time for weaning. It depends on how the baby and mother are getting on. Some babies are weaned at a couple of months, others after a year or more.

A baby's first teeth usually appear about seven or eight months after birth. They are the eight front teeth or incisors. As they grow out of the gum they may make the baby uncomfortable. This is called teething, and some babies cry at this time. Once the first teeth have appeared, the baby can bite and chew its own food and gradually eat a more varied diet. The second batch of teeth, the four "cheek teeth", or molars, appear at about 12 months of age.

Growth and Development

Babies grow and change very quickly. By six months most babies have doubled their birth weight from around 3.5 kilograms (7 pounds 12 ounces) to 7 kilograms (15 pounds 10 ounces). At one year old they may weigh 10 kilograms (22 pounds). Weight gain is quite a good indication of a baby's health. If a baby is not gaining weight over a period of several weeks, it may be ill.

As a baby grows, its muscles become stronger and its brain learns to co-ordinate movements to make them more purposeful. A newborn baby cannot even hold up its head and has to be supported at all times. At about six to eight weeks old a baby will be able to follow moving things with its eyes and start to smile. At around three months it will be able to raise the head to look up when lying facing down. By seven months it will be able to sit up with some support and hold things in the hand, and also babble simple sounds without any real meaning. During the remainder of the first year a baby learns to crawl and pull itself up into a standing position. By about 15 to 18 months a baby is able to walk by itself and say a few words, such as "Mama".

All the ages mentioned above are averages. Not all babies develop at the same speed. Some are able to crawl or walk earlier than usual, others are a little later. This is not important and has no bearing on how clever or athletic the baby will be in the future. Most babies do, however, learn to do these things in the same order.

Cleanliness

Babies must be kept clean in order to remain comfortable and healthy. But they cannot wash themselves, neither can they control their bowels or urine. So a baby must be washed regularly—although a thorough bath every day is not usually necessary. A baby also wears a soft paper or cloth diaper which has to be changed when it becomes wet or dirty.

Most babies begin to control their bowels at between 18 and 24 months, and their urination a few months after.

Gaining Independence

From the moment of birth a baby starts to become independent of its parents. Gradually it learns to look, listen, understand, walk, and talk. This is the beginning of the road to complete independence as an adult.

It is important to remember that a baby has a mind as well as a body. Each baby is an individual and has its own personality, just like children and adults. In general, a baby likes to feel safe and happy. This means being looked after by one or two people, usually the mother and father, to provide reassurance.

At first a baby does not understand that other people have needs and wants. A baby tends to think only of itself. This often leads to what we see as selfish behavior. After a while, though, with loving but firm guidance from parents and others, a baby learns to think of others. Gradually the baby matures and develops normal, happy human relationships with parents, brothers and sisters, and other relatives and friends.

The appearance of babies may resemble that of their parents because many features are inherited from them. Color of hair or eyes, the height to which they grow, or whether they are thin or fat are often related to their parents' characteristics. (See HEREDITY AND GENETICS.) Identical twins usually look exactly the same as each other in all their features because they have developed from the same egg, or ovum. As babies grow, various changes take place and the color of the hair or eyes may become darker or lighter.

At one time it was common for babies to die from disease or neglect before they were a year old. At the beginning of the 20th century in Britain about one in six babies born alive died during the first year of life, but now this figure has been reduced to about 1 baby in 60. (This figure is very much higher in under-developed countries.) Baby clinics exist to advise mothers on the care of their babies and on the correct way to feed them at different ages. They weigh the babies to make sure they are developing normally, and if there is any doubt about their health a doctor is there to examine them. These clinics also vaccinate against illness, for example against whooping cough, tetanus, diphtheria and poliomyelitis.

BABYLON was one of the great cities of the ancient world. It was the capital of the kingdom of Babylonia in Mesopotamia, which is now part of Iraq (see BABYLONIA AND ASSYRIA).

There are still some remains of ancient Babylon today. These were part of the city built by one of the most famous of Babylonian kings Nebuchadnezzar (sometimes spelled Nebuchadrezzar). His father began the rebuilding of the city and during Nebuchadnezzar's reign (6th century BC) it became famous as one of the most wonderful cities in the world.

The ancient Greek historian Herodotus described the great size and magnificence of Babylon, though he may have been exaggerating, as was his habit, in parts of his description. According to him the city was square, surrounded by walls, each side being about 22 kilometers (14 miles) long. The walls were made of baked brick, more than 90 meters (300 feet) high and 25 meters (80 feet) thick, and were so solid that a four-horse chariot could turn round on top of them.

Through the city ran a wide sacred street, the "processional way", along which religious processions passed during festivals. It led out of the city at a huge gate called the Ishtar gate, which was crowned with towers and decorated with carvings of animals. The River Euphrates divided the city into two equal parts and was banked by walls of brick. Where these walls met the ends of the streets, there were gates of bronze.

Among the many fine buildings in the city were the royal palace, built round a vast courtyard, and several enormous temples. One of the temples was dedicated to the god Marduk, the chief Babylonian god. Another, to the god Baal, was a ziggurat, or rectangular building of several stories, each smaller than the one below. The stories were linked by great outside stairways. This temple may have been the Tower of Babel described in the Bible (see BABEL, TOWER OF). The famous "hanging gardens", one of the Seven Wonders of the World, were brick terraces covered with trees and plants so that from a distance the building was completely hidden.

The Jews, who were carried off as captives to Babylon by Nebuchadnezzar, despised the wealth and pagan gods of the city. Babylon gained a reputation as a place where vast wealth was used for worthless or evil ends.

Babylon was captured in 539 BC by the Persian king Cyrus. His successors pulled down the walls and plundered the city. Alexander the Great planned to rebuild parts of Babylon after conquering the Persians, but his successors built a new capital at Seleucia.

BABYLONIA AND ASSYRIA. Babylon and Assur were two of the greatest cities of Mesopotamia, which is now part of Iraq (see MESOPOTAMIA). These cities became the centers of

A stone tablet made to honor a Babylonian ruler by his son. Father and son stand beneath holy symbols.

the empires of Babylonia and Assyria. Their histories were closely connected, as one or the other controlled the fertile region between the rivers Tigris and Euphrates. Their civilizations influenced those of Greece, Rome, and Palestine, and so have had a lasting effect on Western civilization in general.

The Early Settlers

Long before the city of Babylon was built, many different peoples had settled in what came to be called Babylonia. They were attracted by the fertile land and warm climate.

To the north and east the climate was not so pleasant. Moreover, the land became rough and difficult towards the mountains of Asia Minor and Persia. To the south lay the Persian Gulf, and to the west and southwest stretched the deserts of Arabia and Syria.

People moved into northern Babylonia at least 6,000 years ago. Archeological excavations have shown that they lived in small villages. The men were farmers, shepherds, hunters, and fishermen. They made crude dishes and pots of clay, used stone and bone tools, and carried on some trade. When the early settlements were established in the north, a large part of southern Babylonia was under the waters of the Persian Gulf. The gulf extended about 240 kilometers (150 miles) farther inland than it does today. The rivers Tigris and Euphrates, however, regularly deposited large amounts of soil near their mouths. The sand slowly filled the gulf and created swamp land. This land was very fertile and quickly attracted settlers. Some came from the northern part of Babylonia, others from the highlands of Persia. Semitic tribesmen from the deserts to the west also pushed in.

The Rise of Civilization

The earliest people to develop an advanced civilization were the Sumerians. By 3000 BC they were in control of southern Babylonia. Their most famous cities were Ur, Lagash, and Eridu. The Sumerians invented a form of writing in which signs stood for various words. There is a separate entry called SUMERIANS.

About 2300 BC a Semitic king called Sargon of Akkad conquered the Sumerians and established an empire that stretched westward to the Mediterranean Sea. Fierce invaders from Persia destroyed Sargon's kingdom and plundered many Babylonian cities. But in time they were driven out and the Sumerian city of Ur became dominant in Babylonia. It was conquered in its turn by the armies of Elam from across the Tigris. Three city states—that is, independent states consisting of a city and the land round it—then emerged in Mesopotamia. Isin and Larsa were the first two; then came Babylon.

The Age of Hammurabi

After centuries of warfare, Mesopotamia's wisest and strongest king came to the throne. He broke the power of the Elamites in Babylonia, so setting the stage for Babylonia's first period of splendor. By about 1770 BC he had conquered the whole of Babylonia and had extended his power into Persia and Asia Minor. Hammurabi set up a strong central government and tried to form a united country. He drew up a series of laws, now known as the Code of Hammurabi. It was carved on a black pillar, which may be seen in the Louvre Museum in Paris. Many of the laws seem to us fair and just, although some of the punishments for crime were savage, including drowning and the putting out of eyes. Women enjoyed legal rights and privileges. Slaves were protected and could eventually be granted their freedom. There is a separate entry on HAMMURABI.

The Rise of Assyria

After Hammurabi's death central government quickly broke down and waves of invaders brought confusion into the whole area. Hittites, Kassites, and Hurrians all controlled parts of Mesopotamia for varying periods. But another Semitic people, the Assyrians, had become a powerful force in the north of Mesopotamia. Before 2000 BC their capital, Assur, was ruled by weak kings who were often under the control of Babylonian rulers. But in the centuries after 2000 the kings of Assur built up a strong army and conquered parts of Babylonia.

The names and achievements of many Assyrian kings have come down to us, either through archeological investigations or in written records such as the Bible. The first king of whom much is known was Shalmaneser I, who reigned about 1280 BC. The records of his time show that, even at that early time, Assyria ruled a large empire. Two hundred years later Tiglath-Pileser I greatly increased Assyria's power. He claimed to have conquered 42 states and to have extended his rule from Babylon to the Mediterranean Sea. He also built great temples and palaces and laid out gardens and parks. After his death, however, Assyria grew weaker, and the Arameans from northern Syria controlled the area's trade routes.

Under Ashurnasirpal II, who reigned from 883 to 859 BC, the Assyrians reconquered the lands they had lost. The records of his conquests are filled with descriptions of his cruelty. In general the Assyrians, although like the Babylonians in many ways, were a more cold-blooded and savage people. Their empire was a military one, and they often cruelly tortured the captives they took in war.

After another period of decline, Assyria rebuilt its power and empire under the leadership of several exceptionally able rulers. The greatest, Tiglath-Pileser III (745–727 BC), captured Damascus in Syria. Sargon II, an army general who seized the throne in 722 BC, occupied Israel and carried off into exile 30,000 Israelites. Sennacherib (704–681 BC), Sargon's son, defeated the kingdom of Judah and sacked Jerusalem. He destroyed the city of Babylon because it rebelled against Assyrian rule.

During the reign of Esarhaddon (680–669 BC) Egypt was conquered and the Assyrian empire reached its greatest extent. The last important ruler, Ashurbanipal, came to power in 668 BC. He was unable to hold the empire together despite many military campaigns. Egypt freed itself and revolts broke out in Babylonia and in Media, the mountainous area to the east. In 614 BC, 17 years after Ashurbanipal's death, the Medes captured Assur. They then formed an alliance with the Chaldeans, who had moved into Babylonia, and destroyed Nineveh, the Assyrian capital since about 725 BC. So complete was the destruction that all traces of it were lost for more than 2,000 years. Only legends and references to it in the Bible confirmed its former existence. The Assyrian empire fell along with Nineveh because the member states rose in rebellion.

The New Babylonian Empire

When Babylon rose to power again after the fall of Assyria, the Chaldeans formed the ruling class. These people had probably entered Mesopotamia at a very early date, settling round Ur. Nebuchadnezzar II (605–562 BC) was Chaldean and by his time his people had become part of the Babylonian nation. The new Babylonian, or Chaldean, empire flourished under Nebuchadnezzar. It was he who raised the mighty temples, walls, and gates that made Babylon one of the most splendid cities of the ancient world (see BABYLON). It was he, too, who destroyed Jerusalem and the kingdom of Judah in 586 BC, and carried the Jews captive into Babylon. There is a separate entry called NEBUCHADNEZZAR.

The Chaldean empire extended from the River Euphrates to Egypt and from Armenia to Arabia. Thousands of cuneiform (wedge-shaped writing) tablets have given detailed information about this revival of Babylonian power. Trade and industry as well as the arts flourished again. Nevertheless, the recovery was short-lived. When Nebuchadnezzar died, decline again set in.

British Museum photo, Michael Holford

Sennacherib defeated Judah in the 7th century BC. The carving shows his sack of the city of Lachish in 700 BC.

Decline and Fall

Cyrus the Great created the Persian empire between 559 and 530 BC. He captured Babylonia in 539 and made it a province of the empire. Babylonia, however, retained its culture and way of life for a considerable period. When Alexander the Great conquered the Persian empire (334–330 BC), Babylon was still an important and wealthy part of it.

In the period after Alexander, during the Seleucid period, Babylonia kept some of its old traditions. However, in 311 BC the Seleucids built a new capital, Seleucia, north of Babylon. The inhabitants of Babylon were moved to the new city. The history of Babylonia was ended.

Many traces of its civilization remained, however. For example, cuneiform writing was used until the beginning of the Christian era. But by that time most of the old cities of Mesopotamia had fallen into ruin.

Art and Architecture

The Babylonians and Assyrians were influenced to a great extent by the artistic and intellectual achievements of the Sumerians. Like the Sumerians, they built their temples and palaces of bricks made from mud dried in the sun or in kilns. At the center of each city was the shrine of a local god. As a city grew in size and importance, so its shrine became more elaborate until it might end up as a magnificent temple. The temple building was based on a large platform reached by ramps and staircases. It was crowned with a high tower. The Babylonians made some towers in the form of mighty steps up to seven stories, and these were known as ziggurats. The Biblical Tower of Babel (see BABEL, TOWER OF) was probably a ziggurat. On the top stood a small temple usually covered in blue glazed tiles.

The palace that Sargon II built near Nineveh was of enormous size and splendor with nearly a thousand rooms. By it stood a giant ziggurat. Sennacherib built three great palaces at Nineveh. The Assyrians and Babylonians decorated their public buildings in different ways. The Babylonians covered the walls with colored glazed brickwork. The Assyrians preferred carved slabs of limestone or alabaster. The sculptures depicted scenes of war and hunting or religious and court scenes. Many show the king as a distinguished figure with a beard and curly hair, while the people by him look all alike and comparatively insignificant. The hunting scenes are vivid.

Outside the gates of the Assyrians' temples and palaces, lions or bulls with human heads kept guard. The cities were well planned with wide avenues. Great aqueducts were constructed to supply water.

Religion

The Babylonians, like almost all ancient peoples, worshipped many gods and believed many myths, or stories, about them. Most of the myths were originally Sumerian. The Sumerians had myths about the Creation and even a story similar to that about Adam and Eve. Their longest and best-known story concerned the hero Gilgamesh, who set out to find the plant of life. He endured many hardships and adventures before finding the plant. But a serpent came from under the water and snatched it from his boat. The story of Gilgamesh contains an account of the Flood which resembles the Biblical story of Noah.

For the Sumerians, Anu, originally the god of the city of Uruk, was the greatest god. For the Babylonians the greatest god was Marduk, the god of the city of Babylon. In their myths Marduk fought and overcame the dragon Tiamat. He was believed to have created heaven, earth, and mankind. The people thought the king was Marduk's representative on earth. They also worshipped gods of the earth, water, sky, sun, and moon. The Assyrians largely shared the religion and gods of the Sumerians and Babylonians. But for the Assyrians the chief god was Assur, after whom they named their capital city. The chief goddess of both the Babylonians and Assyrians was Ishtar, who was rather like Aphrodite, the Greek goddess of love.

Writing and Learning

The writing of the Sumerians is the oldest that has come down to us. They wrote on clay tablets which were then baked. Archeologists have found many thousands of these tablets, some of which may be more than 5,000 years old. The first writing was picture writing. But this gradually changed into the cuneiform, or wedge-shaped, symbols that the Babylonians and Assyrians used. The tablets found relate to law, religion, mathematics, science, and other subjects. The Assyrians seem to have been the first people to record great events in their history. In addition to these annals (records) they wrote poems and hymns. The Assyrians kept their writings in great libraries. The library of Ashurbanipal at Nineveh yielded about 25,000 tablets covering many subjects.

The Chaldeans laid the foundations of astronomy, although the main reason they studied the heavens was that they believed the future could be foretold from the stars and planets. The word Chaldean later came to mean magician or prophet. The Chaldeans were the first to divide the equator into 360 degrees and to map the stars. They devised a system of weights and measures (see WEIGHTS AND MEASURES) which was afterwards used by the Greeks and Romans.

BACCHUS see DIONYSUS.

BACH FAMILY. The German musician Johann Sebastian Bach is generally regarded as one of the greatest composers and organists of all time. But he was by no means the only member of his family to be involved in music during the 17th and 18th centuries. In fact, the name Bach was so common among musicians in the Thuringia region of Germany that it almost came to be used as another word for "musician". When he was 50 years old, J. S. Bach assembled a list of his forebears in a now famous document called *Origin of the Musical Bach Family*.

The earliest ancestor mentioned in this book was Veit Bach (died 1578), a miller and baker by trade who enjoyed playing the cittern (a type of lute) while he was grinding flour. Veit's younger son Johannes (*c.* 1550–1626) was both a baker and a town musician. His son Christoph (1613–61) became a full-time town and court musician at Weimar, Erfurt, and Arnstadt. Christoph had two musical sons who were twins. One, Johann Christoph (1645–93), followed his father as a court musician at Arnstadt. The other, Johann Ambrosius (1645–95) served in the town band at Eisenach.

The great Johann Sebastian Bach (1685–1750) was the eighth and youngest child of Johann Ambrosius. He was born at Eisenach on 21 March 1685. By the time he was ten, both his parents had died, and he went to live with Johann Christoph (1671–1721) at the small town of Ohrdruf. Johann Christoph taught his young brother the organ and harpsichord, and Johann Sebastian also sang in the choir of the church where Johann Christoph was organist, and probably learned to play the violin at this time. Johann Sebastian also achieved a high standard at school.

In 1700 the 15-year-old Bach went to further his studies at Lüneburg, where he became a member of the choir at St. Michael's School. He also probably continued his organ studies and listened to famous local organists. In 1703 he obtained his first important post as organist and choirmaster of the new church of St. Boniface at Arnstadt. Bach did not find it easy to work with some of his colleagues because they were not very good musicians. In 1705 he got into trouble with the church authorities for fighting with a bassoon-player whom he had called a "nanny-goat". In the same year he was granted a month's leave to go to hear the great Danish-born organist Dietrich Buxtehude at Lübeck. He is said to have walked the 416 kilometers (260 miles) from Arnstadt and eventually overstayed his leave by three months. His employers at Arnstadt did not approve, and in 1707 he took another post as a church organist at Mühlhausen, where he married his cousin Maria Barbara Bach.

In June 1708 Bach accepted the position of organist and court musician to Wilhelm Ernst, Duke of Weimar. Up to this time, he had gained a reputation as a brilliant organist and composer of clever and showy keyboard pieces, and he continued to write such works in his first years at Weimar. At this court he wrote

This engraving from the 18th century shows a group of musicians of the time of the Bach family.

one of his most famous works, the *Toccata and Fugue in D minor*. He also made harpsichord arrangements of works by the Italian composer Antonio Vivaldi. In 1714 Bach was made *Konzertmeister* (director of the court orchestra) and had to compose one cantata (a work for voices and instruments) every month. He had written church cantatas at Mühlhausen, but the ones he now had to compose were secular (non-religious) ones, rather like miniature operas without action.

In 1716 Duke Wilhelm Ernst quarreled with his nephew, for whom Bach sometimes directed musical performances. Seeing no chance of further advancement at Weimar, Bach accepted the post of *Kapellmeister* (court music director) to Prince Leopold of Anhalt-Cöthen. At first the Duke of Weimar would not release Bach from his post and even imprisoned him for a while. Eventually he dismissed Bach, who left under a cloud.

At the lively court of Cöthen, Bach enjoyed good relations with his patron and his musical colleagues and was able to achieve high standards in the music for the court. He composed a large amount of chamber music, following both the French and Italian styles. His works included the six *Brandenburg Concertos*, the six suites for unaccompanied cello, and keyboard works such as the first book of the 48 preludes and fugues of the *Well-Tempered Clavier*. In 1720 his wife Maria Barbara died, and quite soon afterward Prince Leopold got married. The prince's new wife did not like music, and Bach became dissatisfied with the decline in Prince Leopold's own enthusiasm for the art. Bach himself took a new wife, Anna Magdalena Wilken, the daughter of a Cöthen court trumpeter.

In 1723 Bach took up the last appointment of his career, that of Cantor of St. Thomas's School, Leipzig. His many duties in this post included attending to the education of the boys of the school, directing music at several city churches, and composing music for civic occasions such as the swearing-in of the Leipzig town council. As a teacher, choral trainer, and orchestral director, Bach was not very tolerant; he is said to have beaten his choirboys unmercifully if they gave a bad performance. He also found it hard to get on with the school and city authorities, who were often unsympathetic to his needs. In the 1730s he looked actively for another job and in 1736 gained an honorary court appointment as Composer to the Elector of Saxony, which allowed him to visit Dresden and listen to French and Italian operas.

Bach had to provide a church cantata for every Sunday and major feast day in two of his

Mansell Collection

Johann Sebastian Bach, from the portrait painted by the artist Elias Gottlieb Haussmann in 1746.

composition called *The Musical Offering*. In 1749, while working on his last monumental work *The Art of Fugue*, Johann Sebastian Bach went blind. He died at Leipzig on 28 July 1750, a few months after having an operation on his eyes. *The Art of Fugue* was still unfinished when he died.

Bach was the greatest composer of what is called Baroque music. He did not invent new musical forms but brought existing ones to perfection. He is perhaps best remembered for his technique in writing fugues, complex compositions in which voices or parts enter in turn, each having similar music.

Johann Sebastian Bach had 20 children, but only nine of them lived beyond infancy. His eldest son, Wilhelm Friedemann Bach (1710–84) trained as a lawyer but became a brilliant organist under the teaching of his father. He held the post of organist in Dresden and Halle, but he was not very successful in these positions. He composed short symphonies and chamber music in a rather quirky, often conservative style, and eventually died in poverty in Berlin.

Carl Philipp Emanuel Bach (1714–88) was the most successful of J. S. Bach's sons. He also trained as a lawyer but was a skilled keyboard player and became a harpsichordist to the court of Frederick the Great in Berlin. His main job was to accompany the king, who was an accomplished flute-player. In 1768 he became Cantor of the Latin School (grammar school) in Hamburg. He wrote music for the clavichord and the harpsichord, symphonies, and concertos. He also published a book on the art of playing keyboard instruments.

Johann Christian Bach (1735–82) was J. S. Bach's youngest son. He was only 15 when his father died, and so he obtained his instruction in music mostly from his brother Carl Philipp Emanuel. He went to Italy and studied with a famous Italian musician, Padre Martini. In 1760 he became organist of Milan Cathedral. While in Italy, he composed much church music and some opera. He also forsook his family's Lutheran religion and became a Roman Catholic. In 1762, J. C. Bach accepted an invitation to London. Here he promoted a

churches. In his first five years at Leipzig he wrote at least 150 cantatas and revised many others from earlier years. He also completed three major settings of the Passion (trial and death of Jesus Christ) in the versions according to St. John, St. Mark, and St. Matthew. The *St. John Passion* (1724) and the *St. Matthew Passion* (1729) have survived and are still frequently performed. In the 1730s he worked with the *Collegium Musicum*, the student orchestra of Leipzig university, but none of the music he wrote for it survives. In the 1730s and 1740s he wrote much keyboard music, including the second book of the *Well-Tempered Clavier*, the *Clavier-Übung* (Keyboard Course), and the *Goldberg Variations*. These pieces and his greatest choral work, the *Mass in B minor* (mostly adapted from earlier music), seem to sum up his personal philosophy of life. In 1747, while visiting the court of Frederick the Great in Berlin, Bach was given a theme by the king. He improvised a fugue on it and later made it the basis of a very famous series of concerts. He wrote many pieces for these concerts, including symphonies, keyboard concertos, and chamber music. He met and influenced Mozart, who was brought to London as a child. The concerts ran into financial trouble, and Bach died owing £4,000, a vast sum in those days.

BACON, Francis (1561–1626). In an age of many brilliant men Francis Bacon, lord chancellor of England, essay writer, scientist and scholar, was outstanding. He was born in London and was the son of Sir Nicholas Bacon,

National Portrait Gallery, London

Francis Bacon, lord chancellor, essayist, scientist, and scholar, a painting by an unknown artist.

a prominent statesman under Queen Elizabeth I. Francis Bacon, after an education at Cambridge University and after studying law at Gray's Inn in London, also tried to make his mark in politics. He was introduced into the royal court by the queen's favorite, the Earl of Essex, but Elizabeth never liked or trusted the young Bacon, even though he tried to please

her. When Essex was tried for treason, Bacon was one of the lawyers who prosecuted him at his trial.

Under James I, Bacon was much more successful in his career, partly because he wrote much in favor of the royal powers in government. This angered many lawyers and members of the House of Commons. In 1620 Bacon became lord chancellor. But not long after this, he was accused of accepting presents from people whose cases he judged, and at his own trial he was found guilty. Although the king pardoned him and did not enforce the fine of £40,000, Bacon never again held office. He spent the rest of his life in retirement at St. Albans, Hertfordshire. He had earlier been made Baron Verulam and Viscount St. Albans.

Bacon wrote many important books. His essays on the men and customs of the age are still the most popular of his works. He also wrote several books, some of them in Latin, on philosophy and science. Among them were the *Novum Organum* and the *Advancement of Learning*. He tried to encourage people to think along new lines in interpreting knowledge and to explore new subjects. His work gave great encouragement to scientific discovery in England later in the 17th century, even though some of the methods and aims he suggested have since been proved wrong. *The New Atlantis*, a book telling of an imaginary island where Bacon's philosophical ideas were put into practice, remained incomplete at his death but was nevertheless published in the same year.

Partly because of his wide learning and wisdom, some people have thought that Bacon was the real author of Shakespeare's plays and poems. The arguments for Bacon's authorship have never been very convincing, and most people think that there is enough evidence in the plays themselves to disprove his authorship.

BACON, Roger (*c.* 1220–*c.* 1292). In the 13th century the English friar Roger Bacon made many wonderfully accurate prophecies of inventions which came about hundreds of years later, including ocean steamers, railroads, automobiles, flying machines and cranes and bridges without piers to hold them up. In a letter to a friend he wrote: "It is possible that great ships and sea-going vessels shall be made which can be guided by one man and will move with greater swiftness than if they were full of oarsmen, and . . . that a car shall be made which will move with inestimable speed . . . without the help of any living creature." Indeed, Bacon's ideas and experiments were so far in advance of his time that he was accused of possessing powers of witchcraft.

Bacon was born in the west of England, either in Somerset or in Gloucestershire. At the universities of Oxford and Paris he studied Latin and Greek and also learned Hebrew and Arabic in order to read the Scriptures in their original language and Arabic works on philosophy and science.

In the Middle Ages, most learned men were monks or priests, so Bacon became a Franciscan friar. The students Bacon taught at this time called him "the professor of things in general". He advised them always to gain knowledge by experiment and research instead of merely accepting what Aristotle and other ancient thinkers had written. He wrote books and lectured on astronomy, alchemy, chemistry and physics, and he knew of the uses and magnifying properties of lenses. It was he who first taught that the light from the stars does not reach the Earth instantly, and he made unsuccessful attempts to improve the calendar. He also declared—nearly 200 years before Christopher Columbus was born—that the Earth was round, not flat, and that it was possible to reach India by sailing westwards from Europe.

Bacon is often described as the English inventor of gunpowder, and he did in fact hit upon the right way to make it, although he did not appear to be aware of all its qualities.

Between 1257 and 1266 Bacon was ill and had to give up many of his activities; he also seems to have been out of favor with the church because of his teachings. At the end of that time, Pope Clement IV, who had been in England and had heard of Bacon, asked for

some of his writings. The friar felt that he had produced nothing that was worthy to be read by the Pope, so he immediately set to work to prepare a detailed outline of the various branches of knowledge. Within 18 months he had finished three books, the *Opus Maius* (Greater Work), the *Opus Minus* (Lesser Work) and the *Opus Tertium* (Third Work).

After Clement's death in 1268, Bacon again lost the favor of the church for declaring that it was behind the times, and he was put in prison between 1277 and 1279 for an unknown length of time. He went on writing till he died.

BACON AND HAM are made from the meat of specially bred pigs. Such breeds are longer and leaner than others. Originally bacon and ham were made to delay the spoilage of the meat. Refrigeration lessens the importance of

A British Meat Photograph

Several cuts of British bacon. Large joints are boiled and the slices or "rashers" are grilled or fried.

the preservative effect and today bacon and ham are valued primarily for their distinctive flavors and textures.

Bacon is prepared by curing, and often smoking, the back and sides of the pig. It can be dry cured or brine cured. The meat is rubbed with, or soaked in, water mixed with salt, sugar, and sodium or potassium nitrate or nitrite. This pickle can also be injected into the meat. The salt is a preservative but if too much is used the meat will be hard. Sugar is added to keep it tender and balance the flavor. The chemicals prevent the growth of bacteria and help form the typical pink color of cooked bacon. After curing, the bacon may be smoked. This also preserves it as well as developing the color and flavor. Bacon used to be made on a small scale and smoked over open fires. Nowadays the whole process usually takes place in a factory. Bacon is normally cut into thin slices and cooked before eating.

Ham comes from the hind leg of a pig. Like bacon, it may be dry cured or brine cured, and then smoked. Often the ham that is produced in factories has its curing pickle pumped into it. This speeds up processing, increases the weight of the ham, and results in a uniform flavor. Heat processing after curing produces a cooked ham that may be eaten as it is.

Almost all countries where pigs are eaten have their own traditional way of preparing ham. The flavor depends on the breed of pig, what it has eaten, the ingredients used in the curing, and the wood used in smoking. Honey, molasses, brown sugar or corn syrup may replace ordinary sugar and a variety of spices can be added. The wood may be, for instance, oak, hickory, or beechwood. One of the best-known hams in the United States is the Smithfield ham from Virginia. In England there is York ham from Yorkshire, and Bradenham ham from Suffolk. Bayonne ham comes from France, Parma ham from Italy, and Westphalian ham from Germany. Scotch ham is an unsmoked variety.

In some countries, meat other than that of pigs may be processed in an identical manner. In New Zealand, for instance, mutton ham is popular.

BACTERIA are very small living things which can be seen only under a powerful microscope. They were first discovered in about 1680 by Anthonie van Leeuwenhoek, a Dutch draper whose hobby was making small but powerful lenses and using them to study things too small to be seen with the naked eye (see MICROSCOPE). Some of these lenses were no larger than a tomato seed, but they magnified objects as much as 200 times. Probably he noticed the tiny animals in rainwater first and then discovered bacteria, which are even smaller. Later he found bacteria in matter scraped from between his teeth. In this way Leeuwenhoek discovered a whole new world of living things.

A. W. Rakosy/EB Inc.

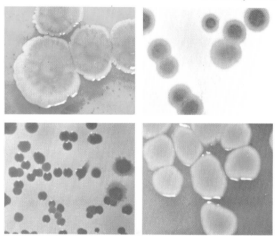

The bacteria shown here are: (top left) *Pseudomonas aeruginosa*, from sputum (spit); (top right), *Chromobacterium violaceum*, from soil; (bottom left) *Serratia marcescens*, from a dirty utensil; and (bottom right), *Pseudomonas aeruginosa*, from urine.

Hardly a spot in the world is free from bacteria. They are found in the soil, in the depths of the ocean, and floating in the air. It is usually bacteria that cause food to go bad. Many diseases of animals and men are due to them and so are some plant diseases.

Bacteria are not plants, or animals, or fungi (yeasts and mushrooms). Most biologists place them in a separate group called monera. Each bacterium (the singular for bacteria) is a single cell. Unlike a plant or animal cell, a bacterium does not have a nucleus (control center) inside. In fact a bacterium is very simply constructed. Some scientists believe that the very first living things to appear on Earth were small, simple bacteria.

All bacteria are very small. If you put 10,000 of them side by side they would measure about

2.5 centimeters (1 inch). Even then you might not see them, for most bacteria are colorless. Under the microscope we can see that they are usually shaped like balls, or rods or corkscrews. Sometimes they are linked in a chain; sometimes like bunches of grapes. Certain bacteria have little hairs called flagella which they wave to and fro to help them to move about. Most bacteria increase in number by splitting in two. If they have enough food, and if other conditions are favorable, they increase very rapidly. One bacterium may breed a million bacteria in 15 hours. After that, suitable food generally becomes too scarce to allow them to increase much more. Also, acids are produced when bacteria multiply and these help to stop them breeding.

Useful and Harmful Bacteria

The bacteria which cause the decay, or rotting, of dead plants and animals are very useful. They destroy the dead tissues and break them down into the simple things out of which they were made. These substances go back into the soil, or into the air or water, and eventually they are used again by other living things. Bacteria are especially helpful in changing sewage into harmless substances. If it were not for these bacteria, the Earth would become cluttered up with dead bodies.

Bacteria help in industry and on the farm. When animal hides have to be tanned to make shoes, and other leather articles, bacteria loosen the hair and make it easier to remove. When linen is being made, the flax is put in water, where bacteria dissolve the gummy cement which holds the flax fibers together. Many fine cheeses owe at least part of their savory taste to bacteria. Other kinds of bacteria help to cure tea leaves and make them black.

Bacteria are used to make vaccines, drugs, hormones, and other chemicals, after having been altered by the process of genetic engineering (see GENETIC ENGINEERING).

One element needed by plants is nitrogen, which makes up four-fifths of the air we breathe. Plants, however, cannot use nitrogen in the form of a gas; instead they need it in the shape of salts called nitrates. Some kinds of bacteria can bring about a change of the ammonia in the soil and convert it into nitrates.

Other bacteria cause many diseases in man and in animals. These are usually the kind caught by touching an ill person, breathing the air near by, or eating and drinking food or water that contains the bacteria. Typhoid fever, cholera, tuberculosis, pneumonia, and leprosy are each caused by a particular kind of bacterium. So are infections that attack open wounds, such as gangrene.

Some bacteria are vital to our health. Our large intestines contain helpful bacteria that digest some parts of our food, absorbing a little for themselves and allowing us to absorb the rest. When we take antibiotic drugs, we kill off most of these intestinal bacteria and so become more likely to get diarrhea and other minor digestive upsets.

Although Leeuwenhoek had sent careful drawings of bacteria to the Royal Society in England in 1683, 100 years went by before other scientists began to make use of his discovery. Several writers in the 18th century suggested that such tiny objects might cause disease, but most scientists thought they were produced *by* decay instead of causing it. Then, in 1860, the Frenchman Louis Pasteur (see PASTEUR, LOUIS) proved that bacteria are living things which reproduce themselves by splitting in two. Soon afterwards Robert Koch, in Germany, managed to grow some bacteria in a dish in the laboratory. Other scientists have since found ways of helping the body to fight harmful bacteria with serums and vaccines (see VACCINATION AND INOCULATION). Drugs such as penicillin and streptomycin are also used today to kill bacteria inside the body (see ANTIBIOTICS). Also, antiseptics (see ANTISEPTIC) are used to kill bacteria on the skin and in wounds.

BADEN-POWELL, Robert, 1st Baron

(1857–1941). Lord Baden-Powell, or B.-P. as he was known, founder of the Scout movement, was born in London, England, and named Robert Stephenson Smyth Baden-Powell. He

BBC Hulton Picture Library

Lord Baden-Powell's interest in outdoor life led him to start the Scouting movement that spread worldwide.

enjoyed a happy childhood at home and at his school, Charterhouse, developing an interest in the outdoor life, particularly camping and tracking, as well as acting and sketching. He followed these interests all his life. After leaving school he became a junior officer in the 13th Hussars and saw active service on India's North-West Frontier and in South Africa. Here he showed his powers of leadership. The Matabele people in South Africa called him *Impeesa*, "the wolf who never sleeps". He became a national hero at the defense of Mafeking in 1899–1900, during the Boer War. Under B.-P.'s leadership the town refused to yield to the surrounding Boer soldiers for 217 days, until help arrived. He was made a major-general, the youngest in the army.

When in the army, Baden-Powell had been shocked at how little young men knew about looking after themselves in the open. When he returned to civilian life he was determined to do something about it and in August 1907 Baden-Powell ran a camp for boys at Brownsea Island at the mouth of Poole Harbour in England. Here he attempted to teach some basic principles and also tried out many of the ideas which he later included in his book *Scouting for Boys*, published in 1908. Many people began to follow its ideas and within a few years the Scout movement had spread to nearly every country in the world.

The rest of Baden-Powell's life is the story of Scouting and Guiding. (The Girl Guides' Association was begun in 1911; B.-P.'s sister Agnes Baden-Powell helped him to found it.) The Scout movement gave millions of boys a chance to take part in activities and learn skills which they would otherwise have missed. When Scouting began, camping and hiking were thought very strange activities. It is largely due to Baden-Powell that camping and walking have become so popular.

Many honors were given to B.-P. He became a baron and Chief Scout of the World. In 1937 he received the Order of Merit. He continued his work for the movement until his 80th year, touring the world to review Scouts and Guides (see SCOUTS AND GUIDES).

Throughout his life, Baden-Powell wanted to help others achieve happiness and it is this idea that lies behind the Scout "good turn" and the Scout law and promise. He was buried in Africa, facing Mount Kenya.

BADGER includes eight species of strong, stocky animals related to weasels, best-known for their burrowing habit. They have powerful claws and a thick, coarse coat. Although their sense of smell is well developed, their eyesight is poor. They tend to be omnivorous—eating both animal and plant food including carrion such as fledglings that have fallen out of their nests. The European badger (*Meles meles*) is distinguished by its white head and black facial stripes. The fur on the back looks gray, but each hair is actually white below, black in the middle, and white again at the tip. The badger is a social animal that lives in woodland in large burrow systems called sets. In Britain the badger is a well-known animal, although few people have actually seen one because they tend to be active at night.

In the past, badgers were hunted for their long fur, used for making shaving brushes. They were also hunted for "sport" and baited—put in a barrel and attacked by dogs. This cruel practice gave rise to the expression "to badger", meaning to worry and annoy.

The North American badger (*Taxidea taxus*) is a powerfully built, slightly shorter animal that lives in the open country of the western

Ernest G. Neal

A pair of European badgers leave their set by night to search for food. They eat insects, small animals, and plants.

United States from southern Canada down to Mexico. It is more carnivorous (meat-eating) than the European badger and preys on ground squirrels and prairie dogs, which it digs out of the ground.

The honey badger or ratel (*Mellivora capensis*) is a small badger of forested regions of Africa and southern Asia. The upper parts of the body are whitish, the lower parts and legs are black. The honey badger lives in burrows and feeds at night on small animals, fruit, and honey. The honey is often located by following the call of a bird, the greater honey guide (see HONEY GUIDE).

The stink and ferret badgers (*Mydaus, Suillotaxus, Melogale*) produce a strong-smelling secretion like skunks when disturbed.

BADMINTON is a fast and skillful game played on a court with rackets and shuttlecocks. The players use light rackets, usually weighing about 140 to 155 grams (5 to 5½ ounces). The shuttlecock, or bird, has 16 goose feathers about 6.5 centimeters (2.5 inches) long fitted into a small piece of cork. The cork is covered with kid for indoor use and rubber for outdoor use. Plastic shuttlecocks are also available. The shuttlecocks travel remarkably fast through the air when hit hard.

The court on which badminton is played is in the shape of a rectangle and is divided in half by a net. On each side of the net are two courts, the left half court and the right half court. Sometimes there are four players, two on each side of the net, in which case it is a

Wardene Weisser/ARDEA

The North American badger is a powerful animal that hunts small mammals by digging them out of the ground. If pursued, it will often dig a burrow, digging down quicker than a man can with a spade.

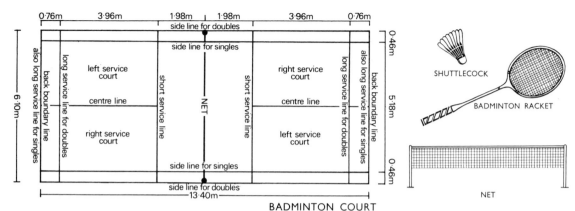

BADMINTON COURT

doubles game. When there are only two players, one on each side of the net, it is a singles game. For a doubles the court is 13.4 meters (44 feet) long and 6.1 meters (20 feet) wide, but it is only 5.18 meters (17 feet) wide for a singles. The net is 1.5 meters (5 feet) high at its center and 25 millimeters (1 inch) higher at the posts that support it.

How Badminton is Played

In badminton, unlike other games in which rackets are used, every stroke of the racket is played as a volley, which means that the shuttlecock must be hit before it touches the ground. This means it is important for the players to be alert and to be able to move quickly. Many kinds of strokes can be played, some depending for their effect on hard hitting, others on a more gentle touch, and there is plenty of opportunity for skill.

At the start of a game, two players face each other and one, standing in his right service court, hits the shuttlecock over the net to the other (his opponent) who is standing in the opposite right service court. This is called serving, and the stroke must be an underhand swing. The opponent hits the shuttlecock back, and it flies to and fro between the players until it either falls to the floor or is hit into or under the net or out of the court.

This hitting of the shuttlecock to and fro is called a rally. If the shuttlecock, after being hit over the net, falls to the floor of the court, the rally is lost by the player on whose side of the net it falls. If it falls outside the court, the player who hit it there loses the rally. A player

who hits the shuttlecock so that it goes into or under the net loses the rally.

There are six basic strokes in badminton. They are the serve, the clear (very high to the back court), the drop-shot (hit just over the net), the smash (a powerful downward stroke), and the forehand and backhand drives.

If a rally is won by the player who served the shuttlecock, he scores one point and serves again; but if he loses the rally, the right to serve goes to his opponent. Although the opponent does not score anything for winning that rally, he scores one point for each rally he wins while he is serving, until he in turn loses and forfeits the right to serve. The game is won by the player who first scores 15 points, or 11 points if the game is a ladies singles.

While a rally is being played, each player naturally does his best to knock the shuttlecock into the part of the court from which his opponent will find it most hard to hit it back.

History of Badminton

Badminton takes its name from the home of the Duke of Beaufort, Badminton House in Gloucestershire, England. It was in this house that a rough and ready form of the game was first played. Toy battledores (wooden bats with strings or parchment stretched across them) and shuttlecocks were used and a cord, instead of a net, was stretched across a large room. That was in or about 1865—the exact date is not known. It was not until several years later that an organized game, with definite rules, really began to be played.

When India was under British rule, some

Mike Powell/Allsport

Badminton is played worldwide: Liem Swie King (Indonesia), in the 1985 All England Championships.

people who had played the early form of the game went to live there and in due course they drew up the first set of badminton rules. It was these people who, after they had returned from India, started the first clubs in England.

Until about 1920, badminton was not played much except in Britain and India, though a number of clubs were scattered here and there in other countries. Since then, however, it has become extremely popular all over the world. In Malaysia and Indonesia it is played all year round, both indoors and out of doors, but in most countries it is only played indoors during the winter. In Europe the badminton season is usually from October to March.

BAGHDAD. Although it did not become the capital of Iraq until 1918, Baghdad has been an important city of the Middle East for many

hundreds of years. Even before it was built an important town had stood either on the same spot or else close at hand. This is not only because it lies at a central point in the Middle East, the natural meeting place of roads and routes across the desert, but also because it is on the banks of the Tigris, at the point where that river and the Euphrates bend towards each other, at the center of an extremely fertile plain.

Baghdad became famous in the 8th century AD when the Arabs made it the capital of their empire. The population even then grew to 2 million, making it the largest city in the world at that time.

Those were the days of the caliph (ruler) Harun al Rashid, of *The Arabian Nights* and Sindbad the Sailor (see HARUN AL-RASHID and ARABIAN NIGHTS, THE). Side by side with trade flourished the new Arab art and learning. The city led the world in the sciences and it was the scholars of Baghdad who rescued the world's knowledge of mathematics, medicine, astronomy, and philosophy from the decay of the Greek Empire. This knowledge was later passed to Europe and produced the great rebirth of scholarship known as the Renaissance (see RENAISSANCE).

All this ended with the Mongol invasion in 1258, however, when Hulaku, grandson of the great Genghis Khan, overran the town, massacred its inhabitants, and murdered the caliph. The destruction begun by the Mongols was completed by the conquering Turks in 1540.

Modern Baghdad spreads over both banks of the Tigris. Even at close quarters the town is not picturesque for, apart from the Quadimain Mosque and the Blue Mosque and the vast, packed bazaars, or market places, little can be seen of its historic past. The town is now crossed by wide streets; government and commercial buildings have been built to meet modern needs; and, particularly since the construction of a big airport, Baghdad has become an important business center. However, the continuing Gulf War between Iran and Iraq since the mid-1980s produced visible shortages in goods and manpower, and subjected the city to occasional Iranian missile attacks.

The beautifully glazed dome and minaret of this mosque in Baghdad are overshadowed by the newer arch.

The population of about 3,400,000 is almost entirely of the faith of Islam. (Islam is the name for the religion of those people who follow the teachings of Muhammad, see ISLAM; MUHAMMAD.)

BAGPIPE. Most people think of the bagpipes as the national instrument of Scotland, but related instruments have been invented in Germany, Greece, Italy, Spain, Turkey, and many other countries throughout Europe and Asia. The instrument has changed in many ways in different countries over thousands of years.

All bagpipes consist of a bag, traditionally made from the skin of a goat or other animal, to which a set of pipes is attached. The bag is kept full of air, which in most cases is blown through the blowpipe from the mouth of the player, and is held under the left arm. Other

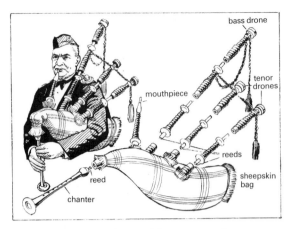

The separate parts of a set of Scottish bagpipes.

pipes of various sizes are fixed in the bag, which when squeezed by the player's arm allows air to pass continuously to the pipes, causing them to make a penetrating sound. The sound is produced by the vibration of a reed as in a clarinet or oboe (see CLARINET; OBOE FAMILY). A bagpipe melody is played on a pipe called a "chanter" that is either pierced with fingerholes or fitted with keys. It usually plays nine notes or tones. The other pipes are called drones and when the instrument is being played they make a steady sound as an accompaniment to the melody. Some nations have developed bagpipes whose drones are more complicated and whose chanter has a larger range of notes.

In Scotland, bagpipes have long been a part of tradition, and music composed for them has come to follow strict rules. The old highland clans used the pipes to provide music for dancing and in the wars which they were fighting for a long period before the 18th century. The piper held pride of place in these wars, and later in history his playing inspired the fighting men of the highland and Scottish regiments. Even the British army's Gurkha regiment recruited from the Himalayas marched to Scottish pipe music.

The highland bagpipe has changed very little since the 17th century, and today it is almost the standard form of the bagpipe all over the world, except for bagpipes used by shepherds in certain European countries. Other forms of the bagpipe still in use in Great

Scottish Tourist Board

A military pipe band is a colorful spectacle on ceremonial occasions or during festivals in Scotland.

Britain and Ireland are the Irish war pipes (mouth-blown), the Northumbrian small pipes and the Irish uillean pipes. These last two have their bags kept filled with wind from a bellows.

BAHA'I FAITH. The Baha'i faith is a religion that was founded in Persia (now called Iran) in the middle of the nineteenth century. It teaches that all people in the world are members of one great family. It also teaches that all religions are basically similar and that all religions worship the same God. According to the faith, one day all the countries of the world will join together as one country with one religion. Practice of the Baha'i faith is intended to work towards this aim. Baha'is believe that science and religion work together; that men and women are equal; that

The headquarters of the Bah'ai International House of Justice in Haifa, Israel.

Courtesy, The Bah'ai Centre, London

education should be provided for everyone; and that everyone should carry on some useful profession.

From 1844 to 1850, the religion was led by Mirza 'Ali Muhammad, who became known to his followers as the Bab. This means the "door" or "gate", and lots of people saw him as the gateway to the truth. Many people in Persia were impressed by the Bab's teachings and his message quickly spread through Persia. However, some of the leaders of the government and Muslim priests hated and feared the Bab. They felt that their wealth and power were threatened by his teachings. They put the Bab in prison in order to put a stop to his preaching. But, more and more people began to believe in his message and he was executed in Persia, on 9 July 1850. More than 20,000 of his converts died in the persecution that followed.

An important part of the Bab's teaching was that another and greater prophet would come after him. In 1863 a follower of the Bab was accepted as the prophet. He became the head of the new religion and became known as Baha'u'llah, which means Glory of God.

Baha'u'llah Strengthens the Faith

Baha'u'llah made the faith much stronger, although the government made him stay out of Persia. He and his family and a few fol-lowers were sent to many countries, and finally to Palestine.

Baha'u'llah added a great deal to the teachings of the Bab. He wrote over 100 religious works including *"al-Kitab al-Aqdas"* ("The Most Holy Book"). He said that the world was paying too much attention to war and not enough attention to religion. He taught that people should turn back to God, and join together to bring peace to the world. He wrote letters to kings, rulers, and heads of religions, asking them to meet and agree to stop war.

When Baha'u'llah died in 1892, he provided for the future development of the religion in his will. It named Abd ol-Baha', his eldest son, as the Interpreter of the Baha'i teachings and the one to whom all believers should turn for guidance. From 1892 until he died in 1921, Abd ol-Baha', gave leadership to the Baha'is. He brought the faith to more than 30 countries around the world. He also wrote books which deal with questions about religion, peace, and social philosophy.

Between 1911 and 1913 he traveled in Europe, Canada, and the United States asking the nations, races, and religions to unite for the sake of peace. While in the United States he met with Baha'is of the Chicago area. They met in Wilmette, Illinois, on the land on which they planned to build a house of worship. This building was opened for public worship in 1953. It has become well-known for its beautiful and unusual style of architecture.

Now the religion has spread to more than 200 countries and dependencies. Literature of the Baha'i faith is published in nearly 400 languages. As well as the temple in Wilmette, Baha'i houses of worship have been built in Kampala, Uganda; Sydney, Australia; and Panama City, Panama.

The Baha'is have no ministers or priests. Their meetings are for worship and spiritual education. Their activities are directed by elected bodies known as Spiritual Assemblies. Every Baha'i should pray daily and fast for 19 days a year, going without food from sunrise to sunset. Alcohol and tobacco are strictly forbidden. The Baha'i calendar has 19 months of 19 days with 4 extra days (5 in a leap year). The year begins on 21 March, the first day of spring and a holy day for Baha'is.

Before his death in 1921, Abd ol-Baha' appointed a new guardian of the Faith. He was Shoghi Effendi of Haifa, Israel. He directed Baha'i activities until his death in 1957. From that time the body of 27 Hands of the Faith has directed Baha'i spiritual affairs throughout the world. In 1963 the International House of Justice was elected as the main administrative body. The world headquarters, located in Haifa, Israel, includes the shrine of Bab, an archives building, and an administrative center.

BAHAMAS. The group of islands known as the Bahamas form an independent parliamentary state in the West Indies. (See WEST INDIES.) They stretch southeastwards from near Florida, in the United States, for more than 1,200 kilometers (745 miles), screening the northern approaches to the Caribbean Sea and the Gulf of Mexico. The group contains about 700 islands and 2,000 rocks and "cays" (a cay is a reef or spit of sand).

The islands are long, narrow, and low-lying; the highest point in all the Bahamas is less than 120 meters (400 feet) above sea-level. They are made of coral and have beautiful beaches of white sand which, with the bright colors of the sea and sky, make the Bahamas

a favorite tourist spot in winter. The climate, also, is one of the most pleasant in the world. On the other hand the soil is mostly poor and there are no mineral products such as coal or iron, so that only 30 of the 700 islands are inhabited. More than half of the people live in the capital, Nassau, on New Providence, which lies in the middle of the group. Most are descendants of freed African slaves but roughly one in eight is of European descent.

FACTS ABOUT THE BAHAMAS

AREA: 13,939 square kilometers (5,382 square miles).
POPULATION: 227,000.
GOVERNMENT: Independent state; member of the Commonwealth.
CAPITAL: Nassau.
GEOGRAPHICAL FEATURES: A group of 30 inhabited and about 670 uninhabited coral islands. There are also more than 2,000 cays (islets).
CHIEF OCCUPATIONS: Tourism is the main industry.
EDUCATION: Children must attend school between the ages of 5 and 14.

The inhabitants earn their living by tourism. Tourists, mostly from the United States, keep Nassau international airport busy, as do the airliners which land temporarily to re-fuel there. The Bahamas export petroleum products and pharmaceuticals, pineapples, tomatoes, crawfish, and handicraft work of straw and shells.

The discovery of the Bahamas was an important event in history. In October 1492, just when it seemed that the Atlantic must defeat him, Christopher Columbus sighted one of its smaller islands and so found the New World. He called the small island San Salvador. After the discovery of the Bahamas the Spaniards took most of the original American Indian inhabitants to work in the gold mines in Hispaniola, and until the middle of the 17th century the Bahamas were almost uninhabited. Then they were occupied by the British, although buccaneers and pirates made the Bahamas their stronghold, too, for half a century or more. Since then, apart from an American naval raid on Nassau during the American War of Independence in the 18th century, and a period of Spanish occupation from 1781 to 1783, the Bahamas have had little violence or disorder.

In 1973 the Bahamas became independent, but is still part of the Commonwealth (see COMMONWEALTH, THE), linked to other independent countries by the British crown. Parliament consists of a senate and an elected assembly, and the government is led by a prime minister.

BAHRAIN. The Bahrain archipelago of 33 islands is an independent Arab state which lies near Qatar off the Persian Gulf (see PERSIAN GULF). It has an area of 685 square kilometers (265 square miles).

The port of Manama, which is also the capital town of the state, is located at the northeastern end of Bahrain island. A deepwater anchorage just off the port provides ample berthing space for the massive oil-tankers that ply along the Persian Gulf. The other major town is Muharraq, a traditional Arab town of narrow streets.

The climate is hot and rather humid in summer but the north of the country is irrigated, and dates, citrus fruits, rice, and vegetables are grown. Traditional industries such as fishing and pearling take place on a small scale, while soft-drink factories, brick-making plants, and a large aluminum smelter have also been established. Most Bahrainis, how-

Picturepoint

Traditional souk (market) in Bahrain.

ever, are employed in the oil industry. Oil was discovered in 1932 and the country's economy depends almost totally on it.

From 1820 to 1971, Bahrain was under British protection, although Iran also claimed the islands. In 1971, when British forces left, Bahrain became an independent country and joined the United Nations. The Emir (ruler) no longer rules personally but is now helped in government by a council of ministers.

The population, mostly Muslim, is 416,000 (1987) and the official language is Arabic.

BAIL. When a person is accused of a crime he, or she, is often released "on bail" instead of having to wait in prison for the trial to take place. This is to avoid inflicting punishment on a person who may be innocent and also to enable the accused person to meet and talk freely with the lawyers who will represent him at the trial. The accused person may still be allowed bail during his trial up to the time when the jury is sent out to come to their verdict. Then bail will not be renewed.

To make sure that a person will appear for his trial, he must show the court that he possesses a certain sum of money which will be paid to the court if he does not appear. Other people, known as "sureties", may "go bail" for the accused person. They will agree to be financially responsible for him and will have to give up the money if he stays away without a good excuse. This is called "entering into a recognizance". The court decides whether the sureties are responsible people and unlikely to be in league with the accused person.

In the United States, if a person has not enough money himself and is not able to find any sureties, he may borrow the money from a bail bondsman. He will have to pay about 10 per cent of the amount borrowed to the bonds-man as a fee.

Sometimes the court makes other conditions of bail. The person may be required to live in a particular place so that the police know where to find him, or he may be required to report to a police station at certain times. If it is thought likely that he may leave the country, he may be required to give up his passport until the trial is over.

The court has to make sure that it is safe for an accused person to be allowed bail. When bail is refused it is not done in order to punish him but because it is thought that he might run away, or try to influence witnesses, or injure himself if he were allowed on bail.

Bail is rarely allowed for murder and not often for other serious crimes of violence. When bail is refused, the accused person may appeal to a higher court, where it may be granted.

See also COURT; TRIAL.

BAIRD, John Logie (1888–1946). John Logie Baird was famous as being the first person to demonstrate true television (see TELEVISION). He was born at Helensburgh in Dumbarton-shire, Scotland, and was educated at the Royal Technical College and at Glasgow University.

In 1906, Baird started research into "seeing by wireless" and moved to Hastings, in Sussex, England. In 1924, in his tiny laboratory at Hastings, he managed to obtain an image or picture of objects in outline on a screen. The following year he had improved his apparatus so that he could transmit in his laboratory in London a recognizable image of human faces with light, shade, and detail. In January 1926 he demonstrated before the Royal Institution

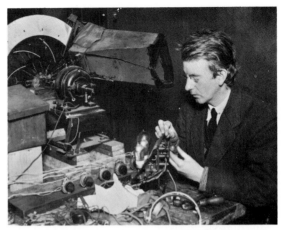

BBC Hulton Picture Library

Baird at work on his television transmitter in 1925. In that year he first transmitted real pictures.

of Great Britain the first true television ever shown.

In 1928 Baird became the first person to transmit television from one side of the Atlantic to the other, and in 1929 the German post office began to broadcast television using his system. The British Broadcasting Corporation (BBC) began television broadcasts the same year and lent their transmitter to Baird to continue his experiments. In 1936, when the BBC started television as a public service, they used two rival systems—one by Baird and the other by Marconi. Eventually, however, they decided to use only the Marconi system.

Just before World War II Baird gave a demonstration of television in natural colors and in 1946, a few months before he died, it was said that he had finished his researches into stereoscopic television. For this, two views of an object are taken from slightly different angles so that when they are put together the picture has a solid or "three-dimensional" appearance, rather than looking flat. Baird's other major invention was a "noctovisor", an instrument for seeing in the dark (what we now call an image intensifier), which he demonstrated in 1927.

BAJA CALIFORNIA (*Lower California*) is a peninsula in Mexico, 1,220 kilometers (760 miles) in length. The northern half, the state of Baja California Norte, has its capital at

Mexicali. The southern half, Baja California Sur, with its capital at La Paz, became a state in 1974.

The peninsula is between 48 and 240 kilometers (30 and 150 miles) wide. It is separated from the Mexican mainland by the Gulf of California and the mouth of the Colorado River. The Pacific Ocean borders Lower California on the south and west, the United States borders it on the north.

Mountain ranges, some with peaks of 3,000 meters (10,000 feet), rise along Lower California's entire length. The land is hot and dry during most of the year. There are many deserts. Because there is little rain, many people live by irrigation farming. The All-American Canal brings Colorado River water to the Mexicali section of the Imperial Valley. There, wheat, barley, alfalfa (lucerne), tomatoes, melons, and cotton are grown. Cotton is also grown in the south-central region in places where water is pumped from wells. Sugar-cane, dates, peanuts, chickpeas, bananas, citrus, and other tropical fruits are grown in the southern territory. Wine grapes and also olives are important agricultural products.

At one time Lower California and the region which later became the state of California in the United States were both a part of Mexico. The present International Boundary was agreed to in the Treaty of Guadalupe Hidalgo (1848), which ended the war between the United States and Mexico. (See MEXICAN WAR.)

The population of Baja California Norte is 1,327,000; of Baja California Sur, 263,000 (1984).

BALANCHINE, George (1904–83), the

Russian-American choreographer, was born Georgy Melitonovich Balanchivadze in the Russian city of St. Petersburg (now Leningrad). His father was the composer, Meliton Balanchivadze, and Balanchine himself had a musical training at the Petrograd Conservatory. He also trained as a dancer at the Imperial School of Ballet in his native city. Graduating with honors, Balanchine joined

BBC Hulton Picture Library

George Balanchine, Russian-born choreographer, was the artistic director and one of the founders of the New York City Ballet.

the ballet company of St. Petersburg (which is now the Kirov Ballet). While on tour with the company in 1925, Balanchine left them to join Diaghilev's Ballets Russes in France. In a very short time he became their leading choreographer, and he created ten ballets for them. Two of these are still performed—*Apollo* and *The Prodigal Son*. With *Apollo*, first performed in 1928, began an association and close friendship spanning close on fifty years with the Russian composer Igor Stravinsky (on whom there is a separate article). Balanchine choreographed many of Stravinsky's compositions, including the well-known *Pulcinella* for the New York City Ballet in 1972.

On Diaghilev's death in 1929, the Ballets Russes disbanded, and Balanchine worked for a few more years in France before accepting an invitation to go to the United States.

In the United States Balanchine played a key role in popularizing ballet. He started the School of American Ballet in 1934, soon to be the leading ballet school in the country. Several ballet companies emerged from this school, the greatest of which was the New York City Ballet, with which Balanchine was involved from the start in 1948 until his death in 1983. In fact, Balanchine's first ballet in

America, *Serenade*, to music by Tchaikovsky and composed for his students at the ballet school, was adopted as the signature piece of the New York City Ballet.

Balanchine created over 150 ballets for the New York City Ballet. Moreover, nearly every leading ballet company in the world has produced his works. He also pioneered choreography for stage musicals, opera, films, and television.

Balanchine commissioned music for his ballets from composers, such as Schoenberg and Ives, who were not popular at the time, and he often used pieces that were difficult to dance to. But he exacted very high standards from his dancers, expecting them to dance at a fast pace to fast music rather than adapting the music to suit the dancers. Many of his ballets did not tell a story, yet they were thrilling and exciting to watch.

Balanchine, known to the ballet world as "Mr. B", was more than anyone else responsible for popularizing ballet in the United States.

BALBOA, Vasco Núñez de (c. 1475–1519).

The Spanish soldier-explorer Balboa is most famous as the man who discovered the Pacific Ocean. He was born in western Spain in about 1475 and at the age of 26 he sailed for the newly discovered West Indies. He began a plantation there, on the island of Hispaniola, but he very soon fell into debt. By hiding in a cask which was put on board a ship sailing to Puerto Rico, another island in the West Indies, he managed to escape. When the crew found the settlement on that island in ruins, Balboa persuaded them to go to Darien, in the land now called Panama, where they founded a new colony. When the leaders quarreled, Balboa took command. Soon after, he set out to conquer the nearby country.

On one of his expeditions inland he heard from an Indian chief about a great ocean on the other side of the mountains and of the gold of Peru, farther to the south. Balboa set out in 1513 with 190 Spaniards and 1,000 natives to cross the Isthmus of Panama; that is, the narrow strip of land joining Central and South

Mansell Collection

Balboa walks into the Pacific Ocean, the first westerner to do so, and claims it for Spain in 1513.

America. At this time he had received news that the king of Spain intended to replace him, so it was to win the king's favor with new conquests and riches that Balboa was spurred on in his life's work of discovery explorations.

Worried by insects, weakened by disease, and weighed down by their armor, Balboa and his soldiers cut their way through the tropical jungle and toiled across the mountains. When they reached the top of the last range they saw before them a vast expanse of sea. They were the first white men to set eyes on the Pacific and Balboa claimed it for the king of Spain!

When King Ferdinand read Balboa's account of his discoveries and received the rich presents sent with it he made him admiral of the Pacific. At the same time, however, he sent Don Pedro Arias de Avila to replace him as Governor of Darien. Jealous of Balboa's plans for further discoveries and fearing he might win back his office as governor, de Avila had Balboa tried for treason, condemned to death, and executed in the public square of Darien, in 1519.

BALEARIC ISLANDS.

A group of islands in the Mediterranean, ranging from 80 to 306 kilometers (50 to 190 miles) off the coast of Spain. The four largest are Majórca, Minorca, Ibiza, and Formentera. The islands form a Spanish province and the capital is Palma, in Majorca, which has a famous 13th-century Gothic cathedral.

Most of the people work on farms, growing fruit and vegetables and raising pigs, sheep, and goats. Olives, wines, fruits, almonds, and salt are exported to many parts of the world, and there are also fisheries. Thousands of people visit the islands every year because of their beauty, their mild and fairly dry climate, much like that of southern California, and their historic interest.

The islands' many good harbors were important to the ancient Phoenicians, Greeks, Romans, and others who traded in the western Mediterranean. When the Moors ruled Spain, the islands were headquarters for pirates (see MOORS).

Except for Minorca, the islands have belonged to Spain for centuries. Great Britain owned Minorca for a large part of the 18th century and it finally became Spanish in 1802.

The population of the Balearic Islands is 699,100 (1982).

BALFOUR, Arthur James (1848–1930), was prime minister of Britain from 1902 to 1905, and, as foreign minister in 1917, the author of the Balfour Declaration. In this statement the British government promised to establish a national home in Palestine for the Jewish people. The plan was carried out in 1948 when the modern state of Israel was formed.

Balfour was born in Scotland. He was educated at Eton College and Cambridge University, and entered parliament in 1874. He did not seem seriously interested in politics, but in 1887 his uncle, Lord Salisbury, Conservative prime minister, made him secretary of state for Ireland. He proved to be a good debater, and he was unafraid of criticism. After holding several cabinet offices, he became prime minister in 1902 when his uncle resigned. His party remained in power until it was defeated by the Liberal party in 1906. Balfour had resigned as prime minister in December 1905. He retired from the party leadership in 1911.

During World War I, he served in Lloyd George's government. He became first lord of the admiralty and later foreign minister. In 1922 he was made a Knight of the Garter and an earl.

BBC Hulton Picture Library

Lord Balfour, author of the Balfour Declaration of 1917 expressing British support for Zionism.

BALI is a beautiful island and province of Indonesia, 1.6 kilometers (1 mile) east of Java. It covers 5,623 square kilometers (2,171 square miles) and has a population of around 2.5 million. The north is mountainous and volcanic. Mount Agung, the highest peak, reaches a height of 3,142 meters (10,308 feet). The climate is hot and wet with most rain falling between December and April. Deer live in the mountain forests; at one time there were Bali tigers, but they may now be extinct.

Rice, the chief food, is grown in the densely populated southern lowlands. Coconuts, coffee, sugar-cane, and tobacco are also grown. Apart from handicrafts, Bali lacks industry, but tourism, especially at beach resorts near Denpasar, the capital and largest town, is expanding rapidly.

The local religion known as Bali-Hinduism is based on Hinduism with elements of Buddhism, ancestor worship, and ancient nature worship. Religion colors all aspects of life. The many ceremonies include painful teeth-filing for youngsters entering adulthood, and funerals with costly cremation ceremonies designed to release the souls of dead people from their bodies so that they may be reincarnated (born again).

Most Balinese live in villages, each of which has its own temple or temples and a *gamelan* (percussion) orchestra. These orchestras, consisting largely of gongs and xylophones, perform at religious festivals and also at dance-dramas illustrating Hindu mythology.

The Balinese are divided into four castes. The largest, comprising 93 per cent of the population, consists of *Sudras*, or peasants. The higher castes are the *Wesias*, made up of merchants and soldiers; the *Satrias*, descendants of old rulers; and the *Brahmanas*, from whom priests are chosen.

BALKANS. The countries in the peninsula that forms the southeast corner of Europe are called the Balkans, or the Balkan States. They are Yugoslavia, Albania, Greece, Romania, and Bulgaria. To the west of the peninsula are the Adriatic Sea and the Ionian Sea, to the south the Mediterranean and the Aegean, and to the east the Black Sea.

Most of the Balkan peninsula is wild and mountainous. Down the whole western side runs a range of mountains which are called the Dinaric Alps in the north. Near the coast of Yugoslavia and Albania the mountains are

of limestone, and in them there are deep narrow gorges between barren rocky heights, rushing underground rivers and many caves. (The name for this kind of limestone country is "karst".) There are dozens of islands and inlets all along this coastline, which is very beautiful.

Eastward of their main ridge, the mountains slope down into wild tangled hills where there are forests on the slopes and green fertile valleys.

The Danube is the most important of the navigable rivers, crossing the Balkans from Germany to the Black Sea. The Morava, Sava, and Tisa in Yugoslavia are three of the many important rivers which empty into the Danube along its course. Others are the Jiu and the Olt in Romania and the Iskur in Bulgaria (see DANUBE RIVER).

There are two great valleys running through the middle of the Balkan peninsula in Yugoslavia, one of the River Morava, which flows north, and the other of the River Vardar, which flows southward. These two valleys are joined together by a low pass over the mountains, and together they make a natural highway down from the north to the south.

How the Balkan Peoples Live

The countries in the Balkan peninsula have not been independent or had their present boundaries for long. (The story of the Balkan peoples and their countries is given later in this article, under the two sub-headings "History of the Balkans" and "The Coming of Independence".) They are young countries and have not had time to become strong economically. There are, however, many valuable minerals in these countries. Yugoslavia produces large amounts of copper, chrome, lead, zinc, and bauxite. There are also large iron-ore and coal deposits. Bulgaria has a variety of minerals; its main mining industry is in the Pernik coalfield near Sofia. Romania has many oil-wells and produces more petroleum products than any other country in Europe except the United Kingdom and the USSR. The oil resources of Yugoslavia and Albania are also being developed.

Courtesy, Yugoslav Tourist Office and Bulgarian Tourist Organization

Top left: Bulgaria, with its Black Sea coast, has built fine new hotels to cater for the growing number of visitors.
Top right: A village on a steep hillside in Bulgaria. **Bottom left**: Buildings in Sarajevo, former capital of Bosnia-Hercegovina in central Yugoslavia, show a mixture of eastern and western influence. The Balkans have been a bridge between the cultures of east and west for centuries. **Bottom right**: A narrow street in Zagreb, capital of Croatia in northwest Yugoslavia. There are many Roman Catholics in Croatia and in Slovenia to the north; elsewhere in the Balkans most Christians belong to branches of the Eastern Orthodox Church.

All the Balkan countries have light industries, the processing of farm produce being the most important. Agriculture is the main industry; the north and central areas of the peninsula produce grain, vegetables and livestock. Tobacco is also produced.

History of the Balkans

So far in this article the inhabitants of the Balkans have been described as if they all belonged to one nation. In fact there are several peoples in the Balkan countries and there may be more than one people in one country. To understand why this is so, it is necessary to go a long way back into history. No part of Europe has been invaded by other peoples quite so often as the Balkan peninsula. Over many hundreds of years waves of invaders pushed their way into the Balkans from the east and north, and each time they destroyed the civilization they found there. The descendants of all these peoples live in the Balkans today.

The first great invaders were Latin-speaking people, the Romans. They ruled over all the Balkans during the first centuries after Christ and made the River Danube their frontier against the barbarians. The Roman empire was divided into two parts in AD 364. The northwest corner of the Balkans remained under Rome's rule, but the rest was ruled from the new capital of the eastern part of the empire, Constantinople. This eastern empire came to be called the Byzantine Empire and the language of its people was Greek (see CONSTANTINOPLE).

After the Romans came barbarian tribes. Two warlike peoples called the Goths and the Huns invaded the Balkans at various times during the 4th and 5th centuries, destroying towns and villages wherever they went. In the 6th century, huge numbers of people called Slavs poured in from the north and settled down to live all over the peninsula, killing the former inhabitants or driving them into the hills. Yet another people, the Bulgars, who were a Turkish tribe, arrived in the next hundred years and set up a great empire, but in the end they were conquered by the Greeks of

the Byzantine empire. Meanwhile, two of the Balkan peoples, the Serbs and the Croats, had formed separate states.

By that time, many different peoples were living in the Balkan peninsula, and it was never peaceful for long. Wars were fought and new peoples seized power and then were conquered in their turn. The Serbian people, for instance, under their king Stephan Dushan, built up a powerful state which was destroyed in the last great invasion. This came when the Turks crossed over to Europe and occupied almost all the Balkan peninsula in the 14th century. Constantinople itself, the capital of the Byzantine empire, was captured. It has remained a Turkish city ever since.

The Coming of Independence

In the 19th century all the different peoples of the Balkans rose against their Turkish rulers. By that time the idea was spreading through Europe that each nation should govern itself and not be under the power of rulers belonging to another nation. One by one the Balkan peoples rebelled and became independent. At last in 1878 a meeting of some of the great powers of Europe, called the Congress of Berlin, decided that Romania, Bulgaria, and Serbia should become free countries. But the Congress allowed Austria—then a powerful country—to occupy the provinces of Bosnia and Hercegovina, which were claimed by Serbia. (This led later to serious trouble, because the people of Bosnia hated their rulers. In June 1914 a young Bosnian killed the heir to the throne of Austria, Archduke Francis Ferdinand, while he was in the Bosnian capital Sarajevo. Austria accused Serbia of being behind the plot, and this was one of the causes of World War I.)

Even after the Congress of Berlin the Turks kept considerable power in the Balkans. But in 1912 the free Balkan states joined together in a war against Turkey and defeated it. However, they quarreled about how the conquered lands should be divided, and in 1913 fought another war between themselves. Serbia and Greece defeated Bulgaria and divided between them most of the lands that had been won from the Turks. A new state called Albania was also set up. It was not until after World War I, however, that the country of Yugoslavia came into existence. In it, several different peoples were united—Serbs, Croats, Slovenes, Bosnians, and Montenegrins.

Since World War II, most of the countries in the Balkan peninsula have become part of the East European group of communist countries that are under the influence of the USSR. Albania, though communist, remains fiercely independent. Yugoslavia, which broke away from Russian influence in 1948, follows a comparatively independent line in home and foreign affairs. (For more information about the Balkan states, see the separate articles on all these countries.)

BALLAD. Ballads—folk-songs or poems which told exciting or romantic stories—were very popular in the Middle Ages. Nowadays other kinds of poems are also called ballads—simple sentimental verses that are often set to music and sung. Sometimes the word ballad now just means a song, usually a lovesong in a slow tempo. The old ballads, which were very different from these modern ones, can still be read in poetry books.

Ballads developed during the late Middle Ages. Nobody knows who composed any ballad originally, but people memorized ballads they heard, and performed them for other people, often changing them a little in the process. At royal courts and great houses, minstrels would entertain their master and his guests with songs that were a personal form of ballad.

Most ballads have fairly short lines which rhyme, and short verses too, so that they are easy to remember. The stories are told in an exciting and dramatic way, sometimes in conversation, like this one from Scotland:

"O where hae ye been, Lord Randal, my son?
  O where hae ye been, my handsome young man!"—
"I hae been to the wild wood; mother, make my bed soon,
  For I'm weary wi' hunting, and fain wald lie down."

"Where gat ye your dinner, Lord Randal, my son?
  Where gat ye your dinner, my handsome young man?"—
"I dined wi' my true-love; mother, make my bed soon,
  For I'm weary wi' hunting, and fain wald lie down."

"What gat ye to your dinner, Lord Randal, my son?
  What gat ye to your dinner, my handsome young man?"—
"I gat eels boil'd in broo'; mother, make my bed soon,
  For I'm weary wi' hunting, and fain wald lie down."

"O I fear ye are poison'd, Lord Randal, my son!
  O I fear ye are poison'd, my handsome young man!"—
"Oh yes! I am poison'd; mother; make my bed soon,
  For I'm sick at the heart, and I fain wald lie down."

Many ballads like "Lord Randal" tell mysterious stories of death, bloodshed, and adventure; others are about love, often ill-fated love that comes to a sorrowful end; and many tell of ghosts and fairies, or of the adventures of famous heroes like King Arthur or Robin Hood, or of great battles and deeds of history, like the battle of Chevy Chase. The language of a ballad, often full of local, or dialect, words, is nevertheless simple and lively because it was the language of ordinary people and not of scholars or courtiers.

Many ballads in English have a chorus or refrain. The last line of each verse in "Lord Randal" is the refrain; sometimes the refrain is in the second and fourth lines. It does not always fit into the story; sometimes it is no more than a lilting chorus like "With a hey lillelu and howlolan, And the birk and the broom blows bonny." Many work-songs, such as the old sea chanteys of the age of sailing ships, were ballads with a refrain. Workers or seamen would join in the refrain, because singing would help them to perform their tasks.

During the 17th century, settlers from England arrived in North America bringing many of their traditional ballads with them. Sometimes these old ballads were changed to fit the new life in the colonies. These American ballads, based on English models, often differ from their English originals in both verse form and rhyme scheme but they still tell a story in poetry and song. Out of the settlement of the West, the American Civil War, the building of the railroads, the rise of trade unions, and other historic events come such literary ballads as "Sweet Betsy from Pike", "Jesse James", and "Casey Jones".

Nearly all countries have traditional ballads of their own. Ballad-like songs are found throughout Europe, especially in Denmark,

Mansell Collection

Popular ballads, printed on broadsides, were sold in the streets of London until the 18th century.

France, Germany, Greece, Russia, and Spain. Some non-English ballads, such as those of Russia, are not divided into verses and do not use rhyme.

The most important development in the history of the ballad in Britain resulted from the invention of printing. When printing became cheap in the 16th century, ballads were sometimes printed and sold on sheets of paper called broadsides. Often these broadsides, which were sold to many people throughout the country, contained references to current events, almost like a newspaper. Many were witty or satirical, but the first big collection of ballads was printed in the 18th century, when Bishop Thomas Percy brought out his *Reliques of Ancient Poetry*. After this people became excited about ballads, and have been interested in them ever since. They have tried to discover others and to write ballads of their own.

The most famous of these poems written in imitation of the old ballads is probably Samuel Taylor Coleridge's "The Rime of the Ancient Mariner".

BALLET. When a ballet is performed in the theater a story is told to the audience, not in words like a play, but in dancing and movement accompanied by music. As well as dancing and music, two other things are very important in ballet—poetry (or drama) and design. (To have poetry in ballet may seem strange, but the way ballet uses it is explained further on in the article.)

The first important thing is the dancing. The dancers in ballet are actors, for they express themselves in movement and must make their story clear without speaking. They have really two jobs to fulfill: to thrill and to please by the beauty of their movements, and to make the audience understand what they are doing and feeling at the moment. This last they can do either by what is called mime, a fixed sign language in which the same signs always represent the same thing, or by free movement and the expressions on their faces, like a charade.

In contemporary ballet the charade method is mainly used, while old-fashioned mime survives only in a few older classical ballets such as *Les Sylphides, Giselle, Coppélia, Swan Lake, The Sleeping Beauty* and *The Nutcracker*. In these ballets there is a definite break in the dancing while the dancers mime the story. In the modern ballet, dancing and acting go on together all the time.

Ballet Music

The music in ballet also has two definite tasks to perform: to beat time, just as the tom-tom, stamping feet, and the clapping hands do in some of the dances of African peoples; and to provide the atmosphere, or set the scene. The first is obvious but the second needs some further explanation.

When you listen to a piece of music, especially if it is the kind called "program" music (that is, music written to express a definite story or idea), you often think you can see a whole series of pictures: for instance, the storm in Rossini's *William Tell*, the lapping of water and the rush of waves in Mendelssohn's *Fingal's Cave*, or the flutter of fairy wings in the same composer's *Midsummer Night's Dream*. The music in fact gives you the background to a story; it shows you the scene and makes you have the same feelings as the composer had. This "scene-setting music" is enormously important in a kind of acting where not a word is spoken and the audience must

The hunters and the swans in a scene from *Swan Lake*. Stage settings in classical ballet are often elaborate.

understand everything by watching the stage and hearing the music. Music of this type is by no means the finest kind of music but it is without a doubt the most suitable for ballet, where it is not just a question of listening but of listening *and* looking together.

The best way is for ballet music to be specially composed for the occasion as was Tchaikovsky's for *Swan Lake* and *The Sleeping Princess*, Stravinsky's for *The Firebird* and *Petrushka*, and Sir Arthur Bliss's for *Checkmate*. Sometimes, however, music that has already been composed fits a ballet perfectly, for example, Schumann's music for *Carnaval*, or Chopin's music in *Les Sylphides*. It needs the greatest skill and knowledge to fit music that has already been composed to a new ballet; the only practical way is to do it the other way round, fitting the ballet to the music.

Poetry, Drama, and Design

Poetry and drama make up the third part of ballet. It is by far the most difficult to understand and it may even seem to be nonsense— poetry and drama yet without words! If you think, however, once again of a charade you will understand. In a charade, as you know from experience, it is only possible to convey something very simple and direct. An audience can be made to understand such sentences as "I love you", "I hate you", "I am cold and hungry", "Leave the room at once", but it cannot be made to understand, "Come and have tea with me some time next week" or "Hello, Uncle". This means that drama in ballet can show only comparatively few things. Yet in another sense it can show more than the spoken word, because if nothing is described very exactly then a great deal is left to the imagination of the audience.

Poetry and drama may be present in ballet in many ways. There need not be a story at all, just a poetic atmosphere, sylphs dancing in a moonlit glade (*Les Sylphides*), or an idea, the fight between good and evil (*Dante Sonata*), or a familiar fairy-tale with a plot (*The Sleeping Beauty*), or a modern story of slum life (*Miracle in the Gorbals*). Another type of ballet is just rhythmic movement to music with no story at all. This is sometimes called "abstract" ballet; *Symphonic Variations* by César Franck is an example.

Ballet Girls on the Stage by the 19th-century French painter, Edgar Degas.

A scene from the film *Tales of Beatrix Potter*, danced by members of the Royal Ballet and choreographed by Sir Frederick Ashton. Michael Coleman, seen here, took the part of Jeremy Fisher.

Designing is the last of the arts involved in the making of a ballet. The designer-artist is responsible for the scenery, or settings, and costumes, and supervises the building of sets, and the painting of the scenery and the back-cloth, which is the huge canvas sheet hanging at the back of the stage. Scenery is often important to the story in classical ballet. The color and shape of the costumes are important to the grouping and dancing, the backcloth is an essential part of the look of the ballet. Abstract ballets depend less on scenery, though skillful lighting and other effects help to project the dancers' movements.

A specialist lighting designer has to make sure that the stage is suitably lit. If scenery or lighting is poor, it is almost impossible to see movement properly, and an unsuitable cos-tume, apart from hindering the dance, may ruin the beauty of the dancer's movements. Also, since there are no words, the costumes and scenery help to make the meaning clear, to show the audience, for instance, that Petru-shka is a pathetic rag doll, or that Aurora in

The Sleeping Princess is a fairy princess living at a luxurious court.

The Choreographer

In the way that has been described above, the dancers, the composer, the author, and the designer are equal partners in the making of a ballet. There is one other partner—the cho-reographer. He is the person who plans and arranges the dance part of the ballet, and to do this he has to be an experienced dancer him-self. In many cases the choreographer also thinks out the story that he puts into move-ment. It is not easy to be a good choreographer, for he must know everything about dancing and about the ways of showing ideas and feel-ings and stories by movements. He must also be a very experienced musician and under-stand the different styles of great painting and sculpture. The choreographer has the task of choosing a good designer. Many choreogra-phers have continued to work until an ad-vanced age. George Balanchine, the Russian-born American choreographer, who died in

These are the five basic positions:

first   second   third   fourth   fifth

1983, is regarded by many as the greatest choreographer of the 20th century. He worked into his eighties.

A ballet can be a success only when all the right ingredients are mixed with care—when the author, the choreographer, the composer, and the painter are expressing the same idea, each in his particular way, and when the dancers fully understand what this is and are skillful enough to make this idea and meaning clear to the audience.

A good example of a successful ballet is *The Three-Cornered Hat*. This brings to ballet a simple tale of the life of Spanish peasants. The composer, Manuel de Falla, has taken Spanish folk music and "translated" it to be played by a symphony orchestra; the painter, Pablo Picasso, has taken the peasant costumes of Spain and altered them to be worn by dancers on the stage; the choreographer, Leonide Massine, has taken the folk dances of Spain and arranged them to be performed by trained dancers on the stage. All three have had the same idea—to use the Spanish music, costumes, and dancing and to make from them a complete ballet to be performed in the theater—and the result of their work together is a masterpiece.

Choreographers and designers are often engaged to create new versions of old ballets. For example, there have been many new versions of *The Nutcracker* since it was first performed in Russia in 1892.

How the Dancers are Trained

Many children take ballet lessons from a very early age, and many thousands of them would like to become ballet dancers. Yet most of them must be disappointed, for there are only a few vacancies a year in the ballet companies; and only a very few people are suited by nature for the hard and difficult life of a career in ballet.

The best age to begin training is between 9 and 11. At first only a daily lesson of about an hour is necessary and then later, after 16, many hours must be spent in lessons and rehearsals. The dancer is ready to appear before the public at about 18 years of age; that is, after nine years of hard physical and mental study for a career that can only last for less than 20 years.

The dancer is really the player of an instrument—not a musical instrument, for her instrument is her body, which she must learn to use perfectly. The female dancer should be comparatively small, between five feet two inches and five feet five inches tall, have a small head well set on the shoulders, well-rounded arms, strong straight legs, straight knees, well-arched feet and toes the proper shape and strength to provide a platform to support the weight of the body. It takes an expert to tell the right type of foot and very great damage can be done if a mistake is made. In any case, no pupil should attempt to get on to points (or *pointe*), that is, on tip-toe, without

Angela Taylor

Amanda Britton and Ben Craft of the Ballet Rambert, London, dance in *Carmen Arcadiae Mechanicae Perpetuum*.

at least two years' training, and then only for very short periods under the strictest and most expert guidance.

The early training is largely physical for what is called "placing the body". Later, artistic training and the training of the mind begins. "You dance with your head," the great Pavlova was never tired of repeating. But even the most perfect physical skill counts for nothing if the pupil is not musical, for dancing is not like athletics or acrobatics, but an art in which movement must be rhythmical and must express a meaning.

Ballet as a career is obviously for only a few, but to learn it under the right teacher is a first-class physical training and an education in the graceful movement of the whole body which is useful and enjoyable for everyone.

There are special schools for training the professional ballet dancer, such as the Royal Ballet School in Great Britain, the Kirov School in Leningrad dating back to 1738, the School of American Ballet in New York. These schools admit would-be dancers from a young age, about seven or eight.

Boys are as important as girls in ballet. Without its male dancers ballet could not exist as an art that shows meanings and ideas in movement. There are today many more openings for the manly athletic boy than for the girl, and the boy does not need to have the perfect foot as the girl does. The words manly and athletic are very important, for this is what the male dancer must be—a ballet needs a contrast of two kinds of movement, strong and manly movements and graceful feminine ones. Strength does not mean that a person cannot be graceful too, for grace is not something that only women and girls have. Great sportsmen—the great cricketer, the boxer, the football player and the bullfighter—are graceful as well as strong. If a dancer is exceptionally promising, then he or she will join the *corps de ballet* of a company and will start to perform minor roles. This gives the dancer some experience of performance. The best dancers then move on to become soloists or principal dancers.

Early History

There was something like ballet in ancient Greece and Rome and even in ancient Egypt, for the peoples of those countries often used dancing to express their religious ideas. But ballet as it is known today really began in the reign of King Louis XIV of France in the 17th century. The King himself loved dancing and the whole court used to take part in the ballets, the King often playing the leading parts. It is because of ballet's beginning in France that the words used in ballet—*pirouette, entrechat*, and the word *ballet* itself—are French.

The actual steps used in ballet dancing have come about in several different ways. Some were taken from the stately dances performed at court, where the dancers could not move very freely because of their heavy court clothes; others came from folk dances and country dances, and also from the leaping and dancing of the acrobats and tumblers who used to wander from town to town during the Middle Ages. At first ballet used to be danced in long heavy costumes, but gradually shorter and lighter dresses began to be worn so that the dancers were more free and could use many different steps. When tights to be worn in the theater were invented at the beginning of the 19th century, dancers were at last able to dance without being hindered by awkward clothes.

Some of the great dancers of the past altered and improved the whole way ballet was danced. Marie Camargo, the Belgian-French ballerina, who made her début (that is, her first appearance) in 1726, was the first outstanding ballerina to wear a shorter skirt which showed her ankles. Because the audience could now see the dancer's feet, the movement of the feet off the ground became important. In 1736, Marie Sallé also introduced changes in costume that were regarded as quite revolutionary at the time. By loosening her skirt and bodice while she danced, she was able to move more freely and could put more expression into her dancing. Sallé was also the first woman to choreograph the ballets in which she danced. In the 18th century, too, Jean Georges Noverre, a choreographer and ballet master to the French queen, Marie-Antoinette, helped ballet to be less tied down by rules and more able to express ideas in a dramatic way, while Maximilian Gardel stopped dancers from wearing masks, so that they could act with their faces as well as with their bodies. An Italian named Carlo Blasis wrote a book in 1830 which for the first time gave a proper system of rules for ballet training.

However, it was the famous ballerina Marie Taglione (1804–84) who made some of the biggest changes. It was because of her delicate appearance and beautiful dancing that the principal female dancer, the *prima ballerina*, became more popular than the male dancer. She was the first ballerina to wear the flimsy white tarlatan dress and probably the first, too, to stand on the tips of her toes as if ready for flight.

The Russian Ballet

Ballet developed as it spread from place to place. From France it spread to Italy, then to Russia, and it was there that ballet as it is today really developed—a style of dancing that combines the gracefulness of the French way of dancing with the strength and variety of the Italian way. The Russian ballet became famous when a Frenchman named Marius Petipa went to Russia in 1847 and took charge of the ballet in St. Petersburg; there he created great ballets like *Swan Lake*, *The Sleeping Beauty*, and *The Nutcracker*, in collaboration with the composer Peter Ilich Tchaikovsky. He worked with the Imperial Ballet in St. Petersburg for more than 50 years.

Among the Russian dancers are some whose names ballet lovers will never forget, such as Vaslav Nijinsky, Tamara Karsavina, Anna Pavlova, and Galina Ulanova. In 1909 a Russian ballet company went to Paris under the leadership of Sergei Diaghilev, who had the finest artists working with him: dancers, choreographers, composers, and designers. Among the choreographers were Michel Fokine, Léonide Massine, and George Balanchine; among the composers were Igor Stravinsky, Claude Debussy, and Erik Satie. The painters of the sets included Pablo Picasso and André Derain.

Much in ballet today comes from Diaghilev. When he began his work, ballet had become an old-fashioned entertainment, but he made it a living and exciting art in which new ballets could be created. Many of Diaghilev's artists later moved to the United States, when that country started to become an innovative center of ballet. More recently, Russian dancers such as Rudolf Nureyev have left the USSR to work with Western ballet companies.

Dame Ninette de Valois, who founded the English national ballet of Sadler's Wells, was one of Diaghilev's dancers, and Dame Marie Rambert, who took ballet to theaters all over Britain, was influenced by him.

In 1956 the Sadler's Wells company became the Royal Ballet and it performs at the Royal Opera House, Covent Garden, in London. From this company came great dancers, such as Sir Robert Helpmann, Dame Margot Fonteyn, and the choreographer Sir Frederick Ashton.

Two contemporary American ballet companies are the American Ballet Theatre, established in 1940 and directed by the Russian Mikhail Baryshnikov since 1980, and the New York City Ballet, with which Balanchine was associated until his death in 1983. It is also known as the Balanchine Ballet. Its stars include Suzanne Farrell, Edward Villela, and Peter Martins, the Danish dancer, who succeeded Balanchine as co-director in 1983. Russia's great companies are the Bolshoi Ballet in Moscow, and the Kirov in Leningrad (the renamed Imperial Russian Ballet). Many famous Russian dancers, including the exiles Baryshnikov, Makarova, and Nureyev, are products of the Kirov. Canada has three major companies, the National Ballet of Canada, founded in 1951, Les Grands Ballets Canadiens of Montreal, and the Royal Ballet of Winnipeg. The Australian Ballet and the Australian Dance Theatre are the major ballet companies of Australia.

Other famous contemporary ballet companies include the Royal Danish Ballet, the Dutch National Ballet and the Netherlands Dance Theater, the Paris Opéra, and Brussels Ballet of the 20th Century, directed by Frenchman Maurice Béjart.

See also DANCE.

BALLOON. The simplest form of aircraft is a balloon. It usually consists of a light bag in the shape of a ball or sausage and made of paper, silk or rubberized fabric, containing hot air, hydrogen, or helium because all three are lighter than ordinary air. To the bag may be attached, by cords or netting, a basket or car for passengers.

Balloons may be allowed to float freely in the air or they may be anchored to the ground by a cable. Free balloons are generally used for upper-air exploration or for racing. Tethered balloons are sometimes used to support radio antennae (or aerials) or advertising signs, and in wartime they may form balloon barrages, like aerial fences, to protect cities or seaports against low-level bombing attacks.

A balloon floats in the air for the same reason that a fish floats in water. Each displaces, by its bulk, more than its own weight of the air or water surrounding it. As long as a balloon and all its equipment weigh less than the volume of air displaced, it will rise. If it loses some of its lifting gas so that its volume decreases, it will sink.

Before take-off a balloon must be held down by ropes or weights. When released, it will rise to a height where the weight of the air displaced equals its own weight, because the density of the air gets less higher up. Then, if the pilot wants to go up or down, he must reduce either his weight or his buoyancy. To do the

1 De Rozier and d'Arlandes take off in a hot-air balloon in 1783.
2 Russian scientists in Antarctica send up a balloon to investigate the weather at great heights. The measurements made by its instruments are transmitted as radio signals.
3 A US personnel-carrying balloon takes off for the stratosphere. As the surrounding air becomes thinner, the bag swells to a sphere 60 meters (200 feet) in diameter.

first, he must throw ballast (sand was used for this) overboard; for the second, he must let out some of the gas. Since neither gas nor ballast can be replaced in flight, the pilot has only limited control in going upwards or downwards. He can also only drift with the wind, for a balloon cannot be steered in flight and so is of little use as a means of getting from place to place. (See AIRSHIP.)

It is strange that no one invented a balloon before the end of the 18th century. A hot-air balloon is a very simple thing known to most people, yet the importance of the fact that smoke over a hot fire always goes up does not seem to have struck anyone until 1782. Then two French brothers, Joseph and Etienne Montgolfier, began to take a scientific interest in the smoke from their kitchen fire. They noticed that it always behaved in the same way and came to the conclusion that this was due to some peculiar property in it which they called "levity".

They decided to catch some smoke in a paper bag and see what would happen. The bag promptly rose to the kitchen ceiling. They had made the first balloon. Then they began to experiment in earnest. They tested several large bags made of silk, feeding their fires with wool and straw, for they did not know that it was heat and not smoke that produced "levity".

After a year they were ready to show their invention to the world. On 5 June 1783, in the market place of their native village of Annonay, they inflated a silk bag 9 meters (32 feet) in diameter over a hot fire. To the astonishment of the crowd it rose more than 1.5 kilometers (1 mile) into the air before it cooled off and floated back to earth.

The news spread rapidly and even the learned men of the French Academy of Sciences took a practical interest. They had the excellent idea of using a light gas to fill the balloon instead of hot air. The English scientist Henry Cavendish had just discovered the gas hydrogen which, being 15 times lighter than air, seemed ideal for the purpose (see HYDROGEN). J. A. C. Charles, a Frenchman, set about the manufacture of sufficient hydrogen to fill a balloon and in August 1783 the first *Charlière* balloon ascended from the

Champ de Mars in Paris. It came down 24 kilometers (15 miles) away, to the astonishment of the inhabitants who had not heard of the experiment.

Hydrogen, however, has the disadvantage of being highly explosive and its use cost many lives in balloons and airships. Much later, the non-explosive gas helium was discovered and took the place of hydrogen as a filling for balloons. (See HELIUM.)

At first all the balloons were sent up by themselves. Then in September 1783 Joseph Montgolfier sent up a sheep, a rooster, and a duck to see what would happen to them. They landed apparently none the worse for the experiment and so the stage was ready for the first human flight.

The first volunteers were Jean-François Pilâtre de Rozier and his friend the Marquis d'Arlandes. In a gaily decorated balloon they made the first passenger flight in history on 21 November 1783. They took off from Paris and stayed in the air for 23 minutes.

In December, 1783 J. A. C. Charles and Nicolas-Louis Robert made a two-hour flight in a hydrogen balloon, and soon afterwards Charles made a solo flight lasting 35 minutes. Charles invented the valve at the top of the balloon to control the letting out of gas, and it was his idea to hang the car from a ring attached to the balloon by nets.

The new science rapidly became popular. J. Tytler, who was editor of the *Encyclopaedia Britannica* from 1776 to 1784, and an Italian, Vincenzo Lunardi, introduced ballooning to England. The first aerial crossing of the English Channel was made by a Frenchman, J. P. Blanchard, in company with an American, John Jeffries, on 7 January 1785. Early in the 1800s ballooning was started in the United States.

The assistance that balloons could give to scientific research was early recognized. Jeffries was the first to study the effects of rarefied air on human behavior. The French chemists Joseph Gay-Lussac and Jean Biot made exploratory flights up to 4,000 meters (13,000 feet) in 1804 to study the structure of the air and the effect of height on animals and insects.

By 1862 balloonists had been up to about 10,500 meters (34,000 feet).

The most dramatic exploit was an attempt by a Swede, S. A. Andrée, to drift across the North Pole in a balloon. With two companions Andrée left Spitsbergen on 11 July 1897. Next day a carrier pigeon brought news that all was well, and that was the last heard of the balloon until 1930 when a Norwegian exploring party accidentally discovered the frozen bodies of Andrée and his companions on White Island a long way east of their intended course.

During the early part of the 20th century ballooning was overshadowed by the rapid development of the airship and airplane. Nevertheless, there still continued to be balloon enthusiasts, and an important international balloon race for the Gordon Bennett Cup took place every year from 1906 until 1939.

A great revival of interest occurred in the early 1930s, when scientists began to use balloons to study atmospheric conditions at very high altitudes. Auguste Piccard and Paul Kipfer reached a height of 16,200 meters (just over 10 miles) in August 1932. They used a spherical pressure-tight cabin in place of the usual open basket. Inside this metal ball they could keep the air at the proper pressure and had sufficient oxygen for normal breathing even at heights where there is far less oxygen in the air than at sea-level. The greatest height that has been reached by a manned balloon is 37,740 meters (about 23 miles) in a United States balloon. This was achieved in South Dakota on 22 October 1965, by Nicholas Piantanida. The official record is 34,668 meters (113,739 feet) made by Malcolm Ross in the Gulf of Mexico in 1961.

In 1958 the first attempt was made at crossing the Atlantic in a balloon. In August 1978 it was finally achieved by Ben Abruzzo, Max Anderson, and Larry Newman. They flew 5,023 kilometers (3,120 miles) from Presque Isle, Maine, in the United States, to Miserey, in France. The journey took nearly six days. In 1981 Abruzzo, Newman, Ron Clark, and Rocky Aoki crossed the Pacific from Nagashima, Japan, to California, United States, a distance of 8,550 kilometers (5,300 miles), taking 84 hours 31 minutes. In 1987 the pop record and airline millionaire Richard Branson and the Swedish balloonist Per Linstrand crossed the Atlantic in the jet stream of the upper atmosphere in a time of 30 hours 41 minutes.

Balloons in War

The first use of balloons in war was during the French Revolutionary wars when two men went up in a balloon over Maubeuge, which was under siege by the Dutch and Austrian forces. The Austrians imagined quite wrongly that their every move could be seen and completely lost their courage, immediately ceasing to besiege the city. The balloon was then moved to Charleroi where the French were defending themselves against the enemy, and again the enemy were so dismayed that they surrendered. On another occasion, in 1794, a balloon rose above the battle being fought at Fleurus where the crew, far above any shots, watched the battle undisturbed. In 1809 Napoleon had a plan for invading England by balloon, but it came to nothing. In the United States, during the Civil War (1861–65), both sides used balloons. During the siege of Paris in the Franco-Prussian war of 1870–71, the French used balloons to take out mail and carrier pigeons; the pigeons in turn brought back news to Paris. Balloons also flew out members of the French government into unoccupied parts of France. In World War I (1914–18) sausage-shaped observation balloons were used on all fronts and simple balloon barrages appeared which acted as a barrier to keep off enemy aircraft.

During World War II (1939–45) balloon barrages with networks of interconnecting cables were used by Great Britain, Germany, and the United States. The object was to entangle enemy bombers or to keep them high up and prevent dive-bombing.

During 1943–44 the Japanese attempted to bomb the United States by balloons launched from Japan itself. Loaded with explosives, thousands were released to drift across the 8,000 kilometers (5,000 miles) of Pacific Ocean

Barrage balloons were used during World War II by both sides to keep enemy aircraft at high altitude.

to the United States. Though a few got across, they did very little damage.

Other Uses for Balloons

Unmanned free balloons are regularly used to explore the upper air. For research at great heights, balloons are released carrying instruments which automatically and continuously measure atmospheric conditions (temperature, pressure, moisture, and so forth) and send down radio reports of their findings. Such devices are known as radiosondes, or sometimes rawinsondes.

In August 1960 the United States launched by means of a rocket the satellite balloon "Echo 1" made of aluminum-coated plastic film. It was inflated after launching and was 30 meters (98 feet) across. The somewhat larger "Echo 2" followed in 1964. These two balloons were used for relaying (repeating) radio messages over long distances by reflecting the signals.

BALSA. The wood of the balsa tree (*Ochroma pyramidale*) is remarkably light and strong and it does not bend easily. It is one of the most rapidly growing trees of the tropical forests of Central and South America, growing up to 4 meters (13 feet) in a single year. Because of this rapid growth, most of the cells of which the wood is made remain thin-walled. When the tree has been cut down and the cells are dead they fill with air, making the wood lighter than cork. The gray-green leaves are as much as 45 centimeters (17 inches) across and the smooth, marbled bark of the trunk looks like that of the plane tree, which can be seen in London and many other large cities.

The name balsa is taken from a Spanish word for raft, because the wood was used by the natives of South America for making rafts and canoes. In 1947 Thor Heyerdahl and his five companions (four other Norwegians and a Swede) made their famous raft *Kon-Tiki* from logs of balsa wood. They used it to sail 7,000 kilometers (4,300 miles) across the Pacific from Peru to an island in the Tuamotu group in the middle of the Pacific, thus showing that Peruvian Indians could have migrated to the Polynesian islands, although this is now thought to have been unlikely.

Balsa wood is very useful for making model airplanes and boats. In World War II the wings and fuselage of a very fast fighter-bomber aircraft, the Mosquito, were made from balsa because it was so light and rigid. A thick layer of balsa was sandwiched between thinner layers of other, stronger woods.

Ecuador grows most of the world's supply of balsa wood.

BALTIC SEA. An inland sea of northern Europe, the Baltic is nearly 1,600 kilometers (1,000 miles) in length. It lies between Sweden on the west, Finland and the USSR on the east, and Poland and Germany on the south. It has three main gulfs. In the north is the large Gulf of Bothnia, between Sweden and Finland, and in the east is the Gulf of Finland, lying between that country and Estonia and reaching to the Russian port of Leningrad, while the Gulf of Riga juts into Latvia. (Estonia and Latvia, like Lithuania further south, have been part of the USSR since 1940.) The Swedish shores are rocky, while those on the opposite side of the sea are low and often sandy, except in the north.

Ships can only reach the Baltic from the North Sea, either via the Kiel Canal through northern Germany, opened in 1895, or through the narrow straits of Skagerrak and

Kattegat, which separate Denmark from Norway and Sweden. From these straits, ships must pass through one of the even narrower channels between or beside the Danish islands. The deepest of these inner entrances is the Sound, between the southern tip of Sweden and the largest island, Sjaelland, on whose shore stands Copenhagen, the Danish capital. The other entrances are the Great Belt and the Little Belt, which is spanned by a bridge.

It is easy to see, therefore, why Denmark in early centuries controlled all the trade of the Baltic. Later, most of it was carried on by the Hanseatic League, which was a union of the merchants in the towns of northern Germany. (See HANSEATIC LEAGUE.) Furs and honey from Russia, wood, tar, iron, and copper from Sweden and timber and wheat from Poland, passed, under their control, to Flanders (now part of France and Belgium) and to Great Britain. It was several hundred years later that Peter the Great of Russia built the city and port of St. Petersburg (now called Leningrad) and so gave Russia its "window on the west".

Navigation in the Baltic has never been easy. The Danish channels and many of the harbors are too shallow for some of the larger ships. Moreover, since many freshwater rivers flow into the Baltic, and it has such a small outlet to the oceans of the world, it is not very salty and this means that it freezes more easily. Wide areas are regularly frozen over for two months of the winter in the southwest and for as many as six months in the north. Some ports and shipping routes are kept open, however, by the use of icebreakers, which are ships specially constructed to break channels through the ice.

Nowadays the chief cargoes carried across the Baltic are timber from the USSR, Finland and Sweden, iron ore from Sweden, and coal from Poland. The USSR opened a canal linking the Baltic and the White Sea in 1975.

BALTIMORE is the largest city in Maryland, and the eleventh largest in the United States. It lies on both shores of the Patapsco River near the northern end of Chesapeake Bay. The first settlers were attracted there by the swift-running tributary streams of the Patapsco River. These could be used for water power in grain mills. The deep harbor of the Patapsco allowed ocean ships to dock for exports and imports. The harbor helped the town, formed in 1729, to grow into a city. Although the grain mills have long ago been replaced by industrial plant, the harbor and port are still of great importance. The city was named after the Baltimore family who founded the colony (now state) of Maryland. During the American Revolution, Baltimore was for a time a meeting place of the Continental Congress (see AMERICAN REVOLUTION) and gained a reputation for building fast sturdy ships that were used as privateers to attack British shipping.

Baltimore is one of the series of large manufacturing and port cities on the Atlantic seacoast. Of all these cities, from Boston, Massachusetts, to Norfolk, Virginia, Baltimore ranks third in population and second as a port. It is just as important as a manufacturing city.

The residential and commercial areas of the city have spread out to the south, north, and northeast toward other cities. The industrial areas have spread out along the shores of the Patapsco River and other nearby inlets of Chesapeake Bay. There the land is flat and the water is deep enough to allow ocean freighters to load and unload. The manufacturing and port activities help each other. The port attracts industries, and the industries enlarge the port.

Baltimore accounts for a large percentage of the industrial and manufacturing work of the entire state. There are many types of industrial plant in or near the city. The fruit and vegetable canneries, grain elevators, stockyards, and copper refineries are old industries. There are also iron and steel mills, car assembly plants, and electrical and chemical industries. One of the more recent industries is electronics. Baltimore's once well-known

ZEFA

The US Navy's first ship, the *Constellation* is permanently moored on Baltimore's harbor front.

aircraft industry has changed completely to missiles, electronics, and nuclear work.

The old business section of the city is near the harbor. It has narrow, winding streets, small pavements, and old buildings, many with modern fronts.

BALZAC, Honoré de (1799–1850).

The French novelist Honoré de Balzac was so dedicated to writing that he sometimes wrote for 15 hours at a stretch. He had set himself the task of looking at human life scientifically and dividing human nature into all its types; to do with mankind what naturalists were doing with animals—studying them in their surroundings, and describing each type. He undertook this immense task in the writing of a huge amount of fiction. Shortly before his death, he chose about 95 of his novels and short stories and gave them the collective title of *The Human Comedy.*

Balzac was born in Tours, France, and studied law for a time before turning to writing. At first he was unsuccessful, but in time he was turning out as many as five novels a year, as well as short stories and articles. His best work, such as *Eugénie Grandet,* the story of a pitiful daughter of a miser, and *Le Père Goriot,* about a self-sacrificing father of selfish children, presents a marvelously accurate picture not only of 19th-century France, but also of men and women of all time.

Balzac worked so hard that he wore himself out and died six months after his marriage to a Polish countess. Though deeply devoted to her, Balzac had delayed marrying her for 18 years.

BAMBOO.

Although they look like bushes or even trees, bamboos are in fact giant woody grasses. The largest kinds reach a height of 35 meters (115 feet) and grow at the astonishing rate of 40 centimeters (15 inches) a day, but they are usually not very thick. Like many other grasses, the stems grow clustered together from roots creeping along under the ground.

All bamboos have smooth, hollow, jointed stems, with a strong partition at each joint.

Herbert G. Ponting

Bamboo can reach a height of 35 meters (115 feet). This thick clump was photographed in Sri Lanka.

The lower parts of the stems are wrapped with curved leaves at each joint during growth, but these soon fall off. Higher up, the stems branch into many smaller ones which bear the main leaves and the flowers. These arching branches with their graceful foliage have inspired Chinese and Japanese artists.

The Different Kinds of Bamboo

The 1,000 bamboo species grow mainly in subtropical and mild temperate regions. There are many in China and Japan, and they extend across Asia into India and Sri Lanka. They are not so common in Africa. In South America they can be found up to the snowline of the Andes Mountains. Many of the larger bamboos have been introduced to the warmer parts of the United States, and in Europe the smaller hardy bamboos are planted in gardens as ornamental plants.

A few bamboo species are climbers and some are armed with thorns. Many have flowers every year, producing, like other grasses, starchy grains which can be eaten. Others flower only after a period of years and then die exhausted, leaving the seeds to carry on the species. One of the common Indian bamboos flowers regularly at intervals of 32 years, and another one flowers every 60 years. When the time comes for flowering, all the bamboos of a particular kind usually flower together over a very large area, such as the whole of India. As this has frequently happened in a year of drought, when the rice crop has failed, the bamboo grain has often saved the people from starvation. The flowering times of certain bamboos have thus become so important that they have been recorded in old Chinese and Japanese writings as long ago as AD 292.

A few bamboos bear fruits like nuts and one kind has a fleshy fruit, looking rather like an apple, which in India is baked and eaten. The Chinese eat the tender young shoots of the bamboo as a vegetable, like asparagus, and also as a sweetmeat or a pickle.

The Uses of Bamboo Stems

Apart from providing food, the great variety of bamboos makes them one of the most useful of all tropical plants. In Asia entire houses are built of bamboo stems. The larger stems serve as posts, while some can be split to make rafters, roofing material, and planks for the floor, the smooth rounded surface being pleasant for the bare feet. The hard outer part is split off, slit into narrow pieces and woven into mats and into lattice-work partitions to separate the rooms.

Single joints of the larger species of bamboo, which may be a foot across, are used as buckets, while smaller ones are kept in the house as water-bottles. The outer parts of some are hard enough to make knives. Strips of bamboo are also woven into strong fish traps and beautiful baskets, or twisted into ropes. Boats may have a single bamboo stalk as a mast while for larger craft several stems are lashed together. A water pipe can be made simply by knocking out the partitions at the joints. In China, a fine paper is produced from the soft fiber inside the hard outer shell and the people

of Java, in Indonesia, use bamboo to make flutes and a musical instrument similar to a xylophone.

BANANA. This popular fruit does not grow on a tree, as many people think, but on one of the largest plants without a woody stem. The stem of the banana plant (*Musa sapientum*) grows from 3 to 6 meters (10 to 20 feet) high, and is really a cluster of leaf stalks rolled tightly round each other. The fully developed leaves spread out at the top, making it look rather like a palm tree; they are often 3 meters (10 feet) long and 60 centimeters (2 feet) broad and they are very handsome. The banana bunches are made up of "fingers" (individual fruits), grouped into "hands", which are arranged in a spiral on the stem.

Bananas are thought to have come from Asia. It is said that missionaries took plants to Central America in the 16th century, and from there the banana spread to many countries. People in the United States now eat more bananas than the people of any other country and, although they grow some of their own in Florida and California, they have to import most of them from other countries such as Mexico, the West Indian island of Jamaica, the Central American republics of Costa Rica and Honduras, together with Brazil, Ecuador, and Colombia in South America. The Canary Islands, off the northwest coast of Africa, grow a famous variety called "Lady's Finger". Bananas are also grown in Ethiopia, Guinea, Nigeria, South Africa, and Australia. Large quantities are shipped to western Europe.

The banana needs a lot of heat and moisture, which is why it grows best in the humid tropics on deep, loose, well-drained soils. The plants are usually placed about 4 meters (13 feet) apart, on land where the trees and undergrowth have been cut and allowed to rot down. A year or two later each plant produces just one stem of bananas which may weigh as much as 45 kilograms (100 pounds), and then dies. After that it is replaced by a new side shoot, or sucker, for the fruit of the cultivated plants hardly ever has seeds.

The fruit has to be cut when it is green, for

Regular spraying (top left) is necessary to control the diseases that affect the banana plant. When the fruit is still green, workers harvest a crop of bananas (top right), cutting down large bunches with machetes. The bunches are hung on cables (bottom left) that carry them from farm to packing station. There they are washed with insecticide (bottom right) before shipping.

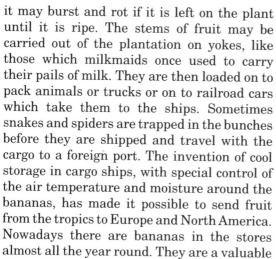

Courtesy, United Brands Company

it may burst and rot if it is left on the plant until it is ripe. The stems of fruit may be carried out of the plantation on yokes, like those which milkmaids once used to carry their pails of milk. They are then loaded on to pack animals or trucks or on to railroad cars which take them to the ships. Sometimes snakes and spiders are trapped in the bunches before they are shipped and travel with the cargo to a foreign port. The invention of cool storage in cargo ships, with special control of the air temperature and moisture around the bananas, has made it possible to send fruit from the tropics to Europe and North America. Nowadays there are bananas in the stores almost all the year round. They are a valuable

food and doctors prescribe them for certain diseases, particularly for children.

Where bananas are actually grown, however, the people not only eat the fruit raw, cooked, dried, or made into flour, but also make a sort of beer from it, use the leaves as plates or umbrellas and the stalks for thatching their homes.

A close relative of the banana is the plantain (*Musa paradisiaca*), which has green fruit larger than a banana. The fruit also contains more starch than a banana does and is not eaten raw. It is usually cooked green, either boiled or fried often with coconut juice or sugar. It is also dried and made into meal and flour. In some parts of East Africa, for example Uganda, the plantain is a staple food crop.

Plants of the banana family show a wide variety of flower type, including large and colorful ones such as the bird-of-paradise flower. (See also CANNA; GINGER.)

BAND. A band playing in a park or in a procession marching through the streets is bound to draw a crowd of people. The words band and orchestra both describe a group of musicians playing their instruments together, but the sound a band makes is often very different from that of an ordinary symphony orchestra. An orchestra usually plays in a concert hall or theater, whereas a band often plays out of doors. Because of this, the stringed instruments, which are so important in an orchestra, are not used in a band, for their sound would not carry well in the open air, and dampness, heat, or cold would soon make them go out of tune. The different kinds of bands, therefore, are made up of wind instruments and percussion.

Brass Bands

Many of the instruments in a brass band belong to the family of saxhorns, a group of brass instruments first introduced in 1845 by a man named Adolphe Sax. The number of instruments in brass bands varies, but here is a list of the ones that are generally used: soprano cornet in E flat; cornets in B flat (which, like the violins in an orchestra, do most of the work); flugels in B flat (the flugel is like a saxhorn but has a wider tube which makes the lower notes easier to play); alto saxhorns in E flat; tenor saxhorns in B flat (also called "baritones"); tenor trombones; bass trombones; tenor and bass tubas; and drums. (See DRUM; HORN FAMILY; TRUMPET FAMILY; TROMBONE.)

Brass bands are a famous attraction in the United Kingdom. The finest brass bands are those connected with factories and coal mines in the north of England. Brass bands became popular in the industrial areas of the Midlands and north of England during the 19th century. They provided enjoyable recreation after work in the factory or at the coal face. Local traditions are still strong and competition is keen. Band membership often runs in the family. At the National Brass Band Contests very high standards of playing can be heard. Test pieces for bands have been written by British composers such as Sir Edward Elgar, Sir Arthur Sullivan, Gustav Holst and Benjamin Britten.

Brass bands, or silver bands as they are sometimes called, are also used in Britain by the Salvation Army in processions and open-air services.

Military and Concert Bands

All the instruments in a military band must be ones that can be played while the army is on the march. Two kinds of wind-instruments are used—woodwind and brass; the third group of instruments is the percussion.

As in brass bands, the way the instruments are combined varies; different countries and even different regiments use different arrangements. These, however, are the instruments generally used in a British or American military band: flute and piccolo; first and second oboes; clarinet in E flat; about twelve clarinets in B flat; two bass clarinets; alto, tenor and baritone saxophones; two bassoons; four horns in E flat; two cornets in B flat; two trumpets; two tenor trombones; bass trombone; euphonium; "basses" and percussion. On the march the basses are tubas, but when a military band plays in a concert hall, string double basses are used instead. A military band usually has a large number of clarinets, which again, like the strings of an orchestra, do most of the work.

A military band is really a special kind of band rather than just a band used in the armed forces. In fact, when it plays in a concert hall, it is very often referred to as a concert band. Concert bands are especially popular in the United States, where school and college concert bands rival professional bands in terms of musical standards.

Other types of band used for marching include the drum and fife band, consisting of fifes (small flutes in B flat) and other flutes,

Barnaby's

Military bands have brass and woodwind instruments. Bassoon, saxophone, and tuba players are included.

both smaller and larger than fifes, side drums, bass drum, cymbals and triangle. A drum and bugle band is like a drum and fife band except that bugles are used instead of the various flutes. Scottish Highland regiments usually have pipe bands, and they march to the skirl (sound) of the bagpipes, accompanied by the bass drum and side drum.

One of the greatest composers for concert band was the United States band conductor John Philip Sousa. His most famous pieces include "The Stars and Stripes Forever". (See SOUSA, JOHN PHILIP.)

Bands in the Past

From the earliest times armies have had their military music and signals. The ancient Roman foot-soldiers had horns, and their horsemen had trumpets. (The trumpet is still the instrument used by cavalry.) The large circular horn the foot-soldiers used was found to be very clumsy and so the bugle came to be used instead. The bugle is really a horn more tightly coiled up and played with a cup-shaped mouthpiece like the one on a trumpet. Only a limited number of notes can be played on it.

In the Middle Ages every important town in Europe had its town band which played at ceremonies and on public occasions. These bands had grown out of groups of wandering musicians. who formed themselves into guilds for mutual protection. In Britain, watchmen called "waits", who used to play instruments to mark the hours, also grouped together to form town bands, usually playing oboes and related instruments. Waits were often heard

One of the most famous dance bands between the two World Wars was the one led by Jack Hylton. This British band had an international reputation. In this photograph, the members of the band are preparing to board an aircraft to become the first group of musicians to broadcast from a plane in flight.

Mary Evans Picture Library

playing carols at Christmas time. The military band began about the 16th century when the waits were used together with the army's horns and trumpets.

The first army bands were composed of civilian musicians who accompanied troops on the march. Later, army regiments used to recruit and train their own bands. In both Britain and the United States, bands attached to the various branches of the armed services have developed from very crude beginnings into outstanding musical organizations.

Dance Bands

A dance band is any group of players which provides music for dancing, particularly for indoor and ballroom dancing. It may be just a piano and drums, or it may be as big as a small orchestra. The choice of instruments varies according to what is fashionable at the time and to what combination of instruments the band leader prefers. In music for dancing, rhythm and "beat" are very important, and thus to provide the rhythm in a dance band drums, cymbals, and all the other percussion instruments are very important. The guitar and the double bass (plucked, not played with a bow) are often used for rhythm too. The most popular instruments that produce the melody or tune in a modern dance band are the saxo-

phone, the trumpet, the trombone, and sometimes the violin. The harmony, that is, the sounds that "fill in" round the melody or accompany it, is made by groups of saxophones, brass instruments, strings or piano accordion. The guitar and the piano, both used a great deal in modern dance bands, can provide rhythm, melody or harmony as required.

In the first half of the 20th century, especially in the 1930s and 1940s, dance bands were extremely popular in both Britain and the United States. In Britain, the great dance band leaders were Jack Hylton, Henry Hall, Ambrose, and Joe Loss. In the United States, the great Glenn Miller, Duke Ellington, and Count Basie were legends in their own time. (See also JAZZ.)

Other Bands

The pop music revolution, which introduced rock 'n' roll and the other great developments from the 1950s onwards, popularized groups consisting of a lead guitar (melody instrument), a rhythm guitar, a bass guitar, and drums. All guitars are now usually amplified electrically. In the 1970s, the rock band arose, in which an important addition to the usual rock group line-up was the synthesizer.

West Indian migration to the United Kingdom has helped to spread the popularity of typical Caribbean musical combinations such as the steel band. A steel band features instruments, traditionally made from household pans, oildrums, and so on, which are specially prepared in order to produce a range of notes or tones. Players make music by striking different parts of their instruments with sticks or beaters. Steel bands produce a highly rhythmical form of music very suitable for a party or carnival atmosphere,

BANDIT AND OUTLAW. Stories about bandits and outlaws have been handed down over 700 or 800 years. For centuries *banditti* (from which comes the English word "bandit") haunted Italy. For until the middle of the 19th century that country was divided into many small states which were often at war with each other. If a bandit was pursued too closely in one state he could flee for safety across the border into another. In about 1600, a famous bandit, Marco Sciarra, who was the leader of a band of about 600 men, often escaped his pursuers in this way but was at last led into a

Mary Evans Picture Library

Ned Kelly, the Australian bushranger, wearing home-made armor, in a shoot-out with the police.

trap and killed when he returned to his old haunts near Naples. In the lawless times when various armies were marching and fighting in Italy during the wars started by Napoleon, bandits again ranged all over the country.

Outlaws, as the name shows, are people who have been put outside the protection of the law and so must always be in hiding to escape capture and death. They usually live by robbery and violence. One of the best-known English outlaws was Robin Hood, an expert archer, who lived in Sherwood Forest, Nottinghamshire, with a band of other outlaws. He fought for the good of the poor people who were oppressed by King John (see ROBIN HOOD). In places where there is wild country in which to hide, outlaws and bandits still operate; in southern Italy, Corsica and Sicily, for instance, bandits are still very active in modern times.

Mansell Collection

Nineteenth-century travelers in England ran the risk of being attacked by robbers on lonely roads.

In the past, travelers were in great danger from brigands. Rob Roy and his band roamed the Highlands of Scotland 250 years ago, and the traveler in England in the 17th and 18th centuries risked being robbed by highwaymen. They were gangs of men, and sometimes women, who attacked coaches on the main roads across the country. They would often wait near an inn where the horses were changed so that they could see who was on the coach and what valuables they had. When the coach was out on a lonely road they would hold up the passengers with pistols. One famous highwayman was Dick Turpin and another was William Page, who dressed in fashionable clothes and drove a carriage with two horses called a phaeton. There was also a highwaywoman called Katherine Ferrers who lived in Hertfordshire, England, and died in 1659 at the age of 25 after being shot during an attack on a coach.

In France in the 14th and 15th centuries there were large bands of hired soldiers discharged from service at various times during the Hundred Years' War, who in desperation

for a livelihood raided the towns and robbed the country districts. The French island of Corsica was another great haunt of bandits and the leaders of the various bands were often regarded as heroes by the islanders.

BBC Hulton Picture Library

Jesse James (right) with his brother, Frank (seated), and a companion, when soldiers in the US Civil War.

Almost everywhere, in fact, at one time or another robber bands have flourished: in the uninhabited wilds of Australia, for example, where they were known as "bushrangers" and were mostly escaped convicts. One of the most notorious was Ned Kelly who, with his gang, was hunted down for killing three policemen. His companions were killed and he was captured and hanged in 1880 in Melbourne.

In the western United States the bandits who robbed the stage-coaches and trains were called highwaymen and road agents. One of the most famous of the train robbers was Jesse James, who was finally betrayed and shot

Mary Evans Picture Library

Ned Kelly photographed the day before he was hanged in Melbourne in 1880. He was aged 24.

by a member of his own gang for a reward in 1882.

During the 20th century Morocco has been a haunt of fierce brigands, and during the civil war in China bandits were a serious threat to travelers. More recently in some South American countries, notably Uruguay, urban guerrillas have robbed banks and kidnapped important people, usually for political reasons. In exchange for their captives' freedom they have demanded money and the release of other guerrillas held in prison. This practice of kidnap and ransom has spread in other countries among groups who have a grievance or oppose the government. A similar practice is the attacking and hijacking of aircraft (see HIJACKING).

BANFF NATIONAL PARK in the province of Alberta, Canada, was established in 1885 to conserve an area of hot sulfur springs for use by the general public. It is Canada's oldest national park and covers 6,641 square kilo-

National Film Board of Canada

Banff, Alberta, is a popular all-year-round resort in the Canadian Rockies not far from Calgary.

meters (2,564 square miles) of spectacular countryside in the Rocky Mountains, 125 kilometers (78 miles) west of Calgary.

As well as hot springs, there are numerous lakes, waterfalls, forests, and alpine meadows. The meadows are covered in flowers in the spring and early summer and are a particular attraction. The forests, which flank the mountain sides, consist mainly of lodgepole pine, Engelmann spruce, and alpine fir. In this part of the park are found black bear, grizzly bear, wolf, cougar, elk, and moose. The park also provides a home for mule deer and bighorn sheep. The region has become an important tourist attraction and is visited by so many people each year that maintaining the park as a conservation area has been found to be impossible and it is now run largely to provide recreation.

BANGKOK is the capital and chief port of Thailand. As the city grew, from the 18th century onwards, it spread over both banks of the Chao Phraya River, about 40 kilometers (25 miles) up from the Gulf of Thailand. At one time most of the houses were built on rafts or stilts, and the easiest way of getting about was by boat along the many canals called *khlongs* in the Thai language. As the city is being modernized, these khlongs are being filled in and paved over with roads to take the ever increasing traffic. The canals are still used by vendors selling all kinds of goods and there are several well-known floating markets.

Bangkok is a busy commercial and tourist center. Each of the city's districts, with its own temples and markets, functions almost as a self-contained small town. The Chinese have their own district called Sam Peng. There is little separation of industrial, commercial, and residential areas; thatched houses and rice paddies can be seen next to stores, Western-style houses, and modern hotels and office buildings.

The newer parts of the city look much like a modern American city, but what makes Bangkok unusually attractive are the palaces and pagodas with their glittering roofs and bell-shaped towers, and the huge carved figures.

BBC Hulton Picture Library

Bangkok abounds with beautifully carved Buddhist monasteries, called *Wats*.

The Grand Palace, a landmark in Bangkok, built in 1782, stands on a bend of the river and is enclosed by walls. Within the enclosure is the royal chapel, *Wat Phra Kaeo* (*Wat* is a temple in Thai). This famous temple houses the Emerald Buddha: high up in a golden shrine with a perpetual light upon it, is an image of Buddha made of jasper, a semi-precious stone. The image's garments of gold and precious stones are changed regularly, according to the time of year. This is the most sacred image of Buddha in Thailand. The many other gilded and shining temples with their circular spires, also contain beautiful golden images of Buddha (see BUDDHA AND BUDDHISM). Sometimes he is sitting in meditation, or he may be standing or sleeping, and sometimes he is shown with his disciples around him.

Most of Thailand's manufacturing industry is in Bangkok, as are most banks and other modern companies. Many international corporations have regional offices in the city. With large numbers of Americans, Japanese, and other foreigners mingling with Thai and Chinese residents, Bangkok has a cosmopolitan air. The city's location makes it the center of communications for Southeast Asia. Its

large and well-equipped airport at Don Muang is one of the principal international air route junctions in the Far East. The population of Bangkok is 5,407,100 (1982).

BANGLADESH has been an independent republic since 1971. It has been under military rule and without a parliament since 1982. It is situated in southern Asia and was once part of Pakistan when it was known as East Pakistan. It is bordered by India in the west, north, and northeast, and in the southeast by Burma. To the south lies the Bay of Bengal. The capital is Dhaka (see DHAKA) and the main port is Chittagong.

Bangladesh is a flat land of many rivers. The great Ganges, Brahmaputra, and Meghna rivers have created the world's largest delta in the Bay of Bengal. Near the coast are mangrove swamps and to the east around Chittagong are forest-covered hills. Bangladesh has a humid, tropical climate, with the monsoon winds bringing high rainfall which makes flooding a frequent hazard to people and crops. The Bay of Bengal has occasional cyclonic

storms, which do great damage when they move north causing flooding that can wash away whole villages. Bangladesh is fringed on the south by the vast marshy forest of the Sundarbans, one of the last sanctuaries for the threatened Bengal tiger and also teeming with crocodiles.

The people of Bangladesh are mostly Bengalis—named after a region of Bangladesh that stretches into India and was once a separate kingdom. The official language is Bengali. Most of the people are Muslims but there are a large number of Hindus and a smaller minority of Buddhists. The people have a rich tradition of music, dance, and literature. Bangladesh is one of the most densely populated countries in the world and its people are among the poorest.

Most of the people are farmers, building their farms on mounds or banks above the level of flood waters. Rice, sugar-cane, tobacco and vegetables are grown, but the country's most important crop and principal export is jute, a plant which is processed to make a fiber used in sacks and rough materials (see JUTE); Bangladesh is the world's chief supplier. Irrigation schemes are helping to improve farming. Clothing and food products are also exported.

Since the population is chiefly rural, there are no really important urban industrial centers. What industries there are tend to be concentrated in villages—in family-run cottage industries, such as cotton weaving or tobacco rolling. Forestry is important and paper is made at Khulna and Chittagong. The country has few minerals, although natural gas has been found. The rivers are still the most important means of communication and there are few modern surfaced roads.

History

The state of Pakistan was created in 1947 when India was divided into two countries, one mainly Muslim (Pakistan) and one mainly Hindu (India). Pakistan's two provinces, East Pakistan and West Pakistan, were separated by more than 1,500 kilometers (930 miles) by India. This separation created a cultural and language barrier, as well as a geographical barrier.

East Pakistan was much the poorer of the two provinces and resentment grew against the West. In 1971 this resentment caused the Bengali people in East Pakistan to rebel against the central government and to proclaim the independent republic of Bangladesh. Civil war broke out as the Pakistan government tried to put down the rebellion. The Bengalis were helped by India and war broke out between India and Pakistan. Indian troops invaded East Pakistan and the Pakistan army was defeated. The Bengalis set up the state of Bangladesh, with Sheikh Mujibur Rahman as President. However, economic problems and food shortages caused discontent, and in 1975 military leaders seized power. President Mujibur Rahman was killed during the revolt, and the new President was Major-General Ziaur Rahman. In 1978 elections were held as a move towards normal democratic government again. Political instability continued to plague the country, however.

FACTS ABOUT BANGLADESH

AREA: 143,998 square kilometers (55,598 square miles).
POPULATION: 105,307,000 (1987).
GOVERNMENT: Republic; under military rule since 1982.
CAPITAL: Dhaka.
GEOGRAPHICAL FEATURES: Low-lying land dominated by world's largest delta in south where Ganges River exits into Bay of Bengal. Marshy, muddy swamps.
CHIEF PRODUCTS: Jute, jute-like fibers, rice, leather, tea, cotton, clothing.
IMPORTANT TOWNS: Dhaka, Chittagong, Khulna.

BANJO. A banjo is a popular stringed musical instrument in which a circular metal frame with parchment stretched tightly across it is attached to a long piece of wood, called the fingerboard. A set of strings is stretched from the top of the fingerboard over a small piece of wood called a bridge which rests on the parchment, and is fixed to the far side of the metal frame. A banjo may have from four to nine strings of catgut or wire. It more usually has five or six strings.

THE NEW VERB.

BANJO, BANJAS, BANJAT—BANJAMUS, BANJATIS, BANJANT!

The popularity of the banjo reached a peak around the end of the 19th and the beginning of the 20th centuries. In both the United States and Britain the so-called Negro minstrel shows spread interest in playing the banjo, and this cartoon of 1886 depicts the craze for banjo-playing sweeping Britain at the time. Banjos were later used in traditional jazz bands, and during the 1930s and 1940s banjo orchestras were very popular in Britain.

Mary Evans Picture Library

To play the banjo a person plucks the strings with the thumb and fingers of the right hand or with a piece of bone or metal called a plectrum. He makes the strings sound different notes by pressing them down on to the fingerboard, on which there are a number of marked spaces, with the fingers of his left hand. This is called "stopping" the strings.

The banjo is thought to have developed in Africa. Black Americans from Africa used to play the banjo on the plantations in the southern part of the United States. It was used a great deal in the "minstrel" shows popular at the end of the 19th century and later in the early jazz bands. It also found its way into white American folk music and "country and western" music.

The banjo is tuned in the same way as a guitar but makes a sharper sound because the strings vibrate over parchment instead of wood. The tenor banjo is tuned like a cello and was invented in the early days of jazz bands so that cellists could play it easily and earn extra money by playing jazz as well as orchestral music. Instruments related to the banjo include the banjolin and the banjulele. These share the features of the banjo and the mandolin and ukulele respectively.

BANKRUPTCY. When a person has no money to pay his debts, the state may take over his property and sell it, dividing the sums obtained from the sale among the people to whom he owes money. When this happens to a person he is described as being bankrupt. In the Middle Ages creditors broke the benches, or trading counters, of Italian merchants who failed to pay their debts. The word "bankrupt" comes from *banca rota*, meaning bench broken. (In England and Australia corporations and limited companies cannot be made bankrupt, but they can be liquidated, or wound up, if they cannot pay their debts.)

With a few exceptions—such as ambassadors from foreign countries—any person may be made bankrupt. He may himself ask to be made bankrupt when he realizes that he cannot pay his debts, or any of the people to whom he owes money, who are called his "creditors", may ask the court to take over his affairs.

When a person is made bankrupt the court appoints a trustee (in England called "the official receiver") who takes over and manages the bankrupt's property. He may run the bankrupt's business for the benefit of the creditors or sell all the bankrupt's property and divide it among the creditors.

The Debtors' Prison, Fleet, London, drawn by George Cruikshank in 1820. People were sent here when they became bankrupt. Prisoners sat at the window hoping for gifts from passers-by.

Without this bankruptcy system each individual creditor might demand complete payment of all the money owed to him—which of course the bankrupt person would not be able to make. Under this system, however, the state protects the bankrupt from these demands, and when he has paid his creditors as much as he can, he may be discharged from bankruptcy owing nothing at all. He can thus begin business again with a clean sheet. The court will only give the bankrupt his discharge if he has behaved with complete honesty, not hiding his property or deceiving his creditors or the court in any way. If he borrows money or makes business deals without telling the person concerned that he is an undischarged bankrupt, he may, in certain cases, be sent to prison.

The present bankruptcy law is less severe than the older laws. In Anglo-Saxon and early Greek and Roman law, for example, a creditor was allowed to sell his debtor into slavery. When the bankruptcy system grew up at the end of the Middle Ages, it was confined to businessmen, or merchants. In England it was not applied to ordinary debtors until 1869; before then, ordinary debtors were usually sent to prison.

In the United States, Congress enacted the first bankruptcy law in 1800. In Canada the various provinces could make their own bankruptcy laws after 1880. In 1919 the Dominion parliament adopted a Dominion bankruptcy act for all Canada. In Australia a federal act governing bankruptcy came into force in 1928 to govern the whole country.

Inside a bank in Germany. The customer is signing travelers' checks; the cashier is counting out bank notes in three different currencies.

ZEFA

BANKS AND BANKING

BANKS AND BANKING. The origin of banking dates back further than 2000BC, when the Babylonians developed a complex system of borrowing, lending, and holding money on deposit. There were no banks as such, financial business being transacted by powerful individuals and families. As in much of banking history, the money in this period was made of precious metals such as gold and silver (called "commodity money"). Later, money came to be made of base metals and paper, but it was still backed by reserves of precious metals held in the banks issuing the notes and coins. It is only in modern times that the issue of money has become the exclusive right of central banks. Because the central banks have the authority of the state or government behind them, the money they issue is legal tender and is not backed by equivalent quantities of precious metals held in their vaults. Such money is called "fiduciary issue". In 600BC Shansi Banks were established in China. With the invention of paper in China in the first century AD, paper money, checks, and certificates of deposit were issued.

In ancient Greece, temples were used as depositories for valuables. They were considered safe because people stealing from them would incur the wrath of the gods. The priests charged fees for providing this service. The Romans developed the Greek banking system into one similar to the modern one in some respects. From the fall of Rome in the 5th century AD to the 11th century, little banking was done.

In 1171, the Bank of Venice was established to help finance a war. The public was invited to lend money to the government through the bank at 4 per cent interest. The word "bank" comes from the Italian word *banco*, which means bench, as the moneychangers often carried on their business on benches in the market place.

In England, at about the same time, goldsmiths were accepting commodity money from merchants for safekeeping. The merchants were given receipts, which began to circulate as paper money. The goldsmiths discovered that it was safe to lend out a portion of the money deposited with them, because all of the depositors were unlikely to ask for all of their money at the same time. They only needed to keep enough money in reserve to meet the expected demands for it. The goldsmiths

Courtesy, The Bank of England

Left: The Bank of England in Threadneedle Street, London. **Right:** Gold bars inside one of the vaults.

charged interest on the loans they made and found that they could attract more deposits by offering to pay interest on them. This was the origin of the modern "fractional reserve" system of banking.

The Bank of England was founded in 1694, to help finance a war in Europe. It developed the various financial practices that had their origins in banking history and became a commercial bank. Other banking institutions sprang up in England, Scotland, and the rest of the world. The Bank of England itself developed as the central bank of the British banking system. Since 1884 it has been the sole issuer of bank notes in England and Wales, although the major Scottish banks still exercise their right to issue bank notes. In 1946 it was nationalized, and since then it has concentrated on purely central banking functions, allowing its private banking business to dwindle. As a commercial, and later as a central, bank it has served as a model for many banking institutions around the world.

The first real United States bank was the Bank of North America, founded in Philadelphia by Robert Morris in 1781. The Bank of the United States was granted a charter in 1791 for 20 years. The state banks opposed it, so the charter was not renewed until 1811. War and financial crisis meant that the Bank retained little power and, although a second Bank of the United States was chartered in

1816, it was not until 1863 that a law was passed allowing state banks to be organized nationally. In 1865 a 10 per cent tax was put on state bank notes, which encouraged the state banks to come into the national system.

In 1933 there was a crisis in banking which forced all the banks to close and they were not allowed to re-open unless they were shown to be reliable. A Banking Act was then passed to put pressure on all the banks to join the Federal Reserve System to improve the supervision of banking. The system is divided into 12 District Reserve Banks with 25 branches. They serve only their member banks and do not deal directly with individuals or business firms. Individuals and businesses deposit money with member banks. The banks then have to set aside a certain percentage of these deposits as a reserve which must then be deposited with the Federal Reserve Banks. This makes it possible to transfer funds to member banks or other districts when needed.

Functions of Banks

Banks are probably the first institutions that come to mind when people discuss financial affairs. This is because the banking system is the most important part of the financial system in most countries. Financial systems contain institutions known as "financial intermediaries". An intermediary is someone who acts between others, so financial intermediaries act between lenders and borrowers, serving their requirements without their having to seek each other out individually. Advanced countries usually have various types of financial intermediary, including banks. Each type of financial intermediary specializes in the provision of a particular group of financial services to their customers. Insurance, banking, and home loan or mortgage services, for example, are commonly provided by different institutions. (See also INSURANCE.)

From the mid-1970s onwards there has been a period of deregulation and change in banking and financial systems, the pace of which accelerated in the early 1980s. Deregulation here means the removal of some, though by no means all, of the regulations imposed by governments on financial institutions. Banks are commonly the most regulated of all financial institutions because many countries have experienced historical episodes in which there were numerous bank failures. A bank fails when it cannot meet its financial obligations because it runs short of "liquid assets". Liquid assets are assets that can be readily turned into money with little or no loss of value.

Deregulation first had its major impact on banking in the United States, where controls over interest rates, for example, were significantly relaxed. "Interest" is money paid, on a regular basis, by a financial institution in order to attract deposits, or money charged by a financial institution to people borrowing from it. (See also INTEREST.) Mainly because the banking systems of the world developed numerous international links during the 1970s, deregulation soon spread to other countries. The result was a period of financial revolution during which the banking and financial systems in the world's major countries were transformed. The traditional distinctions between types of financial intermediary have disappeared and the differences between banks and other financial institutions are no longer clear-cut. Additionally, as financial reforms have progressed, the differences between the banking systems in the various industrial countries have been reduced.

Even before the financial revolution it was difficult to define a bank precisely, and various types of bank and banking systems existed. It is difficult to define a bank, partly because of the range of activities undertaken by banks around the world; and partly because the laws relating to banking vary between countries according to what they regard a bank to be.

One of the fundamental differences between a bank and other financial institutions is usually taken to be the fact that some of a bank's liabilities are money, whereas none of the liabilities of non-bank financial intermediaries is money. This means that checking accounts at banks are regarded as money in the sense that, like cash, they can be used to buy things. The check itself is not money but a token authorizing the bank to transfer money *from* the "drawer's" account *to* the "payee". Imagine, for example, a person who writes a check in a store in order to buy something. In this case, the check is an instruction by the buyer, to the buyer's bank, to withdraw some money from his or her account and to pay into an account held, possibly at another bank or another branch of the same bank, by the storekeeper. Payment is only completed when the account of the buyer is debited, and the account of the store is credited, by the amount indicated on the check. The signature on the check authorizes the buyer's bank to make the transaction. The check itself is a piece of paper which is submitted by the storekeeper to his or her own bank which then submits it to the buyer's bank prior to payment. When payment is complete the check is said to have cleared. In Europe, to prevent the fraudulent writing of checks, account holders usually carry check cards. These are presented to the storekeeper when a check is written so that he can verify whether the signature on the check matches that on the check card. Such a paper-based payments system is clearly old-fashioned in today's world of advanced electronic data processing and communications. It is particularly cumbersome in countries with numerous banking groups and in geographically large countries where many transactions involve customers of different banks which

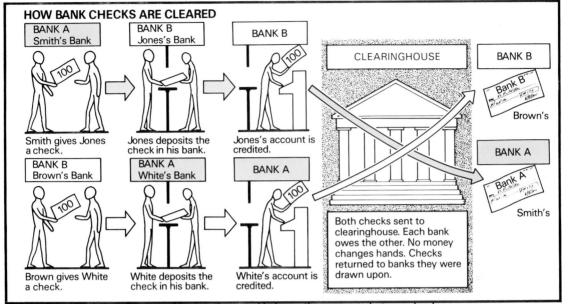

HOW BANK CHECKS ARE CLEARED

BANK A
Smith's Bank

BANK B
Jones's Bank

BANK B

CLEARINGHOUSE

BANK B

Bank B

Brown's

Smith gives Jones
a check.

Jones deposits the
check in his bank.

Jones's account is
credited.

BANK B
Brown's Bank

BANK A
White's Bank

BANK A

BANK A

Bank A

Smith's

Brown gives White
a check.

White deposits the
check in his bank.

White's account is
credited.

Both checks sent to
clearinghouse. Each bank
owes the other. No money
changes hands. Checks
returned to banks they were
drawn upon.

Clearing-houses are used to record transactions and balance the accounts between banks.

may have offices in different parts of the country.

Banking Services

In most industrial countries there are a small number of major commercial banks operating branch networks countrywide. In a few of them, notably France and Italy, some or all of the major banks are state controlled. In most countries, however, most of the banks are owned by their shareholders. They are, therefore, companies or corporations (see CORPORATION AND COMPANY). Their business is that of selling financial services. Their customers usually include private individuals and businesses. The services offered to private individuals are called "retail banking services" and those offered to businesses are called "corporate sector services". The large commercial banks often have a number of subsidiary companies providing a variety of specialized financial services, such as installment credit.

The large commercial banks will accept deposits from their clients into various accounts designed to suit the needs of their customers, and also make loans and grant overdraft facilities to their depositors. An "overdraft facility" allows an account holder to take more money out of an account at the bank than has been put into it, up to a certain agreed limit. For this service the bank charges interest on the overdrawn balance. The bank is effectively lending people with overdrawn accounts sums of money held in accounts which are not overdrawn.

Loans are also commonly made to individuals or businesses which are not depositors. A "loan" is a sum of money lent to a borrower for a fixed period of time. Over the period the borrower is required to repay the loan in regular, commonly monthly, installments and also to pay interest. It has increasingly become the practice for banks to charge a rate of interest which varies over time, in relation to economic conditions. Previously, the interest rate was fixed for the term of the loan. In order to get a loan, the borrower usually has to tell the bank what the money is to be used for and to demonstrate an ability to meet the repayments. This usually involves providing proof of monthly income but occasionally a bank may ask for "collateral". This means that the bank secures the right to assets, such as a proportion of the value of an individual's house, if a person cannot make the required repayments.

There are a large variety of accounts offered by banks, which have developed largely as a result of increasing competition among financial institutions for business. This increase in competition is partly a result of the internationalization of banking, which has brought banks from various countries into direct competition with each other. But competition in banking has also been increased because other companies have entered into commercial banking business. These have included not only other banking and non-banking financial intermediaries but also retail companies who are offering banking and other financial services through their supermarkets and department stores.

There are, however, still basically two types of account: savings and checking. Interest earned on savings accounts is normally higher and access to the money deposited in them is commonly restricted. The account holder is normally required to inform the bank a specified period in advance before taking cash out of a savings account. If the period of notice is not observed but the bank agrees to the cash withdrawal, then interest on the sum withdrawn is normally forfeited. Interest is not always paid on checking accounts because they allow access to checks and other payments services, such as standing orders and direct debits, which allow automatic payment of regular bills. In some countries banks charge fees to their checking account holders for these services in order to cover the costs of providing them. In other countries the fees are waived or are insufficient to cover these costs. To the extent that the costs are not fully recovered, the bank is implicitly paying interest on the account. In some United Kingdom banks "free banking" is offered. This means that the bank does not charge checking account holders for the use of ordinary payments services. They do not pay interest on checking accounts either, even though they can lend some of the money deposited and earn interest. Increasingly, however, interest is being paid on special checking accounts in which people keep large sums of money, the minimum required balance being determined by the bank.

The Commercial Banking System

Commercial banks operate on the basis of the "fractional reserve system". Through experience they have discovered how much money and liquid assets they need to hold in their reserves in order to ensure that they can meet their day to day obligations. The reserves need only to be a fraction of the value of the loans and other liabilities outstanding. The banking system is thus built on trust. If everyone tried to withdraw all the money they held in bank accounts on a particular day, the banks could not pay.

The amount of money that a bank earns depends on the difference between its income and revenue and its costs. The major sources of revenue are fees and charges for services provided and interest earned on loans and overdrafts. In order to provide the services, banks incur costs. Like any other business, they need to pay their employees and to rent or buy their buildings, furnishings, and computer and other equipment. They also have to pay for lighting, heating, and various other utilities. Additionally, in order to attract deposits, they must pay interest, and many banks also engage in advertising. Again, like other companies, they need capital to establish and expand their business and to cover themselves against unforeseen contingencies.

Some countries have many more banks than others. This is because, in addition to the branches of the major commercial banks, there are numerous other independent commercial banks. These are called "unit banks" and they serve the needs of business and households in their localities. Canada and the United States are examples of countries with unit banks. They are particularly numerous in the United States, where nationwide branching of commercial banks is prohibited but statewide branching is permitted in certain states.

The range of services offered by banks also varies between countries. In Japan and the United States, for example, investment and commercial banking operations are required by law to be separated. In contrast, in the Federal Republic of Germany banks have long been known as universal banks because they provide the range of services provided individually by commercial and investment banks in other countries. Furthermore, in Japan, trust banks, which administer properties for individuals, are also required to be legally distinct entities. Since the mid-1960s, the French banking system has also gravitated towards universal banking. In the United Kingdom commercial banks have engaged in investment banking activities largely through their subsidiaries. Investment banks specialize in distributing the securities of corporations to the public.

Merchant banks form an important part of the United Kingdom banking system. As their name implies, their origins lie in international and domestic trade finance. Modern merchant banks provide a range of services to the corporate sector which are similar in nature to those provided by investment banks in other countries. Until 1986, however, merchant banks were not allowed to deal directly in stocks and shares on the London Stock Exchange. Since that date they have merged with other financial institutions and in so doing they have become more like investment banks. The British commercial, or clearing, banks have also converted their merchant banking subsidiaries into institutions like investment banks. It is unclear whether deregulation in the United States and Japan will remove the legal separation of investment and commercial banking, but these two banking sectors have increasingly encroached upon each other's traditional business anyway.

Savings Banks

Most countries have special savings institutions. In some countries they are classified as banks while in others they are classified as "deposit taking institutions". They are often mutual funds or co-operatives, rather than companies or corporations. Their depositors are effectively their owners or shareholders. In addition, in many countries, the Post Office offers savings bank services through its branches. Some of these savings banking institutions provide both retail banking ser-

vices and banking services to local business and agriculture, and local governments or authorities. In many countries such institutions have been the major providers of home loans or mortgages; building societies in the United Kingdom and savings and loan associations in the United States are examples. Financial reform is, however, leading to increasing competition between banks and building societies in the United Kingdom, and banks and savings and loan associations in the United States. This is because of the breakdown of traditional specialization in the financial services industry. Other examples include the selling of insurance through bank branches. The larger banks are thus becoming more like universal banks because they are able to offer a full range of financial services to their retail and corporate customers. They have been called financial conglomerates or supermarkets. Smaller financial institutions may well decide to become specialists in the provision of particular groups of financial services and may analogously become known as financial "boutiques".

Another trend has been the development of wholesale banking. This allows banks to borrow large sums from other banks, domestically in the inter-bank market and internationally in the Euromarkets. Large industrial and other corporations also lend on these markets when they have surplus short-term funds. Banks attract additional funds by issuing financial instruments, such as certificates of deposit and floating rate notes. These developments mean that banks no longer need to receive deposits before they seek out profitable lending opportunities. They can instead first seek out the lending opportunities and then borrow on the wholesale markets. This has become known as "liability management".

Lending itself is beginning to decline in certain sectors of the banking market. Banks have become involved in a process whereby, instead of making loans, they provide finance to certain clients by buying securities, such as bonds, and attempt to convert some of their outstanding loans into tradeable securities. In addition, they have increasingly developed a fee-earning underwriting business. In return for their fee they provide financial assurances to borrowers on the growing Euronote market.

Banks and other financial institutions derive a large proportion of their profits from shouldering the risks that would be borne by their customers if they were to lend to, or borrow from, each other directly, rather than through a financial intermediary. In order to protect themselves against unforeseen losses, banks hold capital reserves. These are distinct from the liquid reserves that they hold to ensure that they can meet their normal, day to day, obligations. They also make bad debt provisions to cover themselves against losses on loans to industries or countries that are not performing well. In many countries banks contribute to deposit insurance funds, so that if a bank does run into difficulties its depositors, particularly the smaller ones, are protected.

Central Banks

Even with capital and liquid reserves and the bad debt provisions, the banking system cannot operate unless it can maintain the confidence of the public. When confidence is lost a bank soon has to close or receive support from its central bank. In such cases, it is important for the central bank in the system to act swiftly

because there is a risk that the loss of confidence will spread to other banks and eventually to the whole banking system. This risk of contagion has increased as banks have lent growing amounts to each other through the wholesale markets. There is a need for a bank with problems to be isolated quickly and this is the responsibility of the central bank. It acts as lender of last resort to the banking system to restore confidence.

Money is usually lent primarily to the ailing bank on the understanding that it will be repaid, with interest if possible, when the bank is restored to health. In order to ensure that banks do not take unwarranted risks, feeling assured that the central bank will come to their rescue if they get into difficulties, central banks are usually also responsible for supervising the banking system. As supervisors, they ensure that banking regulations are adhered to. The central banks of some of the major countries are as follows: Bank of England (United Kingdom); Federal Reserve System (United States); Bank of Canada; Reserve Bank of Australia; Bank of France; Bank of Japan; and Bundesbank (Federal Republic of Germany).

Central banks often perform other functions as well. They usually provide banking services to the government, allowing strict confiden-

First National Bank of Chicago

A modern bank vault is constructed for maximum security. It is usually equipped with a time lock.

tiality to be maintained. They also commonly provide banking services to other banks, especially commercial or clearing banks involved in the payments system. The central bank typically holds accounts for banks offering checking accounts. Following a day's transactions, the amounts owed by one bank to another, after netting out the sum of all payments from one bank to another that are matched by those in the reverse direction, are paid by adjusting the accounts held with the central bank. In larger countries, such as the United States, the central bank has branches to facilitate the regional clearing of checks and the bigger banks often compete with these by offering similar clearing bank (or house) services to the smaller banks in order to earn fees. This provision of banking services by non-central banks to other banks is called "correspondent banking". Central banks are usually also responsible for the distribution of bank notes and coins, or cash, and for monetary policy. The Bundesbank actually decides, as well as carries out, monetary policy in the Federal Republic of Germany, independently of government control. The Bank of England, in contrast, acts on behalf of the treasury or finance ministry. Other central banks vary in the degree of independence they enjoy in formulating and pursuing monetary policy.

In the 1980s central banks have become concerned about the increasing amount of risk to which banking systems are exposed. The major banks lent heavily to the Third-World developing countries in the 1970s and, for a variety of reasons, many of these countries found it increasingly difficult to handle their debts in the early 1980s, thus exposing the banks to risks of losses. In addition, the growth of wholesale banking increased the interdependence of banks, making it more likely that a crisis originating in one part of the banking system would affect other parts.

The spread of the practice of charging variable interest rates on loans also presented the problem that borrowers might find it impossible to pay if interest rates rose sharply, again exposing banks to risk of losses. Furthermore, the growing practice of underwriting has exposed banks to what have become known as off-balance sheet risks. These are risks that do not show up directly in the bank's accounts since they are only commitments of financial support. The worry is that the banks will be called upon to provide support at just the time they are least able to provide it. Central banks and bank regulatory authorities around the world have responded to these perceived threats by requiring banks to increase capital reserves and loan loss provisions.

As a result of the internationalization of the banking system, it has also become necessary for central banks to ensure that the foreign banks operating in their countries are adequately supervised in their country of origin and that their domestic banks are adequately supervised in their operations abroad. The major central banks have come to an agreement concerning the sharing of supervisory responsibilities, known as the Basle Concordat.

The adoption of new technology, especially that connected with information processing and telecommunications, has transformed banking and encouraged the trend towards the erosion of difference between banks and other financial institutions. Eminent economists have argued that in the absence of government regulations, such as those requiring the separation of investment and commercial banking, the differences between the various financial institutions would disappear. If we were to accept the proposition that the two major services provided by the financial sector are broking and financial accounting, then all financial institutions would be broker-bankers, or banks for short, in a fully deregulated financial system. Broking in this context means the practice of acting as a financial intermediary. Eventually people may not even visit bank branches, preferring to use computer, or perhaps even audio-visual, links to transact and negotiate business. Home banking, which involves computer links between homes and banks, with Visual Display Unit terminals at each end, have already been established in many countries. Money itself might even disappear. In the future, if people decide to continue to visit stores rather than buy goods through video catalogues, they are likely to take a plastic card, rather than cash or a check book, to effect transactions. Already banks in the major industrial countries are experimenting with Electronic Funds Transfer at Point of Sale (EFTPOS) systems. The French have developed a chip or memory card which contains a micro-chip and is capable of keeping a record of transactions. The current EFTPOS systems are still based on the idea of effecting payments by moving money between accounts, and will be for a long time. It will also be a long time before electronic payments can be made at local stores, as well as at supermarkets or department stores. In the future, however, it is possible to conceive of a system in which transactions are effected by moving assets, other than money, between accounts.

BANNISTER, Sir Roger (born 1929), was the first man to run a mile in less than four minutes. Born at Harrow, England, and named Roger Gilbert Bannister, he began his athletics career while studying medicine at Oxford University and later attended the medical school at St. Mary's Hospital in London. He competed in the 1952 Olympic Games in Helsinki, finishing sixth in the 1,500 meters race. That same year the Australian John Landy ran a mile in 4 minutes 2.6 seconds and people began to realize that the long-awaited "four-minute" mile could not be far away.

In 1953 Bannister broke the British record for the mile, and on 6 May 1954 he made his attempt on the four-minute mile at Oxford. He was assisted by his friends including Chris Brasher and Chris Chataway, both athletes of note. Bannister broke the finishing tape in 3 minutes 59.4 seconds. His world record lasted only a few weeks before John Landy beat it, but Bannister gained his revenge in the Empire Games at Vancouver in Canada.

At the end of 1954 Bannister retired from the track to begin his career as a doctor. In 1971 he became chairman of the Sports Council, which has the task of encouraging sport and recreation in Britain. Later he served as

Planet News

At the Empire Games in 1954, Roger Bannister beat his own record-breaking speed for running a mile.

president of the International Council for Sport and Physical Recreation. In 1985 he was elected Master of Pembroke College, Oxford.

BANNOCKBURN, BATTLE OF. The battle of Bannockburn was fought between the Scots and the English in the year 1314. Scotland was not then united with England, even though the English king Edward I had managed to conquer the Scots in 1291. The Scots hated their English overlords, and after Edward II became king they managed to drive them out of their country, except for one very important stronghold, Stirling Castle. English soldiers still held this castle, but they came under siege from the army of the Scots led by their great king, Robert Bruce.

The governor of Stirling Castle sent a desperate message to King Edward that the castle could not hold out much longer. An English army quickly marched north. It was very much larger than the Scottish army, and had great numbers of horsemen and archers. Robert Bruce realized that his only hope was to try to trick the English. For his battlefield

Mary Evans Picture Library

At the battle of Bannockburn the English were defeated and had to remove their forces from Scotland.

he chose the ridge at the top of the valley of the Bannock Burn, three kilometers (two miles) south of Stirling, and set up his standard at the highest point, the Bore Stone. He ordered holes to be dug in front of the Scottish battle-line and covered up with sticks and turf so that no one could see that the ground had been touched. His spearmen stood behind these traps, ready for the English.

When the battle began the English horsemen attacked first. They rode up the slopes, only to fall into the pits. As they floundered out, weighed down by their heavy armor, they were met by a wall of pikes and spears they could not break through. The battle became so confused that the archers could not shoot for fear of hitting their own men. Several thousand men who followed the Scottish army but were not actually soldiers themselves were watching the battle from the hillside. They charged down on the English, blowing horns,

brandishing weapons, and shouting, "Slay, slay!" The tired English thought that another whole army was advancing on them, and they turned and fled. Many died in the Bannock Burn and the marshes beyond.

From this time the English had to give up their claim to be masters of Scotland, and for many years they found it very difficult to defend themselves against the Scots. The English learned a lesson from their defeat, however—not to send horsemen in a charge against a solid line of spearmen. After this the English archers always tried to split up an enemy's lines with a rush of arrows before the cavalry mounted an attack.

BANTING AND BEST. Sir Frederick Grant Banting (1891–1941) and Charles Herbert Best (1899–1978) discovered insulin, a hormone used to control the disease diabetes mellitus. Diabetes usually results when the

BBC Hulton Picture Library

The Canadians Charles Best (left) and Sir Frederick Banting (right) worked on extracting insulin from animal pancreas glands and preparing it for use by human diabetics.

pancreas does not produce enough insulin to use the sugar in the blood (see DIABETES).

Banting studied medicine at the University of Toronto in Canada and graduated in 1916. He was awarded the Military Cross for heroism while serving in the medical corps in World War I (1914–18). After the war, Banting returned to practice medicine in London, Ontario, and became interested in diabetes, for which there was no remedy. In 1921, he went to the University of Toronto to do research. His assistant was Charles Best, who was still a medical student, but an expert on measuring blood sugar levels. It took them only seven months to prepare the insulin hormone, which they extracted from animal pancreas glands. They tried insulin on dogs and then on human diabetics. It worked, and the patients became healthy for as long as they took insulin. The first human being to be treated with insulin was a seriously ill 14-year-old boy in the Toronto General Hospital.

For this discovery, Banting and John J. R. Macleod, whose laboratory was used for the experiments, received the 1923 Nobel Prize for Medicine. Banting, however, felt that Best had been slighted, and he shared his prize money with him.

In 1923, Ontario created a Banting and Best department of medical research at the University of Toronto, with Banting as its first head. He was generously funded by the Canadian government for his research. The Banting Foundation was established in 1924, and in 1930 the Banting Institute opened in Toronto. Banting spent the remainder of his life as director of the Banting and Best department, working on problems related to cancer, heart disease, and silicosis (a disease caused by working in the mines).

During World War II, Banting became head of the central medical research commission of the National Research Council of Canada. One of his interests was in the problems raised by flying. In 1940, he was keen to co-ordinate his research with the work of medical researchers in England, and insisted on going to England himself. After his first successful visit, he embarked on a second journey. Sadly, the bomber on which he was traveling crashed when it was forced to land in a remote spot in Newfoundland on 21 February 1941.

Best also continued in medical research. He was the first doctor to use anticoagulants (blood thinners) in the treatment of thrombosis (blood clots). He succeeded Banting as director of the Banting and Best department in 1941, and remained there until 1967.

BANYAN. The strange Indian tree called the banyan (*Ficus benghalensis*) starts life as a seed dropped by a bird on the rough stem of a palm or other rough-barked tree. The young plant sends up shoots that embrace and strangle the tree that supports it, eventually reaching 30 meters (100 feet) or more in height. The wide-spreading branches send down many slender roots. When these reach the ground they take hold in the soil and continue to thicken above it into stout pillar-like trunks which give support to the massive branches. These branches extend further and further until in time a single tree looks like a small woodland. One tree in India was reputed to have 320 large trunks and over 3,000 smaller ones; it was so large that it could give shelter to as many as 7,000 men.

The Hindus of India regard the banyan as sacred. It is a relation of the fig tree and its broad leaves are used by the country people as plates. The crimson fruits, about the size of

Ewing Galloway

This photograph of just one banyan tree shows the pillar-like trunks which grow down from its branches.

cherries, are eaten by birds and monkeys and, in times of famine, by men. The trunk of the tree has a milky white juice, the source of a poor quality rubber and of birdlime, a sticky substance which is smeared on the branches of trees to catch birds. The juice also has a reputation for relieving the pains of bruises and rheumatism. Banyan timber, however, is of very little value.

BAPTISTS. When a person is made a member of the Baptist Church, he takes part in a ceremony of immersion, that is, his whole body is dipped into water. This is known as baptism. Other Christian churches baptize, but their ceremony is different from that of the Baptists because water is poured only on the person's head. Baptists do not baptize babies, saying that only grown-up people understand their faith, and therefore only for grown-up people can baptism be called a sacrament; that is, "the outward and visible sign of an inward and spiritual grace".

In baptizing like this, the Baptists follow the example of Jesus Christ, who, at the age of about 30, was baptized in the River Jordan by St. John the Baptist. The apostles of Jesus were also baptized in this way; in the *Acts of the Apostles* in the Bible it is told that St. Philip went into the water himself when he baptized other people.

The Baptist Church is evangelical, which means that it teaches that belief in the Bible, and particularly in the New Testament, is more important than church ceremonies. The church does not tell people exactly what they should believe, but allows them freedom of conscience, or permission to decide themselves what is right or wrong.

Baptist churches are linked with each other

Church Missionary Society

This young man is about to be totally immersed in water during a baptism service in southern India.

and they form a district association. All the district associations together are called a Baptist Union, or, in the United States, a Convention. The Baptists of Great Britain and of some other lands belong to the World Council of Churches. Most Baptists are connected with the Baptist World Alliance.

There are Baptists in every continent, amounting to more than 30 million in the world. The majority are in North America and they are also found throughout Europe.

History of the Baptist Movement

The Baptist movement began in Europe at the time of the Reformation. Some people declared that the baptism of babies did not mean anything, and in 1525 a man had himself baptized for the second time. This, however, caused an outcry and a year later another man was executed for holding this belief.

Thousands of Baptists were imprisoned and killed in Europe, and many of those that were left fled to Holland, where they were safe. Among them were two Englishmen called John Smyth and Thomas Helwys. Smyth baptized himself and his followers, and at Amsterdam founded the first English-speaking Baptist Church in 1609.

A group of Baptists returned to England with Helwys and, in 1611, they built a Baptist church in London, the first one in England. Helwys was the minister of this church. He aroused much astonishment and indignation when he wrote a book saying that everyone, even people who are not Christians, should be allowed to belong to whichever religion they believe is the true one.

The followers of Helwys called themselves General Baptists, but baptism by immersion was begun by another group of Baptists, known as Particular Baptists. Whereas General Baptists believed that Christ had died to save everyone, the Particular Baptists believed that he died only for a chosen few. John Bunyan, who wrote the *Pilgrim's Progress*, belonged to an early Baptist church.

In the American colonies there were many Baptists, the most famous being Roger Williams, who in 1636 founded the first settlement in Rhode Island state—the first settlement which declared that people were free to worship God in any way they chose. The religion grew quickly in America, becoming particularly popular in the southern states. Baptists became, with the Methodists, one of the two largest Protestant denominations in the country. Many Baptists, being loyal to England, left America at the time of the revolution. Some settled in Canada where they set up the first Baptist Church in Nova Scotia in 1763.

Since 1792, when the British missionary William Carey founded the Baptist Missionary Society and himself went to India, Baptists have sent many missionaries abroad.

BARBADOS, is the most easterly island in the West Indies (see WEST INDIES). It is bordered by the Atlantic Ocean on the east and the Caribbean Sea to the west. Roughly triangular in shape, the island extends 34 kilometers (21 miles) from north to south and 22 kilometers (14 miles) from east to west.

For part of the year Barbados enjoys the cool northeast trade winds (see TRADE WINDS) and this helps to explain why, although it is in the tropics, the weather is not too hot. The island is almost encircled with coral reefs and its highest point, Mount Hillaby in the north central region, is no more than 337 meters (1,105 feet) above the sea. Early Portuguese explorers named the island *Barbados*, meaning "bearded", after the fig trees there which looked like beards.

In spite of its small size Barbados has about 252,700 people, which is more than can comfortably make a living from the island. Over 90 per cent of the people are descended from Africans who were brought as slaves from West Africa in the 17th and 18th centuries. Many earn their living from the sugar industry, either growing and harvesting the cane or manufacturing it into sugar, molasses (syrup), or rum. Tourism is an important industry as is fishing.

There is known to be oil beneath the ground but Barbados has no other mineral resources. Nearly all the original forest was cleared so that sugar-cane could be planted and Barbados now has to import timber. It also has to import most of its foodstuffs.

Barbadians are well known for their Calypso music and the steel bands which play it. Cricket is their national sport and Barbados has produced many famous cricketers.

FACTS ABOUT BARBADOS

AREA: 430 square kilometers (166 square miles).
POPULATION: 252,700.
KIND OF COUNTRY: Independent parliamentary state; member of the Commonwealth of Nations.
CAPITAL: Bridgetown.
GEOGRAPHICAL FEATURES: An island with a gently hilly landscape, its coast almost encircled by coral reefs.
LEADING INDUSTRIES: Sugar, molasses, rum, tourism.

History

The Portuguese were among the first Europeans to sight the island in the 16th century, but the English were the first settlers. When they arrived in 1625 the island had long been abandoned by the original native Indian inhabitants. The English imported slaves from West Africa to work on their sugar plantations and their numbers grew rapidly. Slavery was abolished in 1834, but sugar continued to dominate the economy.

Among their ancient institutions Barbadians are especially proud of Codrington College, founded in 1710, the oldest center of higher education in the West Indies. The capital of Barbados is Bridgetown, founded in 1628, and this is also the only port. It has a deep-water harbor. Bridgetown has a population of about 7,500.

In 1966, Barbados ceased to be a colony of Great Britain and became an independent

Palm trees and coral rocks fringe much of the coastline of Barbados. Some of the shoreline is hilly.

ZEFA

country and member of the Commonwealth (see COMMONWEALTH, THE), with the queen of England as head of state. The government is led by the prime minister. The parliament of Barbados consists of the Senate and the House of Assembly, and the Queen is represented by a governor-general.

BARBARIAN INVASIONS.

The invasions that are usually called by this name were the attacks made against the Roman empire by barbarian tribes beginning in the 4th century AD. The Romans used the word barbarians to describe all peoples who lived outside their empire and who did not share the Roman ideas of a civilized and well-ordered life.

The empire of Rome was weakened by its divisions. In AD 364 it was divided into two parts, each with its own capital; the eastern capital was Constantinople and the western one Milan. Outside the empire were the many barbarian tribes, waiting for their chance to

attack if Rome showed any signs of weakness—tribes such as the Goths, the Vandals, the Lombards, the Franks, the Jutes, and the Saxons. All these might have stayed quietly in the lands to which they belonged, but a great movement of peoples towards the west had started in Asia and the western tribes therefore had to move nearer and nearer to the Roman lands in search of safety.

The Visigoths were the first to trouble Rome seriously. They themselves had been attacked by the Huns, a ferocious tribe of nomads from central Asia. Moving westward away from the Huns, the Visigoths crossed the River Danube and attacked Rome several times. In AD 410 they captured the city, under their leader Alaric. (There is a separate article about him.) Eventually the Goths settled down in Spain and set up a powerful kingdom which stretched from the River Loire in France in the north down to the south of Spain. (There is a separate article on GOTHS.)

Barbarian tribes threatened the Roman Empire from the 4th century AD. Visigoths captured Rome in AD 410.

During this time the Vandals had been gradually moving southwest from their home in Germany, across France and Spain, and had set up a kingdom on the north coast of Africa. Under the command of their leader Gaiseric, the Vandals captured and sacked Rome in AD 455. (There is a separate article on VANDALS.)

Meanwhile yet another people, the Franks, had been moving westward into France, and the Jutes and Saxons had begun raids on the old Roman province of Britain. The Romans had withdrawn their armies from Britain to defend the city of Rome itself.

In Italy there was no settled government for many years. Another barbarian tribe, the Ostrogoths, set up a kingdom there, but it lasted for only 60 years. At last a strong ruler named Justinian became emperor in Constantinople, and he managed to bring back order in Italy during his lifetime. After his death in AD 565, however, Italy was invaded and conquered again, this time by the Lombards.

Two words in our language today have come down from those times: "Hun" is used to mean a brutal attacker, and "Vandal" to mean someone who destroys things senselessly.

BARBERRY is the name for about 450 species of spiny shrubs of the genus *Berberis*. All barberry bushes grow in temperate climates, and they have sharp spines and small, oval leaves that are borne in clusters along the branches. The flowers, inner bark, and wood are yellow.

The fruit is a red berry that sometimes clings to the shrub all winter. The most familiar species in the United States are the common barberry (*Berberis vulgaris*) of Europe, and the Japanese barberry (*Berberis thunbergii*).

NHPA/Brian Hawkes

The red berries of the common barberry grow in clusters. The stems and bark of the plant can be used to make yellow dyes.

The common barberry, introduced into the eastern United States, has been banned from many areas because it harbors the fungus that causes wheat rust, a destructive crop disease. If the shrub is planted near a wheat field, the wheat, or black stem, rust spreads to the wheat plants. The harmless Japanese barberry is understandably more popular. Three points of difference help to distinguish the one species from the other. The common barberry leaves have rough edges, the spines are in

Barbets are related to woodpeckers and use their beaks to drill nesting holes in soft, dead wood. They bite at the wood and carry away the chips, rather than chiseling at it and leaving the chips all over the ground, as woodpeckers do. This pied barbet is bringing the pulped fruit of a fig to its young in the nest.

NHPA/Peter Johnson

groups of three, and the berries are in clusters. The Japanese barberry leaves are smooth-edged, its spines grow singly, and its berries are borne singly or in pairs. The Japanese species is low and compact, reaching about 1.5 meters (5 feet) in height.

Several species of barberry introduced from China and Chile are under cultivation in the United States and England. Most are evergreens.

Birds—including the ruffed grouse, the bobwhite, and the pheasant—eat the fruit of barberry shrubs. Sometimes the berries are used in making jellies and preserves.

BARBET is a stout bird named for the bristles at the base of the bill. The birds are found throughout the tropics, but most of the 78 species live in forests at the very top of the trees. They are mainly fruit-eaters taking wild figs, guavas among others, and also berries and seeds. The prong-billed barbet (*Sem-*

nornis frantzii) of Central America is unusual among birds since it eats flowers. The red-headed barbet (*Eubucco bourcierii*), also of Central America, eats only insects which it searches for under dead leaves on the forest floor.

Barbets are famous for their loud repetitive calls. Sometimes their song goes on endlessly, and when it stops another bird's call takes its place. No wonder that in many places they are called "brain-fever" birds! Some barbets have special names. For example, the Malayan coppersmith bird (*Megalalaima haemacephala*) gets its name from its monotonous call, which sounds just like someone beating on metal with a hammer.

Apart from their calls, barbets have very distinctive coloring. African species have red, blue, yellow, or black plumage. Their Asian cousins are mainly green but with bright patches of red, blue, or yellow around the head.

Barbets are related to woodpeckers. Like them, they have short, stiff tails which are used as supports when climbing trees. They generally nest in holes which are dug out by both sexes. They usually bite at the wood, rather than chisel like woodpeckers. The nest may be used for several years and have more than one entrance hole. Two to five pure white eggs are laid. The chicks are fed mainly on a high-protein diet of insects. When they can fly, the young birds fend for themselves but return to the nest hole at night. They start to live on their own after six weeks.

BARCELONA in northeast Spain is the country's chief port and industrial center and second largest city. It lies in a plain backed by mountains on the Mediterranean coast south of the Costa Brava. The oldest part of the city, near the harbor, occupies the site of the Roman town of Barcino—from which Barcelona gets its name. Here are the cathedral and many fine buildings in the Spanish Gothic style. Since Spain's entry into the European Common Market in 1986, the city's trade and industries, including car manufacturing and furniture design, have been greatly boosted. Much rebuilding has also been undertaken.

The top of the Columbus monument on the waterfront commands a good view of the city. Near by is a copy of Columbus's ship *Santa María* (see COLUMBUS, CHRISTOPHER). From the monument the broad avenue of the Ramblas leads inland to the Plaza de Cataluña, Barcelona's chief square. The Ramblas was once the bed of a mountain torrent (which is what *rambla* means). It is one of Europe's most famous streets, with double rows of trees and busy cafés, stores, and street stalls. From the Plaza runs the Paseo de Gracia, Barcelona's smartest shopping street, at the far end of which is the apartment house called La Pedrera, designed by the Catalonian architect Antonio Gaudí (1852–1926). Other examples of his

ZEFA

Barcelona is a bustling Spanish seaport and commercial center on the Mediterranean. A replica of Columbus' ship *Santa Maria* (in which he sailed to America) can be seen in the harbor.

work are the Guell Palace (now a museum) near the Ramblas and the children's play terrace in the Guell Park. Barcelona is famous for its period architecture.

At the northern end of the harbor is Barceloneta, the picturesque quarter of the sailors and fishermen. To the south of the harbor is Montjuich, a steep hill crowned by an old castle.

Barcelona is the capital city of Catalonia—one of Spain's 17 regions. The people speak Catalan which is quite different from the Spanish most of the country speaks. The city has a population of about 1,700,000.

BARD. The word *bard* is nowadays used as another word for poet. We often speak of Shakespeare as the "Bard of Avon". But among the Celtic-speaking peoples who long ago inhabited Gaul (France) and ancient Britain, bards were gifted poets and minstrels who composed and recited verses in praise of great heroes and heroic deeds. Bards died out as a class of poet in Gaul soon after the time of Christ, but they continued to exist in Wales and Ireland, for centuries. Bards in Ireland were skilled in composing satire, which could be very damaging to its victims.

Bards were a very important class of people attached to the courts of Welsh and Irish rulers. Later on in Wales, they became wandering minstrel-poets. Every so often there was held a great festival of song and poetry called an *eisteddfod* at which bards from all over the country competed. After the time of Queen Elizabeth I these festivals ceased, but they were started again in the 19th century, and are now held regularly. (See EISTEDDFOD.)

BARIUM is a silvery-white, fairly soft, poisonous metal. It melts at 850°C (1562°F) and boils at 1140°C (2084°F). In nature, barium only occurs in combination with other elements, principally as barium chloride in the mineral barite and as barium carbonate in the mineral wetherite.

Barium salts that dissolve in water are very poisonous and must never be taken into the human body. Barium sulfate, however does not dissolve in water and cannot be absorbed by the body tissues. When mixed with water to form a heavy milky liquid called a barium meal, it can be drunk by patients about to have their digestive systems X-rayed. Barium salts are so dense that X-rays can hardly pass through them, and doctors can easily see any blockage or other problem. Barium sulfate is also used in paint pigments (colors), and as a filler for paper (especially wallpaper), rubber, soap, and linoleum.

Another salt, barium carbonate, is a poisonous, heavy, white powder used in rat poison, optical glass, ceramics, paints, and enamels.

BARK. Just as human beings have a skin to protect their delicate flesh, so do trees and shrubs have a covering of bark over their trunks, stems, branches, and roots. Herbaceous plants have no bark.

It is the bark which keeps a tree watertight, but it still allows it to breathe. If you look carefully at a piece of cork, which is the bark of the cork oak tree, you will see the breathing channels running across it like dark streaks.

As a tree grows, it forms new bark to give it a thicker covering. The trunk also grows thicker as it gets older, however, and this may make the bark split. You can identify a tree by the texture of its bark. The bark of the European oak cracks into narrow ridges, while that of the American white oak forms scaly plates.

When a branch is damaged new bark seals up the wound, just as new skin grows on a person's finger when it is injured. In both cases, this prevents germs getting into the wound. If the tree's wound is too large to be healed in this way, however, it is best to paint over the damaged part with a substance which kills disease and fungi.

If the bark is stripped off a tree it will nearly always die. In Australia, trees are often deliberately killed in this way when there are large forests to be cleared so that cattle can graze on the land. The trees have rings of bark stripped from them; this is called ring barking. After a

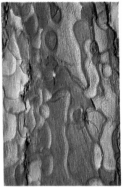

Different trees have different types of bark, some rough, some smooth, some that flake off in big pieces. Even in winter when there are no leaves on the trees you can identify a type of tree by the pattern and texture of its bark.

NHPA/G. I. Bernard
English Elm

NHPA/G. I. Bernard
Black Pine

NHPA/John Shaw
Arizona Sycamore

few years they die and then they can be burned down more easily. Rabbits and deer may kill valuable fruit trees by eating their bark.

Bark has many uses. The cork oak has already been mentioned. Its bark is used for cork mats, lifebelts, and corks for bottles. North American Indians make canoes from thin strips of birch-bark, while some of the people who live on Pacific islands still make clothes from the bark of trees. In the Himalayas, in the north of India, the bark of one tree is used to make paper. Cinnamon, which is sometimes used for flavoring food, is the powdered bark of a tree which grows in India and Malaya. The brown sails and ropes of fishing vessels are dyed (colored) with the powdered bark of the oak, and this is also used for tanning leather. Quinine, for a long time one of the best medicines for treating malaria, comes from the bark of the cinchona tree.

BARLEY, like wheat, is a cereal or edible grain of the grass family. There are many different varieties of the one genus, *Hordeum*. Barley is sometimes described as "bearded" because of the appearance of the long, brittle spikes known as awns that form part of the sheath enclosing the seed. The awns are broken off the grains during threshing.

Barley is a hardy, adaptable plant and charred kernels found in ancient ruins and tombs show that barley was one of man's earliest foods. It was probably first grown in Egypt

in 5000 BC and in northwest Europe by 3000 BC. In some parts of Europe barley bread (rather than wheat or rye bread) was for many centuries the "staff of life", and as such it was

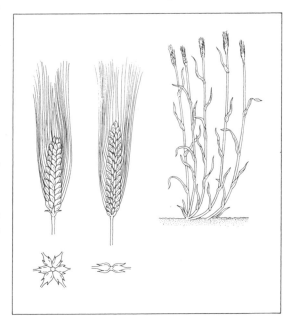

A head of barley grain may have either six or two rows of kernels. Notice the long spikes known as awns.

eaten by the Greeks and Romans. Barley flour cannot be leavened (that is, "raised" as it is baked) and therefore makes heavy bread, and so wheat, which makes a lighter bread, gradually became the favorite grain for this purpose. (See BREAD AND BAKING.)

Because it grows quickly and does not need much rainfall, barley can be grown in many countries. It is found within the Arctic Circle, where it has only two months in which to grow, and in North Africa, where the climate is hot and dry. In Tibet it is grown at heights of more than 4,500 meters (15,000 feet) above sea-level.

A head of barley grain may have either two or six rows of kernels. The kernels may be either black or white and sometimes have no hull, in which case they are called "naked barleys". In Europe the commonest kinds of barley have two rows of white kernels in hulls, but in the United States and Canada, six-rowed types are most common. Some of these at first glance seem to have only four rows of grain and are known as "bere" or "bigg". The naked barleys, grown mostly in India and Japan, can also be either six-rowed or two-rowed.

In Europe and North America most of the barley crop is sown in the spring, although there are also winter varieties which are sown in the autumn. Sometimes spring barleys are used as "nurse-crops" for grasses and clovers that are later made into hay. This means that the seeds of the hay crops are sown soon after the barley and they grow under its shelter until it is harvested.

More than half of the barley grown in the world is used in the form of barley meal to feed farm animals, particularly cows and pigs. A good deal of barley is malted, which means that it is first soaked in water and left to sprout and then dried, after which it is known as malt. Beer is made from malt by adding water and yeast to make it ferment (see BEER AND BREWING). Kernels of barley are made into pearl barley for putting into soups and puddings by being stripped of their sheaths and polished.

Barley is the fourth most important cereal crop after wheat, rice, and corn; the USSR, Canada, China, and France being the largest producers. The states of California, Idaho, Montana, and North Dakota are the main barley-growing areas in the United States, as is the province of Alberta in Canada. Apart from these northern areas where the summers are short, it is also grown in areas of prolonged

sunshine where drought is common, such as Morocco, Spain, and Turkey.

BARNACLE. The barnacle is a small shellfish which belongs to the group of animals called crustaceans and which has a habit of sticking itself to anything convenient. The famous scientist T. H. Huxley described the barnacle as "a crustacean fixed by its head and kicking its food into its mouth with its legs". At low tide you can often see a thick crust made up of millions of barnacles on piers, rocks and breakwaters. They fix themselves on to large

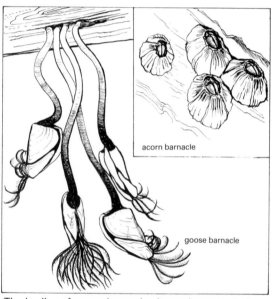

acorn barnacle

goose barnacle

The bodies of goose barnacles hang downwards from stalks. Plated acorn barnacles fix flat to a surface.

objects such as whales, sea turtles, and the bottom of ships. In the days of small sailing ships barnacles were a real danger because they slowed down speed and made steering more difficult. Many a whaler could hardly get home after a two-year cruise because of the masses of barnacles clinging to its hull. Today, ships are treated with antifouling paints (which often contain copper) that prevent the barnacle's larva from settling.

There are many different kinds of barnacle. Acorn barnacles (*Balanus*), named from their acorn-like shape, include the many kinds found on the shore. The body is enclosed by five limy plates. Most are small but the species from the Pacific (*Balanus nubilis*) can reach 30 centimeters (1 foot) across.

Goose barnacles (*Lepas*) get their strange name from the ancient belief that they produced goslings (young geese). They attach themselves to floating debris such as driftwood. The body hangs down from a flexible stalk.

Barnacles feed by thrusting out their feathery feet and withdrawing them with a grasping motion into their mouths. They can trap small animals and plants up to one millimeter long.

When barnacles hatch from their eggs, they look like tiny crabs or lobsters and they can swim about. It is only when they grow older that they find some object to cling to for the rest of their lives. Then they grow a shell, and remain fixed for life with only their six pairs of feathery legs movable. In China, Chile and some other countries, people eat barnacles and find them delicious.

BARNARDO, Thomas John (1845–1905).

Born in Dublin, Ireland, Thomas Barnardo had a religious experience in early manhood which led him to offer his services as a medical missionary in China, and for this purpose he enrolled as a medical student at the London Hospital in England.

He found the streets of the East End of London swarming with children—dirty, ragged, hungry and neglected. Longing to do something for them, he hired a donkey stable and opened a "ragged school".

One cold, wintry night a small boy, aged about 10, clad in rags, begged to be allowed to sleep in the stable. His name, he said, was Jim Jarvis, he had no parents, no home, and there were many others like himself in London. Barnardo took the youngster to his own home and at midnight the two of them went out to track down some of these homeless lads. On the roof of the old rag market in Houndsditch, Jim revealed to his astonished companion 11 boys fast asleep, their hiding place completely concealed by a projecting wall. Later, guided by Jim, Barnardo found a number of other hiding places where homeless boys slept.

Courtesy, Dr. Barnado's Homes

Dr. Barnado worked tirelessly all his life to help homeless children.

One evening, at a large missionary gathering, Barnardo was invited to speak and told his audience about his midnight experiences in London's underworld. But some people doubted these accounts and wrote letters to the papers challenging his statements. Lord Shaftesbury (on whom there is a separate article) read these letters and got in touch with Barnardo who agreed to guide a party to where homeless boys could be found. He took them to the Queen's Shades, Billingsgate, where 73 boys were sleeping under a tarpaulin which covered goods and old bottles.

As the date of his departure for China drew near, Barnardo, still a student, became more and more concerned about what would happen to his projects in London once he had gone away. The ragged school was flourishing in larger premises, a mission he had started for waif boys was going well, and he had boarded out about 20 others. He had a strong and positive influence on these rough, awkward lads, and many friends, including Lord Shaftesbury, urged him to remain in England and extend his work.

The matter was brought to a head with the arrival of a letter from a stranger, offering to provide £1,000 to start a home for destitute boys if Barnardo would take charge of it. Barnardo no longer hesitated; clearly his life's work lay among the poor and homeless in London, not in China.

Homes for the Homeless

Barnardo's first Home opened in 1870 at 18 Stepney Causeway, in the East End of London. He was determined not to run into debt and made a rule only to admit as many boys as he had money to provide for. When little "Carrots" pleaded, one wintry night, to be taken in, he could only be promised the next vacancy. A few days later this boy's body was discovered in an empty cask, and the coroner's verdict was "death from exhaustion due to frequent exposure and want of food". Barnardo was deeply affected by this tragedy and determined that in future he would never turn away a destitute child. That resolution has been kept by Dr. Barnardo's Homes ever since.

In 1873, by then a qualified doctor, Barnardo married Syrie Louise Elmslie, and extended his work to destitute girls. At Barkingside, Essex, a beautiful village gradually took shape, each cottage housing a family of girls with a "mother" in charge. The number in his care grew until there were more than 7,000 boys and girls. Branch Homes sprang up, and over 3,000 children were boarded out in private homes in country districts. Dr. Barnardo also encouraged emigration and settled 10,000 young people in Canada.

Barnardo had unflagging energy, and he seldom left his office before midnight. Again and again he showed up absurdities and injustices in the laws concerned with children, and it was largely his efforts that brought about the passing of the Custody of Children Act in 1891. He edited four magazines—*Night and Day, Children's Treasury, Bubbles* and *Young Helpers' League*. He started a scheme to aid starving infants, and to provide free meals for hungry schoolchildren, free medical and nursing attention for the poor, and financial assistance to elderly women.

Dr. Barnardo had seven children of his own, three of whom died in childhood. He himself died in 1905. In the short space of 40 years he had raised £3,250,000, established a network of Homes for homeless children, and rescued 60,000 destitute boys and girls. His work remains a lasting memorial to him. There are more than 8,000 children and young people being cared for in one way or another by Dr. Barnardo's organization. Some are helped in their own homes by Dr. Barnardo's Family Assistance Scheme.

BARNUM, Phineas Taylor (1810–91). Born in Bethel, Connecticut, Phineas Taylor Barnum worked successively as bartender, newspaper publisher, and theater ticket seller. In 1835 he entered show business by exhibiting a woman said to have been George Washington's nurse and to be more than 160 years old.

Mary Evans Picture Library

Phineas Barnum started "The Greatest Show on Earth" in 1871, merging with his rival, James Bailey, in 1881.

Later he formed Barnum's Museum in New York, an institution which included in its exhibitions a woolly horse, the Fiji Mermaid, a bearded lady, and General Tom Thumb, the famous dwarf. Large signs directed patrons to the "egress", and many visitors who did not know that that word meant *exit* hurried eagerly through the halls, expecting to see some wondrous beast or monstrosity, only to find themselves suddenly on the outside. Tom Thumb became so popular that in 1844 Barnum took him to Europe and exhibited him before Queen Victoria in England and at the French court. Six years later the showman induced Jenny Lind, "the Swedish nightingale", to go to America by contracting to pay for 150 concerts at $1,000 a night.

In 1871 Barnum organized a circus and menagerie which he called "The Greatest Show on Earth". In 1881 he merged with his rival James Bailey. Later they merged with the Ringling Brothers circus. At its peak the Barnum-Bailey-Ringling organization was so large that it traveled in four separate trains consisting of 107 20-meter (70-foot) railroad cars, in total.

BAROMETER. One of the most important of the instruments used in foretelling the weather is the mercury barometer.

The barometer was invented by Evangelista Torricelli, an Italian and a pupil of Galileo, in 1643. His purpose was not to foretell the weather but to show that the air exerts a definite pressure, which is called atmospheric pressure. He filled a glass tube 90 centimeters (35 inches) long with mercury and, without allowing any of it to escape, turned the tube up so that the open end was beneath the surface of some more mercury in a bowl. The mercury in the tube fell until its level was about 76 centimeters (30 inches) above the level in the bowl, leaving a vacuum at the top of the tube. This showed that the air was exerting a pressure on the surface of the mercury in the bowl equal to the pressure produced by the column of mercury. When the atmospheric pressure increased, the level of the mercury in the tube rose.

At about the same time Otto von Guericke of Magdeburg, Germany, made a water barometer 12 meters (40 feet) long. Both Torricelli and von Guericke noticed that the changes in height of the first barometers were connected with the changes in the weather. (When the barometer "falls" it means that the pressure of the air is very low and that air from an area where the pressure is higher will rush in, bringing with it a change in the weather in the form of wind, warmth or rain. When the barometer "rises", it means that the low press-

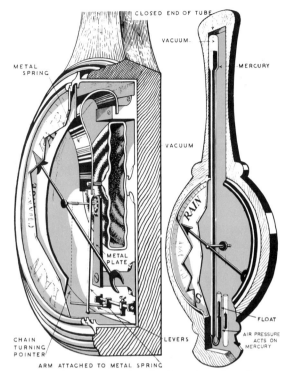

An aneroid barometer, showing how the pointer is linked to the metal box inside. **Right:** A mercury barometer with a dial.

ure area has moved on and that fair weather is likely.) Next a Frenchman, Blaise Pascal, showed that the height of the mercury column fell as the barometer was carried up a mountain and rose again on the descent. This is because atmospheric pressure becomes less as altitude increases. So the chief uses of the barometer began to be seen—by meteorologists and sailors to foretell the weather and by airmen and climbers to measure their height above sea-level.

The usual mercury barometer has a J-shaped tube with a scale marked on it so that the height of mercury can easily be read. A very accurate barometer is the Fortin type: it has an adjustable cistern so that the mercury level can be brought into contact with a fixed pointer before the barometer is read. This overcomes the difficulty caused by the fact that a change in pressure alters the levels in both the column and the cistern.

A portable barometer, originally devised for

the use of airmen and climbers, is the aneroid barometer. The main part of this barometer is a cylindrical metal box with corrugated sides. The inside of the box is almost a vacuum; its thin sides are prevented by springs from being crushed by the air pressure. The sides move in and out as the pressure varies and the movements are magnified by levers which turn a pointer round a dial. This type of barometer is the one most commonly found in ordinary dwelling houses. In the kind called a barograph, the levers cause a pen to trace a line on a paper chart mounted on a rotating drum.

Barometer readings are given in millibars, millimeters or inches: 1,000 millibars=750.1 millimeters=29.53 inches. Roughly, we can say that the barometer falls 12 millibars for every 100 meters (330 feet) of ascent above sea-level.

BARRACUDA. There are about 20 species of barracuda found along the coasts of the warmer seas. The largest is the great barra-

The barracuda's torpedo-shaped body gives it great speed. It has very powerful jaws and sharp teeth.

cuda (*Sphyraena barracuda*), up to 2.5 meters (8 feet) long. It is one of the most ferocious fishes in tropical waters and is especially feared in the West Indies where it is known to have attacked people. Its torpedo-shaped body

is built for speed and with its powerful jaws fitted with knife-like teeth it can do great damage among shoals of other fish, its main source of food. Sometimes it bites through fishermen's nets to get at the fish inside.

As might be expected, barracuda provide great sport for anglers who catch them by a method known as trolling, in which the bait—in this case a live fish—is drawn through the water by a boat. When they are hooked the barracudas fight hard, sometimes leaping high out of the water. In some places, such as off the California coast, they are caught, then salted and sold in markets; but they are not greatly valued as food.

The barracouta (*Leionura atun*) gets its name because it looks like a barracuda and has large, sharp teeth, but it belongs to quite a different family of fishes. It is also known as snoek in South Africa, where it is smoked and canned.

The related king barracouta (*Rexea solandri*) is found only in the waters off southern Australia and New Zealand. At one time it was fished in large numbers, but since 1880 it has lost popularity as a food fish.

BARRIE, J. M. (1860–1937). Sir James Matthew Barrie was a Scottish writer whose most famous play is *Peter Pan*, the story of a little boy who refuses to grow up. Barrie was born in Kirriemuir, Scotland. After studying at the University of Edinburgh, he worked for two years as a newspaper journalist. His first successful book, *Auld Licht Idylls*, was published in 1888. This book, like much of Barrie's work, tells true stories from his own childhood. The town that he calls Thrums in his books is really Kirriemuir, Barrie's home town.

He wrote many novels that were meant for adults but can be enjoyed by younger readers too. They include *The Little Minister* and *The Little White Bird*. In *Margaret Ogilvy* he pictures his mother and tells of his early years with her. The plays that Barrie wrote, however, made him world-famous. *Peter Pan* was first performed in 1904. Barrie had no children of his own but he became guardian to the five sons of a close friend. *Peter Pan* grew out of the stories that he made up for these boys.

Barrie liked to write of a fantasy world, and his other plays, *A Kiss for Cinderella*, *Mary Rose* and *Dear Brutus*, have scenes which, like those in *Peter Pan*, take place in a dreamland. *Peter Pan* has been translated into many languages and is performed all over the world. (See PETER PAN.)

BARROW. Under the Christian culture, which has developed at different periods in Europe, America, and many other parts of the world, people's bodies, or their ashes, are generally buried in graveyards. A cross or stone tablet of some sort is usually put on the grave to mark the place and to show who is buried there. In Europe before the coming of Christianity and in other regions at various periods, people used to put a pile of earth or stones over the grave instead of a cross. This pile is called a barrow, and is usually marked on modern maps as *tumulus* from the Latin word mean-

ing "burial mound". Barrows were often built only over the graves of quite important people, such as chiefs. Sometimes more than one person would be buried in the same barrow. Barrows made from stones rather than earth are also called cairns.

Barrows may be of two kinds, long or round. Both kinds are found in Britain. The long barrows are usually rather older than the round ones. They were built during the New Stone Age and the early part of the Bronze Age, between about 2500 and 1500 BC. Several of them have entrances leading to long passages with little rooms or chambers at the sides. Hetty Pegler's Tump, in Gloucestershire, is one of these, and there is another near the city of Bath. The corpses were buried in the little chambers, doubled-up or in a sitting position. Things which were supposed to be useful to them in their future life, such as cups and plates, and sometimes jewels, were buried with them.

One of these long barrows, near Cheltenham

Ashmolean Museum, Oxford

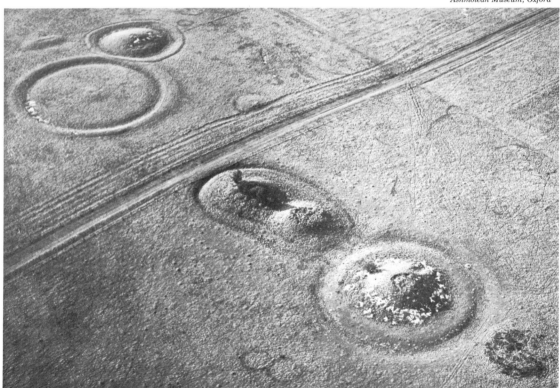

Barrows are round or long. Many round Bronze-Age mounds dating from 1800–800 bc have been found in Britain.

in Gloucestershire, is called Belas Knap. It is cleverly built with a dummy entrance, and the burial chambers are hidden along the sides. The builders of the barrow hoped to deceive robbers who might come to steal the treasures that had been left with the dead bodies.

The first round barrows in Britain were built between 2000 and 1800 BC. Some of the earliest of them have entrances, passages, and chambers built of stone, under the earth mound. Barrows with stone work inside are called chambered barrows. Round barrows made only of earth, built during the Bronze Age (1800–800 BC), have been found on many hills and heathlands in England, such as the Yorkshire wolds in the north and Sussex downs, and in the New Forest in the south of the country. There are nearly 3,000 of them in Wiltshire alone.

Sometimes, if a great warrior died, chariots and horses were buried with his body. This was done during the early Iron Age (500 BC-AD 43). One Iron Age barrow, which was found near Colchester in the county of Essex, contained the bones of a chief, perhaps a king. He had been cremated (burned) first, and his remains had been carried to the tomb on a wonderful funeral carriage, or litter. This was left in the tomb with the bones, along with other beautiful objects made of metal and pottery, including a metal table and some armor. These are now in the Colchester Museum.

The Saxons built many barrows between AD 500 and AD 660. Two kinds have been found, large ones for chiefs and small ones for ordinary people. They are often arranged close together on a large site. At Sutton Hoo, in Suffolk, there is a group of chieftains' barrows. One of these was carefully dug up in 1939, and inside were the remains of a large ship, containing magnificent gold and silver treasures. You can see some of these wonderful things now in the British Museum in London. Many are described in this encyclopedia in the article SUTTON HOO.

After about AD 850 no more barrows were built in Europe. The dead were buried in Christian churchyards.

BARTÓK, Béla (1881–1945). Bartók was a Hungarian composer, generally acknowledged to be one of the great masters of his time. Like Schoenberg and Stravinsky, with whom he ranks in importance, he explored new methods of harmony. Béla Bartók was born in 1881 at Nagyszentmiklos in Hungary (now Sinnicolau Mare in Romania), and was

BBC Hulton Picture Library

Béla Bartók, the Hungarian composer.

first taught music by his mother. Later he studied the piano and composition in Budapest and for some years made his living as a concert pianist and as a teacher.

In 1905 Bartók began to explore the peasant songs of Hungary, Bulgaria and Romania. This folk music was free of the harmonic rules traditional in European music and Bartók began to use elements of folk music in his compositions. He wanted to express the energy of the Hungarian people and to create a national musical style, as other composers had done with the folk music of their countries. The work of Bartók and his fellow composer Zoltán Kodály achieved this and also helped to give a new status to ethnomusicology, the scholarly study of folk music.

Bartók made many expeditions to collect folk songs and traditional peasant melodies. His own compositions reflect the musical techniques he discovered in his homeland's folk music and help to make his works some of the most interesting and original creations of the 20th century.

Before he emigrated to the United States in 1940, Bartók published a vast collection of Hungarian folk music, the result of many years' work. However, he had difficulty settling in the United States and his health broke down. He died a pauper in New York.

Bartók's best pieces are his six String Quartets, the Sonata for two pianos and percussion, and the two Sonatas for piano and violin. He also wrote three piano concertos and two violin concertos. Though Bartók was not primarily a composer for the stage, his opera *Bluebeard's Castle*, his ballet *The Wooden Prince* and his pantomine *The Miraculous Mandarin* are excellent in parts. For young pianists Bartók wrote a collection of 150 small studies called *Mikrokosmos*. These include such titles as "Song of the Fox" and "From the Diary of a Fly".

BARTON, Clara (1821–1912), was the founder of the Red Cross in the United States. Her lifelong efforts to relieve distress proved her to be a generous woman of unfailing resourcefulness and courage.

She was born at Oxford, Massachusetts. In 1854, after 18 years as a teacher, she was appointed a government clerk in Washington, D.C. During the American Civil War she volunteered as a nurse and was so fearless that even under fire during battles she carried food and bandages to wounded soldiers. At the end of the war she organized a bureau of records

to help locate soldiers who were listed as "missing in action". She succeeded also in having the graves of more than 12,000 soldiers identified and marked.

In 1871, during the Franco-Prussian War, Miss Barton went to France, where she led a program to give food and supplies to the starving in Strasbourg and to the hungry people in Paris. She returned to the United States in 1873 to urge United States membership in the Red Cross, which had been founded in Switzerland in 1864. She succeeded in 1881 and was chosen first president of the American Red Cross, an office she held until 1904. Several times she was the United States delegate to meetings of the International Red Cross Society (see RED CROSS).

She was in charge of Red Cross peacetime relief work in many parts of the world— notably after the yellow-fever epidemic in Florida in 1887; the flood at Johnstown, Pennsylvania, in 1889; the Russian famine in 1891; the Armenian massacre in 1896; and the Galveston hurricane in 1900.

BARTON, Edmund (1849–1920) was the first prime minister of the commonwealth of Australia. He was born in Sydney and studied law at the University of Sydney, becoming a barrister in 1871. In 1879 he was elected to the New South Wales Legislative Assembly, serving successively as speaker and attorney general. From 1891 Barton devoted himself to the movement towards federation. He played a leading part in composing a draft constitution and campaigned through the colonies to win approval for the federation scheme. In 1897–98 he chaired a committee which drew up a revised constitution. This won the approval of all the colonial governments.

In 1900 Barton traveled to London to pilot the constitution through the British parliament. He returned successful to Australia and became the first federal prime minister on the day before the commonwealth was proclaimed on 1 January 1901. One of the first measures to be passed by the new parliament was the Immigration Act of 1901. It stated that inten-

The hexagonal columns of the Giant's Causeway, in Northern Ireland, are formed of basalt that has cooled slowly.

ding immigrants should undergo a dictation test. Other restrictions were placed on immigrants, especially kanakas (Polynesians who worked on sugar and cotton plantations). Barton's government also made agreements with Britain on defense and naval matters.

Barton did not enjoy the hurly-burly of Australian politics. In 1903 he resigned and served as a high court judge until his retirement from public life in 1920. He was knighted in 1902.

BASALT is a kind of igneous rock formed by the cooling of a certain type of molten lava (see LAVA).

Basalt is dark gray or black in color and is denser than most other volcanic rocks. It contains less silica and more iron and magnesia than the other common volcanic rocks, such as rhyolite. Its chief minerals are feldspar, pyroxene, olivine, and iron oxides. Although nearly all basaltic rock is crystalline, in some cases, where the lava has cooled rapidly, it has a glassy appearance (see ROCK).

Basalt is produced by the volcanoes such as those in Iceland that erupt from oceanic ridges (see EARTH, THE). It also forms the volcanoes and volcanic islands such as Hawaii, that lie in the ocean basins. The volcanoes of the ocean margins, such as those of Japan and the Coast Ranges of the United States, are made of a more silica-rich lava such as rhyolite which has a composition similar to granite.

Ancient basaltic lava flows may cover enormous areas. In the Columbia and Snake river regions of the states of Washington, Oregon, and Idaho, thousands of square kilometers are covered with basalt. This enormous volume was poured out from great fissures, or cracks, in the Earth's crust. Basalt plateaus of similar size occur in India and Brazil. (See VOLCANO.)

Basaltic lava is very fluid and where it cools slowly and evenly, the newly hardened material shrinks and cracks into columns with several sides. Well-known examples of these columns can be seen at Fingal's Cave on the island of Staffa off the coast of Scotland and at the Giant's Causeway in County Antrim, Northern Ireland. Somewhat similar columnar formations occur in the United States at the Palisades along the Hudson River in New York and at the Devils Postpile near Yosemite National Park in California.

BASEBALL is a team sport, often called the national game of the United States. It is played with a horsehide-covered ball, a wooden bat, and padded gloves. Two teams of nine players each—a pitcher, a catcher, four infielders, and three outfielders—take part. Umpires supervise the game and see that the players follow the rules. The object of the game is to score more runs than the opposing team.

Playing the Game

The infield, or diamond, is a 27-meter (90-foot) square laid out with various markings. The game consists of nine innings unless an agreement has been reached beforehand to shorten it. An inning is completed when each team has had its time at bat. During its half of each inning, a team is permitted to bat until three outs are made. Then it takes its turn in the field, and the other team comes to bat. If the score is tied after nine innings, additional inning are played until one of the teams breaks the tie.

The team in the field tries to prevent the opposing team from scoring runs. The game starts when the pitcher throws the ball towards home plate. The batter tries to hit the ball into fair territory. Fair territory is a V-shaped area. The lines of the V, called foul lines, extend from home plate down the first and third base lines, preferably for a distance of 98 meters (320 feet) or more. The area beyond the infield in fair territory is called the outfield.

Each player of the defensive team (the team in the field) is responsible for fielding any ball in his area. It is generally agreed that the pitcher is the most important player in the field. He works together with the catcher to get the batters to make outs, either by striking out or by hitting the ball in such a way that the batter can be put out by a fielder. The pitcher and catcher are known collectively as the battery.

A *strike* is charged against the batter each time he swings the bat and misses the ball. He is also charged a strike if he fails to swing at a pitch which crosses the plate in the strike zone (an area over the plate and between the batter's knees and armpits). A *foul ball* (a ball that the batter knocks out of fair territory) is also a strike unless the batter already has two strikes. After two strikes, foul balls are not counted. Three strikes make an *out*. If the catcher drops the ball on the third strike, the batter is allowed to try to reach first base before he is thrown out.

A pitch which fails to cross the plate in the strike zone is a *ball*. Four balls entitle the batter to go to first base. This is known either as a *base on balls* or a *walk*. A batter *flies out* when any fielder catches a batted ball, fair or foul, before it hits the ground. A batter *grounds out* when he hits the ball on the ground but does not reach first base before a fielder (usually the first baseman) holding the ball touches first base.

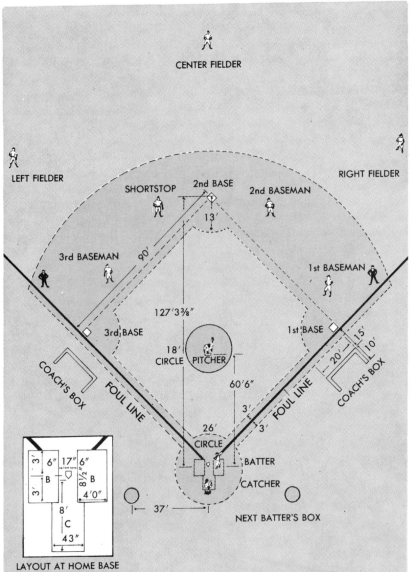

CENTER FIELDER

LEFT FIELDER

RIGHT FIELDER

SHORTSTOP   2nd BASE   2nd BASEMAN

13'

3rd BASEMAN   90'

127'3⅜"

1st BASEMAN

3rd BASE   1st BASE

15'

18'
CIRCLE   PITCHER

20'   10'

COACH'S BOX

FOUL LINE

COACH'S BOX

FOUL LINE

60'6"

3'

26'
CIRCLE

3'

3'

BATTER

CATCHER

37'

NEXT BATTER'S BOX

LAYOUT AT HOME BASE

3'   6"   17"   6"

B   8½'   B

3'   4'0"

8'

C

43"

The official dimensions of a major league baseball field. The distance from the home base to the nearest fence, stand, or obstruction on the right and left field foul lines must be at least 70 meters (250 feet). Ball fields built after 1958 must have foul lines of at least 100 meters (325 feet) or more and a distance of at least 123 meters (400 feet) to the center field fence. Foul lines are marked on the ground in white chalk or lime.

A batter who reaches first base before the ball does is credited with a *hit*. This is also known as a *single*. If he gets to second base while the ball is still in play, it is a two-base hit, or *double*; to third base, a three-base hit, or *triple*. If he makes it back to home plate, it is a home run.

Once on base a batter becomes a base runner. Succeeding batters on his team try to advance him round the bases to score a run. The runner may advance on another hit, on an error by the defensive team, or by stealing. To

steal a base is to advance without the aid of a hit, error, or balk (an illegal act by the pitcher that entitles all runners to advance one base). An umpire calls a balk when a pitcher makes a motion to throw but does not actually throw the ball.

A runner is out if, while not touching a base, he is tagged (touched by the ball held by a fielder or by the hand or glove in which he is holding the ball). He is also out if he is hit by a batted ball or passes a runner who was on base ahead of him. He may be forced out if he

As the pitcher throws he steps towards home base, then follows through with a smooth, quick delivery.

has to run for the next base after the ball is hit by another batter. This happens if runners are on all the bases behind him. He must then run when the ball is hit and not caught in the air. If the ball is caught at the next base before he reaches it, he is out. He is also out if he leaves his base before a fly ball is caught and he does not get back to the base before the ball does.

Special Skills

The best position in the field for a beginner depends on whether he is left-handed or right-handed. If he throws with his right hand, he will not be handicapped in any of the nine positions. If he is left-handed, however, he is more suited to pitcher, first base, or outfield. Speed is most vital at shortstop, second base, and outfield, where the most ground must be covered. Infielders must be both agile and sure ball handlers. Strong throwing arms are most important to the pitcher, outfielders, third baseman, shortstop, and catcher.

Pitcher. Control is probably the most

Pitches are changed by varying the grip of the ball. In throwing a curve the wrist is snapped outward and down so that the ball spins off the fingers.

For a fast pitch, the ball, held firmly by the tips of the fingers and thumb, is delivered with a wrist snap.

For a slow pitch, the loosely held ball is allowed to roll off the finger tips.

important factor in pitching. Often minor-league pitchers can throw as fast and put as much "stuff" (curve or hop) on the ball as major leaguers, but still lack control. A good pitcher seldom places a pitch "down the middle" but tries to pitch to the corners of the strike zone. Of great importance is the ability to throw all pitches with the same motion. A pitcher should throw as much as possible with his shoulders and body. He must not place all the burden on his arm. The ball should be kept out of the batter's view until pitched.

Catcher. The catcher's skills are among the most difficult to develop in baseball. The catcher should be a sure ball handler with a powerful arm. He must be able to throw accurately and swiftly to any base to prevent stealing. Especially important is the catcher's task of studying the opposing batters and discovering their weaknesses. He must signal for pitches that will be difficult for the batters to hit.

First base. A tall and rangy player has an advantage as the first baseman. His extra reach and height enable him to take higher and wider throws, and he provides a big target for the infielders. He must be able to shift to the left or the right in taking a throw from another infielder.

Second base. Speed is important to a second baseman because of the large area he must cover. He has to be able to perform the difficult maneuver of the *double play* in which he must receive the ball from another fielder, tag second base, pivot, and throw to first.

Shortstop. The shortstop's duties are much like those of the second baseman, except that his throw to first base is longer. The shortstop, therefore, should have a powerful arm in addition to great speed.

Third base. The third baseman does not have to cover as much ground as the second baseman or shortstop, but he must be quick and agile and have fast reflexes and a strong arm. His position is closer to the batter, and batted balls come at him at great speed.

Outfield. Outfielders should be able to judge where the ball is going the instant it is hit. The slightest hesitation or move in a wrong direction could result in a hit for the opposition. Outfielders should be able to make long throws from the outfield to any base.

Batter. There are many ways to hold and swing a bat. A beginner should experiment to find the stance, grip, and swing most suitable for himself. Batters should learn to hit the ball where it is pitched, and hit to all parts of the field. Bunting (hitting the ball gently into the infield) is an important part of batting and takes constant practice to master. The essential point for a batter to remember is never to take his eye off the pitched ball.

Boys' Baseball

Organized baseball leagues for boys are well developed in the United States. They provide boys with an opportunity to learn the game and develop skills under competent supervision. Among the more widespread boys' baseball organizations are the Little League, the Pony League, the Babe Ruth League, and the American Legion Junior League. Some major-league baseball players began their careers in these and in some of the other amateur leagues.

Little League Baseball is baseball scaled down so that boys from 9 to 12 years of age can play under conditions matching their size and strength. It differs from regular baseball in equipment, number of innings played, size of the field, pitching distance, and distance between bases. Little League Baseball Inc., is a non-profit-making organization which operates on a large scale with headquarters in Williamsport. Each year a nationwide tournament is played which ends in a Little League world series at Williamsport.

At least two boys on each Little League team must be under 11 years of age. No team is permitted to have more than seven 12-year-olds in the regular lineup at one time. In Little League play, catchers do not have to hold a third strike because the rules say that the batter is automatically out. Runners cannot take leadoffs from the bases until the pitched ball reaches the batter. Bases are 18 meters (60 feet) apart, and the pitcher's mound is 14 meters (46 feet) from home plate. It is recommended that the fence be 55 to 60 meters (175 to 200 feet) from home plate along the foul lines to give the players a chance to hit home runs. The Little League also has a senior division for boys 13 to 15 years of age, which operates under a separate set of regulations. In the mid-1970s, Little League membership was opened to girls.

The Pony League was organized in Washington, Pennsylvania, in 1951 to provide supervised baseball for boys from 13 to 14 years of age. The letters in Pony stand for Protect Our Nation's Youth. The dimensions of the Pony League playing field are scaled down but not so much as the Little League field. The Pony League also holds a world series each year.

The Babe Ruth League provides competition for boys in the 13–15 age group. The league uses the regulation-size diamond and the official rules of baseball.

Oldest of the leagues for boys is the American Legion Junior League. It was organized in 1926. Stan Musial, Ted Williams, and Bob Feller were among the many outstanding players who participated in the American Legion League.

History

The origin of baseball is not clear. It probably grew from the simple game of rounders played by British boys and girls. In rounders a player hits a thrown ball, drops his bat, and runs to a post (base). Some theories tie the early development of the game with cricket. A game called one old cat (or two, three, or four old cat) has also been claimed as an early form of baseball, but some baseball authorities have said that that game was probably a substitute for real baseball.

In the early 1800s, players in the United States developed a game called town ball. It was often played by boys on village greens in New England towns. Typical of such towns was Cooperstown, New York, where Abner Doubleday was said to have laid out a diamond in 1839. At the suggestion of A. G. Spalding, a famous player and the founder of a sporting goods company, a commission to investigate the origin of the sport was appointed in 1907.

The batter keeps his arms away from his body and follows through with the bat at the end of his swing.

The commission concluded that baseball originated in the United States and that Abner Doubleday invented it at Cooperstown. Later research showed the commission's decision to be based more upon legend than fact.

According to more reliable sources, one of the men most responsible for baseball as it is known today was Alexander Cartwright, a surveyor and amateur ballplayer. He headed a group that in 1845 drew up the first known set of rules that resembled those of the modern game. Cartwright's group had the bases 27 meters (90 feet) apart, set the number of players at nine, and made three strikes an out unless the third one was not caught.

Cartwright's club, the Knickerbocker Baseball Club of New York, and another, the New York Nine, met in baseball's first recorded match. The game was played at Hoboken, New Jersey, on 19 June 1846. The Knickerbockers lost 23-1. This event is considered the beginning of organized baseball.

As baseball became more popular and competitive through the mid-1800s, professionalism began to make its appearance. The conflict that grew between the professional and amateur players threatened to ruin the game. The Cincinnati Red Stockings, organized by Harry Wright in 1869, became the first admittedly professional baseball club. The Red Stockings played teams from Massachusetts to California and won every game in their first season. Their undefeated streak stretched to 93 games (one tie) before it was ended by the Atlantics of Brooklyn, New York, who beat the Red Stockings 8-7 on 14 June 1870.

The Red Stockings' success stirred the interest of other cities. In 1871 the National Association of Professional Baseball Players was established with ten teams. They were the Athletics of Philadelphia, Pennsylvania; Bostons of Boston, Massachusetts; White Stockings of Chicago; Haymakers of Troy, New York; Olympics of Washington, D.C.; Forest Citys of Rockford, Illinois; Kekiongas of Fort Wayne, Indiana; Mutuals of New York; Eckfords of Brooklyn; and Forest Citys of Cleveland, Ohio.

In 1876 the National Association was replaced by the National League. The new league promised to stop the gambling that had become common at ball parks and was rapidly destroying the integrity of the game.

The National League's original members were New York, Boston, Hartford, Philadelphia, Chicago, St. Louis, Cincinnati, and Louisville. The formation of the league marked the beginning of official baseball record keeping. So-called modern records are those kept since 1900. These are distinguished from earlier records.

The first game in National League history was played at Philadelphia on Saturday, 22 April 1876. Boston won by a score of 6-5. The first man to get a hit in the game was Boston's Jim O'Rourke. His team-mate Tom McGinley scored the first run, and Ezra Sutton of Philadelphia made the first error. Joseph Borden was the winning pitcher. One month later Borden pitched the first no-hit game.

The National League fought against any attempts to form a rival big league. It lost the battle in 1901 when Byron (Ban) Johnson expanded the Western League, of which he was president, and renamed it the American League.

The National League objected to the new league, but in 1903 it agreed to let its pennant winner meet the American League's winner in a five-out-of-nine game World Series. To the National League's surprise, the American League Boston Red Sox defeated the Pittsburgh Pirates five games to three. In 1904 the New York Giants won the National League pennant, but manager John McGraw refused to play the Red Sox, who again were the American League champions. Since 1905 there has been a World Series to end each baseball season.

In 1903 the American League had a membership of eight teams that remained unchanged for half a century. The clubs were the Philadelphia Athletics, St. Louis Browns, Boston Red Sox, Chicago White Sox, Cleveland Indians, Washington Nationals (later the Senators), Detroit Tigers, and New York Yankees.

Tony Duffy/Allsport Photographic

The San Francisco Giants playing away from home at the Dodgers' stadium in Los Angeles.

The National League remained stable at eight teams from 1900 until 1953, when the Braves moved from Boston to Milwaukee, Wisconsin. This started a series of moves. The St. Louis Browns moved to Baltimore, Maryland, and became the Orioles in 1954. In 1955 the Athletics of Philadelphia moved to Kansas City, Missouri, remaining until 1968 when they moved to Oakland, California. In 1958 the Brooklyn Dodgers moved to Los Angeles, California, and the New York Giants moved to San Francisco, California.

The American League grew from eight to ten teams in 1960. The Washington Senators moved to Minneapolis, Minnesota, becoming the Minnesota Twins. A new Washington Senators team was then formed, but it moved to Dallas-Fort Worth in 1971 to become the Texas Rangers. The second new team was the Los Angeles Angels (later renamed the California Angels). In 1966 the Milwaukee Braves moved to Atlanta, Georgia. In 1969 two more teams were added to the American League— the Seattle (Washington) Pilots, which became the Milwaukee Brewers, and the Kansas City Royals. In 1977 the Seattle Mariners and the Toronto (Ontario) Blue Jays were also added. In 1966 the National League added two teams—the Houston (Texas) Colt .45's (later renamed the Astros) and the New York Metropolitans (Mets). In 1969 two more were added—the Montreal (Quebec) Expos and the San Diego (California) Padres. Both leagues grouped their teams into divisions.

Professional baseball has gradually developed into a big business. In 1964 80 per cent of the New York Yankees was bought for more than $11 million. The team had come to New York from Baltimore, Maryland in 1903 for $18,000.

Modern baseball's greatest crisis occurred in the years 1919 to 1921, when it was proved that eight Chicago White Sox players had been bribed to lose the 1919 World Series (the American and National League Championships). The incident is known as the "Black Sox Scandal". Though the eight players were barred for life from baseball, the prestige of the game suffered greatly. One outstanding player George Herman (Babe) Ruth helped baseball to survive the scandal. The colorful Ruth became an idol who aroused new interest in the sport.

Professional baseball includes a chain of minor leagues, where most future major-league players learn their skills. Many of the minor-league clubs serve as "farm" teams for major-league clubs. The farm team may be owned by a major-league team, or there may be a working agreement between the two teams.

Only a few important changes occurred in professional baseball rules after 1900. In 1968 the maximum height of the pitcher's mound above the level of home plate was reduced from 38 centimeters (15 inches) to 25 centimeters (10 inches). In 1954 the sacrifice-fly rule was adopted. This rule says that an outfield fly that enables a runner to score does not count as a time at bat. In 1968 the strike zone was reduced from the area between the batter's shoulders and knees to the area between the tops of his knees and his armpits. In 1973 the American League began using a tenth player, called a "designated hitter," who bats instead of the pitcher.

In 1972 a 13-day strike by players over pensions delayed the opening of the season. A 49-day strike in 1981 forced the cancellation of one-third of the season. The strike was settled when players and owners agreed that a "player pool" would be used to compensate teams losing players who became free agents and signed with other teams.

Records and Awards

Both major leagues keep complete records of every game and ever player. The records are used to calculate batting, pitching, and fielding averages and to determine individual player awards. The Baseball Writers' Association each year presents awards in each league, including the Most Valuable Player award, the Rookie of the Year award, and the Best Pitcher award. An All-Star game is played each season between teams made up of outstanding players from each league.

Perhaps the highest baseball honor is membership in the National Baseball Hall of Fame. The National Baseball Hall of Fame and Museum was opened at Cooperstown, New York, in 1939. It contains the most complete baseball library in the world. It includes record books dating from American Civil War days; almost every book published on baseball; and countless documents, scrapbooks, and letters.

Every year each member of the Baseball Writers' Association of America lists ten people worthy of the Hall of Fame. The players named must have been retired for at least five years. Only baseball writers who have been members of the association for at least ten years may take part. To be elected, a player's name must appear on 75 per cent of the ballots. A Hall of Fame committee also elects veteran players and other people who have contributed significantly to baseball. Annually since 1971 one or more players have been chosen from the leagues of black players, which flourished before blacks were accepted into the major leagues.

The first players elected were known as the "select five". They entered the Hall of Fame when the first vote was taken in 1936. They were Ty Cobb, Babe Ruth, Christy Mathewson, Honus Wagner, and Walter Johnson. Cobb, the first elected, won 12 batting championships and had a lifetime batting average of .367. He stole 892 bases during 24 years with the Detroit Tigers and the Philadelphia Athletics.

Babe Ruth, baseball's most famous player and the game's greatest home-run slugger, followed Cobb into the Hall of Fame. In 1921 Ruth hit 59 home runs. In 1927 he hit 60—a record that still holds for a 154-game season.

Roger Maris, a 26-year-old Yankee outfielder, hit 61 home runs in 1961, but his feat was accomplished in 162 games. Considerable controversy arose over whether or not Maris had broken Ruth's record. Baseball Commissioner Ford Frick, however, ruled that Ruth's record could be broken only if a player hit 61 home runs in 154 games; any home run hit after that would establish a separate record. In 1974 Hank Aaron of the Atlanta Braves exceeded Ruth's career record of 714 home runs. Although he had taken more games than Ruth had to accomplish the feat, Aaron's achievement was generally regarded as a new record. Throughout his career he hit 755 home runs. In 1975 Aaron broke Ruth's record for runs batted in.

METHODS OF BASKETMAKING

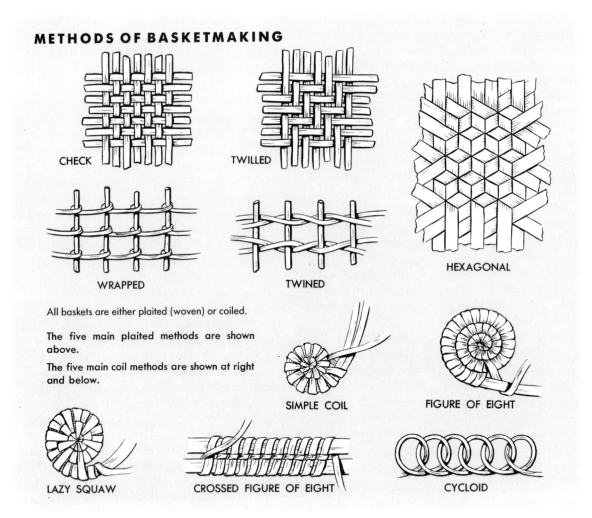

CHECK

TWILLED

WRAPPED

TWINED

HEXAGONAL

All baskets are either plaited (woven) or coiled.

The five main plaited methods are shown above.

The five main coil methods are shown at right and below.

SIMPLE COIL

FIGURE OF EIGHT

LAZY SQUAW

CROSSED FIGURE OF EIGHT

CYCLOID

BASKET is a container made of woven or coiled synthetic or vegetable fibers, such as canes, grasses, or roots. Baskets are sturdy, unbreakable containers that can be used to transport goods and food.

The making of baskets is probably the oldest industrial art. In many parts of the world examples of baskets have been found dating from prehistoric times. Ancient Egyptians and Britons made huts of a kind of rude basketwork daubed with clay, much like houses that people build today in parts of Australia and Africa. The Egyptians also had basket boats similar to those still used on the Tigris and Euphrates rivers in Iraq and on rivers in many districts of India. In 1970 the Norwegian scientist-explorer Thor Heyerdahl crossed the Atlantic Ocean in a woven papyrus boat named *Ra* built by the Aymara Indians of Lake Titicaca in South America.

People in various parts of the world are still using basketwork for skirts, hats, and sandals, as well as for sleeping mats and coffins. Some tribes have wicker shields and helmets and build forts of sand-filled baskets the size of small houses. Often baskets are used during ceremonies and religious rites.

The Hupa Indians in California produced waterproof baskets, shaped like vases. They were used as cooking vessels or for carrying water and were made of a fine fibrous root and decorated with shells, bird feathers, or the colored quills of the porcupine. Magical symbols or figures from ancient legends were often

The Hutchison Library
Basketry is the most widespread craft in Africa. These baskets are being sold at a market in Nigeria.

woven into the design. Frequently, too, the designs displayed the Indian love of nature and suggested such things as running water, the flight of birds, or the footprints of animals.

The Japanese and the Chinese make fine baskets of bamboo, which is split very thin and woven into small and intricate shapes. Of coarser material, they also make chairs and tables and other articles of the furniture known as wickerwork. Crude types of baskets are also used sometimes in these countries for packing goods for transportation.

Palms are used to weave baskets in the tropical parts of the world. Rattan, abundantly used in Malaysia, is a kind of palm, as is raffia. In the colder parts of the world a number of plants, including reeds, sedges, and rushes, provide basket materials.

The most familiar baskets made in the United States and Europe are usually woven of osier or willow twigs. Basket willow is grown mostly in Europe and imported into the United States. The New England farmers also make excellent baskets out of ash and oak saplings. Very slim saplings are peeled, and the wood is beaten until it comes apart in long, fibrous strips suitable for weaving. The remaining Indians of New England and northern New York State still make their traditional fragrant sweet-grass baskets, which are sold to summer visitors.

The methods used in basket-making have changed little over the past several thousand years. The art is still a handicraft, and no machines have been perfected that are able to produce baskets. Machines do produce the coarse vegetable and fruit baskets sometimes seen in food markets, but no machine can manufacture the finely woven product of the basket-maker. People can learn basket-making by using their sense of touch and therefore many blind people are taught how to do it.

BASKETBALL is one of the world's most popular sports. It is the only major world sport that began and developed in the United States. More Americans watch basketball

Courtesy, Amateur Basketball Association

Basketball is a fast passing game where the ball must go through a ring and down into the basket to score.

than any other sport. The Olympic Games have included basketball since 1936, and the United States has won the gold medal on each occasion except 1972.

Playing Area and Equipment

Basketball is usually played indoors on a hardwood court. The dimensions of the court vary but are generally 26 meters (85 feet) long by 14 meters (46 feet) wide. At each end of the court a backboard, 1.8 meters (6 feet) wide by 1.2 meters (4 feet) deep, is suspended, overhanging the court, 1.2 meters (4 feet) inside the end line. On the backboard, 30 centimeters (1 foot) from the bottom, at a height of 3 meters (10 feet) from the ground, is the goal or basket. This consists of an iron ring, 45 centimeters (18 inches) in diameter, from which is suspended a bottomless white net. Points are scored by throwing a ball so that it goes through the ring from above and down through the net.

The ball is round and has a circumference of about 75 centimeters (30 inches) and a weight of about 600 grams (21 ounces).

Playing the Game

Each team has five players on court, but can have up to seven substitutes. There is no limit to the number of substitutions that can be made by a team. A team consists of a center, two forwards, and two guards. The center is usually the tallest man in the team. At the start of each game and each period of play the ball is thrown up between two opposing players in the center circle, higher than either player can jump. The ball must be tapped by one or both of the jumpers after it reaches its highest point. Whichever team gets possession of the ball tries to advance with it towards the basket by passing or dribbling (bouncing) the ball. The player with the ball may take only one step before passing to a team-mate. If the player advances by dribbling and stops, he must pass the ball or attempt a shot. If he begins to dribble again, he will be guilty of a violation called a double dribble.

A player may shoot the ball at the basket from any angle. A jumping player may "stuff" or "dunk" the ball right into the basket. If the ball goes through the rim, it is a basket, or field goal, and counts two points. When a field goal has been scored, a player of the opposing team gets the ball out of bounds beyond the

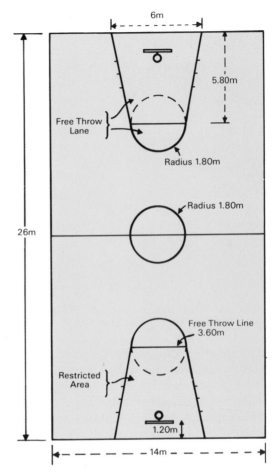

end line. He then has five seconds to put the ball in play by throwing it to a team-mate in the court. If the ball is thrown into the player's backcourt (the half of the court farthest from a team's goal), his team then has ten seconds to advance it beyond the center line to its front court. If the team with the ball fails to do so within ten seconds, the ball is awarded to the opponents out of bounds.

A team may not first touch a ball it has caused to go from its front court to its backcourt. The ball must be first touched by an opponent; otherwise, it is a violation.

Fouls and Violations

Fouls. Basketball is meant to be played without deliberate physical contact between players. Whenever illegal contact occurs, such as pushing or holding, the referee blows his whistle and calls a foul on the offending player. This is a personal foul and entitles the player fouled to a free throw at the basket from the free throw line, 4.6 meters (15 feet) from a point below the backboard. The opposition may not interfere with the free throw. If the foul is committed against a player in the act of shooting, or if it is a deliberate foul, two free throws are awarded. After a specified number of personal fouls by a team, bonus free throws are awarded. A successful free throw counts one point, and the player committing the foul is charged with one personal foul. A player with five personal fouls must leave the game.

For certain violations, such as delay of the game, grasping the basket, unsportsmanlike conduct, or having more than five players in the game at one time, the official may call a technical foul. When a player commits a personal foul while the ball is in possession of his team, the ball is awarded to the other team. After a double foul, when two players foul each other simultaneously, the ball is put in play by a jump ball at the center circle.

Violations. Infractions of the rules other than fouls are called violations. When a player is the last to touch a ball before it goes out of bounds, or when he steps on a boundary with the ball in his control, he commits a violation, and the ball is awarded out of bounds to a player of the opposing team. The same penalty applies to an offensive player who does any of the following: remains in the free throw lane more than three seconds; double dribbles; travels (takes more than one step without dribbling); kicks the ball; or strikes it with a fist.

Timing and Strategy

In the United States, college games are played in two halves of 20 minutes each, with an intermission of 15 minutes. High-school games are played in four quarters of 8 minutes each, with an intermission of 1 minute after the first and third quarters and 10 minutes between halves. Teams younger than high-school age play 6-minute quarters. Professional teams play 12-minute quarters. If the score is tied at the end of the second half or fourth quarter, play continues for one or more extra periods. The game ends if at the end of any extra period one team is ahead. Extra periods in college games are 5 minutes, and in high school, 3 minutes. In Britain a game consists of two 20-minute halves with a 10-minute interval at half time.

The clock starts when a jump ball is legally tapped, when a ball put in play by a throw-in touches a player, or when the ball touches a player after an unsuccessful free throw. The clock stops whenever the official blows his whistle and uses a hand signal to indicate a reason for the stoppage. A raised arm with a closed fist indicates a foul; an open hand indicates that a time-out has been called. These are short breaks called by a team, during which the coach can give instructions. Teams may take five time-outs during a game, plus one extra time-out for each extra period.

American professional basketball has the 24-second rule; a professional team must take a shot at its basket within 24 seconds from the time it obtains possession of the ball or puts it in play. Failure to shoot within 24 seconds causes the ball to go to the opposing team. In Britain the time limit is 30 seconds.

Offense. Many teams will react to certain game situations by using a fast break. That is, when they recover the ball near the basket they are defending, they try to beat the defense to its backcourt by a combination of speed and passing and make the field goal before the opponents have time to form a defense.

When a team recovers the ball and does not have the opportunity for a fast break, it may play a deliberate style of offense. The guards bring the ball down the court toward the basket carefully, passing, dribbling, and screening (blocking the path of an opponent) in an effort to set up a play that will free a player for a shot. Generally, set patterns of play use one or two men playing near the free throw area as pivot, or post, men. These players are in position to receive passes, pass to team-mates, shoot, screen for team-mates, and rebound (recover missed shots).

Defense. When a team loses the ball to its opponents, it goes into a defensive formation to try to stop the offense from scoring. There are three standard defenses—the zone, the man-to-man, and a combination of the two. In a zone defense, each player has an area that he must guard. In the man-to-man defense every player has a particular opponent whom he must guard. The combination defense allows players to switch to other opponents when they are screened. In another combination defense, some players may be playing man-to-man while others guard zones.

One of the most effective defensive techniques is the zone press, or all-court press, in which defensive players extend their zones far into the opponent's backcourt. The zone press can often prevent the offense from bringing the ball across mid-court within the required ten seconds or force a bad pass or other violation that could cause loss of the ball.

History

James A. Naismith, a physical education instructor at the International YMCA Training School at Springfield, Massachusetts (now Springfield College), invented basketball in 1891. He had been asked to devise an interesting indoor, non-contact game.

After unsuccessful attempts to modify existing games, Naismith decided to design an entirely new game. He noted that team games in general are played with some kind of ball. Football was rough because the players could run with the ball, so he eliminated that feature. To discourage roughness still further, he placed the goals above the heads of the players and had the goal opening horizontal rather than vertical. For goals, he hung peach baskets on the walls at the ends of the gymnasium. A soccer ball was used in the first games. Thirteen rules governed the original game, most of which are still observed. Basketball was an immediate success and spread rapidly throughout the United States and the world.

See also NETBALL.

BASLE is the second largest city of Switzerland. It is the country's chief gateway, as it stands at the meeting-point of Switzerland, France, and Germany and is a busy inland

ZEFA

Market day in the Marktplatz (market place) of Basle. The reddish building in the center is the town hall.

port for traffic on the Rhine River, which flows through the middle of the city.

The abbey church, formerly a cathedral, towers over the city from a terrace high above the south bank of the Rhine. It is of mixed Romanesque and Gothic styles, built of red sandstone with a roof tiled in patterns of green and yellow. The university, which dates from the 15th century, is the oldest in Switzerland and was founded by Pope Pius II. Among famous men who lived in Basle were the painter Háns Holbein and the scholar Erasmus. (See the articles ERASMUS, DESIDERIUS; HOLBEIN, HANS.)

The Swiss Industries Fair is held in the city every spring, allowing the public and trade buyers to see the latest products. Basle is an important banking center. It also has a large chemical industry which develops and makes drugs used in medicine; the insect-killing powder DDT was invented here.

Basle lies in the German-speaking part of Switzerland and the German spelling Basel is often used. The population is 174,600 (1986).

BASQUES AND THE BASQUE REGION.

The Basques live in a region straddling the Franco-Spanish border around the southeastern corner of the Bay of Biscay. Many experts think that they are descendants of Western Europe's earliest inhabitants. Their language, called Euskara, is not related to other European languages and many Basque words do not resemble those of any other known language. The Basques also differ physically from other Europeans, notably in blood type.

The number of Basques has been estimated at about 700,000. Roughly six out of every seven live in Spain, mainly in the provinces of Guipúzcoa, Vizcaya and Álava. These provinces, which are together called "the Basque Country", have a combined area of 7,261 square kilometers (2,803 square miles) and a population of 2,135,000, which includes many non-Basques.

The Basque Country is rugged, with a mild, rainy climate. The thickly forested upland areas contain many mineral resources, including coal, copper, iron, and zinc, while the fast-flowing streams are used to generate hydroelectric energy. Fishing and farming, particularly sheep rearing and the cultivation of corn, sugar beet, and grapes for wine, are traditional occupations. But manufacturing is now the leading activity. The main industrial center and largest city is Bilbao, the capital of Vizcaya province. Bilbao is one of Spain's leading iron and steel producers. Other major cities are Guernica, the traditional center of Basque culture, northeast of Bilbao; the coastal resort of San Sebastián, capital of Guipúzcoa province; and Vitoria, the capital of Álava province and also nominal capital of the entire Basque Country.

The French Basques live in the western part of the Pyrénées-Atlantiques department. This area lacks resources and many Basques have moved to the French industrial cities to the north.

Most Basques are bilingual and are Roman Catholics. But they are proud of their distinctive culture with its ancient dances, poetry and songs, which they have struggled to preserve since Roman times. The fast-moving ball game jai alai originated in the Basque area. They have contributed to Spanish culture and several important writers, including Miguel de Unanumo (1864–1936) and Pío Baroja (1872–1956), were Basques.

Some Spanish Basques support the nationalist organization Euzkadi ta Azkatasuna (ETA). *Euzkadi* is the Basque name for their region. ETA translated means "Euzkadi and Liberty". Supporters of ETA have used violence in their attempts to persuade the Spanish government to give them independence. In 1980, a parliament was elected for the Basque Country, giving the people more control over local matters.

BASS is the name for many different kinds of fish that come from two main families. The largest group are marine and perch-like and

Most members of the two bass families are carnivorous. Both saltwater and freshwater varieties are popular game fish.

include the European bass (*Dicentrarchus labrax*) of the eastern Atlantic, Mediterranean, and Black Sea. This strong, silvery, blue-gray fish lives in the surf around rocks and just below the low-tide zone of beaches. It feeds mainly on other smaller fish such as sprats and sand eels. Fishermen rate it as a first-class game fish and it is also good to eat. So, too, is the striped bass (*Morone saxitilis*) of the North American Atlantic coast (and introduced into the Pacific). It can weigh as much as 45 kilograms (100 pounds).

The black bass (*Centropristis striatus*), also of the Atlantic, shows a feature peculiar to some sea basses. When young this fish tends to be female but after five years it changes into a male. Some other species of bass are hermaphrodite, that is they have both male and female sex organs throughout their life. One example is the belted sandfish (*Serranus subligarius*) of coastal Florida. It is a common fish over rocky bottoms and spawns in small shoals.

Freshwater Basses

The other main grouping of bass come from the sunfish family, all from North America. The largemouth bass (*Micropterus salmoides*), native to the eastern states, has been widely introduced into ponds and lakes throughout the United States. It is one of the most popular freshwater game fishes with a record weight of 10 kilograms (22.25 pounds). It can live in muddy water, and feeds on other fish, frogs, crayfish, and insects. The smallmouth bass (*Micropterus dolmieui*) prefers the cool, clear waters of northern lakes and rivers, while the attractive spotted bass (*Micropterus punctulatus*) lives in slow streams and deep pools of the Midwest and South of the United States.

BASSOON see OBOE FAMILY.

BASSWOOD includes trees of the genus *Tilia*, also known as linden or lime. Some basswoods are popular street and ornamental trees, and some yield lumber. There are about 40 species, mainly in the North Temperate Zone. The American basswood, or linden (*Tilia americana*), is the species that grows in the United States and Canada, from Nova Scotia to southeastern Manitoba south to Florida and Texas. Some botanists, however, think that 4 to 15, instead of just 1, species of basswood occur in the United States. In parts of northern United States, basswood is a common forest tree. American basswood may grow 43 meters (140 feet) tall, but the usual height is 18 to 24 meters (60–80 feet) tall. The tree often has several trunks.

The tough, fibrous inner bark (the bast) of basswood was made into fishing-nets, maps and rope by the American Indians. Recalling this use, the name basswood was derived from

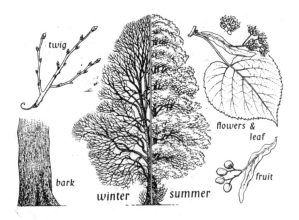

"bastwood". The wood of basswood is soft, easily worked, and light in weight and color. It is used for boxes, Venetian blinds, beehives, furniture, and piano keys. It is good for food containers because it is odorless and tasteless and so does not affect food placed in it.

Basswoods are deciduous trees (their leaves fall off in autumn). The leaves are alternate on the stem, toothed along the edges, long stalked, and heart shaped but usually lopsided. The flowers, blooming in early summer, are fragrant and have five creamy, yellowish or pale pink petals. They grow in drooping clusters. A narrow, leaf-like structure is attached to the stalk of each cluster. Basswood flowers are pollinated by insects, especially bees. Basswood honey is well known. In Europe the flowers are dried and used to make a tea-like infusion.

Fossil basswood leaves, about 40 million years old, have been found in Alaska and Greenland, where no basswoods grow today.

BASTILLE. Every year, on 14 July, school children in France have a holiday. Their parents too have a day off work to join in the general fun and rejoicing. Bastille Day is a national holiday because it was on this date in 1789 that the people of Paris captured the grim stone prison called the Bastille. The Bastille was surrounded by a moat 30 meters (100 feet) wide, and within its massive walls and eight big gray towers were 70 or more cells. One of the most famous of the prisoners was the mysterious "Man in the

The storming of the Bastille marked the beginning of the French Revolution. It was torn down after its capture.

Iron Mask", who died there in 1703. In its dungeons some prisoners spent their lives in complete darkness.

The Bastille was built in 1370, not as a prison but as a fortress for defending Paris. It became the special stronghold where the kings of France shut up their enemies, very much as traitors in England were sent to the Tower of London. The French king was able to sign secret warrants, known as *lettres de cachet*, by which a person would be imprisoned as long as the king desired. In other words, the king could get rid of anyone he chose without a trial. It was for this reason that the Bastille got its evil name and in people's minds came to stand for a cruel and unjust way of government. It is also why, in 1789, when the people of Paris were on the brink of the greatest revolution in their history, almost the first thing they did was to storm the hated Bastille.

By that time it was thought to be worse than it really was. King Louis XVI did not use his tyrannical powers of imprisonment much, and when the governor surrendered the prison to the mob they found only seven prisoners in it. Nevertheless, to Parisians it seemed like a miracle that they had made so great and famous a fortress surrender to them. It meant new freedom for them, and so they sang and danced for joy in the streets. The old prison was completely destroyed, but Bastille Day still stands for the freedom and independence of France. Between 1940 and 1944, when France was occupied by the Germans, it was made a day of national mourning. But after the liberation of France it again became a great national holiday.

BAT. Of all mammals, the bats are the only ones that fly. Several different mammals have developed membranes (sheets of skin) between their fore and hind legs on which they can glide from tree to tree, like the flying squirrels; but only the bats truly fly. Their long arms and their hands, with specially long fingers, are covered with very thin membrane and make efficient wings. The membrane extends to the tiny legs and in many kinds to the tip of the tail as well.

With these wings, bats can steer a very accurate course, avoiding any obstacle which may lie in their path. Experiments have shown that they can do this even when blindfolded, and it has been proved that they tell where objects are by means of the echoes they hear when they send out very high-pitched sounds. (This is rather like the way in which radar works.)

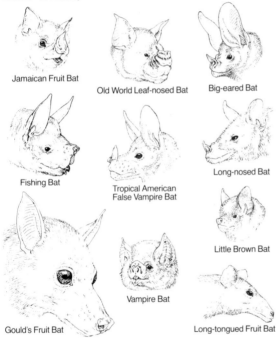

Jamaican Fruit Bat

Old World Leaf-nosed Bat

Big-eared Bat

Fishing Bat

Tropical American False Vampire Bat

Long-nosed Bat

Little Brown Bat

Vampire Bat

Gould's Fruit Bat

Long-tongued Fruit Bat

There is great variety in head size and shape among bats. Of about 900 kinds of bats, 10 are illustrated here.

Bats usually rest during the day, hanging upside down by their toes in a cave or the belfry of a church or some other dark place where they may collect in large numbers. They come out in the evening and the early morning to feed, and some kinds fly about all night. One or two young are born in the spring. At first a young bat clings to its mother's breast and is carried about on her flights, but later she leaves it hanging up in the roost until, towards the autumn, it is old enough to fly. Bats are long-lived for animals of their size, 10–15

years being not uncommon among the smaller species. Larger fruit bats have lived up to 19 years in captivity.

There are about 900 species of bats, more than any other group of mammals except rodents. Bats are found in temperate and tropical regions, with most species in the tropics. Their size varies greatly. The Philippine bamboo bat (*Tylonycteris pachypus meyeri*) weighs just 1.5 grams (0.05 ounce) with a wingspan of 15 centimeters (6 inches), while the flying fox (*Pteropus vampyrus*) may weigh 1 kilogram (2.2 pounds) and have a wingspan of 1.5 meters (5 feet).

Most bats of temperate regions feed on insects such as moths and mosquitoes which they catch as they are flying, but in other parts of the world they have a very different diet. One or two kinds catch fish by dropping on them and taking them in their claws. Several species are carnivorous including the greater spear-nosed bat (*Phyllostomus hastatus*) that feeds on a variety of prey including birds, smaller bats, rodents as well as insects. The famous vampire bats of South and Central America feed only on blood which they lap from tiny wounds made by their front teeth in animals or humans, but they are not the serious menace that some people think. Some tropical species feed only on the nectar and pollen of flowers. To do so, they have very long tongues. These bats are important since they pollinate flowers (see POLLINATION). The flowers of certain cacti and those of trees such as the banana and baobab tree are pollinated by bats. In Australia they are known as blossom bats.

Fruit-eating bats are found only in warm regions because they must be able to find fruit of some sort all the year round. In many parts they can be seen in countless thousands and, just before dark, they fly in great clouds from their roosting trees to the feeding places. These bats include the flying foxes named because of their fox-like heads, although they are not related to foxes in any way. Seeds from the fruits these species eat are often carried and dropped at the roosting places; in this way the bats help to spread plants.

In cold climates insect life becomes very scarce in winter, so bats must either hibernate, or else migrate to warmer places, as many birds do. As far as is known European bats all hibernate, but many insect-eating bats of North America spend their winters in the warm south and in Central America.

BATH is a well-known English spa, or medicinal watering place, in the county of Avon.

There is an old motto which says that "Manners makyth man", but at Bath in the 18th century, manners actually changed a city. Ever since the days of the Romans, Bath had been noted for the hot springs that come bubbling up from the interior of the Earth. The Romans built baths, which can still be seen, and a town grew up, visited by invalids who bathed in the "healing" waters. However, the baths were ill-kept after the Romans left, and by the 17th century Bath was known as a rather rowdy, unfashionable vacation resort.

The man who "made" Bath was Richard Nash, a leading figure in 18th-century society, also known as Beau Nash because of his dress and manners. He made a list of dos and don'ts for visitors, which was really a lesson in good manners. In a remarkably short time the town was transformed into a fashionable and pleasant place. People began to flock to Bath and it became necessary to build houses and inns where they could stay. Fortunately, at that time Bath had a wealthy and able citizen, Ralph Allen, who engaged the two John Woods, father and son, as architects, and together they built the most beautiful part of the city, including the famous Royal Crescent. Today, Bath is an attractive mixture of terraces, crescents, and squares built largely of a local yellowish stone, Bath stone, in the 18th century. The abbey, built in the 16th century, is a fine example of Gothic architecture.

Bath lies in the deep valley of the River Avon and one of its bridges, the only one left in Great

The Roman baths at Bath, England. Hot mineral springs reaching 49°C (120°F) attracted the Romans who founded the town. The baths were rediscovered in 1755 and are now a popular tourist attraction.

Britain, is still lined by a continuous row of stores. This beautiful bridge was designed bv the celebrated architect Robert Adam, on whom there is an article. Besides one of the finest botanical gardens in the west of England, Bath has a museum in which can be seen Roman monuments, inscriptions and statues. There is some light industry, clothing manufacturing, and printing carried out in the city.

Because it was such a fashionable place, Bath has had a number of things named after it or its inhabitants. Perhaps the most famous is the Bath chair—the original wheel-chair.

BATHS AND BATHING. For someone today, the word bath conjures up a plastic or enameled metal tub with taps at the end—one for hot water and one for cold. This is a modern bath, but of course for thousands of years people have washed themselves, although they haven't always used baths.

Early bathing was usually done in the rivers. The Egyptians used to bathe in the Nile as part of their religion. Later, in India, people started to wash in the Ganges to clean both their bodies and their souls, a practice which continues to this day. There are also stories about bathing in the Bible: you may remember that Naaman the Syrian bathed in the River Jordan to cure his leprosy.

The first people to make bathing a part of everyday life were the Greeks. In ancient Greece every town of any size had its public baths, which were used for swimming as well as washing. There were bathrooms with water supply and drainage in the palaces of Knossos and Phaistos in Crete, and in the mainland cities of Pyros and Tiryns, between 1700 and 1400 BC. The Greeks also built baths in most of the towns they captured in other countries.

The Romans were even keener than the Greeks on building baths. From about the third century BC, wealthy Romans built baths in their private houses. They heated them with furnaces, which channeled hot air through the walls and under the floor. They constructed great palaces, three stories high, with floors of priceless marbles and mosaics.

As well as swimming tanks, there were warm baths, steam baths and hot-air baths. Wealthy citizens met their friends in the public baths, called *thermae*. There were people to massage the bathers, and there were hairdressers, valets, restaurants, and even theaters.

The ruins of the Emperor Caracalla's public baths can still be seen in the center of Rome. These were set in spacious gardens, and the water was supplied from reservoirs, via aqueducts. The bathers were so extravagant that the men often washed in wine and the women in milk. The wife of the Emperor Nero used to keep 500 asses to supply the milk for her bath.

Bathing plays a part in both the Christian and Muslim religions. From John the Baptist new members of the Christian faith inherited the practice of being dipped in a flowing river, and John himself baptized Christ in the River Jordan.

Muhammad said that Muslims should pray five times a day, washing themselves beforehand, and as a result all their mosques have washing fountains. When European Crusaders first went to the Holy Land in 1096, they quickly copied the Muslims and bathed to keep cool. By the time of Saladin, in the 12th century, the Muslims had public baths in all their large towns, and later the Turks imitated them. The public bath of the Islamic Empire was called a *hammam*. It included a cold bath, warm bath, and a dressing room. The heating system was similar to that of the Romans.

Arab and Turkish baths are different from Greek and Roman ones. There is usually no swimming pool and the cleaning is done by heat, steam, perspiration, and massage. Other countries have copied the idea. The real Turkish bath, as found in Turkey itself, is in a low, arched cellar of great beauty. The temperature is kept up by roaring fires under the floor. Women can use them only on special days; for example, a Muslim bride is allowed to invite all her girl friends to bathe with her on the day before her wedding.

The European cities of the 11th and 12th centuries had public baths. A few people had wooden tubs in their own homes. In England, in the 13th century, King Henry III built him-

Bathing "ghats", or steps, line the banks of the Ganges River in India. Hindu pilgrims come to purify themselves in the river's sacred waters.

ZEFA

self a bathhouse supplied with hot and cold water in his Westminster Palace. But for most people during the Middle Ages washing was not considered fashionable, and some even regarded it as an unhealthy habit. Instead they used perfumes to overcome the smell and standards of cleanliness declined. Queen Elizabeth I was proud that she took a bath as often as four times a year, "whether she needeth it or no".

Little progress was made in washing equipment until the 19th century, when permanent tubs were first introduced to replace portable ones (which were in any event not common). Hot water had to be carried to the bath. Gradually, however, people realized how important bathing was for health, so they began to use soap more, particularly when the tax was taken off it in the middle of the 19th century. For the poor, who lived in overcrowded and inadequate housing, public bathhouses were introduced into the cities, the first of which

was built in Liverpool in 1842. They are not much needed nowadays, as almost every house has a bath.

In Japan every home has its circular wooden tub. This is usually out of doors and is used in public by all the family. In Iceland the warm water from the famous natural geysers is tapped for domestic use in houses and hotels. The Finnish sauna bath (in which water is poured on to hot stones to produce steam) is popular in many countries. Some hardy Finns rush from the steam room, beat themselves with twigs and then dive into cold water or even roll in the snow. Sauna baths have become popular outside Finland, in other parts of Western Europe and the United States.

Spas were used for medicinal purposes in ancient Greece and Rome. When the Romans occupied Britain, they found natural hot springs at Bath, and they made full use of them. Vichy and Aix-les-Bains in France,

Baden-Baden in Germany and Spa in Belgium became fashionable in the 18th century and are still popular. Many other old Roman spas have survived to this day.

There are natural hot springs in Japan, and in the United States, where the most famous ones are Hot Springs in Arkansas; White Sulphur Springs, in West Virginia; and Warm Springs, in Georgia.

BATIK is a method of decorating cloth with design and color. The art of batik has been practiced in Celebes, Java, and Mandura for more than 1,000 years. In recent years there has been a great interest in batik both in Europe and in the United States. Craftsmen can produce beautiful designs by batik dyeing. The earliest batiks used only one color, but from the 18th century the Indians introduced a technique for producing multicolored fabrics. The finest work requires great skill and a knowledge of dyes and their uses.

The process used for batik is called resist dyeing. Instead of painting or printing a color directly on a cloth, as in most patterned fabrics, the worker covers parts of the fabric with wax. The cloth is then dyed and dried. When the wax is removed, only the areas that were not waxed are colored. The amateur artist can make simple designs with one or two colors and the skilled artist can produce intricate designs in a variety of colors. The process is slow and requires careful planning. Batik articles are usually used for pillow cases, curtains, wall hangings, scarves, or dresses. The colorful Javanese sarong, worn by both men and women, is decorated with batik design.

A design typical of the Javanese batiks includes rows of triangles, either facing each other in the center of the cloth or forming borders on the ends, with a richly patterned allover background of geometrical or floral designs. Many of the same designs have been used for generations. Bird, animal, and butterfly patterns show some Chinese influence. Elephant, cobra, and dragon designs were originally borrowed from India. Although the human figure is not common in batik designs,

grotesque figures patterned after the marionettes of shadow pictures are sometimes used. These figures are usually done in dark brown shades. Traditionally, the elaborateness and beauty of the batik design reflected the social position of the wearer.

Traidcraft

These Indian women are making batik by applying wax to a design, which is first drawn with charcoal.

In Java, where the batik process is a national art, some of the ancient batiks are among the most beautiful textile designs produced anywhere in the world. The Javanese batik process is a long and tedious one. The fabric is washed, kneaded by hand or trodden by foot, and dried. It is treated with oil and lye (to make it soft and pliable), boiled in rice starch and dried (to keep the wax from going too deeply into the fibers), and then pounded with a mallet (to make it smooth). The men usually prepare the cloth and dye it.

The cloth is hung over a frame. Women trace the pattern with charcoal and apply the wax. Originally, the wax was applied by a strip of bamboo shaped in a certain way. But in the 17th century, a small copper cup with a number of spouts called a *tjanting* was invented, which improved the technique of applying the wax. The worker dips the *tjanting* in the warm wax and holds it just above, but not touching, the fabric. The liquid wax is applied in lines of varying thickness over the parts that are not to be dyed. Then the waxing is repeated on the reverse side. The cloth made with the wax is called a *tuli*.

The fabric with the waxed pattern is then steeped in dye. Originally all dyes were natural vegetable dyes, but some manufactured ones are being used today. The fabric is then boiled to remove the wax. The entire process is repeated for each color used. Blue, yellow, and brown are the most common ones. Certain designs and colors are characteristic of specific regions.

A faster and cheaper way of applying wax was introduced in the 15th century with a copper stamp or block forming a design, which is called a *tjap*. Most Javanese, however, think that these *tulis* are inferior to the ones done in the old way. The block is dipped in a pan of melted wax, then placed on the cloth to be decorated. Another block, with an identical but reversed design, is then pressed on the other side. With this process, usually carried out by men, ten to twenty batiks may be waxed in a single day.

Many beautiful designs are produced by the *tjap* methods, and it may take an expert to tell the final product from one made by hand. The steps used by modern Western designers are similar to those used by the Javanese, although efforts to make batik techniques more commercial have resulted in a decline in craftsmanship.

BATTERY, ELECTRIC. Electric batteries may be used for lighting a flashlight, ringing bells, running a portable radio, or, on a large scale, for giving the power for a telephone exchange. The name battery, however, is used to describe a number of electric cells connected together.

In 1794 an Italian physicist called Alessandro Volta discovered that if he used a piece of wire to connect two different pieces of metal standing in a salt solution, an electric current passed along the wire. This simple electrical device is called a Voltaic cell. Volta then went on to put a number of pairs of the same two metals together in the salt solution, each pair being separated by a sheet of cardboard. This he called a "pile", and he found that by touching the metals at each end he received a small electric shock.

This was the earliest electric cell. Although many improvements have been made, any cell is an apparatus that yields an electric current from chemical changes taking place inside it.

There are two main kinds of cell. The *primary cell* will generate an electric current until the chemicals are exhausted; it cannot be recharged. The *secondary cell* can be recharged with electricity when it has run down. Batteries of secondary cells are sometimes called storage batteries; an example is the battery in a motor vehicle.

The primary cell most used is Leclanché's cell, first used in 1868 by the French engineer Georges Leclanché. It may be made up in two ways: as a wet form in a glass jar; or, more usefully, as a dry form in a metal container. This dry form is often called a dry battery. Leclanché cells, or dry batteries, are useful for supplying small quantities of electricity, as for electric bells, flashlights and portable radios. Secondary cells can supply larger quantities. They are usually made in the form of lead accumulators (groups of connected cells).

The force with which a cell can pass a current is described as the electromotive force (e.m.f.) and is measured in volts. The e.m.f. varies according to the nature of the metals and solution used in a cell. That of a Leclanché cell is 1.5 volts, and that of the accumulator is 2 volts.

It is possible to link a number of cells together, as did Volta, and obtain a much larger e.m.f. If, for instance, ten cells are wired together so that the positive terminal (that is, the terminal from which the electricity is said to flow) of one is linked to the negative terminal of the next, and so on, the e.m.f. of the battery of cells is now $10 \times 2 = 20$ volts. It is in this way that "dry batteries" are linked together to give the high-tension battery (over 100 volts) used for portable radios. This is called wiring in series. If the cells are connected so that all the positive terminals are linked, and all the negative terminals are linked, the e.m.f. is still only 2 volts, but the result is a large battery of great capacity, capable of giving a low current for a long time. This is called wiring in parallel.

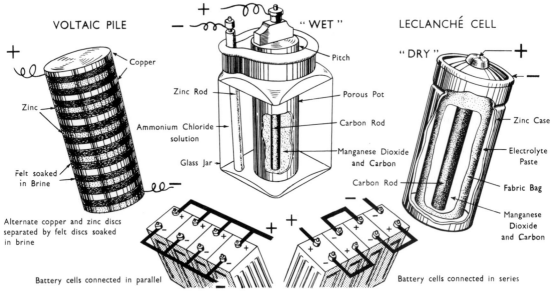

There are three basic types of electric battery: the voltaic pile and the "wet" and "dry" Leclanché cells.

The fuel cell, invented in 1959 by the British scientist F. T. Bacon, works by combining oxygen with the hydrogen in the cell so as to form water and give off electricity directly and very efficiently. (The principle is the exact opposite of that in electrolysis; see ELECTROLYSIS.) Fuel cells are used for supplying electric power in spacecraft and have been tried in electric cars. The efficiency of fuel cells and the cheapness of the fuels they use make them a very convenient source of electric power.

BATTLE OF BRITAIN see WORLD WAR II.

BAUDELAIRE, Charles Pierre (1821–67),
was a French poet and critic born in Paris. When he was six years old, his father died, and his mother married an army officer. Charles rebelled against his stepfather. After Charles had finished his education at Lyons and Paris, he fell into bad company and wasted both time and money. Thus his stepfather sought to remove him from the unhealthy influence of his Paris friends, by sending him on a voyage to India in 1841. Although he did not get as far as India, he became fascinated with the Orient.

When he returned to Paris, he quickly spent the small fortune his father had left him. In order to raise money, he began to write articles about artists. He knew many painters, including Ferdinand Delacroix and Edouard Manet, and found it easy to write about them. He was also interested in politics. In 1848 he became a member of a group that tried to change politics in France.

He became interested in the tales of the United States writer Edgar Allan Poe and enjoyed reading the stories so much that he translated them into French. The first book of his own poems, *Les Fleurs du Mal* ("Flowers of Evil"), was published in 1857. The poems tell about the struggle men face in choosing between good and evil. Before Baudelaire began to write poetry, most poets had been interested in nature. He was interested in city life. He believed that "flowers of evil" bloom because men plant seeds of evil. Because his poems offended many people, he was arrested. The French authorities refused to let his book be printed unless six of the poems were left out. (The ban on these six poems was lifted in 1945.) In 1866 Baudelaire wrote *Little Poems in Prose*.

Baudelaire believed that by appealing to the senses, a poet could say things in poetry that could not be said in prose. His poetry is full of sadness, curiosity, and a dream-like quality.

Charles Baudelaire, the French poet.

He lived an unhappy life and died a poor man in a Paris hospital at the age of 46.

BAUDOUIN (born 1930). King Baudouin of Belgium was born near Brussels, the second child of Prince Leopold, later King Leopold III. When Germany invaded Belgium in 1940, early in World War II, the young prince and his sister and brother sought refuge first in France and then in Spain. Later in the war they returned to Belgium.

After the liberation of Belgium, King Leopold was forced to live abroad, and in 1950 he gave up the throne in favor of his son. In the early years of King Baudouin's reign Belgium was troubled by arguments about education, as some supported and others opposed special help for Roman Catholic schools. This dispute was settled in 1959. Even more troublesome was the struggle of the Belgian Congo (now Zaire) for independence, which was finally won in 1960.

King Baudouin married his queen, Fabiola, a Spanish aristocrat, in 1960. About that time

disputes between the Flemings in the north and the French-speaking Walloons reached their height. The king continually tried to bring the communities together. He is a popular ruler who gained the confidence of his countrymen during the difficult post-war period.

BAUM, Lyman Frank (1856–1919), a writer of children's books, is best known as the creator of the Land of Oz.

Baum was born in Chittenango, New York, United States. He was at first a journalist and started writing children's books to earn more money for his growing family. In 1899 *Father Goose: His Book* became a best-seller. It was illustrated by W. W. Denslow, who the following year did the now famous drawings for the first Oz book, *The Wonderful Wizard of Oz*. It tells the story of Dorothy, a Kansas farm girl, who is blown by a cyclone to the land of Oz where she meets a tin woodman, a scarecrow, and a cowardly lion.

By 1910, when he published *The Emerald City of Oz*, Baum had grown tired of the land he had created. In that book he said that Oz had been cut off from communication with the rest of the world. He relented, however, and in 1913 published *The Patchwork Girl of Oz*, telling how telegraphy had been discovered so that communication between Oz and the rest of the world could be re-established.

In addition to writing the books mentioned, Baum wrote a number of others under the pen names Edith Van Dyne, Schuyler Stanton, and Floyd Akers. In 1939 a film was made of *The Wizard of Oz* that was popular then and has remained a favorite movie of children ever since.

BAUXITE. The rocks and soils from which metals are obtained are called ores, and bauxite is the principal ore of aluminum. This metal combines very readily with oxygen to form aluminum oxide (alumina) and bauxite is impure alumina. It takes its name from the town of Les Baux near Arles in southern France, where it was first found in 1821.

Over the course of the ages many different kinds of rock have been changed into bauxite

Courtesy, Geological Museum, London

Bauxite varies greatly in color, texture, and hardness, depending on where it is found. This piece comes from Ghana in West Africa.

by weathering, or the action of rain, wind and sun. Bauxite may exist as lumps of rock or in the form of gravel, clay or sand. In color it is generally reddish, buff, gray or white. It is found in many countries, usually on or near the surface, and tends to be most plentiful in tropical lands. The largest deposits mined are those in Surinam, Guyana, Jamaica, West Africa, Arkansas (United States) and Queensland (Australia).

The bauxite is removed by strip mining and treated with chemicals—usually caustic soda—to obtain the alumina. This is then smelted by electrolysis, which is done by passing an electric current through it. Usually it takes about four tonnes of bauxite to yield a tonne of aluminum. (See ALUMINUM; ELECTROLYSIS.)

BAVARIA is the largest state in the Federal Republic of Germany (West Germany). It covers 70,551 square kilometers (27,240 square miles) and is in the southeast of the country. It has a population of 10,969,000.

Bavaria is a tableland surrounded by mountains. The Bavarian Alps in the south include the country's highest peak, the Zugspitze, which reaches 2,968 meters (9,738 feet). The chief rivers are the Main in the north and the Danube in the south. Bavaria has cold, snowy winters, but hot summers in the valleys.

Forests cover a third of the land and farms just over a half. Agriculture and forestry are important activities and barley, oats, potatoes, sugar beet, and wheat are major crops. Dairy farming and cattle rearing are other leading occupations, though Bavaria's best-known industry is probably brewing. Since World War II, many light and heavy industries have been set up, especially in the capital, Munich, and the cities of Nuremberg, Augsburg, and Regensburg.

The Romans ruled Bavaria from about AD 15 until the fifth century, when Germanic people from the east (the Baiuvarii) conquered the area. For much of its history, Bavaria was a duchy (dukedom). It became a kingdom in 1805 before joining a united Germany in 1871. Today, 70 per cent of Bavarians are Roman Catholics and 26 per cent Protestants. The Bavarians have a distinctive national costume: *Lederhosen* (leather shorts) worn with long socks, for men; and *Dirndlkleider* (a patterned dress with a full skirt and puffed sleeves) for women. They are worn on special occasions. Many tourists visit Bavaria to see its magnificent palaces, scenic mountain resorts, and attractive towns, especially Bayreuth, which is renowned for its music festivals, and the village of Oberammergau, where the famous Passion Play is performed every ten years.

BAY. The sweet bay tree (*Laurus nobilis*) is one of the laurels and a member of the Lauraceae family. It grows on both sides of the Mediterranean Sea, where the winters are wet and not too cold and the summers are dry and warm. It can grow to a height of 18 meters (60 feet). However, it is generally seen as a bush,

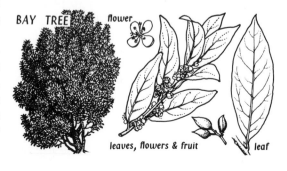

BAY TREE   flower

leaves, flowers & fruit   leaf

The Bavarian Alps form a magnificent backcloth to the autumn-colored trees and roofs of Garmisch-Partenkirchen. The highest peak here is the Zugspitze.

ZEFA

sometimes cut into formal shapes. It has evergreen lance-shaped leaves with smooth edges and a pleasant scent. In the spring the bushes have clusters of greenish-yellow flowers and later the female ones turn into dark purple berries.

The sweet bay is not a showy kind of laurel but people have long used it as a sign of distinction. To the Romans it was a symbol, or sign, of courage and they also believed that it would protect them from lightning. It was the tree of Apollo, the Greek god of poetry and archery among other things, and world conquerors and national poets alike have been proud to wear a wreath of bay. Nowadays the sweet-scented leaves are popular in cooking to flavor stews, fish, and soups.

BAYEUX TAPESTRY. The Bayeux Tapestry is a piece of embroidery made in the time of William the Conqueror over 900 years ago. It is a long narrow strip, about 50 centimeters (20 inches) wide and 70 meters (230 feet) long. The pictures stitched on it tell the story of the conquest of England by the Normans.

About the year 1066, William's half-brother Odo, the bishop of Bayeux, in Normandy, is believed to have given orders for this tapestry to be made to hang in his cathedral. The pictures were worked in eight different colored wools on small strips of canvas, and then sewn together into the long piece when they were finished. The colors are gay, with blue trees, horses with oddly-colored legs, and red and green beasts in the margin. At one time the tapestry was hung round the walls of Bayeux Cathedral when festivals were held.

The story is told in 72 scenes. One shows Harold with his hand on a chest covered with a decorated cloth. He is making a solemn promise to allow William of Normandy to become king of England when Edward the Confessor dies. The chest contains holy relics.

The tapestry then shows how Harold broke his promise and became king himself. It shows in great detail Duke William's preparations for war. His ship, with a figure-head of a boy blowing on an ivory horn, is shown crossing the English Channel. The last scene shows the English fleeing after the death of Harold at the Battle of Hastings in 1066. The end part of the tapestry has, however, been lost.

The Bayeux Tapestry is an important historical record. It shows the weapons and armor used at the time of the Norman conquest. It has the only known picture of Edward

The Bayeux Tapestry was worked in eight different colored wools. It tells the story of the Norman Conquest.

the Confessor's Westminster Abbey, which was pulled down in 1245. The bright colors are now faded and the tapestry is kept under glass in a museum at Bayeux. A copy of the tapestry is in the Victoria and Albert Museum, London.

BEAD is a small object made of glass, wood, metal, shell, nuts, teeth, bird quills, plastic, or some other material. A bead usually has a hole through it so that it can be strung together with other beads.

The word bead comes from the old Germanic word *bidden* meaning "to pray". This is because strings of beads helped people to count

their prayers (*bedes*). Beads are still used as religious or magical objects in many parts of the world. Christians, Buddhists, Hindus, and Muslims have rosaries for counting their prayers. In many Arab countries, a single blue bead attached to an object, person, or animal, is supposed to ward off bad luck.

Another use of beads is for ornamentation. Beads decorate clothing and can be made into various articles of jewelry. Holes pierced through the ears, nose, or lips attach beads to the body. In the branch of needlework which we call beadwork, beads and other materials, such as pearls and corals, are sewn onto a fabric to make a pattern. Beadwork as an art

Michael Holford

This long-necked gourd, covered in beads, was the
Royal Calabash of the Bamum people of Cameroon,
West Africa.

flourished in Elizabethan England and 17th-century Italy, when nearly all clothing had some decorative beadwork. The art experienced a revival in Victorian times. Beadwork is still common in most of Africa, among American Indians, and in the Pacific. American Indian beadwork is noted for its bold geometric and floral designs, found on dwellings, costumes, and even horse gear. The best-known examples are to be found among the Crow, Sioux, and Blackfoot Indians. In Africa, beads are used to decorate head-dresses and leggings, to cover vessels for carrying water, and for aprons and necklaces, some of which convey messages. The Zulu love letter is made of many different colors of bead, each of which has a special meaning. In Southern Africa, every group has its particular color combination. Melanesians and New Guineans mostly use shell beads.

A most important use of beads is for trade. This also dates back many thousands of years. Archeologists have found shell beads made into necklaces very far from the coast where they originated, which suggests that they were used in barter. We do know for certain that European explorers to all parts of the world in the 17th and 18th centuries exchanged beads for local products and offered beads as gifts to the local people. Beads made in Renaissance Venice found their way as trading objects to Brazilian Indians, who wore them until fairly recently. Christopher Columbus noted in his diary on the day he discovered America that he offered a gift of beads to the people of San Salvador Island.

In North America, after contact with Europeans, the Indians used beads for money, or *wampum*, as it was called. The practice continued until the middle of the last century in some parts of the United States. Wampum was usually made of polished clam, oyster, or periwinkle shells or pieces of whelk. They were strung on strands made of sinew or bark thread. Wampum necklaces and belts were also valued as ornaments and used as a form of ceremonial gift exchange. To make treaties binding, wampum belts were exchanged by Indian tribes, or between the Indians and the early white settlers on the eastern seaboard of the continent.

Earliest Beads

The ancient Egyptians were wonderful bead-makers. They had workshops, 6,000 years ago, which turned out colored stone beads carved with beautiful designs of flowers and fruits. We know this because mummies have been found that were wrapped in cloths decorated with elaborate beadwork. A mummy robe, found in the tomb of the daughter of an Egyptian priest, was made of beads held together by pieces of solid beadwork, closely woven in patterns of fish and scarabs. (The scarab was the sacred beetle of ancient Egypt.)

The Phoenicians perfected the art of making glass beads and were responsible for the first brilliantly colored beads. They were also noted for their comic beads depicting humorous human and animal faces.

Around 1100 BC, the civilization of the Aegean world (around the eastern Mediter-

In the early 17th century, strings of wampum beads were used as money by whites and Indians in what is now the eastern United States.

Michael Holford

ranean) produced famous workers in metal—especially gold—and ivory. Fluted beads, in shapes of flowers, and made from ivory and amber, came from Crete. (Amber is a substance made from fossilized tree resin, and was common among the early Greeks.) Amber beads were also being produced before the Roman Conquest in the area which is now Brittany, in Northern France.

Bead Manufacture

Today, one of the chief commercial producers of beads is Czechoslovakia. The industry began there with the manufacture of celluloid beads made to look like coral, and later grew to include beads of wood, horn, tortoiseshell, and glass.

Venice, Italy, has long been famous for its beautiful glass beads, the craft of making them dating back to the 13th century. Venetian beads are often gilded and decorated with bits of colored paste blown on to them in the making. A mass of glass is used in the manufacture of glass beads. It is either white, black, or colored to resemble some precious stone. The glass is blown and pulled out into a hollow rod which may be as much as 30 meters (100

feet) long. These rods are then cut into pieces about 30 centimeters (1 foot) in length and heated. Small pieces are cut off and cooled, a process which toughens the glass and fixes the colors. The rough beads are placed together with charcoal and plaster or ashes in a rotating drum and treated over a furnace. The

Michael Holford

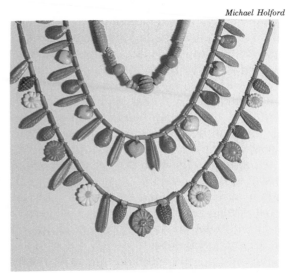

Glazed Egyptian beads from the 18th dynasty, 1550–1100 bc. At banquets, guests were given collars of these beads.

beads are rounded and polished by rubbing together in the drum, while the plaster or ashes keeps them from sticking together. Finally, they are washed in order to remove waste matter and to clean the hole in the center through which a thread or wire is run to string the beads together.

BEAN is the seed and pod of certain plants of the Legume family (*Leguminosae*), which also includes peas and lentils. (See PEA.) The name bean is also given to the plant itself.

NHPA/G. I. Bernard

A colorful mixture of dried beans: lima, kidney, black, mung, haricot, aduki, black-eyed, and butter beans.

The blossoms of bean plants are relatively large, borne singly or in clusters. The fruit of the plants are the pods. The seeds are arranged in a row within the pod. There are many differences in the size, shape, and color of the pods. They range from 5 to 20 centimeters (2 to 8 inches) in length, and they may contain 1 or 2 seeds or as many as 12 to 20, as in some of the edible cowpea types. (See SEED.)

All beans are annuals and are grown from seeds. Some are spreading vines, sometimes called pole beans because poles or trellises must be used to support them. Others are low and bushy, sometimes called dwarf beans.

Because beans provide a nourishing food, they are an important crop all over the world. They are so rich in protein that they are often used as a meat substitute. In several species only the seeds are eaten. In others—varieties such as the string bean, so called because of the string like fibers in the pods—the pod is also eaten. Both pod beans and seed beans may be canned or preserved by freezing. Seed beans are also preserved by drying.

Bean plants serve as food for animals and also help in the growth of other plants. Beans, like many legumes, are among the plants on which nitrogen-fixing bacteria live. (See LEGUMINOUS PLANTS.)

The most important of the world's beans is the soybean. It is an extremely important crop in the United States; in fact the United States and China produce most of the world's soybean supply (see SOYBEAN).

The second most important bean of the world is the common green or kidney bean (*Phaseolus vulgaris*), also called snap, string, French, wax, navy, or field bean, as well as Boston pea. It is grown mainly for food. It is native to Central and South America but is now grown throughout the world. The many varieties differ greatly in size, shape, and color. The frijoles of Latin America are also varieties. Some of these varieties are grown for their edible pods, which may be green, yellow, or red. The seeds range from white to green, yellow, tan, pink, red, brown, purple, black, and multicolored. They are known by many different names, the best-known being haricot (white), flageolet (green), kidney (red), and borlotti (brown). Haricot beans are the ones used to make "baked beans".

The broad bean (*Vicia faba*), also called the Windsor or horse bean, is an important bean in Europe. It is the bean mentioned throughout Anglo-Saxon history and the bean that appears in the story of "Jack and the Beanstalk". The broad bean is native to the Mediterranean region and the middle eastern region of Asia. Although it is widely grown in Canada and Latin America, it is little known in the United States because it cannot withstand the summer heat of most of the country.

The cowpea or horse bean (*Vigna sinensis*) is native to India. The pod of one variety grows 60 to 90 centimeters (2 to 3 feet) in length and is appropriately called the yard-long bean. Another variety is known as the black-eyed bean. The tiny mung bean (*P. aureus*) is also native to Asia. It is little known in Europe and the Americas, but in the Orient it is an important food, especially as bean sprouts. The aduki bean is a very small red bean, also eaten in China and Japan.

The lima bean (*P. limensis*) is native to tropical America and an important food in the United States. The scarlet runner (*P. coccineus*), also native to tropical America, is grown in the United States as an ornamental plant because of its bright red flowers. In Europe it is popular as a food plant.

Enemies of Beans

The bean is often destroyed by plant diseases and insect enemies. A dangerous enemy is the bean weevil, common in the southern United States. It lays its eggs on the young pods and is found also in dried beans. Common diseases are anthracnose, which is a fungus disease attacking any part of the plant, rusts, blights, and various diseases. A bean field should never be worked during wet weather because the diseases spread most easily at that time. Another pest, especially common in Europe, is the black fly, which attacks and eats bean plants. (See PLANT.)

An insect causes the curious behavior of the Mexican jumping bean. This bean has a three-celled bean pod used by the bean moth as a shelter for its eggs and larvae. The egg is laid in the flower and after a time is surrounded by the meat of the bean pod. The larva eats away the meat and lines the pod with silk from a gland in its head. This completed, it enters the seed. Every now and then the larva moves suddenly, and the bean seed jumps. Warmth causes the larva to jump more actively. The larval stage lasts for several months, after which the insect pierces the side wall of the seed and emerges as a moth.

BEAR. Although bears differ a good deal in size and color, it is quite impossible to confuse a true bear with any other animal. Bears form a very distinct family of the carnivores, or flesh-eating mammals. They are heavily built, with a fairly long muzzle. Their ears are short, rounded and furry, and they have hardly any tail. Their feet are strong and have five toes, each with a powerful claw which is sometimes long; they are almost flat-footed in their walk. In most bears the coat is rather thick and coarse, though in some of the tropical kinds it is shorter and thinner. There is sometimes a white mark on the chest and throat, but the coat is generally of one color—either black, brown, or white.

Although they are carnivores, most bears, apart from polar bears, are very mixed feeders; in fact they are omnivores, or eaters of everything. They eat a wide variety of vegetable food, especially roots and fruits, as well as many grubs and other insects. Their liking for honey is well known and they also love molasses.

The seven species of bear have a wide distribution in the northern hemisphere. There are two kinds in Europe and several in Asia, but none at all in Africa south of the Atlas Mountains. North America has four distinct kinds. Only one species, the spectacled bear (*Tremarctos ornatus*), extends well into the southern hemisphere, down to Bolivia along the Andes mountain chain.

Polar Bears

The polar bear (*Thalarctos maritimus*) is the only one with creamy white fur. It lives in the Arctic and has furry soles to its feet which help it to run safely over smooth ice, and a membrane between its toes for swimming. It is one of the biggest bears; a very large adult may weigh nearly 770 kilograms (1,700 pounds), which is the best part of a tonne. It lives more on flesh than most other bears, feeding on walruses and seals for much of the year. One blow of its powerful paw can kill a seal and lift it right out of the water. In some places it also eats fish, especially salmon, and in the arctic summer it is known to feed on berries.

Towards the end of the autumn the mother polar bear gets very fat and she then retires into a snow cave to have her tiny cubs, weighing little over a pound each. She stays there

Five of the seven bear species (clockwise from the top): spectacled, grizzly, Malay (sun), polar, and black.

and feeds them until the spring, without having any food herself.

Local people have always hunted polar bears for their skins. In the second half of the 20th century there came hunters of a different kind—those who use long-range rifles from helicopters. Thousands of polar bears were killed in this way. By the 1970s the total population of the bears was thought to be down to about 20,000. In 1973 conservationists agreed to save the polar bear, and now it is protected by all countries bordering the Arctic Circle and may not be hunted except by local peoples such as the Eskimos or for scientific research.

Brown Bears

The one species of brown bear (*Ursus arctos*) includes many different kinds, including the Kodiak bear which lives along the coast of Alaska and on some nearby islands. This is the largest flesh-eating land mammal, and can reach a massive 3 meters (10 feet) long and weigh a massive 780 kilograms (1,700 pounds). At full stretch when standing on its hindlegs, a bear can reach 3.3 meters (11 feet) tall. Kodiak bears gorge themselves on salmon as they move up river to spawn. They scoop the fish out of the water with great accuracy and flick them on to the river banks. Their paws are tremendous and can give a smashing blow, but the bear is generally peaceful enough if not interfered with.

The grizzly bear was once found from Alaska down to southern Mexico and from the Rocky Mountains to the Pacific coast, but it has been killed off in many areas and is now common only in parts of Canada. In the days of the pioneers the grizzlies were much feared, especially when they became cattle raiders, but they cannot stand up to modern rifles. Most adult grizzlies weigh between 180 to 400 kilograms (400 to 900 pounds), but some may weigh as much as 450 kilograms (1,000 pounds). They are a rather light brown or brownish yellow, often with a sprinkling of white tips to the hairs on the back and face. They also have very long and rather straight claws on their fore feet. The name "grizzly" refers to their color. Grizzlies feed on small mammals, fish, berries, and plants.

Centuries ago brown bears were found over nearly all of Europe, though now they are rare except in parts of eastern Europe and some mountainous regions. Their color varies from silvery gray-brown to nearly black. They are not as big as polar bears and seldom weigh more than 340 kilograms (750 pounds). Also their heads are a very different shape, being broader and much more pointed, with larger ears. They have two or three cubs at a time, generally in January or February. Those that live in the colder countries fatten up enormously before going into a cave for their long winter sleep. Brown bears are tamed fairly easily and "dancing bears" are to be seen in many parts of the world, especially in the Balkans. The bear pit at Bern in Switzerland has been occupied for many centuries and it was here that one bear was known to live for almost half a century, showing that bears are among the most long-lived animals.

Black Bears

The American black bear has a short, glossy black coat, though a pale form is seen from time to time. It lives in the forest regions of North America and is found from Mexico northward to Alaska. It has been heavily hunted but is still common in many places. It is about 1 meter (3 feet) high at the shoulder with a length of 2 meters (6 feet). The black bear eats roots and other vegetable matter and small animals such as mice, frogs, and fish. Sometimes it raids domestic animals, but it seldom attacks man. Unlike the grizzly, it is a good climber.

These black bears are the ones commonly seen in the American national parks, where they often become so tame that they beg for sweets along the roadside. Their fur was very popular among the Indians for making robes and blankets.

The only other New World bear comes from South America. This is the spectacled bear (*Tremarctos ornatus*), so-called because of the light-colored rings round the eyes. Its home is in the Andes Mountains of Chile, Bolivia, Ecuador, and Peru and it is very different from any other kind. The general color is black, with white on the throat and chest, and it is quite small, growing to 2 meters (6 feet) long.

The Malayan bear (*Helarctos malyanus*) is the smallest species, with a normal length of 1.2 meters (4 feet). The black coat is very short and smooth and it has a very pale patch on the chest and a pale muzzle. This little bear has a wide range—from Indonesia in the south, through Malaya and Burma to northeast India. It is a forest animal and an expert climber.

The Himalayan black bear (*Selenarctos thibetanus*) is easily recognized by its black coat and a broad white or cream V on its chest. It is a good deal smaller than the American black bear and weighs only a little over 90 kilograms (200 pounds). Its coat is short and smooth and its ears rather large and furry. It lives in the forests and is found from Iran in the west through India to China. One form of this bear is also found in Japan. In the Himalayas it can be found up to a height of over 3,000 meters (10,000 feet). In the colder parts it hibernates for part of the time, but does not go into a very deep sleep.

The last of all is the sloth bear (*Melursus ursinus*), an ugly creature found only in parts of India and Ceylon and rather smaller than the Himalayan black bear. Its black fur is shaggy and its claws are long and powerful. It feeds mostly on fruit, honey and insects, sucking them up with its long muzzle and lips. Its favorite food is ants and termites that are sucked up by a vacuum-cleaner type action of the lips and long tongue. Like most bears it also eats meat, if it can get it. Baloo of Kipling's *Jungle Book* is a sloth bear.

BEAVER. The beaver is the second largest rodent after the capybara (see CAPYBARA), weighing over 25 kilograms (55 pounds). It is a powerfully built creature with a body up to 76 centimeters (30 inches) long and a tail of 38 centimeters(15 inches).

The beaver has wonderful waterproof fur and its hind feet are webbed like a duck's, making it a very powerful swimmer. It can stay under water for as long as 15 minutes, during which time its ears and nose are automatically closed by valves. The broad paddle-shaped tail acts as a rudder in the water and also makes a firm support on which it can sit back while it is building its lodge, using its front feet as hands. When the tail is slapped on the water it warns the other beavers of danger.

Like all rodents, beavers have front teeth which never stop growing. These broad gnawing teeth have hard enamel in front with a softer part behind and they have to be used constantly if they are to be kept sharp and not grow too long. A remarkable thing about the beaver is a special double claw on the second toe of the hind foot which is used for cleaning the fur when it becomes muddy.

Two Kinds of Beaver

There are two species of beaver, the European (*Castor fiber*) kind and the North American (*Castor canadensis*). The first was once common in central and northern Europe. It was plentiful even in Britain before the Norman Conquest, and nobody knows quite when it disappeared. In western and central Europe it has been hunted very heavily and at one time seemed likely to be exterminated, but it was protected just in time. There is a colony in the Rhône Valley in France, also in northern

Germany and in Norway, and the beaver has been reintroduced into Sweden and into Switzerland, where it was once common. Fossil beavers have been found, some more than 2 meters (7 feet) long.

The American beaver, too, has suffered very much through hunting. At one time it was found from the Mexican border right up to Alaska and Labrador, but it disappeared long ago from most of the United States and is rare in many parts of Canada. It is now protected by the governments of both these countries. Beavers have been reintroduced into some of the eastern parts of the United States.

Although its meat can be eaten, the reason why the beaver is so heavily hunted is that its fur is valuable. The beaver fur which makes such splendid coats is not the thick outer coat of shiny reddish-brown hair, but the waterproof underfur which is soft, dense, of a rich brown color, and with a beautiful silver tinge.

The Way Beavers Live

Beavers are probably best known for their activities in damming rivers, but the European beaver does little of this work and generally lives in the river banks. The American beaver can fell small trees by gnawing away at the base and then using them to make large dams; one in Montana, in the United States, measured more than 600 meters (2,000 feet)

NHPA/Michael Leach

A European beaver using its front feet as hands while gnawing a log. Note the webbed hind feet.

Beavers building a lodge. One beaver swims out from the shore; another brings a branch through a tunnel.

across. Beavers mainly fell trees to provide food. During most of the year they live on the tender bark and buds of the trees they fell, choosing especially small aspens and willows.

Later the beavers trim the branches off the tree and cut the trunk into lengths for use in their dams and the lodges in which they live. The dams hold up the water and make it possible for the animals to have permanent underwater entrances to their homes, deep enough to avoid being frozen up in cold weather. The beavers drag the branches and brushwood to the water by holding them in their mouths and then floating them to where they are wanted, but the logs are not so easy to manage. If these are on a hill they can be rolled or pushed and the beavers will clear a trail through the brush for this purpose. In this way they sometimes move logs up to 3.5 meters (12 feet) in length. When all the trees near their home have been cut down they sometimes dig canals to a swamp or another pond and use them to

help transport logs which may be lying much further away.

The beavers also cut up the thinner branches of the trees and store them under water as their winter food supply. In winter, too, they swim under the ice in their deep ponds and find the roots of water plants to eat. In this way they avoid wolves, coyotes, bears, and other enemies.

The beaver's work is never done and that is why people say that a man who works hard "works like a beaver". If a flood causes a break in the dam the animals must quickly repair it by adding logs and brushwood and piling mud and stones on top to keep everything in place. When the stream washes down silt and stones which fill up the pond, the beavers must increase the height of the dam, and when this causes the water to run round the ends of the dam, the dam has to be lengthened. Although over-eager beavers sometimes damage the river banks, they also do a great deal of good by their work. By holding up water they often help to prevent floods in wet weather, while in a dry spell their dams help to prevent the streams drying up.

Beavers are rather sociable animals. Sometimes a colony may consist of only one family in one lodge, but often the colonies are much larger, with a number of lodges. A lodge may be built of sticks, logs and branches in the pond itself or it may be a stick-covered burrow in the bank of the stream. The older it is the larger its size, for the owners are always adding material to it. Some of the largest found have measured over 6 meters (20 feet) across and were raised over 2 meters (7 feet) above the water line. Inside, the living chambers may be so large that a man could lie full length in them in either direction. They are ventilated by air-holes and in winter, when everything is frozen, these can sometimes be seen to let out a faint "smoke" like a human being's breath on a frosty morning. Beavers do not hibernate, or sleep during the winter, though they are not so active in the cold months as in the summertime. The young are born in the spring, usually from two to five at a time, though families of eight have been known.

BEAVERBROOK, William Maxwell Aitken, 1st Baron (1879–1964). Max Aitken was born in Maple, Ontario, Canada and was at first a stockbroker in Montreal. He amalgamated the entire cement industry of Canada, which made him a wealthy man. In 1910, after moving to England, he was elected to the House of Commons as a Conservative Member of Parliament. In 1916 he took over the *Daily Express* newspaper, and later started the *Sunday Express* and took over the *Evening Standard*. In 1916 he accepted a baronetcy and the following year a peerage. In 1918 he was a member of the Cabinet as Chancellor of the Duchy of Lancaster and Minister of Information in charge of propaganda.

During World War II (1939–45) he was a member of Winston Churchill's War Cabinet as Minister of Aircraft Production and later Minister of Supply. He was one of only three people to sit in the British Cabinet during both World Wars I and II.

BBC Hulton Picture Library
Max Aitken, Lord Beaverbrook, financier, politician, and newspaper proprietor.

Beaverbrook was a supporter of individual enterprise, free trade, and imperialism. He was a close friend of Churchill, who valued him for his energy and flair for improvisation, but he never fully achieved the political power that he sought.

BECKET, Thomas (1118–70). Thomas Becket, or Thomas à Becket, was Archbishop of Canterbury from 1162 to 1170, during the reign of King Henry II of England. It was a troubled time of quarrels between the king and the Church. Though Henry and Thomas were great friends at first, they became deadly enemies through these quarrels, which led to Becket's murder in 1170.

After he had been educated in London and had studied in Paris and at Bologna, in Italy, Thomas became an archdeacon to Archbishop Theobald of Canterbury. It was then that King Henry met him, liked him, and made him his chancellor, one of the highest positions in the state. The king and the chancellor became great friends. Thomas helped Henry in the task of trying to restore order in the country, which had been disturbed by civil wars during

Becket was murdered in Canterbury Cathedral in 1170 by the soldiers of Henry II. This picture comes from a book of Psalms made in about 1200.

eror or Henry I. He set out his claims in 1164 in a document known as the Constitutions of Clarendon. Becket refused to accept them and fled to France, where he stayed in exile for six years. Some of the English bishops supported the king and this made the quarrel even more bitter.

In 1170 the quarrel was settled. Becket returned and immediately tried to punish his opponents. Henry was furious and, so the story goes, he cried out "Who will rid me of this turbulent priest?" Four knights who heard him left at once for Canterbury and there, shouting out "King's men", they struck Becket down with their swords in the cathedral itself.

The Christian world was shocked by the terrible deed and in 1173 Becket was made a saint. Henry was forgiven by the pope and walked barefoot in penance to Becket's shrine in Canterbury. The shrine became the most popular place of pilgrimage in England in the Middle Ages, and many miracles were said to have taken place there. The pilgrims in Chaucer's *The Canterbury Tales* were on their way from London to the shrine at Canterbury.

the reign of Stephen, the previous king. Henry hoped that Thomas, after becoming Archbishop of Canterbury, would continue to be his right-hand man.

However, in 1162 when Thomas became archbishop he ceased to be the king's servant and became the servant of the Church. He gave up his life of luxury, wore a hair shirt under his robes, and did penance for his sins. Unfortunately he was sometimes very proud and stubborn, refusing to give way at all in an argument.

At that time the Church was rich and powerful but the clergy owed duties to both the king and the pope. During Stephen's reign the Church had won more independence from royal control. Henry II wished to restore the royal powers and have a voice in Church affairs as strong as that of William the Conqu-

BEDE (672 or 673–735) was a Benedictine monk who lived during the early years of Christianity in England. From one of the books Bede wrote comes the famous story about Pope Gregory the Great. The pope saw some fair-haired English children in the slave market at Rome, and asked where they came from. When told they were Angles, he exclaimed "Not Angles, but angels", and after this he sent St. Augustine to convert England to Christianity.

When Bede was seven years old, his parents handed him over to be brought up by the monks of Wearmouth in what is now County Durham. He spent all his life in this monastery and in the nearby one at Jarrow, studying the scriptures and taking part in all the ceremonies and services of the Church. When he wrote a short description of his life he told how he had always loved learning, teaching, and writing. He became famous as a scholar in a time when not many men were learned. He

Bede's most famous work, *The Ecclesiastical History of the English Nation*, described England and its Church.

knew Latin, Greek, and Hebrew, and used his learning wisely.

His most famous work is a history book called the *Ecclesiastical History of the English Nation*. In it he tells the story of England and its Church up to his own time. (The story of Pope Gregory comes from this book.) He also wrote books about the Bible and about scientific subjects. He was interested in the study of the stars, not for scientific but for religious reasons. He wanted men to be able to tell the day of the year by the movements of the sun, moon, and stars, so that they could celebrate the Christian festivals on exactly the right days.

Bede's writings influenced the Church throughout western Europe. Manuscripts of his work, copied out by monks hundreds of years ago, are in many of the great libraries of the world.

He is usually called "the Venerable Bede". The word venerable sometimes means old as well as respected, but in early times it was often used to describe holy men. Bede's last hours were spent, like the rest of his life, in praying and teaching—a good end to a good and gentle life.

BEDFORDSHIRE is one of the smaller counties in the south midlands of England. It lies between Buckinghamshire to the west, Northamptonshire to the northwest, Cambridgeshire to the east, and Hertfordshire to the southeast. It is 1,235 square kilometers (477 square miles) in area and has a population of 515,700 (1984).

Much of eastern Bedfordshire is flat. The remainder of the county is mostly gently rolling land, with the Dunstable Downs, part of the Chiltern Hills, providing the highest points, in the southwest. The downs are chalk hills, rising to nearly 240 meters (800 feet) and are the home of many interesting species of chalk-loving plants, some of which are protected at Knocking Hoe nature reserve near Shillington. There are other nature reserves at Felmersham and at Sandy, which is the national headquarters of the Royal Society for the Protection of Birds.

The main river of Bedfordshire is the Great Ouse, which enters the county in the northwest and follows a winding course to Bedford, the county town, before flowing northeast into Cambridgeshire. Its tributary, the Ivel, crosses the eastern part of Bedfordshire.

Where the soil is well-drained, the land is fertile and good for farming. The pastures of the Ouse Valley provide grazing for dairy cattle. Wheat and barley are the chief crops, but root crops are also grown. Market gardening takes place in the eastern part of the county and most of the produce is sent for sale in London.

Towns and Industries

Although farming is still an important activity, the number of people who earn their living from the land is small. Most now work either in industry or in commerce, and many travel daily by road or rail to jobs in London.

Brick-making is a traditional local industry and at Stewartby is one of the largest brickworks in the world. Sand for making glass and bricks is dug near Leighton Buzzard, while

Totternhoe is known both for limeworking and for building stone (stone from here was used in the construction of Windsor Castle).

Bedford, standing on a main crossing of the River Ouse, is an important commercial and industrial center. It has manufacturing, electrical, and food processing factories, and on the outskirts of the town, at Thurleigh, is an aeronautics research establishment. Bedfordshire played a part in aviation history: at Cardington near Bedford stand the sheds built to house the famous airships R100 and R101 (see AIRSHIP). Cranfield is the site of an aeronautical college.

The largest center of population in Bedfordshire is around Luton and Dunstable. Luton is a busy industrial town, with vehicle-building, electrical engineering, and scientific instrument-making. Luton was famous in the past for its straw hats, and hat-making still goes on there. Dunstable is noted for engineering, cement, and printing works.

British Tourist Authority

John Bunyan, the author of *The Pilgrim's Progress*, lived for much of his life in Bedford.

Two attractions for visitors interested in animals are Whipsnade Zoo where the animals roam inside huge enclosures, and Woburn Safari Park, a large wildlife park in which animals are allowed to roam unrestricted. Woburn Abbey is the home of the Duke of Bedford, and is among the most popular of Britain's "stately homes". It is visited by thousands of people each year. Luton Hoo, near Luton, is another fine country house. Here the gardens were laid out by the famous landscape gardener Lancelot "Capability" Brown.

History

The humps on Dunstable Downs are barrows, or graves (see BARROW) made by ancient Britons. Just west of Dunstable is a circular earthwork known as Maiden Bower. The town itself stands at the crossing of the prehistoric Icknield Way and Watling Street (the road built by the Romans that ran from London towards Wales). Another famous highway in eastern Bedfordshire is the Great North Road, which has several old coaching inns.

Probably the most famous person connected with Bedfordshire is John Bunyan, writer of *The Pilgrim's Progress*. He was born in 1628 at Elstow. The old "Moot Hall", a 15th-century half-timbered market house contains a collection of objects illustrating the life and times of Bunyan and at the top of Bedford High Street is a statue of the writer. On the site of the barn in which Bunyan preached is a modern meeting house. Its bronze doors are carved with scenes illustrating his famous book. The building contains most of the surviving relics of Bunyan.

Sir Joseph Paxton, who designed glasshouses and built the Crystal Palace for the Great Exhibition of 1851 in London's Hyde Park, and John Howard, who did much to reform English prisons in the 18th century, are two more distinguished persons born in Bedfordshire.

BEE. Like all insects, a bee has six legs. Its body consists of three main parts—the head, with eyes, antennae (feelers), and mouth parts; the thorax, or mid-section, with the legs and wings; and the abdomen, or rear portion.

During its development a bee passes through four stages. It starts as an egg and hatches into a larva, which consumes large quantities of pollen and either nectar or the honey made from nectar. Next it becomes a pupa, or chrysalis, during which time it is changing its shape to emerge as a winged bee.

Bees are found all over the world, particularly on flowers. Over 20,000 different species are known, including some that are parasitic, that is, they live or lay their eggs in the nests of other bees. Most bees are hairy, usually on their hind legs or on the under side of their abdomen. They have special brushes to help them gather the pollen they need for their diet. A special character of all bees is that some of their body hairs are branched. These features help to distinguish them from their nearest relatives, the wasps, which usually have few body hairs. Some bees, however, especially the parasitic species, are remarkably wasp-like, and only the presence of some branched hairs on the thorax reveals that they are in fact bees.

Bees and the Flowers

Although bumble bees (*Bombidae*) and honey bees (*Apidae*) are often active in cloudy weather, most bees are very much creatures of the sunshine. They are never found far from the flowers which provide the nectar and pollen food. The bee has a tube-like tongue, sometimes as long as its whole body, through which it sucks up nectar. Only the females collect pollen, however, and their methods of doing so make them among the most interesting of insects. The female bumble bee and the female honey bee have a smooth, slightly hollowed-out space on the outer side of the hind leg. It is called a pollen basket and the bee, with certain movements of her legs, combs her body clean of pollen grains and gradually packs them in a solid lump in her pollen basket. The leaf-cutter bees pack the pollen they gather on the underside of the abdomen.

Bees do much to fertilize the flowers of plants and trees, for some of the pollen from the male flowers gets brushed off on to the female flowers. These will then turn into seeds or fruit and produce new plants, they in turn providing pollen and nectar for later generations of bees. (See FLOWERS.) Bees are so useful in this way that beekeeping has often had to be specially encouraged in places where the wild bees have been reduced in numbers by, for example, chemical insecticides.

When a bee sucks some nectar from a flower, it flows into a special sack in its abdomen called the honey-stomach or crop. There it is held without being digested, and when the bee

returns to its nest it regurgitates it to feed the young or stock the nest.

It is only the female bee that stings; males cannot defend themselves and spend their time searching for the females or feeding among the flowers. They take no part in either making a nest or collecting food for their offspring.

Most bees are solitary; they nest alone and a female receives no help from others during nest construction or in looking after the brood. They nest in tunnels in the earth, in the hollowed-out stems of plants, and other similar places. However, some solitary bees are gregarious; they like to nest very near other bees of their species and sometimes even share a common entrance to their respective tunnels. Some gregarious bees are cultured for the pollination of crops (see BEEKEEPING). A few species of bees are social. These have a queen and live as a colony, or family, consisting mostly of workers; that is, females that cannot lay eggs but do the day-to-day work of the colony. Social bees can also produce wax, which no solitary bee is able to do. It first appears on the bee's body in the form of thin scales or flakes sticking out from between the segments, or plates, that make up the bee's abdomen. The bees use it for making combs in which to store honey or pollen for the winter, or in which the eggs are laid, and it does not melt even at quite high temperatures. The best known social kinds are the bumble bees and the honey bees.

Honey Bees

For thousands of years colonies of bees have been kept by man for their honey (see BEEKEEPING). Often a swarm of honey bees escapes the notice of the beekeeper and settles down in a hollow tree or in a chimney. Here the bees may live and go about their business for many years, no worse off than in the hive from which they came. Each hanging comb of the honey bee is double-sided with many hundreds of cells opening on each side of it. The cells are six-sided and made of the thinnest wax. To suit his convenience the beekeeper gets the bees to build their combs within wooden frames which can easily be lifted out of the hive.

Honey bees arrange their storekeeping so

Bees feed on the nectar and pollen of flowers, but only female bees collect pollen. Female honey and bumble bees have a pollen basket on the outer side of the hind leg. They comb their bodies free of pollen grains with their legs, and pack the grains in the pollen basket. The pollen is then taken back to the nest for the whole colony of bees to use. In moving from flower to flower, bees also do much to fertilize plants and trees.

Athos Millington-Ward

that the honey-cells form an arch across the top of the comb and half way down the sides. Beneath the honey is a narrow strip of cells in which the workers pack their loads of pollen, and all over the middle and lower part of the comb are the cells in which the queen lays the eggs that hatch into grubs and later become bees. A big colony may contain as many as 60,000 workers, females all of them and ready to sting if roughly treated. (Unlike most kinds of bee, the female honey bee has a barbed sting and this stays in the wound; the loss of its sting causes the bee to die.) There is also the queen bee, the one fertile female in the colony, and many males, called drones. The drones are big with very large eyes and their only use is to mate with the young queens at swarming time. At the end of the summer the workers drive or drag the drones out of the hive, to die of neglect and starvation. During the summer, when the work is hard, worker bees live for only about six weeks, but many of those born at the end of the summer live through the winter and keep the colony going.

From the time she emerges from her cell the worker bee performs various jobs. For about the first three weeks, as a "house bee", she cleans and polishes the cells. Then she helps with nursing duties, feeding the newly hatched larvae in the cells. Later she produces wax and builds this into the honeycomb. At the end of the three weeks she becomes a field bee and goes off to gather pollen and nectar from the flowers, although she may still have duties to perform in the hive, such as fanning with her wings to reduce the temperature in hot weather. These house duties are of course performed subject to the needs of the colony, and a "house bee" will become a "field bee" and vice versa, if the colony's needs so dictate.

When a worker bee finds a supply of nectar, such as a field of clover, she will fill her crop, come home and tell the other workers where she found it. She does this by two special dances. In the round dance she runs round on the comb in a small circle, first one way and then the other. This tells the others that they must hunt for food round about the hive but not more than about 45 meters (50 yards) in any direction. If the food is more than 90 meters (100 yards) away, she does a tail-waggling dance by tripping lightly over the comb so as to mark out a figure of eight, all the while waggling her abdomen. During the dance, she gradually moves over the comb followed by her excited sisters. The direction she takes and the number of times she waggles her abdomen while doing each figure of eight movement tell the other bees in what direction and how far they must fly to find the honey.

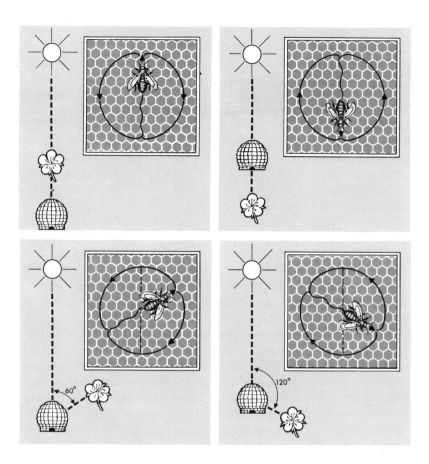

The dance language of bees.
Top left: The bee runs *up* on the vertical comb on the wagging part of the dance to tell other workers to fly *towards* the sun.
Top right: It runs *down* to tell them to fly *away* from the sun. The number of runs in a given time tells the distance.
Bottom left and right: The angle at which the bee runs on the wagging part of the dance gives the angle of the food source in relation to the hive and the sun. The drawings do not show that the scout bee is surrounded by workers who follow its movements with their antennae.

The Queen of the Colony

Although the queen is the only female that can lay eggs and therefore the most important member of the community, she is also the most helpless. Unlike her cousin the queen bumble bee, she cannot collect pollen. She is even unwilling to feed herself, preferring to receive droplets of food direct from the mouths of the workers, which are always around her. Although timid in the ordinary way and never stinging even when picked up in the fingers, the queens will, nevertheless, fight savagely if two of them chance to meet.

At swarming time, therefore, when the workers have built the special cells in which they raise young queens, the old queen runs the risk of being stung to death by one of her royal daughters, so she leaves the hive with a swarm of about 15,000 bees and sets up home elsewhere. When the first young queen leaves her cell she too goes off with a swarm, or "cast"

as beekeepers call it, and her example may be followed by several of her sisters. However, since each swarm means fewer bees left in the hive, a time comes when the colony needs to keep every worker it has and no longer feels the urge to swarm. A young queen is then allowed to remain and after the bees have destroyed, perhaps with her help, any queens still in their cells, she goes off on a marriage flight, mating in quick succession with about ten drones. She soon returns and becomes the head of the colony.

Swarming does not take place every year. A great deal depends on how much honey there is in the hive, the state of the weather, and whether the bees are cramped for space. One of the most wonderful things about the honey bee is that the workers can make themselves a new queen if anything should happen to the old one. To do this, they select a grub which in the ordinary way would become a worker and

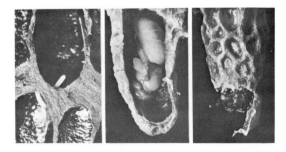

Worker   **Queen**   **Drone**

Top: The queen lays tiny, white eggs in the cells of the honeycomb (top left). These develop into workers, drones, or new queens. When a new queen is needed she is reared in a specially large queen cell (top center). She emerges when fully developed (top right). The queen larva is fed only royal jelly, a thick, white nutritious substance made in glands in the heads of worker bees. **Center:** a queen surrounded by her workers. The queen secretes a substance craved for by the worker bees that keeps the members of the hive together. **Below:** Relative sizes of honey bee worker, queen, and drone.

feed it on a special secretion of glands in their heads, called royal jelly, which causes the grub to grow into a queen. A queen may live for several years and in that time produce as many as 1,500,000 eggs.

Bumble Bees and Stingless Bees

Bumble bees live chiefly in the cooler parts of the world, one kind being found as far north as Lapland. Typically, the young bumble bee queen passes the winter asleep in the ground, but with the coming of spring she wakes and sets about finding somewhere to live. The deserted burrow of a mouse with its supply of dry grass makes a suitable nesting site. Inside she makes a waxen cell in which she lays about six or seven eggs. She also builds a large wax pot to hold a supply of honey. The grubs that hatch from the eggs need a great deal of food and the queen is busy from dawn to dusk and in all weathers collecting honey and pollen for them.

After two weeks the grubs are fully grown and each spins a tough, silky case called a cocoon for itself. The cocoons are fastened together and the queen presses her body very closely against them so that her warmth passes through to the resting pupae, or chrysalises. About two weeks later young worker bumble bees bite their way out of their cocoons and are soon out foraging, or searching, for more food to raise further broods of workers, which, as in the case of the honey bees, are smaller than the queen.

Towards the end of summer there may be as many as 100 workers in the nest. It is at this time that some of the grubs grow into young queens while others turn into males. These fly from the nest and mate, after which the young queens hide away in the ground until the following year. The males, the old queen and the workers all die. Thus, unlike the colonies of the honey bee which survive the winter and may flourish for many years, the life cycle of the bumble bee lasts a year and then starts all over again. It is only in the tropics that bumble bee colonies last from one year to another and give off swarms like the honey bees.

Bumble bees, like honey bees, can inflict a sting, but in the tropical countries there are bees with hardly any stings at all. Although some of these stingless bees (*Meliponidae*) are very gentle in their behavior, other kinds will, if their nest is disturbed, fly at the intruder in great numbers, crawling into his eyes and ears and sometimes smearing his face with an unpleasant sticky liquid. In South America some stingless bees gather enough honey to make it worth while for people to keep them in rough hives made out of hollow logs (see BEEKEEPING). Their combs are very crude compared with the beautiful six-sided cells of the honey bee.

The walls of their cells are made of a substance called cerumen, a mixture of resin, wax, and sometimes mud.

Solitary Bees

Of the great number of species of bee in the world most live a solitary life.

One of the common types is the mining bee (*Adrenidae*). When the female wants to make her nest she digs down about 20 centimeters (8 inches) into the ground, often choosing a bare spot in an area of sparse grass and betraying her presence by the small mound of earth she throws up. At the end of the burrow she makes several side galleries one below the other, each forming a cell just big enough for the growth of a bee from egg to fully winged insect. She stocks each cell with bee-bread, which is simply a mixture of honey and pollen, lays an egg on it, and then seals up the entrance with earth. The eggs hatch into legless grubs, or larvae, which grow to their full size on the food provided by the mother. They then turn to pupae, or chrysalises, and the following spring come out of the ground as winged bees. As with the bumble bee, the life cycle lasts a year. Most solitary bees are short-lived as adults, spending all but a few weeks in the immature stages. In temperate climates solitary bees pass the winter in their cells, as mature larvae or as young adults.

Although most solitary bees nest in the ground, there are some that make burrows in wood or use the holes made by other insects such as beetles. Among these are the leaf-cutting bees (*Megachile*), common the world over. The female gnaws a burrow into the rotten wood of an old tree stump. Each separate cell in the burrow is made out of pieces of leaf which she cuts with her sharp jaws from various plants, a rose bush being one of her favo-

rites. She uses large pieces of leaf for the walls of each cell and smaller, circular pieces to plug the ends. If a row of these cells, placed one on top of another, is lifted from a burrow, it looks just like a long thin cigar. Before laying eggs in them, the female stocks each cell with a paste of honey and pollen as food supply for the grub when it hatches from the egg. Leaf-cutting bees collect pollen on the underside of the abdomen. Some species of leaf-cutters are remarkable in that they make their nests only in the abandoned shells of land snails.

Bees that use cement are the mason bees (*Osmia*) found in the warmer countries. The female mason makes an elaborate nest, building her cells in a cluster, about the size of half an orange, in a sheltered place beneath a rock or the eaves of a house. She lays in a store of honey and pollen in the manner of all solitary bees.

The important thing to notice about solitary bees is that the female seals up each egg in a cell with enough food to last it while it grows into a bee and then takes no further interest in her family, whereas the social bees feed their grubs from day to day. Also, since the solitary bee has to do so much work for every egg she lays (there are no workers to do it for her), it is not surprising that the number of her offspring is small—there are usually only about 12 in the nest.

Cuckoo Bees

Cuckoo bees (*Anthophorinae*) are brightly colored wasps—like bees that parasitize the nests of other bees. They are of worldwide distribution. Like cuckoos that lay eggs in the nests of other birds, they lay their eggs in the nests of other bees. The female flies slowly over the nesting ground of solitary bees. When she finds a burrow she slips in quickly and lays an egg on the food gathered by the solitary bee for her own young. The grub of the cuckoo bee apparently grows faster than the grub of the bee that made the cell. It finally eats the other grub and the plentiful supply of honey and pollen around it

There are also cuckoo bees that live at the expense of the bumble bee and look almost exactly like them. The female seeks out the nest of a bumble bee in the spring and tries to enter. The worker bumble bees, which are able to recognize her as a stranger, attack her and try to keep her out, but she is well protected against their stings by the horny skin of her body and she is not easily turned from her purpose. After a while the workers leave her alone and she settles down quietly among them. Her next move is to kill the unfortunate bumble bee queen and take her place. The workers do not seem to realize what has happened and now raise her family with the same care that they gave to the brood of their own mother. None of the eggs of the cuckoo queen becomes a worker. They develop into females exactly like herself or into males. After they have flown from the nest and mated, the young cuckoo queens hide away until the following year when they creep from shelter and fly off again in search of bumble bee nests.

BEECH is any one of 10 species of trees (*Fagus*) of the northern hemisphere, as well as several species (*Nothofagus*) from the southern hemisphere.

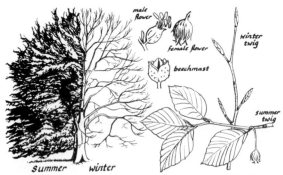

Beechwood makes good timber. The nuts, called beechmast, are used to feed deer, pigs, and poultry.

Northern beeches are hardy, decorative trees with smooth, light-colored bark. They grow up to 30 meters (100 feet) and cast a dense shade, allowing little undergrowth to develop. The American beech (*Fagus grandiflora*) and the European beech (*Fagus sylvatica*) are the best-known species.

The American beech ranges across the eastern half of North America from New Brunswick to Florida. The slightly taller European tree ranges from southern Scandinavia to the Mediterranean. The copper or purple beeches are ornamental varieties of the European birch.

Beechwood produces good timber, used for furniture, flooring, and paper pulp. The nuts, called beechmast in Europe, are, in some parts, ground to make an oil used for cooking. Good beechmast harvests provide abundant food for forest animals.

Southern Beeches

Southern beeches are important timber trees. The largest is the 46-meter (150-feet) high Australian beech (*Nothofagus moorei*) from New South Wales. The Australian red myrtle (*Nothofagus cunninghamii*) is famous for its fine-grained wood. Both trees are evergreens. The "black birch" forests of southern New Zealand are made up largely of evergreen southern beeches.

The Antarctic beech (*Nothofagus antarctica*) from the Argentine and Chile produces a pink-brown hardwood.

BEE-EATER. There are 25 species of bee-eater found throughout the warmer parts of Eurasia, Africa, and Australia. They are among the most brilliantly colored and graceful birds. The cock and the hen of the common bee-eater (*Merops apiaster*) are alike, with chestnut backs, yellow throats, and greenish-blue underparts. Their bills are long and pointed and their tails are also long, with the two middle feathers longer than the others.

These birds live on insects—chiefly bees, of course—and they can be a great nuisance in places where there are beehives. They also eat wasps and dragonflies which they catch on the wing, hunting in small groups with a gliding flight like swallows. They like to perch on dead boughs, telephone wires or poles, darting off to catch a fly and then back to their perch again. Once caught, large and stinging insects are banged repeatedly against the perch, until lifeless, and then swallowed whole.

Bee-eaters have a flute-like, single note which they keep on repeating.

Usually, bee-eaters keep together and nest in colonies. They dig out a tunnel in a soft

S. C. Porter/Bruce Coleman

Bee-eaters often perch on a dead bough, dart off to catch an insect on the wing, and then return to eat it.

sandbank, throwing the sand backwards with their feet as they peck it out. These tunnels can be 2 meters (6 feet) long and there is a round nest chamber at the end. The hen lays her five or six white eggs on the bare sand.

During the summer common bee-eaters are found in southern Europe from Spain to Bulgaria. Now and again the odd bird visits Britain. In the autumn they migrate in large flocks to Africa and India.

Most species of bee-eater are found in Africa and one of these, the carmine bee-eater (*Merops nubicus*), often rides on the backs of large birds such as bustards and storks, jumping off to catch the grasshoppers and other insects they disturb. It has also been seen to follow trucks, catching the insects that are disturbed by their passing. There is an Australian bee-eater (*Merops ornatus*), which is sometimes called the rainbow bird because of its brilliant blue, green, and orange plumage. The bird nests in southern Australia and winters in New Guinea and the Celebes.

BEEKEEPING. Bees are kept for the harvesting of bee products, such as honey and wax, and for the pollination of crops. Pollination is by far the most important reason for keeping bees. About one third of human diet comes directly or indirectly from crops that require, or are benefited by, insect pollination, and bees are the chief pollinating insects (see POLLINATION). In addition many wild flowers depend on bee pollination for survival. In the absence of bee pollination these flowers would disappear and many wild animals would be deprived of an important food source.

Beekeeping with the Honey Bee

The common European honey bee, *Apis mellifera*, is one of the few domesticated insects. (Another example is the silkworm.) It has been introduced into many parts of the world where it previously did not exist, including the continents of America, Asia, and Australasia. In Brazil it has hybridized (intercrossed) with another introduced race, the African honey bee, *Apis mellifera adansonii*. The hybrid, or "Africanized" honey bee is aggressive and has spread over most of South America; it could possibly invade the United States.

In very early times bee-keepers kept their bees in hives made of wicker or in hollowed-out logs, and later in straw baskets called "skeps". But in all such hives the bees fixed their combs to the hive walls and the honey could not be taken out without harming the colony. At the end of the summer it was then the custom to select the heavier skeps, kill the bees with sulfur fumes, and then cut out the combs and press the honey from them. In the following year the bee-keeper filled the empty skeps with swarms from the remaining colonies.

Honey bee colonies are now housed in rectangular wooden boxes, called "chambers", that are open top and bottom. The chambers are stacked to accommodate the seasonal growth of a colony. For winter a colony may consist of one queen and about 8,000 workers, but by mid-summer the population may increase to some 60,000 workers. In each chamber, the beekeeper hangs a number of wooden frames containing a thin sheet of bees-

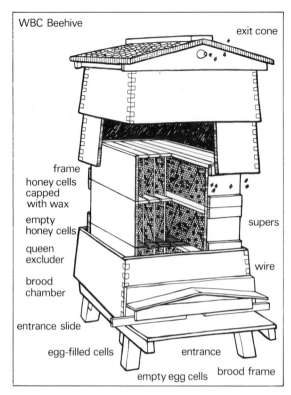

WBC Beehive

exit cone

frame
honey cells
capped
with wax

empty
honey cells

queen
excluder

brood
chamber

entrance slide

egg-filled cells

empty egg cells

entrance

supers

wire

brood frame

The WBC beehive designed in 1884 by William Broughton Carr. The boxes inside contain wax supported by wire which forms the foundation on which the bees build cells. This becomes honeycomb. A queen excluder keeps the queen bee in the lower box, called the brood chamber, where she lays eggs and where honey is stored. The worker bees can move into the upper boxes, called supers, where they also store honey; this is the honey that will be removed by the bee-keeper. The entrance can be made smaller in the winter to keep the hive warm. The exit cone allows the bees to leave the hive but not enter.

wax called "foundation". On it, printed in relief, is the hexagonal shape of bee-cells. The bee workers secrete more wax from glands in their body to construct cells on each side of the foundation. The use of frames enables the beekeeper to lift each comb individually out of the hive to look at the colony more closely. The cells that make up the comb are used by the bees to store honey and pollen, as well as for the rearing of their young. The combs that hang in the middle of a hive are built, predominantly, of rather small cells. The side combs and the margins of most combs often have noticeably large cells. In normal colonies only the queen lays eggs. As she walks from comb to comb she inspects the cells, and lays fertilized eggs in the smaller cells, and unfertilized eggs in the large cells. From the fertilized eggs develop workers, and from unfertilized eggs develop drones (males). (See BEE.)

The Founding of New Hives

The population of a hive also varies with the food situation. The more food, especially pollen, coming into the hive, the more brood is reared. At the height of the summer the queen may lay 1,500 eggs per day. When the colony reaches a certain size, it may swarm, weather permitting. A swarm consists of the old queen plus about half the bee population of the hive. The swarming bees all leave the hive together and settle temporarily in a compact cluster on some nearby branch or other object. Meanwhile, scout bees are sent out in search of a near, permanent nesting site. Swarming seriously weakens a colony, and this may affect the bee-keeper's prospect of harvesting honey. However, beekeepers know in advance when a colony is planning to swarm, since before the event the colony takes precautions to ensure that the half of the colony that stays behind will not remain queenless for long. Before swarming the colony builds a few distinctive cells in which young queens are reared. These young queens develop, like the workers, from fertilized eggs, but during the larva stage they are fed with a special diet of royal jelly, a substance produced by certain glands of young workers. The presence of these queen or swarm cells warns the beekeeper that the colony is planning to swarm. Swarming is the natural way by which a bee colony multiplies, and cannot be prevented indefinitely.

The beekeeper can, however, delay it, or even make an "artificial swarm" by dividing the colony at a time that is least harmful to his prospects of a honey harvest. The queenless half of the colony can produce a new queen by converting worker cells containing very young larvae into emergency queen cells, and feeding the young larvae in them with royal jelly. The colony may also be allowed to swarm naturally if the time of the year is not harmful to the beekeeper's interests. The swarm is removed from its temporary resting

Courtesy, Australian News and Information Bureau

A veil and "smoker" are essential for the bee-keeper. The brush is used to remove bees from the comb.

place by knocking or brushing it into a box. Later it is shaken into an empty hive containing new frames with foundation.

Honey and Wax

To obtain honey, the beekeeper uses a "queen excluder". This is a screen with slots through which the relatively smaller workers can pass, but not the queen. The queen excluder may be placed between the chambers, confining the queen to the lower point of the hive. The queen is thus prevented from laying eggs in the upper chamber, and the workers only store honey there. This can be extracted without interfering with any brood.

Honey is made from the nectar of flowers, or from sweet secretions produced by some other parts of plants or even some insects. The bees gather the nectar, and transfer it to the combs in their hive. In the process enzymes are added to it, and its water content reduced to 16 to 20 per cent. The honey is then "ripe" and the bees seal all the cells with a wax cap. At this stage the beekeeper may remove the fully sealed frames and extract the honey. The wax cappings are first removed with a knife or fork, and the frames put in a centrifugal honey extractor. The honey is spun out of the combs, filtered, and allowed to stand a few days so that air bubbles rise to the surface. It is then bottled.

Honey was formerly used for nearly all foods that required sweetening. Nowadays cheaper sweeteners made from sugar beet are available. Most of the honey harvested in the world each year is eaten as a spread on bread. A very small proportion is fermented to produce a wine called mead, which is reputedly the oldest alcoholic drink known to man.

Wax is harvested by melting down old combs. There are 125 listed uses for wax. Some of the most important are in the cosmetic industry (as an ingredient of cold creams and lipstick, for instance), in making candles, and in the manufacture of foundation for beekeepers.

After the honey has been removed from a colony, the beekeeper usually feeds the colony with syrup, so that the bees will not starve during the winter. The amount fed depends on the length of the winter. In northwestern Europe about 14 kilograms (30 pounds) of sugar is sufficient. In the colder parts of the United States and Canada much more food is required, but in regions with a Mediterranean climate little or no feeding is necessary.

Beekeeper Protection

While handling bees, beekeepers usually wear a veil to protect the head from stings; this is draped over a broad-brimmed hat so that the material is kept well away from the face. Some use gloves, too, but they are rather a hindrance in handling the frames and other equipment. In addition they use smoke to subdue bees or drive them away. The beekeeper uses a "smoker", which is a kind of bellows filled with the burning material. As he puffs smoke into the top of the hive, the bees are driven to fill themselves with honey; this honey makes them feel good-tempered, so that they can then be handled with no more than an occasional sting.

Beekeeping with Wild Bees

Some species of bee are better adapted than the domesticated honey bee for the pollination of certain crops. The leaf-cutter bee (*Megachile pacifica*) is extensively kept for the large-scale pollination of alfalfa in the United States and Canada. It is a gregarious, rather than social, species (that is, it likes to nest very near other bees of the same sort, but each bee looks after herself and her own nest). The leaf-cutter bee nests in tunnels in wood. A common way of keeping it is to provide it with thick pieces of wood into which thousands of holes have been drilled about 9 centimeters (3.5 inches) deep and 0.5 centimeter (0.25 inch) in diameter. A female leaf-cutter bee fills a tunnel with a

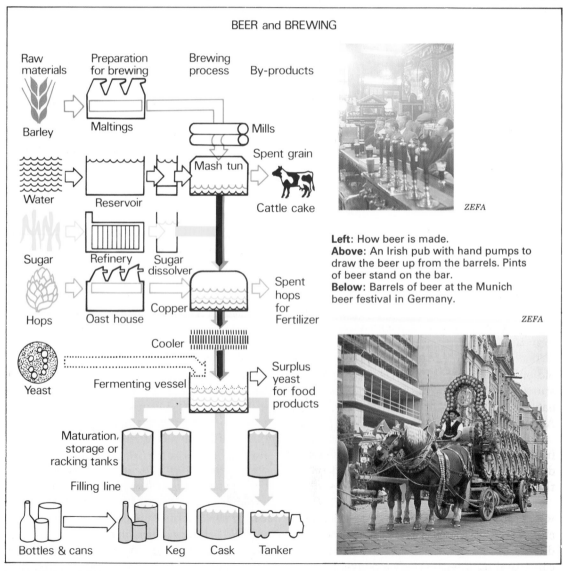

BEER and BREWING

Raw materials — Barley
Preparation for brewing — Maltings
Brewing process
By-products

Water — Reservoir
Mills
Mash tun
Spent grain
Cattle cake

Sugar — Refinery — Sugar dissolver
Hops — Oast house — Copper
Spent hops for Fertilizer

Cooler
Yeast — Fermenting vessel
Surplus yeast for food products

Maturation, storage or racking tanks
Filling line
Bottles & cans   Keg   Cask   Tanker

ZEFA

Left: How beer is made.
Above: An Irish pub with hand pumps to draw the beer up from the barrels. Pints of beer stand on the bar.
Below: Barrels of beer at the Munich beer festival in Germany.

ZEFA

Courtesy, The Brewer's Society

chain of cells. In the tunnel, each cell is constructed from a rolled piece of leaf half filled with the nectar and pollen with an egg on top. Each cell is individually capped with a circular piece of leaf.

The alkali bee (*Nomia melandri*) of northwestern America is also kept for alfalfa pollination. It nests in tunnels about 12 centimeters (5 inches) long, dug in salty ground. It is also gregarious. Its nesting requirements, however, make it more difficult to keep and less easy to transport to the crop than the leaf-cutter bee.

Other bees of significance are the bumble bees (*Bombus*), and the "stingless bees" (*Melipona beechii* and *Trigona*), all of which are social. *Melipona beechii* has been cultured for honey by the Yucatecan Maya of Mexico since prehistoric times. These bees are hived in hollow logs, approximately 56 centimeters (22 inches) long by 25 centimeters (10 inches), in diameter. The ends of the logs are fitted with wooden stoppers and the entrance is a small hole in the middle. Honey is stored at the two ends of the logs and can be harvested by removing the wooden stoppers. The harvesting of the honey among these Mexican peoples is part of a complex religious ceremony.

BEER AND BREWING. Beer is a drink made from the grains of cereal, such as barley, and flavored with hops (see HOPS). The grain is first made into malt and the process of making the malt into beer is called brewing.

The making of beer is probably nearly as old as the growing of grain crops for food. It started in the countries surrounding the eastern shores of the Mediterranean. (See AGRICULTURE, HISTORY OF).

Bread made from wheat, and beer made from barley are still the characteristic food and drink of such peoples as the Scandinavians, the Germans, and the English.

For many centuries, before tea became widely available at a reasonable price, even children drank beer. Water was often a filthy, disease-carrying liquid to be avoided at all costs, and milk was not always available.

The First Brews

Beer is now often made in huge breweries which turn out thousands of barrels, but the process is very much the same as the process carried on throughout the ages from the kitchens of Egypt to the abbeys of Europe in the Middle Ages. It must have been a happy accident that produced the first bread and the first beer, for both need yeast, and yeast in its natural condition cannot be seen by the naked eye (see YEAST). Nobody could have guessed that the addition of yeast to wet sprouting barley would produce a sparkling drink. Probably some barley grains were left about in a damp spot and started to grow or "germinate" as all seeds do if they are kept warm and wet. They must then have been crushed in water so that the sugar from inside the grain was dissolved in the water. Yeast from the outside of the grain started the fermentation and produced the first beer.

This beer had no hops in it. Throughout the centuries various herbs and other flavoring materials were put into beer, but it was not until the 14th century that hops became commonly used. Even then for many years in England hops were not always used. But the improvement in taste, the saving on malted barley, and above all better keeping qualities (the hop acted as a preservative) ensured the successful use of hops. The word "beer" was kept for the hopped variety and unhopped beer was called "ale".

Beer and Brewing Today

Today the name "beer" is applied to all kinds of beer. In England there are milds, bitters, stouts, and barley wines; in the United States all beer is the "lager" type, but there are different varieties, such as steam beer and malt liquor. Sometimes in Europe and the United States the word "ale" is used for the English type of beer and "beer" is kept for the European type—called "lager" in Great Britain—which has less hops in it and is made somewhat differently.

The first step in making beer is changing the grain, usually barley, into malt at "maltings". The grains are steeped in water, which causes them to germinate, turning the starch into sugar, before being heated in a kiln to end germination. This biscuity-tasting malted grain is then brought to the brewery where it is crushed between rollers and mixed with hot water in a large circular vessel called a "mash tun". Sometimes small quantities of other grains such as corn or rice are used; these are not malted but are specially treated before being added to the mash tun.

In this vessel the changes that started in the maltings continue until nearly all the contents of the grain have been changed into sugar. This is not quite the same sugar as that sold in the stores but it is very similar and is called "maltose". The maltose and small quantities of other substances dissolve in the water, which is called "wort". This is then run off from the mash tun and boiled in a copper for one or two hours with hops. After this the hops are strained off into a "hop back", the hopped wort is cooled, and yeast is added to start the fermentation. This continues for three or four days during which time the yeast grows and multiplies (see FERMENTATION) and converts the sugar into alcohol.

During fermentation carbon dioxide is released creating a thick "head" on top of the vessel. Lager uses a different strain of yeast, called "bottom-fermenting" as it settles to the bottom of the vessel.

When the fermentation is complete the "rough" or "green" beer is allowed to settle for three or four more days, and is then run into casks or storage tanks, where it is kept for various periods according to the type of beer and whether it is to be sold draft or bottled. "Draught" beer means beer sold to the customer straight from the cask. Sometimes extra hops and priming sugar are added to encourage a strong secondary fermentation in the cellar. This is called "cask-conditioned" beer. Isinglass or finings are also added to clear the beer.

The various kinds of beer depend on the mixture of malts used and different treatment throughout the course of brewing. Dark beers are made with malts which have been heated more strongly than malts for the pale beers;

stouts are made with roasted malt or roasted barley. "Keg," canned, and most bottled beer is chilled, filtered, and pasteurized in the brewery to give the beer a longer shelf-life. This "dead" beer is pressurized with carbon dioxide to provide a semblance of life when served. Such processed beers often contain additional chemicals to give them foaming heads and extra sparkle. All lagers made in Great Britain are processed.

Lager Beers

The word "lager" is the German for a storehouse. The beer is stored for several months at a low temperature during which time the flavor matures and carbon dioxide is released. Pilsener is a particular type of light lager, first made in Pilsen, Czechoslovakia. Munich beer is darker and has a more malty taste.

German immigrants to the United States started to brew lager there in the mid-nineteenth century and this soon became more popular than the English type of beer. In the Prohibition period in the 1930s the drinking of alcohol was banned in the United States, and afterwards beer started to be brewed only by large companies, rather than small family breweries. The largest brewery in the world is Anheuser Busch of St. Louis, which brews more beer than the whole of the United Kingdom breweries put together.

In Australia and Canada commercially produced lager is also the predominant type of beer. This may have something to do with the climate, as a light, fizzy beer is more refreshing in warm weather than the traditional English beer. It is also easier to transport long distances once it is canned or bottled, and it can be stored for longer periods and in more varying conditions than cask beer.

Revival of Real Ale

During the 1960s almost all the small regional breweries in Great Britain were taken over by six large breweries. These national companies, producing eight out of every ten pints, needed national beer brands. Traditional ales with their local character and shorter shelf-life, could not be easily sold nationwide, across the country. So the companies turned to processed keg beers—filtered and pasteurized and then served under heavy carbon dioxide pressure to give a semblance of life. They threatened to eclipse Britain's heritage of traditional cask-conditioned ales—living beers which continued to mature in the cellar right until they were served.

This change, for the convenience of the industry rather than the benefit of the beer drinker, sparked a unique consumer revolt, which forced the brewing industry into a reverse trend. Hand-pumps—the traditional method of serving cask beer—reappeared on thousands of bars. The remaining independent breweries were revived and the national breweries reintroduced their own real ales. During the next ten years over 100 new breweries were established and 80 home-brew public houses were set up.

In the 1980s North America started to follow this revival. By 1985, 25 small breweries were set up in the United States, and Canada added 12, all producing more distinctive beers than the national brands available. After years of driving towards mass market products, traditional beer was beginning to come back into favor.

BEET. The vegetables known as beets probably came from a plant called by the Latin name of *Beta vulgaris* which still grows wild along the shores of the Mediterranean. Beets have thick, solid roots, and in the first of the two years of their growth only the roots and leaves appear. Farmers usually dig up the beets during the first year, so the flowers and seeds which develop in the second year of growth are not normally seen.

There are four different kinds of beets, some of which are grown for people to eat and others for animals. The beetroot, also known as the red beet or garden beet, has a round, purplish-red root which is cooked and served in salads or made into soup. The Swiss chard (also known as perpetual spinach or spinach beet) is grown for its leaves which taste very like spinach. The stems are eaten like asparagus. The mangel-wurzel is valuable for feeding livestock during the winter, for it can be kept from autumn until late spring.

The most important type of beet is the sugar beet. This is a white root and from it about two-fifths of the supply of sugar in the world is made. The rest comes from sugar-cane.

BEETHOVEN, Ludwig van (1770–1827).

When people talk about Beethoven today they think of him as a composer of great music of all kinds, yet in his own time he was admired more because he was a wonderful pianist. People especially marveled at his astonishing power of playing a piece of music on the piano at the same time as he was actually composing it in his head (this is called improvisation or extemporization), but his written music was often too difficult for them to listen to and too hard for them to play. Through the course of time, however, he has come to be regarded as one of the greatest composers that has ever lived.

Beethoven's Life

Beethoven was born at Bonn, a town on the River Rhine in Germany which is now the capital city of the German Federal Republic. He was baptized on 17 December, 1770. His cruel and lazy father was a singer at the Court of the Archbishop-Elector of Cologne. When the little boy Ludwig showed signs of being musical, it is said that his father thought he might get rich quickly by showing off his son as an infant wonder, as the great composer

Red Beet
Garden Beetroot

Mangel

Sugar Beet

Ludwig van Beethoven, from a portrait by J. K. Steiler.

Mozart had been when he was young. According to some traditions, four-year-old Ludwig was locked into a room with a harpsichord and violin and told to practice, often in tears. By the age of eight he was also learning the organ. When he was 11 years old he was appointed assistant to Christian Gottlob Neefe, court organist to the Elector and the young Beethoven's first real teacher. The following year he succeeded to a post in the court theater where his duty was to accompany the orchestra on the harpsichord. In this way, he gained valuable experience in music and was already trying his hand at composing music himself.

The first important event of Beethoven's life was his visit to Vienna in 1787. There he met Mozart, who heard him play and said: "Pay attention to him; he will make a noise in the world some day." The visit to Vienna was cut short by the death of Beethoven's mother and he returned to Bonn. Here he now met the von Breuning family, his first real friends, and Count Waldstein, who provided him with a piano and helped him in other ways.

Beethoven's father had by now become an alcoholic, and at the age of 18 Beethoven found himself the breadwinner of the family, earning money to support his younger brothers. Beethoven was stocky and rugged in appearance, ill-mannered, hot-tempered and obstinate. But people were already aware of his great gifts as a musician, especially as a pianist. When he was not occupied in the court orchestra or with teaching he would go for long walks alone in the country, jotting down tunes that occurred to him in a little notebook, something which he did all his life. From these little notes he would work out the themes for his sonatas and symphonies.

In 1792 Beethoven again left Bonn for Vienna to study composition with the great Joseph Haydn. Beethoven's arrogance made him a reluctant pupil, and Haydn, preoccupied with other work, did not take as much trouble with him as he might have done. The lessons ended when Haydn went to England in 1794. Beethoven then studied with J. G. Albrechtsberger, a strict teacher who could not understand the reason for his pupil's rebellious nature.

Beethoven now settled in Vienna, trying to earn his living as a pianist and composer and trusting in the generosity of his patrons, Count Waldstein and the Prince and Princess Lichnowsky. Beethoven proved difficult to get on with, quarreling about his lodgings or falling out with his servants. But as his friends eventually learned, there was a tragic reason for this behavior.

Toward the end of the 1790s Beethoven started to become deaf. By 1801 it was becoming more and more serious and in the end he could hear nothing at all. It was a terrible thing to happen to a musician. Beethoven even thought about committing suicide, discussing the idea in his famous document, the Heiligenstadt Testament of 1802. Although his friends helped him even more when they learned of his deafness, Beethoven withdrew into a world of his own, a world in which only music was important. He wrote some of his most wonderful music—music which he never heard himself, except inside his head. At the first performance of his ninth symphony in 1824 he was so completely deaf that a friend had to turn him round to see the thunderous applause for his music. He remained in Vienna until his death on 26 March, 1827, aged 57.

Beethoven's Music

Before Beethoven's time the music of great composers such as Haydn and Mozart was graceful and delicate, full of beautiful and charming tunes and perfectly planned. Beethoven's music was stronger and more romantic, full of personal feelings; it could express the most unbearable sadness, or joy and delight, or even laughter, as the composer wished. This seemed like a revolution in music at the time and was one of the reasons why people did not altogether realize Beethoven's greatness during his lifetime. His own strong and stubborn character comes out in his vigorous music.

He was chiefly a composer of music to be played on instruments rather than to be sung, although he did write choral masses, an oratorio called *Christ on the Mount of Olives*, a *Choral Fantasia*, featuring a solo part for piano, and an opera called *Fidelio*, and the last movement of his ninth symphony is also choral. His greatest works are his nine symphonies and 17 string quartets. Musicians think of the nine symphonies of Beethoven in the same way as writers think of the plays of Shakespeare: they are among the greatest creations of any artist.

Beethoven also wrote several overtures, five piano concertos and one violin concerto, 32 piano sonatas and a great deal of other music.

BEETLE. These are very easy insects to recognize, though they are all sorts of shapes and may be as small as a pin's head or as big as a man's fist. True beetles have the scientific name of *Coleoptera*, which means sheathwinged, and they all have one thing in common: what should be the front pair of wings are not wings at all, but thick, usually tight-fitting sheaths, or covers (called *elytra*), which completely cover the real pair of wings

and so protect them. Only beetles have sheaths like this and they usually meet in a straight line down the middle of the back. Sometimes bugs are mistaken for beetles, but instead of the powerful biting jaws of beetles they have sharp-pointed beaks through which they suck their food. (See BUG.)

When a beetle flies, it lifts up its wing covers and then spreads out the wide, thin wings behind them. All beetles were, at one time, flying insects but many of them, like the common ground beetles, have given up flying and depend on their six legs for traveling about.

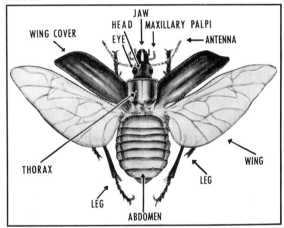

Although beetles are of all shapes and sizes, they all have the parts shown in this diagram in some form.

Although most beetles have eyes with which they can quickly see approaching danger, their most useful organs (parts of their bodies) are those with which they smell. These are chiefly contained in the antennae, called feelers by most people, and help them to find their food and recognize others of their own kind. However, there is little doubt that male and female fireflies and glow-worms, which are beetles in spite of their names, find each other partly by means of their lights. (See FIREFLY AND GLOW-WORM.)

Many beetles can make chirping or squealing sounds by rubbing one part of the body against another. Often this is done by scraping the legs over very fine close ridges on another part of the body, rather as a bow is used to scrape the strings of a violin. This noise is called stridulation. The deathwatch beetle

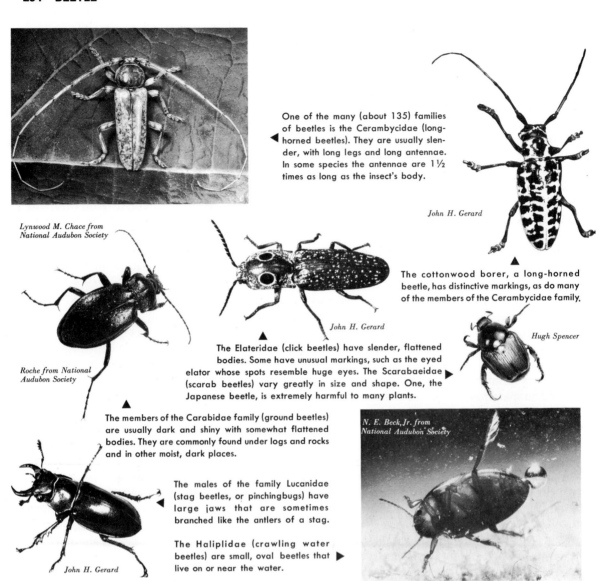

One of the many (about 135) families of beetles is the Cerambycidae (long-horned beetles). They are usually slender, with long legs and long antennae. In some species the antennae are 1½ times as long as the insect's body.

Lynwood M. Chace from National Audubon Society

John H. Gerard

The cottonwood borer, a long-horned beetle, has distinctive markings, as do many of the members of the Cerambycidae family.

Hugh Spencer

The Elateridae (click beetles) have slender, flattened bodies. Some have unusual markings, such as the eyed elator whose spots resemble huge eyes. The Scarabaeidae (scarab beetles) vary greatly in size and shape. One, the Japanese beetle, is extremely harmful to many plants.

John H. Gerard

Roche from National Audubon Society

The members of the Carabidae family (ground beetles) are usually dark and shiny with somewhat flattened bodies. They are commonly found under logs and rocks and in other moist, dark places.

N. E. Beck, Jr. from National Audubon Society

The males of the family Lucanidae (stag beetles, or pinchingbugs) have large jaws that are sometimes branched like the antlers of a stag.

The Haliplidae (crawling water beetles) are small, oval beetles that live on or near the water.

John H. Gerard

(*Xestobium rufovillosum*) makes a tapping noise by banging with its head, usually against wood. This is believed to be a mating call. (See DEATHWATCH BEETLE.)

In one respect beetles are like bees and wasps, butterflies, and moths. They are not born as little beetles which grow gradually into large ones, but instead start as eggs from which larvae, or grubs, hatch. These spend all their time eating and as they grow they keep on shedding their skins, which become too tight for them, until eventually they turn into pupae. In this stage, like the chrysalises of butterflies, they rest and when they hatch out they are fully grown beetles.

Most beetles are careful to lay their eggs where the larvae will find plenty of food. This is not difficult, for most of them feed on leaves, flowers, stems and roots of plants, and even the wood of trees.

Some, however, have to go to much more trouble. The dung beetles make burrows beneath cow dung and stock the holes with dung for the larvae to feed on. The scarabs, once the sacred beetles of Egypt, first make balls of manure and then pull and push these balls into holes they have already prepared, after which they lay their eggs on top of them. (See SCARAB.) Burying beetles have much the same habit; underneath small dead animals they make a pit into which they pull the carcase and on this they lay their eggs so that their grubs can feed as soon as they hatch. All these kinds lay only a few eggs because the food for their offspring is plentiful and they are all likely to survive.

The blister beetles and the oil beetles go to the other extreme and may lay as many as 10,000 eggs. Each tiny grub that hatches needs to feed first on the egg of a bee and then on honey and pollen. To reach the bee's nest it lies in wait for a bee visiting a flower. It then fastens itself to the insect's hairy body and so gets carried to the hive. No wonder these beetles have to lay so many eggs; it is surprising that even one in a thousand should find the right kind of flower and the right kind of bee.

Harmful Beetles

One of the most destructive beetles is the Colorado beetle (*Leptinotarsa decemlineata*), a terrible pest on potatoes in North America and Europe, where it has been introduced. Both the beetle itself and its grub eat the leaves, stems and even sometimes the roots of potato plants. (See COLORADO BEETLE.) The Colorado is one of a very large family of beetles which feed on plants. The family includes the pretty little asparagus beetle (*Crioceris asparagi*), another pest, and also the tiny but troublesome flea beetles which eat the leaves of cabbages, turnips and other plants, often killing them when they are small. If it is disturbed it hops off the plant just like a flea.

Much bigger than this are the handsome long-horned beetles, whose "horns" are really antennae. The grubs of these beetles burrow into the wood of trees and often take years to grow up, so that they may not come out of the wood until it has been made into timber and used in houses and elsewhere. The bark beetles, which look just like the bark of the trees they live on, are among others that cause serious damage to valuable timber.

There are a large number of beetles called weevils that are serious pests of crops such as corn, rice, cotton, palms, and nuts.These were the beetles that were often found in ship's biscuits. (See WEEVIL). Among the harmful beetles which live in the house are the carpet beetle and the furniture beetle (*Anobium punctatum*). Carpet beetles are pretty little oval insects and it is their larvae that do most of the damage to carpets and clothes as well. The furniture beetle (*Xestobium rufovillosum*), a relation of the notorious deathwatch beetle which causes such damage to the woodwork of old churches, lays its eggs in cracks or crevices of the furniture. When they hatch, the grubs eat their way through woodwork and turn it into powder inside. When nearly full fed the grubs bore their way outwards until they are just below the surface of the wood, so that when they turn into beetles they can escape easily through the holes known as "worm-holes". The so-called woodworm is in fact the grub of the furniture beetle.

The mealworm is the larva of the flour beetle (*Tenebrio*) and the wireworm (the larva of click-beetles), lives in the soil and feeds on the roots of plants. Wireworms can do great damage to corn and other crops. Buprestid beetles, which are big brothers of the click-beetles, live mostly in very hot countries and some are destructive to timber. Nearly all of them are brightly colored and many are so highly polished that they look like metal. The Indians of South America use these beetles as ornaments for this reason.

Chafers are stout-bodied, mainly brown beetles that include many pests, for their grubs feed on the roots of crops, and the beetles into which they change feed on the leaves of fruit trees and other kinds of tree.

Harmless and Helpful Beetles

The well-known ladybirds (see LADYBIRD), which are also beetles, are often very useful, for many of them eat huge numbers of the harmful greenflies (see APHID) and scale insects (see SCALE INSECT).

A great many beetles live by scavenging the useless rubbish that collects in houses, hedges, old tree stumps, birds' nests, and similar places. Among these are many of the rove beetles which are very easily recognized, for they are narrow and their wing cases cover only about half their bodies. Most are very small. Other beetles, such as the burying beetles, are useful in helping to clear away dead animals.

Among the most active species are the brightly colored tiger beetles that may be found in hot, sandy places, flying about very actively in the sun. The grub lives in a tube-like burrow in the ground, lying in wait with its head sticking out over the top, to seize and eat other insects that walk over it. Ground beetles are very similar and might be called hunting beetles because, both as grubs and as beetles, they spend their time searching out other small creatures to eat. The largest ground beetles are about 5 centimeters (2 inches) long and the smallest is only a little bigger than a pin's head. The smaller ones live among rotting leaf-mold, under stones and in caves, often being quite blind. When frightened some of them squirt out a nasty-smelling liquid from the end of the body.

Water beetles form another very large group. They are all of the same rounded, "streamlined" shape and propel themselves through or over the water with their hairy hind legs, which act like oars. The middle pair of legs is generally used for clinging to weeds and the front pair for seizing the beetle's prey, which may be an insect or even a large creature such as a tadpole or a small fish. Other water beetles feed on plants, however. All water beetles have to come to the surface for air from time to time and often they leave the water and fly long distances to other ponds and streams.

Male stag beetles have great jaws which look like antlers (see STAG BEETLE). They sometimes frighten people but in fact the jaws are not of much use for biting. In hot countries stagbeetles are common and it is there, too, that their cousins the Hercules and Goliath beetles live. These are among the biggest of all insects, as big as a man's fist and very hard and tough. It is not always the jaws which grow into "antlers"; sometimes other parts of the head or of the thorax grow horns.

BEETON, Isabella Mary (1836–65). Isabella Mayson was born in London, England, the eldest of four children. When her father died in 1841 her mother married a widower who also had four children, and the family increased so that eventually Isabella was the eldest of a family of 21 children. At the age of 20 she married Samuel Beeton, a publisher.

A French kitchen of the 19th century. This picture was in Mrs. Beeton's book *Household Management*.

Although Isabella was used to caring for her younger brothers and sisters, she was surprised how little she knew about cooking and running a home and was amazed to discover how difficult it was to find the information in books. She began to collect recipes and was helped by a request in her husband's *Englishwoman's Domestic Magazine* for people to send them to her. During the next four years she worked on her *Book of Household Management*, which was first published in monthly installments between 1859 and 1861. She wrote, "What moved me, in the first instance, to attempt a work like this was the discomfort and suffering which I had seen brought upon men and women by household mismanagement. I have always thought that there is no more fruitful source of family discontent than a housewife's badly-cooked dinners and untidy ways." She tested the recipes herself in her own kitchen. The book had a comprehensive index and each recipe was set out with a list of ingredients, method of preparation, estimate of the cost, the number of people it served, and the time when it was seasonable. A large part of the book dealt with running the home, the duties of the many different servants that people employed in those days, caring for children and invalids, and medical and legal advice.

Mrs. Beeton later wrote the *Englishwomen's Cookery Book* and the *Dictionary of Cookery*. As many as 60,000 copies of *Household Management* were sold in the first year and it eventually became the best-selling book after the Bible. Mrs. Beeton was famous not only for cooking. She and her husband went to Paris to arrange for fashion plates (prints of fashionable clothes, colored by hand) to be sent regularly to them, which they then reproduced in their magazine. Readers could send in for paper patterns from which they could make up the clothes at home. This was the first time that such patterns were available to the general public.

Mrs. Beeton died at the age of 29, after giving birth to her fourth child; only two of her children survived her.

BEGONIA

BEGONIA is a genus of about 1,000 species of flowering plants. They may be herbs, vines, or shrubs, and they grow mainly in moist, tropical climates. Many garden varieties are cultivated in greenhouses.

The first species was introduced into the United States about 1865. Since that time many species of begonia have become popular worldwide as house and garden plants. There are over 10,000 cultivated varieties. Although all species are relatively small and have juicy stems, their blossoms and leaves may be different. The blossoms may grow singly, doubly, or in clusters, and their colors may be scarlet, orange, yellow, white, or shades of pink or deep rose. The leaves of all begonias are smooth and shiny with a waxy covering, but they may differ in color and shape.

Begonias are classified according to their roots. Those with tuberous roots have the largest blossoms and bloom in the summer. The fibrous-rooted types are used as house plants and may bloom in winter. Rex begonia (*Begonia rex*) and its many varieties, all fibrous-rooted types, are among the most commonly cultivated begonias. They have few blossoms but are grown both indoors and out for the beauty of their spectacular heart-shaped leaves.

Like most plants, begonias may be grown from seeds, but unlike many plants they also may be raised easily from cuttings. When a leaf from a begonia plant is cut and laid on wet sand or soil, some of the cells at the cut surface will grow and develop into a new plant. New plants may also develop from pieces of stems or roots. The begonia was named in honor of the French botanist Michel Begon.

BEIJING

BEIJING (Peking) is the capital of China. It lies at the northern end of the fertile agricultural plain of northern China, close to the main routes leading to the Mongolian uplands and to Manchuria. Beijing under various names has been important since about the 12th century BC. In AD 1267 the Mongol conqueror Kublai Khan made it the capital of his empire and in 1275 it was visited by the Venetian traveler Marco Polo, who was full of admiration for the splendors of the city. After the Mongols were driven out, the Ming emperors changed their capital from Nanjing (Nanking "Southern Capital") to Beijing ("Northern Capital").

The Mings were overthrown in 1644 by the Manchu emperors, who in turn were replaced by the Republic of China in the revolution of 1911. Beijing remained the capital until 1928, when the Chinese Nationalists renamed it Peiping and moved their capital back to Nanjing. Peiping was held by the Japanese from 1937 to 1945. In 1949 the Nationalists were defeated and driven to Taiwan by the Communists, who restored the old name Beijing and made the city the capital of the People's Republic of China.

Despite all these changes, Beijing has altered little since Marco Polo's day. It is a fascinating city. It has very hot summers and bitter

The Summer Palace to the north of Beijing is a favorite spot for city dwellers to stroll in and relax.

winters. The air is generally dry and can be dusty, as sands from the Gobi Desert are whipped down from the plains. This is why you often see pictures of Beijing cyclists and pedestrians wearing face masks. Thanks to the spacious way in which it was laid out by Kublai Khan, Beijing has broad main streets, unlike most Chinese cities. The main streets are lined with trees, behind which the stores are decorated with painted fretwork. Along the roads pass buses, trolley-buses, trucks, a few cars, pony carts, mules, and hundreds of thousands of bicyclists. Beijing must be the bicycling capital of the world.

Beijing is laid out on a rectangular grid pattern, with wide roads criss-crossing north–south and east–west. All the city's outer and inner walls, wall-gates, temples, palaces, and market places were built according to this layout. The city is made up of the northern or Tatar city and the southern or Chinese city, both of which are surrounded by walls. The Tatar city is roughly square. Inside it is the Forbidden City containing the palace of the emperors, once "forbidden" to ordinary Chinese. It is now a restored national museum open to all. Inside the series of inter-connecting courtyards are buildings roofed with dazzling yellow tiles and staircases of white marble. Outside the Forbidden City there is a chain of artificial lakes surrounded by pleasure grounds and temples. Famous landmarks include the Summer Palace to the north, the Temple of Heaven, the Beijing Hotel, and right in the middle is the largest city square anywhere in the world—Tien-an-Men Square (also known as Red Square). The mausoleum of Mao Tse-tung, founder of modern China, is at the center. Other public buildings, including the massive Great Hall of the

After the hardships of the "Cultural Revolution", Beijing is beginning to look like any major western city, with giant advertising billboards encouraging the Chinese to buy once-forbidden western consumer goods such as cameras, washing machines, and TVs.

Frank Spooner

People (which can seat 5,000 people for a banquet), are located around the square along with many colorful flags and giant portraits of Karl Marx, Lenin, Stalin, and Mao Tse-tung (see COMMUNISM). The Chinese enjoy strolling across this gigantic paved area and many use the vast space to fly all sorts of kites from it. Up to 1,000,000 Chinese gather in the square to celebrate the country's National Day on 1 October. The Communist government, which was set up in October 1949. has done much to improve Beijing, improving sanitation, providing parks, and expanding industry. The broad main road leading south from the Forbidden City to the gate of the Chinese city is lined with modern government buildings. Away from the wide, busy avenues are much narrower alleyways where many traditional home compounds, complete with courtyards, house family groups in a way of life that seems remote from the hustle and bustle of the city. Farther out new housing developments, factories, suburban towns, and new parks have been added to the city in recent years. Main industries include the manufacture of railroad equipment, machine tools, electronics, agricultural machinery, and chemicals. Beijing is a center of learning, with universities and scientific institutes.

The population of the city area is more than 9,540,000 (1983), and Beijing is the second largest city in China, after Shanghai.

BEIRUT is the capital and chief seaport of Lebanon in the Middle East, situated on a promontory at the eastern end of the Mediterranean Sea.

Beirut was founded by the Phoenicians in the 15th century BC, and first achieved fame under the Romans in the 3rd century AD when the chief school of Roman law was set up there. In 551, however, an earthquake destroyed the town and it never returned to its previous splendor. It revived a little under the Crusaders in the 12th century, but it was not until the 14th century that it started to be a prosperous seaport. Late in the 19th century French companies built the harbor and the railroad to Damascus. French is the second language, after Arabic.

After World War I (1914–18), Beirut became the capital of the new state of Lebanon, which became independent during World War II (1939–45). Modern high-rise buildings built after the war and other improvements transformed Beirut into one of the Middle East's most modern cities, and the chief center of trade and banking.

In 1975 a Christian-Muslim civil war began in Lebanon and caused extensive damage to Beirut. The central city was largely destroyed, and the important hotel district badly damaged. (See LEBANON.) Since then Beirut has become the most war-torn city in the world. Bombings, shootings, shellings, and kidnap-

Jill Brown/MEPA

Sadly, a typical scene of modern-day Beirut, torn by bitter fighting among rival militia factions.

ping of foreign residents are almost daily occurrences, yet the city's population, which has declined from roughly 475,000 before the civil war, continues against these odds to carry on a normal urban life.

The city is effectively divided into two—a Muslim-militia-controlled West Beirut, and a Christian-militia-controlled East Beirut. There is also a large Palestinian refugee population in Beirut.

The once bustling airport is virtually closed. It has been the scene of several terrorist hijackings (see TERRORISM).

BELFAST is the capital city of Northern Ireland, a province of the United Kingdom. It is a great seaport and lies at the point where the River Lagan joins the arm of the sea known as Belfast Lough. It is the chief industrial center of Northern Ireland.

Like London and many other cities, Belfast was built at a point where a river could be forded, or crossed by wading. The city was founded in the 17th century. It is low lying, but surrounded by hills.

During the English Civil War Belfast was, in 1648, occupied by Cromwell's forces under George Monck. It was quite a small town until the end of the 18th century, but then grew rapidly. Linen was introduced at the end of the 17th century and Belfast became one of the world's chief centers of linen manufacture. Nowadays it is also a center of the synthetic textile industries.

Belfast is also a great shipbuilding center. Small shipbuilding yards were at work in Belfast at the close of the 18th century. In 1847 the River Lagan was deepened by dredging, and in 1858 was founded the great firm of Harland and Wolff, which grew to be at one time the largest shipbuilding establishment in the world. (The liner *Titanic* was built by Harland and Wolff.) More recently, the shipyard has built bulk carriers and warships.

Belfast's large city hall, built in 1906, copies the style of Wren's famous 17th-century St. Paul's Cathedral.

As well as textile factories and shipyards, Belfast has engineering works, an aircraft factory, chemical, tobacco and clothing factories, one of the biggest ropeworks in the world, iron foundries, and a large industry making mineral waters and soft drinks. (Ginger ale was invented in Belfast). It was in Belfast, too, that John Boyd Dunlop invented the pneumatic tire (see TIRE OR TYRE).

Belfast is also the chief transportation and commercial center of Northern Ireland. Much of Ulster's trade passes through the city, including many of the products of Northern Ireland's important farming industry. Belfast harbor, with its network of basins and channels, has 16 kilometers (10 miles) of waterfront. Regular shipping services link Belfast with ports in Britain and many other parts of the world. The civil airport at Aldergrove, about 20 kilometers (12 miles) west of Belfast near Lough Neagh, is one of the busiest in the United Kingdom.

The disturbances in Northern Ireland between the Protestant population and the Roman Catholic minority which began in 1968 have seriously affected life in Belfast. Bombings and gun battles have taken place in the streets and the army has imposed security measures in the city. The Northern Ireland parliament sat at Stormont, east of the city, until 1972 when it was suspended by the British government. To find out more about the troubles in Northern Ireland, see the article IRELAND, NORTHERN. The population of Belfast is 322,600 (1983).

BELGIUM. Wedged between France on the southwest, Germany and Luxembourg on the east, and the Netherlands on the north, with only a short coast on the North Sea, Belgium is one of the smallest European countries. It has become one of the most heavily industrialized nations on the continent of Europe as well as having one of the highest concentrations of population per square kilometer in the whole world.

It is a low-lying land with three rivers, all rising in France, to form the main branches of a complicated system of waterways, including canals. The Scheldt helps to water the flat plain of Flanders in western Belgium and then flows on through a corner of the Netherlands to the North Sea. Entering Belgium halfway along the border with France, the Sambre flows through a hilly coal area to join the Meuse at Namur. The Meuse itself follows a northeasterly course through wild and beautiful country, passes Liège and further on becomes part of the boundary with the Netherlands where that country juts southward.

South of the Meuse are the Ardennes Hills and there the countryside is much like the neighboring part of Germany, with woods, bogs, and moors.

Agriculture and Industries

In the northern part of the fertile central plain the farmers grow oats, rye, flax, and potatoes for export to other countries, while in the south their main crops are wheat and sugar beet. A large number of cattle, pigs, sheep, and horses are raised in the country.

Most of Belgium is intensively farmed land. Although farming is important, it was the coal deposits which in the past led to Belgium's chief wealth. The main coal belt lies towards the south where limited quantities of other minerals were found, such as iron, zinc, lead, and copper. These supplies of raw materials, combined with Belgium's central situation in Europe, have encouraged the setting up of steel and glass works, sugar refineries, woolen and cotton mills, and industries producing machines and chemicals. These are spread all over the country, with the main centers at

Courtesy, Belgian Embassy, London
Metal-working is an important industry in Belgium. Metals are exported to many other countries.

Liège in the south and the ports of Antwerp and Ghent in the north.

Belgium exports metals, machinery, machine tools, transportation equipment, chemicals, and textiles. For the size of its population, Belgium is one of the leading exporters of industrial products in the world. Much of this trade is with Belgium's partners in the European Economic Community (see EUROPEAN COMMUNITIES).

Cities and People

Side by side with all the industrial activity, Belgium preserves in its cities much of the architecture and beauty of the Middle Ages. Brussels and the great port of Antwerp, on which there are separate articles, together with Ghent, Louvain, Malines, Bruges, Ypres, and Tournai were all built between the 13th and 16th centuries. Old gabled houses with red roofs line the clean, tree-bordered streets and often the carved house fronts are reflected in the clear waters of the canals that wind through the cities. Some of the medieval fortifications still remain and there are many impressive Gothic town halls with tall belfries. The cathedrals with their famous carillons, or

The ancient city of Bruges is famous for its picturesque canals and fine old houses.

chimes of bells, contain paintings by the Flemish masters Hubert and Jan van Eyck, Peter Paul Rubens, and Anthony van Dyck.

Much in Belgium's everyday life goes back to its medieval days. The country is famous for its many colorful carnivals. In the older parts of some of its cities, women may still be seen outside in their white lace caps making the lace for which the towns of Malines, and in particular Brussels, have long been noted.

On the canals, barges float along carrying crowds of vacationers, while Ostend, which is a favorite vacation resort, looks from the sea as if it were composed entirely of glittering hotels and casinos (where people dine, dance and gamble).

There are universities at Brussels, Louvain, Antwerp, Mons, Hasselt, Namur, Ghent, and Liège, the last two belonging to the state. Primary schools and secondary schools are also run by the state.

Although most of Belgium is Roman Catholic, the people are free to choose their own religion. The country has two languages. In the northern parts Flemish is spoken. The Flemings are much like the Dutch. In the south French, and in some parts Walloon, a dialect of French, are spoken. The Walloons are very like the French. People who live in the region round Brussels speak both languages with equal ease.

Early Belgian History

The earliest mention of the Belgians, or Belgae, from whom the country takes its name, is that made by the Roman Emperor Julius Caesar in his account of his campaigns. Beginning in 57 BC., it took him seven years to conquer these people, whom he called "the bravest of the peoples of Gaul". In the 4th century AD the Franks, crossing the Rhine from Germany, practically controlled the Belgians, and when Charlemagne was the Frankish emperor in the 8th century (see CHARLEMAGNE) they came under his rule and were converted to Christianity. Travelers between Aachen, Charlemagne's capital in Germany, and France, had to pass through Belgium and it soon became the central market place of the vast Frankish empire.

FACTS ABOUT BELGIUM

AREA: 30,518 square kilometers (11,783 square miles).
POPULATION: 9,858,000.
GOVERNMENT: Constitutional monarchy.
CAPITAL: Brussels.
GEOGRAPHICAL FEATURES: The country is a plain rising gently towards the southeast, the highest level being the plateau of Botrange (690 meters) [2,264 feet].
LEADING INDUSTRIES: Steel, machinery, machine tools, glass, textiles, leather, diamond cutting, chemicals, food.
CHIEF PRODUCTS: Coal, iron, copper, zinc, lead, grain, sugar beet, hops, cattle, pigs, and horses.
IMPORTANT TOWNS: Brussels, Antwerp (chief port), Liège, Mons, Ghent, Namur, Bruges.
EDUCATION: Children must attend school between the ages of 6 and 15.

In those days the area that is now called Belgium, together with Holland and French Flanders, made up the Low Countries, so named because there was not much land above sea-level anywhere and some even below it in places. During the Crusades the towns gained in wealth and importance and in the 11th and 12th centuries became fairly independent. Bruges, Ghent, Ypres, and Louvain imported

Courtesy, Belgian Embassy, London

Two aspects of work in Belgium: traditional lace-maker (left) and chicory grower (right).

wool from England and wove cloth for all Europe, while ships from Bruges and Antwerp carried the rich trade of the northern seas.

In 1385 the Low Countries came under the powerful dukedom of Burgundy. The peaceful reign of Philip the Good was a golden age for art and architecture in Belgium, but it was followed by oppression and revolt under Charles the Bold. The towns recovered their liberties under the rule of his daughter Mary but it was her marriage to Maximilian, Archduke of Austria, that led to the Low Countries first becoming the battleground of Europe, for Mary's son married a daughter of the King of Spain and thus both Spain and Austria had a claim to the land.

The Protestant teaching of Martin Luther and John Calvin, on whom there are separate articles, made great progress in the Low Countries in the 16th century. However, their followers suffered cruelly under the Spanish Inquisition (see INQUISITION), and when the people were preparing to revolt against their Roman Catholic rulers, the Spanish king sent an army under the merciless Duke of Alva to suppress them. Holland fought for and won its independence, but what is now called Belgium remained under Spanish rule for another 70 years.

From 1701 to 1713 the country was the battleground of the general European war known as the War of the Spanish Succession and by the Treaty of Utrecht it was given to Austria. Then in 1792 the Austrians were defeated at Jemappes, in Belgium, by the French republican armies and Belgium became a province of France during the French Revolution and Napoleonic periods until Napoleon was finally defeated at the Battle of Waterloo, also on Belgian territory, in 1815. Belgium was then united to Holland, but in 1830 the people revolted and the Dutch were forced to retire.

A year later the Belgians chose Prince Leopold of Saxe-Coburg, a German, as their king and in 1839, by the Treaty of London, the great European powers recognized the independence of Belgium and promised not to invade it in time of war. (This was to be the treaty the Germans broke in 1914 when they invaded Belgium.)

During the 19th century Belgium developed its industries and railroad system under King Leopold II. He also personally started the huge Congo Free State in central Africa; in 1908 this was taken over as a colony by the government and named the Belgian Congo. Belgium obtained great wealth from the

Congo. Though it was a sparsely populated country, it contained great mineral wealth, especially in copper and zinc, in the Shaba district in the southeast, and was also a source of rubber and ivory. The colony became the independent state of Zaire in 1960.

Two World Wars

When the Germans invaded Belgium in 1914, much of the devastation and fighting of World War I took place there and Belgium fell under German control for four years. After the Armistice of 1918 the Belgians enjoyed a period of peace and prosperity until 1940, when war struck them again, the German troops marching in without warning this time. Neither the Belgians nor their French and British allies could withstand the fury of the German onslaught and after 18 days of fighting King Leopold III accepted the German terms of surrender.

After the defeat of Germany in 1945, the Belgian parliament would not permit King Leopold's return. He was criticized for having surrendered so quickly in 1940. In 1950, however, the king won a small majority in a popular vote. He then re-entered his country but, because of popular unrest, soon stepped down from the throne in favor of his 19-year-old son, Prince Baudouin. Baudouin was made regent in 1950 and became king in 1951 when Leopold abdicated. Baudouin, unlike his father, had the support of the people. The day-to-day running of the country is carried out by parliament.

The Belgians were able to recover fairly quickly from the effects of World War II, despite great losses, chiefly because the Belgian resistance forces, together with the Allied invasion forces, advanced so rapidly that the Germans were given little time to destroy important industries and means of communication as they withdrew. Post-war progress was especially good in the chemical and metal industries.

Belgium joined a customs union with Luxembourg in 1922 and with the Netherlands in 1948. This union, called Benelux, abolished trade barriers between the three countries even before they joined the European Economic Community, or Common Market, which is a much larger customs union (see EUROPEAN COMMUNITIES). The Common Market headquarters are in Brussels and the North Atlantic Treaty Organization (NATO) moved its headquarters to Brussels in 1967.

BELGRADE is the capital and largest city of Yugoslavia. It is situated to the center and east of the country, in one of the republics called Serbia. Belgrade is also the Serbian capital.

Yugoslav Tourist Office

Belgrade, capital of Yugoslavia, is an industrial city. It has many government and institutional buildings.

The city has a commanding position on a spur of the Serbian Hills jutting northwards into the plains where the River Sava joins the Danube River, which gives it control of this important trade route.

As Belgrade also guards the gateway from the Balkans to central Europe, armies have fought for possession of it throughout the ages. Founded by the Celts in the 3rd century BC, it has been held by Romans, Greeks, Huns, Bulgarians, Hungarians, Turks, and Serbs.

The Serbian name for the city is Beograd, meaning "White Fortress". The old fortress, now ruined, stands at the tip of the hill spur, where it ends in a cliff 60 meters (197 feet) high. The outworks have been leveled and made into a public garden from which there are magnificent views of the two rivers and of the great plains which stretch away to the north. Behind the park, on the ridge of the hill, is the old city with the main hotels and stores, and the old royal palace. The slopes fall steeply to crowded commercial and industrial areas beside the river. Several bridges across the Sava link the city with New Belgrade, developed since 1945, and a railroad bridge spans the Danube. Belgrade's modern airport also lies on this side of the Sava, and the city's air, rail. road, and river routes make it the communications center of Yugoslavia.

In 1918 Belgrade was still half Eastern in appearance, with mosques and bazaars like those of Turkey. The large new buildings which have replaced them are more European in style, less attractive, though tidier, than the old. Nevertheless, thanks to its situation Belgrade is still one of the most impressive cities of Europe.

Modern factories in Belgrade build machinery and process foods, leather, and textiles. Handicraft industries also employ many workers. The city is an important educational and cultural center, and has a university, other institutions of higher learning, and libraries. Its population is about 1,470,000. (1981)

BELIZE is a small, thinly populated country on the Caribbean (eastern) coast of Central America. Coral reefs and mangrove cays (or keys) separate it from the open Caribbean, and inland it is bordered by Mexico and Guatemala. It was a British colony until 1981 when it became independent, and it was formerly known as British Honduras. There are still some 1,800 British troops stationed in Belize to protect the borders against claims by neighboring Guatemala.

First discovered by the Spaniards at the end of the 15th century, Belize was considered too inhospitable a land to live in. It was the English who first settled the area in the 17th century, particularly because of the logwood forests in the interior from which textile dyes were made.

The city of Belize was founded on low, marshy ground at the mouth of the Belize River, which permitted easy access to the interior forests and was used to float logs to the coast. The city prospered until the 19th century, when dyes from coal tars largely replaced natural dyes on the market. Logging mahogany helped the economy temporarily, but after the 1920s its value decreased. Logwood

---

FACTS ABOUT BELIZE

AREA: 22,965 square kilometers (8,867 square miles).
POPULATION: 166,400 (1985).
CAPITAL: Belmopan.
GOVERNMENT: Constitutional monarchy, member of the Commonwealth.
GEOGRAPHICAL FEATURES: Low and swampy coastline; northern part of territory is flat but in the south there are mountains; many rivers; most of the country is forest land.
MAIN EXPORTS: Timber, chicle gum (for chewing gum), citrus fruits, sugar, bananas, and tinned fruit and juice.
EDUCATION: Children must attend school between the ages of 6 and 14.

---

is no longer sent abroad; instead the country exports some mahogany, cedar, and pine. Another export obtained from a tree is chicle, from which chewing gum is made, although now the manufacturers also use artificial ingredients.

The country exports sugar and bananas, and a profitable citrus fruit (lemons, oranges and grapefruits) industry has been built up.

Tourism, too, is beginning to thrive, particularly with the attractions of the second largest coral reef (after Australia's Great Barrier Reef) as well as many ancient Maya Indian sites in the interior.

Although Belmopan is the administrative capital, its population is only 2,940, whereas Belize City has 39,770 (1980) inhabitants. It also boasts the oldest Anglican cathedral, St. John's, in all of Latin America.

Maya and Carib Indians live in the interior and there are also many descendants of the African slaves who were brought over by the early settlers to work in the forests. There has been much inter-marriage between the races. English, Spanish, and American Indian languages are spoken in Belize. Most schools are Roman Catholic, but there is no official state religion.

BELL, Alexander Graham (1847–1922), was famous for his invention of the telephone in 1876. He was born in Edinburgh, Scotland, where his father was a teacher of elocution. In 1870 Alexander emigrated with his family to Canada. In 1872, at Boston in the United States, he opened a school for training teachers of the deaf. The next year he became a professor at Boston University, studying the science of speech.

Much of his spare time was spent in trying to discover a way in which people could talk to each other over long distances. He realized that the actual sound waves of speech traveled only short distances even through a speaking-tube, or through string or wire stretched between two hollow vessels. He therefore experimented with the vibrations caused by sound and at last found that these could be sent from one place to another by using electric currents (see SOUND).

Bell's telephone consisted of two similar instruments each having an electro-magnet (that is, a piece of iron made into a magnet by a wire carrying an electric current coiled round it) with a very thin sheet of iron called a diaphragm supported near it. The coils of the electro-magnets were connected to the live wires,

Mansell Collection
Alexander Graham Bell, the inventor of the telephone.

joining the transmitter to the receiver. Speech waves caused the diaphragm to vibrate and the vibrations gave different currents to the coil. The currents flowing round the coil of the receiving instrument caused its diaphragm to vibrate in tune with the transmitting dia-

Bell's telephone consisted of two instruments like this. One was a receiver, the other a transmitter.

phragm and so the sounds delivered to the receiver were heard coming from the transmitter. Bell's instrument is still used as a receiver, but not as a transmitter. The first complete sentence was transmitted in 1876. In 1877 Bell married Mabel Hubbard, who had been one of his deaf students.

Bell made several other inventions. One was the photophone, which used a beam of light to carry speech over a short distance. Bell's graphophone—a kind of record player—in 1883 played the first records, made of wax. Later he experimented with kites, and worked with Glenn Curtiss, an American, to develop an aeroplane. In 1918 the world water-speed record was taken by a hydrofoil developed by Bell and the Canadian inventor Casey Baldwin. (See HYDROFOIL.)

BELL. A bell is a hollow, vessel-like object that can be made to vibrate, or ring, and give a musical sound when struck or shaken. The sound can be produced in a number of ways: by means of an internally fixed "clapper" that strikes the inside of the bell, as in a church bell; by means of a hammer or mallet hitting the outside of the instrument, as in the case of certain bells played in China; or by means of tiny grains or pellets hitting against the inside of the bell, as in sleigh-bells or jingle bells. Bells are usually made of metal (copper, bronze, silver, or iron) but may in some countries be made of clay, glass, animal horn, or wood.

Bells are made in many shapes and sizes all over the world, depending on the purpose for which they are made and the cultures in which they have appeared. These purposes include rain-making ceremonies, the casting or lifting of spells, protection against evil spirits, and communication with the gods. The most important use of bells is in signaling—calling people to worship, tolling the hours, mourning and rejoicing, announcing news, and sounding an alarm. Bells are hung on animals, so that their owners can keep track of them, and are found on vehicles for various purposes, such as telling other road users that the vehicle is there. On ships, a bell is used to indicate time. Eight bells, for example, are rung every four

hours to indicate to the crew the main changes of watch.

Bells can be spherical or egg-shaped, but the typical bell shape people know in Western countries is that of the church bell. Church bells are designed to be heard a long way away. The rim of the bell is circular and quite thick, forming what is called a sound bow. Above the sound bow, the bell forms the shape of an upside-down "cup" with a central attachment by which the bell is hung from its frame. A wheel mechanism turns the bell from below, operated by long ropes. As the wheels revolve the bells swing and are sounded.

There are two ways of sounding church bells—by chiming or by ringing. Chiming is a gentle method in which the wheel moves just enough for the clapper to hit the side of the bell. Ringing is a vigorous method in which the bell is swung full circle, starting from an upside down position. Bell-ringing, or campanology, is hard work, and each bell requires a person to pull the rope.

Bells are tuned to different musical notes according to their size, the largest bells giving the deepest sounds. A set of such bells in a tower

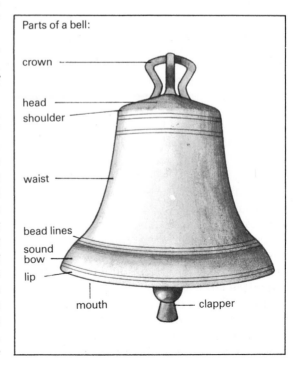

Parts of a bell:

crown

head
shoulder

waist

bead lines
sound
bow
lip

mouth   clapper

In India many different kinds of bells are in everyday use. Among them are the bells shown here. **Top row, left to right:** camel bell, water carrier or bheestee bell, sacred cow bell, Hindu temple bell; **center row:** Sadhu wandering monk bell, elephant bell, tango (one-horse or two-wheeled taxi) bell; **bottom row:** sweetmeat bell, wedding bell, bullock bell.

S. S. Sarna

is called a peal. Usually, there are from 5 to 12 bells in a peal. Church bellringers in Britain practice an art called change ringing, which is based on varying the order in which the bells are sounded according to a complicated plan.

Another method of bell-ringing is practiced in some countries, particularly in the Netherlands and Belgium. In many cities there, a large number of bells (sometimes as many as 70) are hung in a special tower and are played by means of a large keyboard and sometimes a pedalboard as well, rather like an organ. A set of such bells is called a *carillon*. The *carilloneur* (carillon player) plays on these bells by pressing down the keys with his fist, protected by gloves. The most famous carillon is that at Bruges, Belgium. The largest carillon in the world is the Laura Spelman Rockefeller Memorial carillon in Riverside church, New York City. It consists of 74 bells, and weighs 92 tonnes. The bourdon bell (bass bell) of this carillon weighs 16.5 tonnes and is the largest bell in the United States.

In an orchestra the sound of bells is imitated by metal tubes of different lengths hung on a stand and known as "tubular bells". Similar tubes are sometimes hung in church towers in place of true bells, particularly in America. They have the advantage of weighing less than ordinary church bells.

How Bells are Made

Bells are a very ancient form of sound-producing instrument and have been made by the process of casting, or founding (that is, pouring molten metal into a mold), since the Bronze Age, some 4,000 years ago. Modern bell-founding remains a great art today. A bell is still made by the process of casting in a bell foundry. The procedure for making a church bell is usually as follows. After the dimensions of the bell have been worked out, a mold is made. This consists of a core of brick covered with a coating of loam or sand shaped to the inside of the bell, around which the cope is constructed. The cope, also made of loam or sand, is shaped to the outside of the bell and fits over the core in such a way that a space is left between them. Molten bronze or bell metal (a type of bronze in which the tin content is 20–25 per cent) is poured into the space at a temperature of 1100°C (2000°F). The cooling of the metal is carefully controlled to prevent the finished bell from cracking. Large bells

Courtesy, Whitechapel Bell Foundry Ltd.

To make a bell, a mold is first built up for both the inside and the outside shape (top left). The two molds are placed one on top of the other (right), and molten metal is poured into the space between them (left).

may take up to two weeks to cool. After the bell has cooled, the mold is broken up, and the rough casting of the bell is sand-blasted and polished. The bell-founder tunes the completed bell by revolving it and grinding away bits of metal from the inside. This is one of the most delicate operations in the whole bell-founding process.

The greatest bell-makers in history were the Chinese during the 1,000 years before Christ. In Europe the art of bell-founding was lost during the next few centuries. Bells of the Roman period were made of pieces of iron forged and riveted together. Bell-founding as a craft was rediscovered by monks about the 8th century AD. The finest European bell-founders were those of Belgium and the Netherlands, who were the first to learn the mysteries of precise tuning.

The biggest bells were those made in Russia. The Tsar Kolokol, now in the Kremlin in Moscow, is the name of the largest bell ever made. Cast in 1733–35, it was cracked before it was ever rung. It measures 5.8 meters (19 feet) high and weighs more than 196 tonnes (216 US tons). The largest bell still in use is the great Mingun Bell of Burma weighing 90.6 tonnes (99.8 US tons).

The note or tone made by a bell is a very complex sound. When a bell is rung, it first emits what is called a strike note or strike tone. This sound is quite short-lived and is composed of a "root" pitch and many overtones or harmonics (see SOUND). After this has died away, a deeper sound persists, which is called the hum note, or hum tone. It too consists of a "root" and various overtones and takes a long time to die away.

Bells in History

Many legends are told about bells, and some of them are facts of history. In 1282 a peal of bells in Sicily gave the signal for a great massacre of Frenchmen known as the "Sicilian Vespers". (A massacre is the killing of many people.) William the Conqueror, who became king of England in 1066, ordered the curfew bells to sound at eight o'clock as a signal for putting out fires.

In the United States the Liberty Bell, which hangs in Independence Hall, Philadelphia, Pennsylvania, rung in 1776 after the signing of the American Declaration of Independence. The bell was made in 1753 by a London bell foundry but cracked while being transported to America. It had to be recast twice before its tone was satisfactory. But it cracked again in 1835. After 1848 people started calling it the Liberty Bell from the inscription it bears— "Proclaim Liberty Throughout the Land".

In modern times the ringing of a special bell called the Lutine Bell at the headquarters of Lloyd's in London, the great insurance business, gives warning of important news—a ship has been lost or a missing ship found. The bell was recovered from H.M.S. *Lutine*, a frigate that sank in 1799.

Bells figure in the famous nursery rhyme "Oranges and Lemons", which is a song about various churches in the City of London. Many bells in Britain have affectionate names, such as Big Ben, the hour bell on the clock of the Houses of Parliament in London, and Great Paul, the largest bell in Britain, which is located in St Paul's Cathedral and weighs 16.9 tonnes.

The bell is an instrument that is known all over the world and has inspired famous works of literature. For example, Edgar Allan Poe wrote a poem called "The Bells", which was set to music in a Russian translation by Sergei Rachmaninov. In *The Nine Tailors*, a murder mystery by the British author Dorothy L. Sayers, the art of change-ringing forms an important part of the plot.

BELLBIRD is the name given to several unrelated birds with bell-like calls. Probably the loudest are made by four species of cotingas that live deep in the forests of Central and South America. Only the male bird has a penetrating call. He uses it to attract the female over large distances.

The white bellbird (*Procnias alba*) has a black, feathered spike on its forehead. The other three species have fleshy lobes, called wattles that hang from the throat, and flap around when the male dances in front of the female.

Bellbirds build a fragile nest at the end of a branch. They usually lay only one egg.

Australia has two species of birds with bell-like calls. The crested bellbird (*Oreoica gutta-ralis*) is a plain-colored, thrush-like bird with a most beautiful call—at a distance it sounds like the chiming of bells. This bird has the strange habit of stocking its nest with paralysed caterpillars before the eggs have hatched. The bell miner (*Manorina melanophrys*) belongs to the family of honeyeaters. It is an olive-green bird about the size of a starling. It lives in colonies and each member of the flock utters an individual tinkling call that adds up to a sound like the ringing of a number of small bells. The bell miner feeds on nectar and scale insects. It suspends its cup-shaped nest from bushes and trees.

BELLINI, Giovanni (*c.*1430–1516) was one of the greatest painters of the "Venetian School". His father, Jacopo (*c.*1400–70), and brother, Gentile (*c.*1429–1507), were also noted artists, but Giovanni was far greater than either of them and was responsible for turning Venice into one of the most important art centers in Italy during the Renaissance (see RENAISSANCE). Bellini progressed from a flat way of painting to one which used colors and light. Having begun in his father's workshop, Bellini started his own workshop in 1459, where he trained younger artists. His best-known pupils were Giorgione and Titian (on whom there is a separate article). He taught them a great deal, but was also willing to learn and be influenced by their styles.

Venice in the 15th century was a major seaport and trading center. Expensive color pigments, such as lapis lazuli, were among the items that Venetians imported from the East. It is therefore hardly surprising that Venetian paintings, particularly Bellini's, were famed for their beautiful use of color. Artists from all over Italy came to Venice to paint, among them

Bellini's beautiful painted panel *The Agony in the Garden* is one of his finest works.

Bellini's portrait of the Doge Leonardo Loredan painted about 1501.

the great German artist Dürer from the north of Italy, and Mantegna and Antonello from the south of the country. Their particular painting styles affected the development of Venetian art.

Andrea Mantegna, who married Bellini's sister, was a landscape painter. Bellini learned much from him, but Bellini's own landscapes were far more life-like than Mantegna's, whose figures resembled cardboard cut-outs placed on top of a landscape. A famous Bellini landscape is *Agony in the Garden*, painted in the 1460s, which hangs in the National Gallery in London. The Sicilian, Antonello da Messina, had worked in oils and trained in the workshops established by Flemish painters from northern Europe in Naples and Rome. Antonello came to Venice in 1475, and he influenced Bellini and other Venetians in the way they painted portraits. Bellini's *Doge Leonardo Loredan* (*c*.1501) also in the National Gallery, London, is typical of the Flemish school; there is a ledge in front of the sitter, the head is turned slightly away, the painter uses vivid colors and manages to bring out the textures of the cloak as if it were real.

Bellini became painter to the Venetian Republic in 1483. But by this time his fame had spread far beyond Venice, and wealthy patrons from all over Italy commissioned work from him. He was a versatile artist, who painted small pictures, huge altar pieces (of which the *San Zaccaria Altar* of 1505, in the church of San Zaccaria in Venice, is a particularly fine example), and frescoes. He also painted on a wide range of subjects: biblical, religious, mythological (for example, *Allegory*, *c*.1505, in the Louvre Gallery, Paris). One of his most famous non-religious works, which we call "secular", is *Feast of the Gods*, or *Bacchanal*, commissioned by Alphonso d'Este, Duke of Ferrara. It was later worked on by Titian. It is on a mythological theme, depicting gods, satyrs, and beautiful women, and was painted when Bellini was well into his eighties. The painting now hangs in the National Gallery, Washington, D.C.

Bellini died at 86. Ten years before his death, Dürer visited his workshop, and said of Bellini, "Although he is old, he is still the best in painting."

BELLOW, Saul (born 1915), American writer, was born in Quebec, Canada, and spent his early years in a poor Jewish area of Montreal. His parents were Russian Jewish immigrants from Eastern Europe. The family moved to Chicago when Bellow was nine, and

Saul Bellow, the American Jewish writer, winner of the Nobel Prize for Literature in 1976.

he continued to live there for most of his adult life. After studying anthropology and sociology at the University of Chicago and Northwestern University, from which he graduated in 1937, Bellow taught briefly before becoming a full-time writer. He married four times and had three sons.

Bellow wrote about contemporary American society, and concentrated on the educated city dwellers, particularly Jews. In his writings he expressed his feelings of alienation from American society and criticized its values. His works show concern about the lack of feelings people have for one another, the absence of kindness, and about the self-centered nature of many Americans. He said that "the novel is an instrument for delving into human truths . . .", and has done just that in his own writings. Bellow's first novel, *Dangling Man*, was published in 1944. The first of his works to receive wide acclaim was *The Adventures of Augie March* (1953), which has been described as a modern-day *Huckleberry Finn*. It is about a young person growing up in Chicago.

Bellow is the only writer to receive the United States National Book Award three times. He also won the Pulitzer Prize, another prestigious literary honor. He was twice nominated for, and then, in 1976, received the Nobel Prize for Literature. The Swedish Academy, awarding him the Nobel Prize cited him "for the human understanding and subtle analysis of contemporary culture".

Bellow has written plays and essays and is best-known for his nine novels: *Dangling Man* (1944); *The Victim* (1947); *The Adventures of Augie March* (1953); *Seize the Day* (1956); *Henderson the Rain King* (1959); *Herzog* (1964); *Mr. Sammler's Planet* (1970); *Humboldt's Gift* (1975); and *The Dean's December* (1982).

BELORUSSIA. The Belorussian Soviet Socialist Republic is one of the westernmost republics of the Soviet Union. It is bordered by Poland to the west, and Lithuania and Latvia to the northwest separate it from the Baltic Sea. The Russian SFSR is to the north and east, and the Ukrainian SSR to the south.

Victory Square in the center of Minsk, capital of Belorussia, and seventh largest city in the USSR.

Belorussia has an area of 207,598 square kilometers (80,154 square miles)—about the same size as the state of Kansas.

The history of the Belorussian area is largely one of claims by stronger neighbors, Russia and Poland, to control its territory. It began around the 9th century when it was the home of Eastern Slav tribes. In later centuries Belorussia came under the rule of Kiev (an early Slav state), then Lithuania, and then Poland. It was made part of the Russian tsarist empire as a result of the partitioning of Poland between 1772 and 1795. Poland retook the western part after World War I, and the Communists established the eastern part as a Soviet republic. In 1922 Belorussia became

one of the four original republics of the USSR. When Poland was partitioned by Germany and the USSR in 1939, western Belorussia was incorporated into the Belorussian SSR.

During World War II Belorussia became a battleground when the Germans invaded the USSR in June 1941. Many people, including large numbers of the native Jewish population, were killed, and many of the cities and rural areas were devastated. Modern Belorussia has its own government and Communist party, both of which are under Soviet government control in Moscow.

The northern part of Belorussia has an irregular terrain—including lowlands, hills, ridges, lakes, and rivers. A level, swampy plain called the Polesye covers much of the southern area. The Polesye is so flat and poorly drained that each spring when the rivers thaw and overflow their banks, much of the area appears as a large lake. The Pripet Marshes cover a large part of the plain. Summers are cool and winters are quite mild in the republic, temperatures being less extreme than in the central USSR.

Agriculture is a major occupation despite poor soils, which often require fertilizers or extensive drainage to make them productive. Emphasis is placed on livestock raising, dairy production, and flax, hemp, and potato growing. Grains, sugar beets, and fruits are also important. More than a quarter of the area is covered by forests, and lumbering is one of Belorussia's most important activities.

The principal industries include machine building, metalworking, textile manufacturing, and the processing of forest and agricultural raw materials. Among the major industrial centers are Minsk, Gomel, Vitebsk, and Mogilev. Minsk, the capital and largest city, produces agricultural machinery, tractors, and heavy trucks. The chemical industry is growing.

Belorussia has a good transportation network of railroads, highways, and waterways. The most important rail line links such cities as Brest and Minsk to Moscow and Warsaw.

The population is over 9,000,000. About 80 per cent of the inhabitants are Belorussians and are also known as White Russians. Other major groups living in the republic are Russians, Poles, Jews, and Ukrainians. The Belorussians speak an Eastern Slavic language that is closely related to Russian and Ukrainian. The written language uses the Cyrillic alphabet. The traditional religion of Belorussia is Eastern Orthodox, but years of Communism have weakened its influence.

BENEDICT, Saint (*c.* 480–*c.* 547). Benedict of Nursia was the founding father of the Benedictine Order of Monks. He laid down the rules which were later followed in almost all the monasteries of Europe. Today there are still a great many Benedictine monas-teries and convents. (See MONK AND FRIAR.)

Of Benedict himself very little is known. He was born at Nursia in Italy in about AD 480 and was sent to be educated in Rome. However, Benedict was so horrified by the wickedness he saw around him that he ran away, eventually coming to the ruins of one of the Emperor Nero's palaces at Subiaco, not far from Rome.

There he lived in a cave as a hermit. The local monks asked him to be their head, but found his ways so strict that they tried to poison him! However, in time Benedict set up 12 monasteries in the neighborhood of Subiaco, with 12 monks in each. Later he journeyed to Cassino, a town halfway between Rome and Naples. On the high mountain overlooking the town he built the great monastery of Monte Cassino.

It was probably in 529 that Benedict estab-lished what is known as the Rule of St. Benedict. The great difference between this rule and earlier ones was that the monks were taught that work and study have as much value in the eyes of God as a life of prayer. Between their services, Benedictine monks, wearing their black habits or robes, worked on the farms attached to the monasteries and in the vineyards, which became famous for their produce and orderliness. A fine liqueur (a kind of drink) first made by monks in Normandy, France, in the 16th century is still called Benedictine. Boys were, and still are, edu-cated in the monasteries and much study and copying of manuscripts went on. An example of Benedictine learning is the *Ecclesiastical History* of the Venerable Bede, about the early English Church.

It is not known exactly when Benedict died, but it was probably in about the year 547. His sister, Scholastica, who died shortly before him, is generally thought to have founded the Benedictine convents.

BEN-GURION, David (1886–1973), one of the founders of the state of Israel and its first prime minister, was born at Plonsk, Poland. Under his father's influence he became actively interested in the Zionist movement aiming to create a Jewish state in Palestine. In 1906 he went as a laborer to Palestine, which was at that time under Turkish control.

BBC Hulton Picture Library

David Ben-Gurion became Israel's first prime minister in 1945 and held office almost continuously until 1963.

He remained there until shortly after the outbreak of World War I, when the Turks expelled him for his Zionist activities. He then went to the United States and helped to organize the Jewish Legion of the British forces. He served in the Legion in the Near East during the war.

After the war Ben-Gurion returned to Palestine, which had passed to British control. He continued to work towards the founding of a Jewish national state. He was an organizer of the Jewish Labor party (Mapai) and of the General Federation of Jewish Labor (Histadruth). Mapai later became the most powerful political force in Israel.

In 1933 Ben-Gurion joined the Jewish Agency for Palestine, which was in charge of Jewish immigration, settlement, and welfare in Palestine. In 1935 he became the Agency's chairman, and for several years he was the outspoken leader of the struggle to make Palestine an independent Jewish state. On 14 May 1948 Ben-Gurion read the declaration of Israel's independence. The following day the Arab nations invaded the new country. By February 1949 Ben-Gurion had succeeded in

defeating the invaders and in uniting Israel. In that month the first election was held and Ben-Gurion became prime minister. He held that post until 1963, except for a brief period of a year and a half, from 1953 to 1955.

BENIN. West of Nigeria on the Guinea Coast of Africa is the republic of Benin, which until 1975 was called Dahomey. It has frontiers with Niger and Upper Volta in the north, and is bounded by Togo in the west. Its coast is fringed with lagoons (saltwater lakes). Then comes a swampy strip and a belt of rain forest. Inland there are grassy uplands rising eventually to the Atakora Mountains. The chief river is the Ouémé, which flows into the Nokone Lagoon. At the frontier with Togo, the Mono River flows into the sea at Grand Popo. The climate is hot and damp, with a heavy rainfall.

Most of the people are Negroes. They cultivate millet, corn, yams, and cassava, and keep cattle and sheep on the uplands. The chief products are palm kernels and palm oil, groundnuts (peanuts), coffee, and cotton.

FACTS ABOUT BENIN

AREA: 112,600 square kilometers (43,450 square miles).
POPULATION: 4,000,500 (1985).
GOVERNMENT: Republic with one party and president.
CAPITAL: Porto-Novo.
GEOGRAPHICAL FEATURES: Low-lying coastal region, only 110 km (70 miles) long; network of lagoons along coast. Inland there is a fertile plateau that gets hillier to the north. The Ouémé is the longest river.
LEADING INDUSTRIES: Agriculture.
CHIEF PRODUCTS: Cassava, corn, yams, palm kernels, peanuts.
IMPORTANT TOWNS: Cotonou (chief port), Abomey.
EDUCATION: (Almost 50 per cent of population under 15 years old!). Education compulsory for children aged 5–12.

The chief towns are the capital, Porto-Novo with a population of 208,000, and the port of Cotonou which has a larger population of 487,000 and is located on a narrow strip of land bordering a lagoon. Inland the main center is the old capital, Abomey, now with only 54,000 inhabitants. Porto-Novo displays several interesting buildings, some of which were built during the time of French colonial rule, while others are older, going back to the days of the Dahomey kingdom. The history of that kingdom is illustrated in detail in the museum at Abomey. Traditional dances are regularly staged in that ancient town, and there is a flourishing trade in local craftware.

In the 17th and 18th centuries many of the native people were carried off as slaves and the coast became known for this reason as the Slave Coast. In 1899 the French made Dahomey part of French West Africa after overcoming the Dahomey kingdom that had existed since about 1625. Dahomey became independent in 1960, though French is still the official language and there are strong links with France. Political instability has held back economic progress and, as a result, Benin is a poor country, depending on foreign aid.

BENTHAM, Jeremy (1748–1832), English philosopher and reformer, and his followers, are known as "Utilitarians" because they asked of everything "What use is it?" Utility means usefulness.

Bentham was born in London and at the age of 7 he went to Westminster School. At 12 he went to Queen's College, Oxford University, and before he was 16 he had taken a degree in law. He had attended the lectures of Sir William Blackstone (see BLACKSTONE, SIR WILLIAM) whom he later criticized for not

Mansell Collection

Jeremy Bentham, the philosopher and reformer.

attempting to reform the law in England. Although Bentham had been trained to practice as a lawyer, he quite soon turned his efforts to trying to reform both the law and the prison system. Between 1785 and 1788 he traveled in Russia with his brother Samuel. In France his reputation was so great that the Revolutionary assembly elected him a French citizen and in Spain his writings were printed at the public expense. In England he lived the life of a recluse, perfecting his philosophical theory that all human action, especially action by the government, should aim at the greatest happiness of the greatest number of people. In 1789 his book *An Introduction to the Principles of Morals and Legislation* was published, presenting this idea.

Only gradually, and then largely through his disciples or followers, did his teachings bring practical results, but by the time of his death his influence was already great. He played an important part in sweeping away many stupid and brutal punishments, such as transportation to the colonies and imprisonment for debt, in getting rid of corrupt practices, in overhauling the law concerning paupers (poor people), in making the civil service more efficient and in hastening parliamentary reform. The first Great Reform Bill was passed in the year he died and others followed later. In his will he gave his skeleton to University College, London, which he helped to found.

BENZENE is a clear, colorless liquid with a strong odor. It is highly flammable and burns with a bright, smoky flame. It is one of a large group of chemical compounds that are known as hydrocarbons, because they contain only the two elements hydrogen and carbon. Benzene is found in nature in some petroleums and has a formula of C_6H_6. It reacts easily with many substances to form a variety of useful compounds.

Benzene was discovered in 1825 by the English scientist Michael Faraday, who first separated it from the waste products of whale oil gases. In 1845 a German scientist called A. W. Hofmann obtained benzene from coal tar (see

The structure of benzene consists of a ring of six carbon atoms with a hydrogen atom linked to each one. The structure was supposedly revealed to the German chemist F. A. Kekulé in a dream.

CREOSOTE). The largest single source of benzene up to the end of World War II was in by-products of the steel industry. In the processing of coal used to make coke for steel furnaces, coal tar and gases containing benzene are driven off and collected. Benzene used to be recovered from the tars and gases by distillation. This process is still used, but because of greater industrial demands for benzene in recent years, petroleum has become an increasingly important source.

Two of the most important substances made from benzene are styrene (phenylethene) and phenol (carbolic acid). Styrene is widely used in the manufacture of plastics and synthetic rubbers. Carbolic acid is most commonly used as a disinfectant. Benzene is also used in motor fuels and as a solvent for fats, oils, resins, and rubber. Aniline dyes and many insecticides, such as DDT, are made from benzene.

BEOWULF, one of the oldest poems in the English language, tells of a powerful hero who alone, through physical strength, loyalty and courage, defeated evil and malevolent monsters. It was written, probably in the 8th century AD, in Anglo-Saxon or Old English, the earliest form of the English language. But the story goes back even farther. Perhaps it was told among the Angles and Saxons before their arrival in England. A manuscript of the poem is in the British Museum in London.

The story begins at the court of Hrothgar, King of Denmark. He and his warriors would have been happy in their magnificent gold-roofed hall had it not been for the dreadful monster Grendel who came out of the lonely marshes near by. Every night for 12 years Grendel burst into the hall where the warriors were sleeping and dragged away one or more of them to devour; nobody in Hrothgar's realm was strong or brave enough to tackle him.

Then at last Beowulf, who was the nephew of the king of the Geatas of Sweden, heard of Hrothgar's misery and came to Denmark with 14 chosen companions to help him. Hrothgar welcomed Beowulf with joy, but feared that even he would not be able to defeat Grendel. All evening the warriors drank and made merry together, but when night came fear fell on them at the terrible thought of Grendel's coming.

Beowulf stood on guard waiting, and as usual Grendel came. Before the hero could do anything Grendel had seized and devoured one of his men. Then he came for Beowulf, and in the struggle between them Beowulf tore one of Grendel's arms right off. Howling and bleeding, the defeated monster returned to the marshes to die.

The next night, however, Grendel's mother, an even more dreadful monster than her son, came to the hall seeking revenge, and carried off the king's chief counselor. Beowulf followed her down to her lair at the bottom of a muddy lake. There was a terrible fight in which Beowulf was nearly killed, but in the end he slew the monster with a magic sword called Hrunting.

Some years later, when the king of the Geatas died, Beowulf succeeded him as king and reigned happily for 50 years. At the end of this time, however, a dragon appeared in his kingdom and began to destroy the land. Once more Beowulf took up his shield and sword and went out to challenge the monster. Beowulf, helped by his one faithful follower, managed to kill the dragon and so save his country, but in doing so he received such a terrible wound from the beast's poisoned fangs that he too died.

BERGSON, Henri (1859–1941), was a French philosopher. He was born in Paris of Irish-Jewish parents. He was educated in French schools, where he showed remarkable ability in mathematics, science, and Greek. After completing his studies, Bergson taught philosophy in the provinces of France and in Paris. In 1900 he became professor of philosophy at the Collège de France.

BBC Hulton Picture Library

Henri Bergson believed change and truth were one; most other philosophers thought truth never changed.

In 1914 Bergson received the high honor of being elected to the French Academy. After World War I he was the first president of the Commission for Intellectual Co-operation of the League of Nations. In 1927 he won the Nobel Prize for Literature. In his later years Bergson became interested in Roman Catholicism. He did not declare himself a convert, however, but instead proudly called himself a Jew because he wanted to show his fellowship with French and other European Jews being persecuted by the Nazis.

Throughout Bergson's career he was noted for his brilliant lectures and for the clear and graceful way in which he presented his ideas. His most important idea came to him when he was 25 years old. He realized that what he knew best in all the world was himself. But he also realized that he was always changing.

At any instant in the present, he (or anything else) was the total result of whatever had happened in the past. This experience of constant change Bergson called "duration." He believed that intuition was more trustworthy than intellectual reasoning.

Since Plato's time philosophers had tried to find truth in an idea of eternity. They thought that truth never changed. Bergson's idea was the exact opposite. He believed that change and truth were one. All of his books developed this idea. Among them are *Time and Free Will*, *Creative Evolution*, and *Matter and Memory*.

BERING SEA is the body of water that lies between Alaska in North America and Siberia in the Soviet Union. On the north the Bering Strait connects the sea to the Arctic Ocean. On the south the Aleutian Islands form a boundary between the sea and the Pacific Ocean. The chief islands in the Bering Sea include St. Lawrence, Nunivak, and the Pribilof group in the north and east, and the Commander, or Komandorski, group in the west.

The Bering Sea is the fourth largest sea in the world. It covers an area of about 2,293,000 square kilometers (885,000 square miles) and has an average depth of about 1,500 meters (5,000 feet). The sea is deepest in its southwestern basin, which has an average depth of more than 3,660 meters (12,000 feet). The greatest depth is 4,773 meters (15,659 feet).

The sea water is very cold, and ice forms in

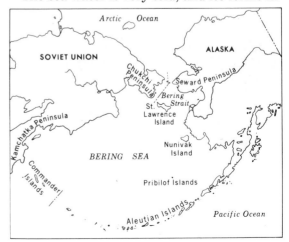

it during much of the year, making it one of the most difficult seas for ships to cross. Its average annual temperature is only –4°C (25°F). Water currents and wind during the winter force the ice into large clusters called pack ice. Southwesterly winds during the summer drive the ice northward, out of the way of shipping. The islands and coasts of the Bering Sea are unforested and have little vegetation. However, on some islands, such as the Commander and Aleutian groups, thick carpets of grass cover the ground. Animal life on land surrounding the sea consists mostly of birds and seals, as well as bears, moose and wolves.

Aleuts, Eskimos, Koryaks, and Chukchi, live in the Bering Sea area. The Eskimos inhabit the Alaskan coast and islands near the center of the sea. The Aleuts, similar to Eskimos, live on the Aleutian Islands. The Chukchi and Koryaks are Siberians who live on the Kamchatka Peninsula in Asia.

Russia was one of the first countries to explore the Bering Sea. In 1724 Peter the Great, tsar of Russia, appointed Vitus Bering, a Danish navigator, to find out if Asia and America were connected by land. In 1728 Bering sailed into the narrow passage named after him as the Bering Strait. Satisfied that water separated the continents, he retraced his route home in 1730. Eleven years later he again sailed across the Bering Sea. This time he reached the coast of Alaska. On his return trip, he died on the island that today bears his name.

Bering Strait

The Bering Strait is the narrowest stretch of the Bering Sea, with only some 90 kilometers (56 miles) separating the northeastern tip of the Asian continent from the northwestern tip of the North American continent. Until 1867 Alaska was actually part of the Russian Empire, but it was bought by the United States in that year. The boundary between these two powers passes between the two Diomede Islands in the Bering Strait, and at this point there are only a few kilometers between United States and Soviet Union territory.